Music and Fantasy in the Age of Berlioz

The centrality of fantasy to French literary culture has long been accepted by critics, but the sonorous dimensions of the mode and its wider implications for musical production have gone largely unexplored. In this book, Francesca Brittan invites us to listen to fantasy, attending both to literary descriptions of sound in otherworldly narratives and to the wave of "fantastique" musical works published in France through the middle decades of the nineteenth century, including Berlioz's 1830 *Symphonie fantastique* and pieces by Liszt, Adam, Meyerbeer, and others. Following the musico-literary aesthetics of E. T. A. Hoffmann, such works allowed waking and dreaming, reality and unreality to converge, yoking fairy sound to insect song, demonic noise to colonial "babbling," and divine music to the strains of water and wind. Fantastic soundworlds disrupted France's native tradition of marvelous illusion, replacing it with a new form of magical materialism inextricable from republican activism, theological heterodoxy, and the advent of "radical" romanticism.

Francesca Brittan is Assistant Professor of Music at Case Western Reserve University. Her work focuses on music of the long nineteenth century, and has been published in a range of scholarly journals including *19th-Century Music*, the *Journal of the American Musicological Society*, and the *Journal of Popular Music Studies*. She was the 2012 winner of the American Musicological Society's Alfred Einstein Award.

New Perspectives in Music History and Criticism

General editors

Jeffrey Kallberg, Anthony Newcomb, and Ruth Solie

This series explores the conceptual frameworks that shape or have shaped the ways in which we understand music and its history, and aims to elaborate structures of explanation, interpretation, commentary, and criticism which make music intelligible and which provide a basis for argument about judgments of value. The intellectual scope of the series is broad. Some investigations will treat, for example, historiographical topics, others will apply cross-disciplinary methods to the criticism of music, and there will also be studies which consider music in its relation to society, culture, and politics. Overall, the series hopes to create a greater presence for music in the ongoing discourse among the human sciences.

Published titles

Leslie C. Dunn and Nancy A. Jones (eds.), *Embodied Voices: Representing Female Vocality in Western Culture*

Downing A. Thomas, *Music and the Origins of Language: Theories from the French Enlightenment*

Thomas S. Grey, *Wagner's Musical Prose*

Daniel K. L. Chua, *Absolute Music and the Construction of Meaning*

Adam Krims, *Rap Music and the Poetics of Identity*

Annette Richards, *The Free Fantasia and the Musical Picturesque*

Richard Will, *The Characteristic Symphony in the Age of Haydn and Beethoven*

Christopher Morris, *Reading Opera between the Lines: Orchestral Interludes and Cultural Meaning from Wagner to Berg*

Emma Dillon, *Medieval Music-Making and the 'Roman de Fauvel'*

David Yearsley, *Bach and the Meanings of Counterpoint*

David Metzer, *Quotation and Cultural Meaning in the Twentieth Century*

Alexander Rehding, *Hugo Riemann and the Birth of Modern Musical Thought*

Dana Gooley, *The Virtuoso Liszt*

Bonnie Gordon, *Monteverdi's Unruly Women: The Power of Song in Early Modern Italy*

Gary Tomlinson, *The Singing of the New World: Indigenous Voice in the Era of European Contact*

Matthew Gelbart, *The Invention of Folk Music and Art Music: Emerging Categories from Ossian to Wagner*

Olivia A. Bloechl, *Native American Song at the Frontiers of Early Modern Music*

Giuseppe Gerbino, *Music and the Myth of Arcadia in Renaissance Italy*

Roger Freitas, *Portrait of a Castrato: Politics, Patronage, and Music in the Life of Atto Melani*

Gundula Kreuzer, *Verdi and the Germans: From Unification to the Third Reich*

Holly Watkins, *Metaphors of Depth in German Musical Thought: From E. T. A. Hoffmann to Arnold Schoenberg*

Davinia Caddy, *The Ballets Russes and Beyond: Music and Dance in Belle Époque Paris*

Brigid Cohen, *Stefan Wolpe and the Avant-Garde Diaspora*

Nicholas Mathew, *Political Beethoven*

Julie Brown, *Schoenberg and Redemption*

Phyllis Weliver, *Mary Gladstone and the Victorian Salon: Music, Literature, Liberalism*

Francesca Brittan, *Music and Fantasy in the Age of Berlioz*

Music and Fantasy in the Age of Berlioz

Francesca Brittan
Case Western Reserve University

CAMBRIDGE
UNIVERSITY PRESS

University Printing House, Cambridge CB2 8BS, United Kingdom

One Liberty Plaza, 20th Floor, New York, NY 10006, USA

477 Williamstown Road, Port Melbourne, VIC 3207, Australia

4843/24, 2nd Floor, Ansari Road, Daryaganj, Delhi – 110002, India

79 Anson Road, #06–04/06, Singapore 079906

Cambridge University Press is part of the University of Cambridge.

It furthers the University's mission by disseminating knowledge in the pursuit of education, learning, and research at the highest international levels of excellence.

www.cambridge.org
Information on this title: http://www.cambridge.org/9781107136328
DOI: 10.1017/9781316479803

© Francesca Brittan 2017

This publication is in copyright. Subject to statutory exception and to the provisions of relevant collective licensing agreements, no reproduction of any part may take place without the written permission of Cambridge University Press.

First published 2017

Printed in the United Kingdom by Clays, St Ives plc

A catalogue record for this publication is available from the British Library.

Library of Congress Cataloging-in-Publication Data
Names: Brittan, Francesca author.
Title: Music and fantasy in the age of Berlioz / Francesca Brittan.
Description: Cambridge, United Kingdom ; New York, NY : Cambridge University Press, 2017. | Series: New perspectives in music history and criticism | Includes bibliographical references.
Identifiers: LCCN 2017024708 | ISBN 9781107136328
Subjects: LCSH: Fantastic, The, in music – History – 19th century. | Music and literature – History – 19th century. | Music – 19th century – History and criticism.
Classification: LCC ML3849 .B837 2017 | DDC 780.944/09034–dc23
LC record available at https://lccn.loc.gov/2017024708

ISBN 978-1-107-13632-8 Hardback

Cambridge University Press has no responsibility for the persistence or accuracy of URLs for external or third-party internet websites referred to in this publication and does not guarantee that any content on such websites is, or will remain, accurate or appropriate.

For Nicholas

Contents

List of Figures and Table *page* x
List of Music Examples xii
Acknowledgments xiv
Note on Translations xvi
List of Abbreviations xvii

Introduction: Hearing Fantasy 1
1 The *Fantastique moderne* 14

Épisode de la vie d'un artiste 51
2 Melancholy, Monomania, and the *Monde fantastique* 53
3 *Le Retour à la vie*: Natural Magic and the Ideal Orchestra 89
4 Grammatical Imaginaries 136

Of Demons and Fairies 189
5 Listening in Hell 191
6 Fairyology, Entomology, and the *Scherzo fantastique* 268

Bibliography 326
Index 351

Figures and Table

Figures

2.1 Théodore Géricault, *Monomanie du vol* (*The Kleptomaniac*), ca. 1820–24. Oil on canvas, 61.2 cm x 50.1 cm. Museum voor Schone Kunsten, Gent, Belgium. Photo: Scala / Art Resource, NY. *page 70*

4.1 Jacques Callot, *The Temptation of St. Anthony*, 1635. Etching; third state of five (Lieure). Sheet: 36.1 cm x 47 cm. The Metropolitan Museum of Art, Bequest of Edwin De T. Bechtel, 1957. www.metmuseum.org. 162

5.1 "Adoration of the Golden Calf." From Gabriello Simeoni, *Figure de la Biblia, illustrate de stanze Tuscane*, Illustration XXXII (Lione: Appresso G. Rouillio, 1577), Woodcuts by Pierre Eskrich. © British Library Board, Shelfmark C.51.b.2. 247

5.2 "Amusemens de l'empereur après son dîner." From Antoine François Prévost, *Histoire générale des voyages, ou nouvelle collection de toutes les relations de voyages par mer et par terre*. Volume 12, Plate 14 (Paris: Didot, 1754). Harvard University, Baker Library. 248

5.3 "The Cullemgee of the Negroes." From Jean-Baptiste-Léonard Durand, *A Voyage to Senegal; or, Historical, philosophical, and political memoirs relative to the discoveries, establishments and commerce of Europeans in the Atlantic Ocean, from Cape Blanco to the river of Sierra Leone*. Plate facing p. 104. (London: Richard Phillip, 1806). Manuscripts, Archives and Rare Books Division, Schomburg Center for Research in Black Culture, The New York Public Library, Astor, Lenox and Tilden Foundations. 249

6.1 Sir Joseph Noel Paton, *The Quarrel of Oberon and Titania*, 1849. Oil on canvas, 99 cm x 152 cm. Reproduced by permission of the National Gallery of Scotland. 274

6.2 "The classic Cicada, the grassy Grullus, and the deep-toned Dor." From L. M. Budgen (Acheta Domestica), *Episodes of Insect Life* (London: Bell and Daldy, 1867), 237. *Episodes* was originally published by Reeve, Benham, and Reeve in three volumes, 1849–51. Reproduced by kind permission of the Syndics of Cambridge University Library. Classmark MA.14.33. 299

6.3 Title page of Adolphe Le Carpentier, *La Ronde des farfadets, Danse fantastique* (Paris: Meissonier, ca. 1872).   317

Table

4.1 Symphonie fantastique en 4 parties. – *Épisode de la vie d'un grammairien*. Parodic symphonic program printed in *Le Ménestrel* (May 8, 1836).   180

Music Examples

3.1 Berlioz, "Le Pêcheur" with *idée fixe* interpolation (1855), mm. 58–79 *page* 96

3.2 Berlioz, "Chant de bonheur," mm. 1–19   98

3.3 Berlioz, "La Harpe éolienne," mm. 1–12   101

3.4 Berlioz, "Fantaisie sur la tempête de Shakespeare," mm. 1–6   106

3.5 Berlioz, "Fantaisie sur la tempête de Shakespeare," coda   109

4.1 Berlioz, *Symphonie fantastique* I, thematic emergence, mm. 232–41   168

4.2 Berlioz, "Chant de bonheur," mm. 14–31 (strings omitted)   171

4.3 Berlioz, " Élégie en prose," mm. 1–17   173

5.1a Berlioz, "Méditation," *La Mort de Cléopâtre*, mm. 11–13   194

5.1b Berlioz, "Choeur d'ombres," mm. 12–14   195

5.2 Berlioz, "Hymn des Francs-juges" with janissary strikes, mm. 46–48   210

5.3 Berlioz, *Les Francs-juges*, Overture, fortissimo clashes (in context), mm. 42–49   212

5.4 Berlioz, *La Damnation de Faust*, Méphistophélès's first appearance, Part II, scene v   215

5.5 Berlioz, "Orgie des brigands," *Harold en Italie* IV, *ombra* music with entry of trombones, mm. 211–16   219

5.6 Meyerbeer, "La Valse infernale (Choeur dans la caverne)," *Robert le diable*, Act III, scene ii (offstage orchestra only)   241

5.7 Meyerbeer, "Bacchanale des nonnes," D-major section with line-end clashing, *Robert le diable*, Act III, scene vii   244

5.8 Adam, "Bacchanale des Wilis," *Giselle ou les Wilis, ballet fantastique en deux actes*, Act II, scene xiv   253

5.9 Gounod, "Chant bachique," *Faust*, Act V, scene i ("From this bewitching goblet / Let us drink everlasting oblivion!")   255

5.10 Schindelmeisser, Bacchanale for Gounod's *Faust*, mm. 1–5   256

5.11 Boito, Witches' dance ("Ridda e fuga infernale"), *Mefistofele*, Act II, scene ii   257

List of Music Examples

5.12 Boito, Mefistofele revealed ("What a noise!"), *Mefistofele*, Act I, scene i   259

5.13 Liszt, *Faust* Symphony III ("Mephistopheles"), opening gesture with Berliozian clash, mm. 1–5   260

6.1   Mendelssohn, Octet, Op. 20, mm. 1–10   277

6.2   Mendelssohn's "buzzing fly," *Midsummer Night's Dream* Overture, Op. 21, mm. 264–70   280

6.3   Berlioz, "La Reine Mab," *Roméo et Juliette*, mm. 1–40   288

6.4   Berlioz, "La Reine Mab," trills at the close of the scherzo leading into the opening of the trio, *Roméo et Juliette*, mm. 349–70   290

6.5   Adolphe Bazzini, *La Ronde des lutins, Scherzo fantastique pour violon avec accomp. de piano*, Op. 25 (Paris: Richault, 1852), mm. 64–79   309

6.6a Liszt, *Gnomenreigen [Danse des lutins]*, mm. 1–4   309

6.6b Liszt, *Gnomenreigen [Danse des lutins]*, beginning of round dance proper, mm. 21–26   310

6.7   J. Ascher, *Les Diablotins, Polka fantastique pour piano* (Paris: Lemoine, 1858), mm. 1–20   311

6.8a Mendelssohn, Octet, Op. 20, closing ascent, mm. 237–41   312

6.8b Berlioz, "La Reine Mab," closing ascent (strings only), *Roméo et Juliette*, mm. 761–69   313

6.8c Liszt, *Gnomenreigen [Danse des lutins]*, closing ascent, mm. 165–68   313

6.8d F. A. Kummer, *Ronde fantastique*, closing ascent (cello only), *Pièce fantastique pour le violoncelle avec acc. d'orchestre ou piano*, Op. 36 (Paris: Richault, 1846), mm. 243–56   313

6.8e Gennaro Perrelli, *Rondo fantastique pour piano*, Op. 35 (Paris: Flaxland, 1869), closing ascent, mm. 376–86   314

6.9   Richard Kleinmichel, *Fée Mab, Scherzo für piano*, Op. 27 (Mainz: B. Schott's Söhnen, 1876), mm. 1–17   316

6.10 Adolphe M. Blanc, *La Farfalla, Scherzetto fantastique pour alto-viola avec acc. de piano*, Op. 7 (Paris: Richault, 1853), mm. 1–13   318

6.11a J. Schiffmacher, *Les Abeilles, Scherzo*, Op. 68 (Paris: Michelet, 1868), mm. 22–27   319

6.11b Schiffmacher's "buzzing bee," *Les Abeilles, Scherzo*, Op. 68, mm 38–40   319

Acknowledgments

There is a poem by Shel Silverstein that reads, "I'm writing these lines / From inside a lion / And it's rather dark in here." I've read this poem to my daughters many times over the past several years, always with a sense of eerie recognition. Good ideas come out of a ferociously dark space, and only because our friends reach in with candles, ropes, and words of encouragement. The first to do this for me were the members of my Cornell dissertation committee, who helped root this project and give it shape, and to whom I offer deep thanks: Neal Zaslaw, Annette Richards, James Webster, and Julian Rushton. The slow transformation from dissertation to book was aided by colleagues on both sides of the Atlantic, who listened, read, and illuminated what was murky. Roger Parker, David Rosen, Thomas Christensen, Annette Richards, Benjamin Walton, Jonathan Kregor, Ross Duffin, and Sarah Hibberd read individual chapters (sometimes more than once) and saved me from innumerable errors. Later, James Webster, Alan Rocke, Gary Moulsdale, and Mark Evan Bonds looked at big swaths of the manuscript and offered keen insight. Others provided last-minute advice and general good cheer: Judith Peraino, Emily Green, Catherine Mayes, Davinia Caddy, Ralph Locke, Nick Mathew, James Davies, and Sherry Lee.

I extend my warm thanks to the members of the Network for Francophone Music Criticism for their practical support, fellowship, and good wine. And I salute the Berlioz community, especially Julian Rushton, Katherine Kolb, Peter Bloom, Hugh Macdonald, and Stephen Rodgers, who were unfailingly welcoming and knowledgeable. Annegret Fauser, in her capacity as editor of *JAMS*, honed the article version of Chapter 6 with an expert hand ("On Microscopic Hearing: Fairy Magic, Natural Science, and the *Scherzo fantastique*"), and James Hepokoski, as editor of *19th-Century Music*, shaped the first incarnation of Chapter 2 ("Berlioz and the Pathological Fantastic: Melancholy, Monomania, and Romantic Autobiography"). I extend my gratitude to both, and to the University of California Press for allowing me to republish portions of these earlier essays.

My musicological colleagues at Case Western Reserve University have been supportive in too many ways to count. For their patience and rigor (not to mention the dinners, coffee breaks, and Berlioz jokes) I thank Peter Bennett, Ross Duffin, Georgia Cowart, Daniel Goldmark, Susan McClary,

David Rothenberg, and Robert Walser. Jean Toombs of CIM's Robinson Music Library and Stephen Toombs of CWRU's Kulas Music Library offered bibliographic advice, found obscure documents, and forgave a mountain of library fines. Fabienne Bernard and Christine Cano leant me their expertise with French translation, offering clever and funny ideas. My research assistant Jarryn Ha set the music examples carefully and swiftly. And our graduate students, especially the members of my 2015 "Romantic Shapes" seminar, enriched and challenged me. The best parts of this book are a testimony to the critical acumen and altruism of these friends and colleagues; it goes without saying that all remaining weaknesses are mine alone.

Support for this project came in the form of a Junior Research Fellowship at Queens' College Cambridge, and then a series of generous awards from Case Western Reserve University, including a W. P. Jones Presidential Faculty Development Award, a Glennan Fellowship, and funding through the Baker-Nord Center for the Humanities. I would also like to thank the music departments at King's College London, the University of Cambridge, the University of Southampton, Cornell University, Princeton University, the University of British Columbia, Youngstown State University, Dalhousie University, and the University of Michigan for giving me a chance to develop my ideas in guest lectures and colloquia.

To the relatives and friends near and far who saw me not just through the writing of this book, but through the two difficult pregnancies and special exhaustions of early parenthood that accompanied that process, I am eternally grateful: Jackie Wille, Greg Wille, Carol Holley, Gary and Wendy Moulsdale, Tsitsi Jaji, Meg Elliott, Wendy Fu, John Duncan, Kirsty Money, Peter Shulman, Jo Willmott, Sheila Harper, Dori and Irv Katz, Jen Meyers, Eric Dunn, Julie Andrijeski, Tracy Mortimer, Debra Nagy, Ana Boe, Vera Tobin, Steve Cook, and the other precious neighbors and chums who have made our lives possible. My oldest and most profound debt is to my three sisters, Alice, Jennifer, and Suzannah, and to my parents, Eric and Cora. This book could not have been written without you; indeed, its claims about the power of magic, make-believe, and spirit were fostered by your love and imagination. Finally, I thank my husband, Nicholas, to whom this book is dedicated, and who read the entire manuscript, offering me strength and affection when it mattered most. And I blow a kiss to our two small fairies, Rose and Lucy, who remind me daily that musicology is not, in the end, at the center of things. To you three, via Victor Hugo: "L'amour fait songer, vivre et croire. / Il a pour réchauffer le cœur, / Un rayon de plus que la gloire, / Et ce rayon c'est le bonheur!"

Note on Translations

Translations are mine unless otherwise indicated. Original language is given in footnotes only when the source text is not readily available either via digital collections or modern editions. Thus, it appears in the case of individual journal reviews and serialized tales but not for Berlioz's own critical writing and correspondence, nor for the majority of French novels and scientific texts. The spelling of original texts has been left intact; thus, for instance, "attroupemens" rather than "attroupements."

Abbreviations

CG: Berlioz, *Correspondance générale*. General editor, Pierre Citron. 7 vols. and *supplément*. Paris: Flammarion, 1972–2003.
CM: Berlioz, *Critique musicale*. General editor, Yves Gérard. 7 vols. Paris: Buchet/Chastel, 1996–present.
NBE: *New Berlioz Edition (New Edition of the Complete Works)*. General editor, Hugh Macdonald. Kassel: Bärenreiter, 1967–2006.

Introduction: Hearing Fantasy

Among the earliest fantastic tales published by French authors were those of Théophile Gautier and Jules Janin, whose work set the stage for an explosion of *contes fantastiques* through the 1830s and 1840s. Gautier's "La Cafetière" (1831) tells a brief but alluring story revolving around Théodore, an art student who, as the tale begins, departs Paris for a vacation at an old house in Normandy. The trip involves a full day of travel and when Théodore arrives with his friends, he is tired and retires to his room. It is a cavernous space that, oddly, already seems to be occupied – combs, boxes, and discarded dresses lay all about. Uneasy, he tries to sleep, but as the room darkens, strange shapes begin to dance on the walls, figures from the innumerable portraits and murals on the wall, which appear as flickering, distorted silhouettes. This unsettling visual show is accompanied by an increasingly acute experience of hearing: Théodore describes the persistently sighing wind and ticking clock, whose effects usher in a series of hallucinatory events. As the clock strikes eleven, its lingering resonance brings the room to life. The candles light themselves, a coffeepot hops down from the mantle and settles itself on the embers of the fire, armchairs walk about on their ornamental feet, and characters from the paintings step out into the realm of the real. All listen intently. Finally, the clock sounds the stroke of midnight and an unknown voice declares, "The hour is here, let us dance!" And now a more powerful magic takes hold. An orchestra woven into the great tapestry on the wall stirs into being, calling all to participate in a whirling entertainment whose speed and intensity hint at violence:

The horn player and the musicians [of the tapestry] who until then had given no sign of life bowed their heads in acknowledgement. The conductor raised his baton and the musicians struck up a lively dance tune. First, the company danced the minuet. But the rapid notes of the score played by the musicians did not match the stately movement of the dancers. After a while, each pair of dancers began to spin round and round like a top. The women's silk dresses made a curious noise as they whirled, like a flight of pigeons or a beating of wings. Puffed up from beneath by the draught, they looked like bells ringing. The musicians' bows attacked the strings so vigorously that they struck electric sparks from them, the fingers of the flautists moved up and down like quicksilver, the huntsmen's cheeks swelled out like balloons and the resulting deluge of notes was so rapid and tumultuous that even the demons of hell could not have kept up the pace for more than a few seconds.[1]

Music animates the inanimate and even, as the story unfolds, brings a dead girl back to life, allowing her to participate in the action. But as the orchestra fades and the light of dawn glimmers, the magic ends. Théodore loses consciousness and, when he wakes in the morning, finds himself dressed in peculiar clothes, bewildered, and unable to explain the events of the night previous.

Jules Janin's first *conte fantastique*, "Kreyssler," published the following year (1832), contains many of the same tropes. Here again, fantastic magic is ushered in on a wave of sound – another fanciful orchestra, this one made up of clinking glasses and booming kegs of beer described at the outset of the tale by the fictional musician Johannes Kreyssler (Kreisler):

I was still at the tavern the *Grand-Frédéric*; indeed, I had passed the entire night there. Oh what a night! A brilliant concert in the midst of a thick cloud of smoke! Pitchers knocking against pitchers, glasses clinking together, beer foaming and rising to the rim. Like a rustic flageolet married to a bagpipe, the cork pops to more clearly mark the beat; the barrel serves as bass drum in the corner of the orchestra. Well played, musicians! Bravo, music! We have executed a whole drinkers' symphony, allegro, in all keys and every meter. My goodness! When the sparkle of a robust wine glimmers at the brim of my glass, I feel like I am witnessing a magic spectacle.[2]

Intoxicated by wine and by the sound of his imagined orchestra, Janin's Kreyssler (like Théodore before him) begins to see dancing shadows on the wall of the tavern, grotesquely shifting as if with a life of their own. He enters a space akin to Shakespeare's "Midsummer Night's Dream" in which fairies, ghosts, and even the Princess Helen seem to appear. As light breaks, he wanders the streets surrounding the tavern carrying on an (imagined?) conversation with the princess. Finally, she disappears into her palace – or perhaps, Kreyssler muses, she ascends into the heavens. He continues on his walk, only to find himself back at his favorite watering hole the following evening, asking "Did I dream all of that?"

These tales, hallucinatory, sonorous, ontologically unstable, were written in the wake of E. T. A. Hoffmann's introduction to France in the late 1820s (in many cases, as both Gautier's and Janin's protagonists indicate, as a direct response to the German author's work).[3] They mark the beginning

---

[1] Gautier, "La Cafetière," 8.   [2] Janin, "Kreyssler," 33.
[3] Théodore is a reference to Ernest *Theodore* Amadeus Hoffmann. The point is made by Whyte, who also draws attention to the continuities between Gautier's animating coffeepot and Hoffmann's magical pot in *Der goldene Topf*; see his "Théophile Gautier, poète-courtisan." Janin's Kreyssler points (obviously) toward Hoffmann's musical alter ego, Johannes Kreisler.

of a new culture of literary fantasy stretching through Balzac, Baudelaire, and Nerval to Maupassant and de l'Isle Adam. The *contes fantastiques* of these authors were much read – serialized in major journals, reissued in collections, lauded by some, denounced by others, emerging from (and perpetuating) a deep fascination with fantastic worlds. Common to the delineation of many of these is a species of multisensory description in which narrative, musical, and visual elements are woven together. Their synesthetic quality has attracted while also confounding critics, placing fantasy just outside the grasp of conventional analytical methodology and therefore legibility. Its disciplinary slippages make stories like Nodier's and Gautier's (and behind these, Hoffmann's) difficult to master; though cast in narrative form, they often seem to emerge from and be sustained by sound, which itself perpetuates otherworldly modes of seeing and knowing.

Studies of fantasy have only slowly begun to approach the kind of interdisciplinarity the mode itself seems to require. They originated in the domain of literary criticism, which has long emphasized the importance of the fantastic, situating it as central to mid-nineteenth-century novelistic and poetic production and, in a broader sense, to the articulation of French romanticism. Texts documenting the arrival and impact of E. T. A. Hoffmann (whose tales were translated under the rubric *contes fantastiques*) are numerous, as are accounts of France's response. Between Pierre Georges Castex's seminal *Le Conte fantastique en France de Nodier à Maupassant* (1951) to the wide-ranging overviews and anthologies of recent decades, including Neil Cornwell's *The Literary Fantastic from Gothic to Postmodernism* (1990) and David Sandner's *Fantastic Literature: A Critical Reader* (2004), dozens of books on fantasy have appeared, many detailing from various angles the ways in which the mode reshaped conceptions of supernaturalism (and therefore also naturalism), blurring entrenched boundaries between real and unreal, waking and dreaming, marvelous and mimetic. Structuralist accounts of fantasy (famously, that of Tzvetan Todorov) abound, as do poststructuralist, psychoanalytic, thematic, and postmodern readings, which demonstrate how the genre plumbed new psychological depths, played with archetypal images, undid existing narrative conventions, and confounded language itself.[4] Work emanating from the literary community has been extended and enriched by visual historians including Marina Warner, Barbara Stafford, Wolfgang Kayser, and Roger Schlobin, who have linked the rise of fantasy with the wave of modern

---

[4] Todorov, *The Fantastic*. Many later studies expand, modulate, or refute Todorov. For a range of methodological approaches, see as starting points: Jackson, *Fantasy*; Olsen, *Ellipse of Uncertainty*; Armitt, *Theorising the Fantastic*; Leonard, ed., *Into Darkness Peering*; Andrès, *La Fantaisie dans la littérature français du XIXe siècle*.

bogeymen – newly "real" and "human" monsters – pictured by romantic engravers and painters from Francisco Goya to Eugène Delacroix, Gustave Doré, and Odilon Redon. And moving further afield, cultural historians have theorized the fantastic in conceptual terms, as a liminal social space generated by revolutionary notions of state and self.[5]

The result is an increasingly rich and multifaceted understanding of fantasy, including the ways in which it operated as a textual, visual, and psychological impulse. What remains persistently underdeveloped is a sense of its aural dimensions. Music, as seems so often the case, is the final hurdle, the most difficult medium to capture and theorize. But in the case of fantasy it is – quite obviously – crucial. Hoffmann's tales and, as I have highlighted, those of his French champions, are woven through with sonorous description and evocation, their narratives of enchantment often propelled by acts of listening. In both Gautier and Janin, the *conte fantastique* is inextricable from the orchestre fantastique – from a newly debauched, magical, and intoxicating domain of instrumental sound. One thinks right away of Berlioz's *Symphonie fantastique*, which premiered just before the publication of the first fantastic tales and was clearly entwined with them. Musical fantasy, in a strict sense, preceded French literary fantasy. So why has so little been written about it?

One explanation lies in the widely held sense of Berlioz's symphony as a singular work, a lone exemplar of the musical fantastic in an era dominated by the *conte fantastique*, a "transient, marvelous exception," as Wagner put it.[6] But the idea is misleading. As literary fantasy proliferated so too did *fantastique* musical production, the two inextricably conjoined. Berlioz's symphony, with its famously literary program, was followed quickly by two other Fantastic Symphonies (also attached to otherworldly narratives), both of which premiered by 1835.[7] And around the same time, a corpus of other compositions bearing the rubric began to appear: sonatas, concerti, character pieces, and dramatic works, some by known composers (Liszt, Schumann, Moscheles), others by more obscure figures (Antonio Bazzini, Adolphe Blanc, Adolfo Fumagalli, Benjamin Godard). The term

---

[5] Warner, *Fantastic Metamorphoses*; idem, *No Go the Bogeyman*; Stafford, *Body Criticism*; idem, *Devices of Wonder*; Schlobin, *The Aesthetics of Fantasy Literature and Art*; Kayser, *The Grotesque in Art and Literature*; Siebers, *The Romantic Fantastic*; Monleón, *A Specter Is Haunting Europe*. An ever-widening sense of fantasy's interdisciplinary appeal is evidenced by the yearly proceedings of the International Conference on the Fantastic in the Arts.

[6] *Dresdener Abendzeitung* (5 May 1841).

[7] One of these (now lost) was composed by Berlioz's compatriot, violinist François-Laurent-Hébert Turbry. The other was the work of a young Belgian composer, Etienne-Joseph Soubre, who began his *Sinfonie fantastique* in 1833 while a student at the *Conservatoire royale de Liège* and premiered it in 1835, only months before Turbry's. Soubre's work, which is clearly a response to Berlioz's, survives. For detail, see my edition of his *Sinfonie fantastique à grand orchestra*.

fantastique was applied to operas by Weber and Gounod, to a collection of mid-century ballets, and to several of Berlioz's later otherworldly evocations, including *Harold en Italie*, *La Damnation de Faust*, the *Messe des morts*, and parts of *Roméo et Juliette*. It was as meaningful in the musical sphere as in the literary and visual worlds, though neither the corpus of *fantastique* works nor the term itself has received sustained musicological attention.[8]

It is this lacuna that the present book aims to fill. It is concerned with the ways in which music interfaced with literary and visual fantasy and, more pointedly, with fantasy's emergence as a compositional category. What did the term mean in a musical context? What do the pieces to which it was attached have in common? How are they related to the procedures of pictorial and poetic fantasy? To shifting notions of supernatural representation? To theories of instrumental, especially orchestral, sound? Asking these questions goes some way toward resolving fantasy's elusiveness. As we shall see, many literary accounts of the mode begin and end with claims around its indefinability – the impossibility of saying what it is or how it means. Here, I have no pat definition to offer nor do I hope to simplify or contain fantasy, but I do suggest that its opacity arises in part from a neglect of its sounding dimensions, which were crucial from the outset. The fantastic is accessible only via multipronged inquiry, residing, as I argue in the pages to follow, in an interstitial space between reading, hearing, seeing, and sensing.

My musical point of departure is the same as that suggested by Gautier's and Janin's "orchestral" tales and by French music critics: the work of Hector Berlioz, who was bound up from the 1830s onward with fantastic rhetoric, positioned as the promulgator of a newly literary, Hoffmannesque, and more broadly "German" musical mode. This strand of the composer's reception has not gone entirely unnoted; indeed, the sense of a connection between the *Symphonie fantastique* and the wider discourses and aesthetics of fantasy stretches back to Christian Berger's *Phantastik als Konstruktion* (1983) and carries through later work by Wolfgang Dömling, Laura Cosso, Andrea Hübener, and Marianna Ritchey.[9] These authors argue, among other things, for a link between Berlioz's rhetorical and formal strategies and those of contemporary *contes fantastiques*, mapping literary theory onto musical practice. They also draw attention to Berlioz's programmatic

---

[8] There are several interesting and recent exceptions, especially in scholarship on staged music. These include Meglin's series of three articles under the umbrella title "Behind the Veil of Translucence"; also, Lacomb and Picard, *Opéra fantastique*.

[9] Berger, *Phantastik als Konstruktion*; Dömling, *Hector Berlioz*; Cosso, *Strategie del fantastico*; Hübener, *Kreisler in Frankreich*; Ritchey, "Echoes of the Guillotine." See also my own dissertation, "Berlioz, Hoffmann, and the *Genre fantastique* in French Romanticism," and that of Ritchey, "Echoes of the Guillotine."

borrowings – the overlaps between his otherworldly imagery and that of Hoffmann, Gautier, and Charles Nodier. These ideas are important and play a role in the chapters to follow, although I also complicate, extend, and in some ways reorient them. The musical fantastic was not, I suggest, simply responding to literary or visual impulses but was, from the beginning, intertwined with them. Authors of fantastic tales also reviewed fantastic musical works; composers of *musique fantastique* themselves published *contes fantastiques*. Fantasies seen, read, and heard were always already inextricably linked. More importantly, the shift produced by fantastic aesthetics extended well beyond Berlioz's symphony and Berlioz himself, transforming notions of otherworldly sound on a broad scale.

I am especially interested in Hoffmann's role in establishing a framework – literary, visual, and especially musical – for French fantasy. Both he and his alter ego, Kreisler, had a wide and deep impact (as Janin's tale indicates and Hübener's study confirms), importing a new kind of artistic consciousness as well as what French critics understood as a "modern" conception of the fantastic. The term, as both Hoffmann and his Parisian champions applied it, was not synonymous with "fantasy" in a loose sense. It did not refer, in other words, to imaginative worlds at large, but to a new form of rational enchantment first introduced in the literature and aesthetic theory of the late eighteenth century.[10] At its heart was a breakdown of entrenched barriers between reason and imagination, reality and the unreal. Modern fantasy emerged on one hand from idealist philosophy, which posited a new relationship between nature and the supernatural, and on the other from political upheaval – the forces of both revolution and imperialism – which collapsed entrenched social and intellectual boundaries, forcefully enjambing reason with the irrational. In tandem, these impulses disrupted the old domain of the marvelous (what the French regarded as a native magical tradition, a theatrical mode associated with make-believe, illusion, and mythology), replacing it with a new species of "real" supernaturalism (*le surnaturel vrai*). No longer divorced from reason, magic became newly entwined with it; indeed, romantic science itself midwifed the birth of fantasy, bridging the divide

[10] An important distinction, since the term is sometimes applied to a much broader swath of literary material; see, for instance, James and Mendlesohn, *The Cambridge Companion to Fantasy Literature*, which clubs together tales of make-believe from the Renaissance to the present day. *Fantastique* as I invoke it here should also be separated from the "fantasy" (*phantasie, fantaisie*) as a musical form. Though certain connections between the mode and the form obtain, French lexicons do not make them synonymous. *Fantastic* as applied to Berlioz's work was connected to a new kind of orchestral sound and a novel approach to magical representation rather than to the improvisatory procedures associated with the *stylus phantasticus*.

between otherworldly belief and modern skepticism. Novel microscopic and telescopic inventions rendered invisible worlds visible, new geographical exploration made imaginary worlds actual, emerging theories of matter and mind penetrated beyond the surfaces of things to reveal hidden, distant, and ideal spaces. In musical as in literary and visual arenas, modern technologies (philosophical, physical, compositional) reinvented magic. They reinvested sound with an old incantatory influence and the musician himself with occult power.

Understanding how this power was regained means examining shifting boundaries among musical, theological, and empirical discourses, placing *fantastique* soundscapes against broader histories of supernaturalism. This is, in part, the project of Chapter 1, which begins with French Hoffmann reception – with the wave of reviews, commentaries, and analyses sparked by the arrival of the German author's *Fantasiestücke* in the late 1820s. As we shall see, critics were much exercised by the intertwining of science and folklore in these stories, which seemed at once alluring and disruptive, introducing new modes of reading and listening (the two sometimes blurred). They separated Hoffmann's fantastic mode not just from the French "marvelous" tradition, but from English Gothic aesthetics, and the "ancient" magic of Renaissance mythology, introducing a set of distinctions that would later be taken up by a host of twentieth-century critics. Here, I devote some time to fleshing these out, surveying a body of writing on seventeenth- and eighteenth-century musico-magical ontologies by (among others) Claude Palisca, Gary Tomlinson, and Penelope Gouk, and a corpus of work on eighteenth-century marvels initiated by Marian Hannah Winter and extended, most recently, by David J. Buch.[11] Together the work of these scholars sketches out a shift from an enchanted to a disenchanted reality, from a world animated by sonorous magic to one in which music was relegated to the merely aesthetic. Buch's study takes us up to the 1790s, to the period André Grétry termed the "third age of the marvelous." What followed, as French critics suggested, and as I argue here, was the *next* moment of musico-magical negotiation: the birth of modern fantasy, which reinvested sound with some of its lost Neoplatonic power and therefore magic with "real" efficacy. It was this shift that Parisian readers sensed in Hoffmann's tales, which destabilized their own magical tradition, introducing a new narrative wavering that was also an enchanted (metaphysical,

---

[11] This is not the place to give a full account of the literature on music and magic, although a rich selection of writing on the topic will be represented in the chapters to follow. The works I mention here are well-known points of departure: Palisca, *Humanism in Italian Renaissance Musical Thought*; Tomlinson, *Music in Renaissance Magic*; Winter, *The Theatre of Marvels*; Buch, *Magic Flutes and Enchanted Forests*.

socially radical) form of listening. From the outset, they situated the fantastic as both a fictional and musical category, identifying Hoffmann as the primary exponent of the former and Berlioz of the latter. The *Symphonie fantastique*, according to many, was the flagship work of a burgeoning école fantastique, a piece ushering in a new kind of sounding supernaturalism and a modern model for the inspired musician.

Close readings of Berlioz's first symphony and its sequel *Le Retour à la vie* form the subjects of the following two chapters, which examine the ways in which these works rendered Berlioz a musical Hoffmann, translating into practice what the German *conteur* had only imagined in fiction and, in so doing, providing a template for the French "school" of fantastic composition. Berlioz's original title for the first symphony was *Épisode de la vie d'un artiste: Symphonie fantastique en cinq parties*, but very quickly, he shortened this to *Symphonie fantastique* and later, in the letters, referred simply to the *Fantastique*. His rhetorical telescoping is interesting, inviting us to consider how the term sums up the work. How fantastic was the Fantastic Symphony? How was it shaped by the twin philosophical and political impulses associated with the *surnaturel vrai*? Part of listeners' struggle to place and read the work, in Berlioz's time as well as now, I suggest, emerges from a difficulty theorizing fantasy itself, understanding its central ontological and disciplinary hesitations and the fractured persona of the Hoffmannesque artist himself.

This persona (and, in a larger sense, the nature of fantastic selfhood) is the subject of Chapter 2, which looks at Berlioz's first symphony as an autobiographical work, exploring its adoption/adaptation of the alienated, mad, and obsessive identity celebrated in Hoffmann's fiction. Accessing fantasy's "hesitating" domains is possible, in the German author's tales, only via spiritual suffering, a form of self-estrangement wrapped up with the German condition *Sehnsucht*, which he attaches to his own musical alter ego, Kreisler, and to a host of other "artistic" protagonists. In the program of the *Fantastique*, Berlioz diagnoses himself with a similar form of longing, although now his ailment is not just philosophical, but medical. Idealist yearning is conflated in his program with a form of unhealthy fixation: the famous *idée fixe*. Here, I examine the relationship between these pathologies, the ways in which metaphysical, psychiatric, and nervous discourses converged to produce the figure of the modern fantasist, allowing him to occupy while also escaping his own materiality – to exist as a doubled self. In pursing this line of inquiry, I gesture toward a familiar psychoanalytic approach to the fantastic (the array of Freudian, Jungian, and Lacanian readings of the mode) while also departing from it.[12] I am less concerned

---

[12] For an overview of such approaches, see Butler, "Psychoanalysis."

with twentieth-century psychoanalytic thought than with the psychiatric theory of Berlioz's and Hoffmann's own moment – in concepts eventually taken up and expanded by Freud and his generation. The birth of modern "mental science," I argue, produced a new kind of creative (literary, musical, visual) fantasy and, along with it, a form of unstable autobiography suspending artists between reality and fiction, madness and transcendental perception.

Chapter 3 moves from the *Fantastique* to its little-known sequel, from a consideration of Berlioz's fantastic self to an interrogation of his fantastic soundworld. In *Le Retour à la vie*, the composer reveals himself not just as a Kreislerian sufferer, but a Hoffmannesque listener – one whose access to the ideal was rooted, seemingly paradoxically, in acute perception of the real. The work was, as Berlioz put it, an extended contemplation of "his art" and the *monde fantastique* from which it sprang, an explanation of the symphony and its central theme. In it he located the *idée fixe* not just as a dream melody, but also as a natural sound drawn from the sighs of the breeze, the songs of birds, and the noises of water and earth. The intertwining of imaginary and actual worlds at the heart of the *Fantastique* is reflected in *Le Retour* by a parallel musical blurring: a collapse of supernatural into actual sound. This was not simply a form of "imitation" or orchestral materialism (a common complaint in the work's reception), but, as Berlioz argued, a new kind of vitalist "expression." He, like Hoffmann, associated the fantastic soundworld with a sonorous enchantment that worked on and through the body, transmitting the divine energy of the natural world and in so doing an intimation of the metaphysical beyond. As we shall see, the idea was difficult for mainstream critics to grasp and explain; instead, it was explored through a series of *contes fantastiques* published by Berlioz's proponents through the middle 1830s, which positioned the composer's orchestra as an instrument of transformation and magico-nervous revelation.

If fantasy disrupted representational and epistemological binaries (distinctions between expressive and imitative, aesthetic and scientific), it also played with stylistic and formal ones. In the *Fantastique*, *Le Retour*, and a host of Berlioz's surrounding works, critics complained not just of orchestral noise, but of structural disorder: faulty harmonies, tortured rhythms, and syntactical illegibility. Fantastic music emerged, they claimed, both from imported philosophical impulses and, equally clearly, from revolutionary linguistic innovations – the lexical "reforms" of Louis-Sébastien Mercier, Charles Nodier, and Victor Hugo. Chapter 4 teases out these ideas, connecting the "natural" sound embraced by Berlioz and his proponents to romantic theories of "natural" language and, behind them, the "natural" rights of man. New phraseology and syntax, as we shall see, were central to both the ontological uncertainty and political volatility of modern fantasy. In Hugo's much-read Preface to the drama *Cromwell*, neology itself – the invention of new words and sounds – undid the artificial reality of the old marvelous world, replacing it with an aesthetics of all-embracing grotesquerie. High and low, poetry and prosody, ugly and beautiful, material and ethereal intermingled in his literary imaginary, its poetics indebted to aesthetic and political ideologies of organicism. It was this syntax that Berlioz associated with his own work and that of the *fantastique* pieces he admired, including Weber's *Der Freischütz* and *Oberon*. For him, as for his critics, the imaginative grammar of these pieces was also a radical semiotics – onomatopoeic, cabbalistic, electric – poised to materialize new creative and social spaces.

The final chapters of this book move outward, concerned with the ways in which *fantastique* selves and soundworlds proliferated through the middle decades of the century. Berlioz remains, however, a center of gravity, largely because he was perceived as the chief representative – in many accounts, the pioneer – of the fantastic style. But he was not its only adherent, nor was the idiom itself monolithic. Berlioz himself acknowledged at least two subtypes central to his own work and that of his contemporaries: the *fantastique terrible* and the *fantastique gracieux* (an echo of Nodier's 1830 distinction between "religious" and "poetic" fantasy). Both invoked, in quite different ways, the rational and more pointedly real and scientific otherworldliness associated with the modern fantastic. They emancipated fiends, elves, sprites, and other imaginary creatures from the confines of the marvelous, allowing them to creep back into the realm of materiality, to hover between reason and unreason in spaces of ontological hesitation generated (as in the *Symphonie fantastique*) by structural and orchestrational innovation.

The dark or "terrible" fantastic is the focus of Chapter 5, which examines novel kinds of infernal sound in the work of Berlioz and his contemporaries, tracing a move away from the mythological terrains associated with eighteenth-century underworlds toward the semi-real and terrestrial landscapes of romantic hells. Like God himself, demons were naturalized, rendered proximate by fantastic evocation, although the "real" with which they were associated was not the divinely saturated nature theorized by romantic idealism, but an artificial terrain constructed by imperialism – what we might understand, drawing on H. L. Malchow, Patrick Brantlinger, and others as a kind of Gothic naturalism. The new infernal power of these creatures was generated and revealed via science, especially the burgeoning disciplines of anthropology, geography, and comparative philology. In making this argument I return again to the intersections between fantasy and language that underpinned Chapter 4, but now I am less concerned with the "energized" lexicon of revolutionary reformers, more so with the inert, animalian languages Berlioz associated with France's incipient colonies (though, as we shall see, the two were not always separable). For Berlioz, as for Meyerbeer, Liszt, Gounod, and many of their contemporaries, it was the sound of "barbaric" tongues and the rituals attached to them that underpinned fantasies of the inferno. No longer contained by mythology or biblical legend, the modern fiends of these composers were relocated to the fringes of the civilized world, where they hovered between human savagery and supernatural evil, "ethnographic" and otherworldly effects.

The aural vacillation – the confluence of actual and imaginary tropes – that marked the *fantastique terrible* also, as I argue in Chapter 6, underpinned romantic fairy music (Berlioz's "gracious" fantastic). Here, the sounds of miniature magical realms began to blur into microscopic scientific domains, elves and imps into butterflies and bees. In musical works, as in visual fairy-scapes and literary *contes de fées*, fairies were materialized, recast as creatures secreted within rather than held outside the realm of the real. They wavered between the two domains, the product of botany and entomology as much as dream and make-believe. The result was the elfin mode showcased in Berlioz's "Queen Mab" scherzo and prefigured in Weber's and Mendelssohn's fairy-scapes, which drew together established otherworldly tropes with new "natural" effects. In France, such evocations became associated with a genre called the *scherzo fantastique*, which extended well beyond either Mendelssohn or Berlioz, through Liszt, Bazzini, Godard, and, at the turn of the century, Stravinsky. The fairies it conjured were new versions of Paracelsian spirits, emblems of archaic enchantment recalled, in Hoffmannesque fashion, by the technologies of an orchestral present.

In mapping the emergence of these "real" supernaturalisms – the rise of a musical *genre fantastique* – I do not mean to imply that other kinds of magical soundworlds ceased to exist. The lure of and demand for purely escapist spaces (those of the old marvelous) persisted even while new fantastic terrains came into being. As with all aesthetic transformations, the rise of fantasy was messy, inconsistent, and contested. In France, it was wrapped up with various forms of theological and nationalist resistance, perceived by many as a Teutonic import. Gautier, among others, argued that the French were not, by nature, fantastic: "the demi-light so necessary to the fantastic does not exist in France, either in thought, language, or domestic life."[13] Tracing fantasy's musical unfolding and reception means, in part,

---

[13] "Le demi-jour, si nécessaire au fantastique, n'existe en France ni dans la pensée, ni dans la langue, ni dans les maisons." Gautier, "Hoffmann," *La Chronique de Paris* (14 August 1836).

mapping the impact of German literature and aesthetic philosophy in French circles, and especially that of Hoffmann's instrumental metaphysics. As both Gautier's and Janin's tales make clear, the mystique of orchestral sound was central to the mode's emergence; indeed, the orchestra itself was perceived as a novel Hoffmannesque and Berliozian technology, an agent of transformation, coded communication, magical magnification, even mesmerism. Katherine Kolb, in her pioneering 1978 dissertation on Berlioz, suggested as much, arguing that the composer's Orchestration Treatise was essentially a "treatise on the fantastic." And more recently, Inge van Rij has positioned both Berlioz's writing on orchestration and his orchestra itself as devices of exploration and revelation, key portals to the composer's "other worlds."[14]

Chief among these, as I argue here, was what Nodier termed the "intermediate world" (*le monde intermédiare*), the liminal space of fantasy that, for him, was synonymous with a liberated imaginary. Nodier argued that fantasy ushered in new ways of perceiving and being, escaping boundaries and limits, articulating a revolutionary poetics. Music theorists understood the mode as similarly transformative. Charles Soullié, in his 1855 *Nouveau dictionnaire de musique illustré*, defined *fantastique* as a form of "radical romanticism" (*romantisme outré*) crucial to the 1830s and 1840s, but difficult to sum up or contain, seeming to exist just outside established musical practice. His description of the mode is also an apt assessment of Berlioz, whose music, like the *contes fantastiques* with which it was so pervasively entwined, hovered between aurality and textuality, art and science. The composer's wavering other-worlds generated (and reflected) his own uncertain place in the musical canon, explaining to some degree our sense of him as both central and marginal, legible and illegible. At the heart of his musical imaginary, as we shall see, was a form of "radical" sonorous experimentation whose very liminality was the marker of a fantastic modernity.

The danger and promise of contemplating Berlioz's fantastic worlds, as with those of his literary and visual contemporaries is, as Soullié suggests, that they undo legibility; they lead us out of the conventional world of cultural criticism into unstable spaces of poetic invention, hallucination, and speculation. Nineteenth-century descriptions of the fantastic often begin as prefaces or essays, only to shade into anecdotes, autobiographies, or scientific demonstrations. And Berlioz's own criticism hovers constantly on the edge of (sometimes tipping over unashamedly into) fiction and

---

[14] Reeve, "The Poetics of the Orchestra in the Writings of Hector Berlioz," 242. Van Rij, *The Other Worlds of Hector Berlioz.*

confession. To discover where fantasy resides and how it works, we must be willing to be similarly mobile. We must slip from visual and musical discourses through literary, medical, philosophical, and technological ones, often occupying between-spaces. This kind of intermediality and disciplinary blurring can feel precarious, compromising our status as experts, forcing us into foreign or uncertain territory. But it is also emancipatory, allowing musicological questions to become broader inquiries about the nature of intellectual (poetic, magical, made-up) history. Nodier, in his first essay on the *genre fantastique*, sounded a note of caution about (while also clearly delighting in) the slippery nature of his own project. As he put it, "Questions on the fantastic *themselves* reside in the domain of fantasy."[15] But perhaps history and fantasy, and even criticism and fantasy, are not so far apart. Perhaps what we imagine and what we know can be reconciled. Let's see.

[15] "Les questions sur le fantastique sont *elles-mêmes* du domaine de la fantaisie." Nodier, "Du Fantastique en littérature," 109.

1 ❧ The *Fantastique moderne*

Do not, then, cry out so against the romantic and against the fantastic. These supposed innovations are the inevitable expression of extreme periods in the political life of nations and without them I hardly know what would remain to us today of the moral and intellectual impulse of humanity.

– Charles Nodier[1]

This impassioned embrace and defense of fantasy appeared in an essay titled "Du Fantastique en littérature" (November 1830) by Charles Nodier, Parisian author, critic, and early champion of romanticism. Published in the fashionable *Revue de Paris*, and responding in large part to a wave of French enthusiasm for the tales of E. T. A. Hoffmann, it was a landmark piece – a twenty-one-page manifesto – announcing the dawning of a new age in the history of art and aesthetics: that of the fantastic. All that was most innovative and truthful in the human psyche, according to Nodier, all that was truly modern, was expressed through the medium of fantasy, which captured the tenor of the age, representing "the only essential literature in the time of decadence or transformation in which we find ourselves."[2]

These claims were rooted in a panoramic, quasi-Hegelian theory of human intellectual development laid out in the opening pages of the essay, which began with the earliest poetry and led inexorably to the "fantastic" authors Nodier and the members of his circle most admired, including Shakespeare and Goethe. In the "first age" of man, according to this history, "the simple expression of feeling" (*l'expression naïve de la sensation*) gave rise to the birth of language and to a primitive literature rooted in material experience. In the second age, that of man's spiritual development, he invented religion and science, contemplating philosophical truths as well as purely physical realities. Finally, in a third stage of development, he embraced "the lie" (*le mensonge*), hallucinations and dreams widening his imaginative compass to a hitherto unknown degree. As his visions took form, they opened up an

---

[1] "Il ne faut donc pas tant crier contre le romantique et contre le fantastique. Ces innovations prétendues sont l'expression inévitable des périodes extrêmes de la vie politique des nations, et sans elles, je sais à peine ce qui nous resteroit aujourd'hui de l'instinct moral et intellectuel de l'humanité." Nodier, "Du Fantastique en littérature," 210.
[2] "Voilà ce qui a rendu le fantastique ... la seule littérature essentielle de l'âge de décadence ou de transition où nous sommes parvenus." Ibid., 209.

"intermediate world" (*le monde intermédiaire*) – the space of the fantastic – which hovered between the material and the ethereal, embracing both the sensational realm of the first age and the spiritual domain of the second.

The synthesis that produced the *monde fantastique*, the eradication of partitions among the seen, unseen, and imagined, was in part the legacy of political upheaval: "The fantastic demands, in truth, a virginity of imagination and belief that is lacking in lesser literature, not evident in it except in the wake of those revolutions whose passage renews everything."[3] Fantasy, in Nodier's account, was a social force emerging at moments of historical transition during which the impediments to free thought were suddenly (in some cases, temporarily) removed. Such a development had been impossible in France until recently; certainly, Nodier argued, it could not have taken place under the "academic and classical sun" (*le sol académique et classique*) of Louis XIII and Richelieu but only once their repressive regime (and its legacy) had dissolved. Aesthetics are inextricably yoked to politics in his account; those critics who resist the fantastic also resist the tide of ideological change sweeping France. They, the absolutists of the literary world, cling to classical forms, to Quintilian, Boileau, and La Harpe. But classicism, for Nodier, is the mark of a lesser literature, a "partial, momentary, impersonal" mode (*l'expression partielle, momentanée, indifférente*). The Aristotelian unities themselves can no longer be enforced in art, he insists, when "the great unity of the social world is everywhere destroyed" (*quand l'immense unité du monde social se rompoit de toutes parts*). Fantasy offers a larger, more universal vehicle for expression not only proper to the modern world, but irresistible, having already infiltrated drama, elegy, novels, painting, "and all the products of the spirit, as with all the passions of the soul."[4] It would, Nodier insisted in his rousing closing lines, flourish despite all efforts at suppression.

If these were grandiose pronouncements they were also prescient. The new fantastic mode did, as Nodier's essay prognosticated, prove crucial for authors of the 1830s and 1840s, who embraced Hoffmannesque aesthetics eagerly. The first *contes fantastiques* by Théophile Gautier and Honoré de Balzac were in print by 1831 and, hard on their heels, those of Jules Janin, Prosper Mérimée, and Gérard de Nerval. Fantastic impulses wove equally clearly through the writings of Alexandre Dumas, George Sand, and Charles Baudelaire – a debt such authors were quick to acknowledge; indeed, Gautier

---

[3] "Le fantastique demande à la vérité une virginité d'imagination et de croyances qui manque aux littératures secondaires, et qui ne se reproduit chez elles qu'à la suite de ces révolutions dont le passage renouvelle tout." Ibid., 209.

[4] "De ce moment le fantastique fit irruption sur toutes les voies qui conduisent la sensation à l'intelligence ... dans le roman, dans la peinture, dans tous les jeux de l'esprit, comme dans toutes les passions de l'âme." Ibid., 223.

spoke for many when, in 1831, he hailed Hoffmann, *fantastiqueur*, as a beacon of the aesthetic future, an artist piloting a ship in full sail toward the "literary horizon."[5] Nor, as we shall see, were he and his fellow poets and novelists alone in their embrace of the fantastic, which impacted equally clearly the visual world, shaping the outpouring of supernatural imagery (and critical reception of same) produced by Eugène Delacroix, Louis Boulanger, Théodore Géricault, and others through the early-middle decades of the century.[6]

Equally obvious, though less well explored today, was the impact of the fantastic on French musical production. Berlioz's first major work, the *Symphonie fantastique*, remains the best-known – indeed, the only known – representative of sounding fantasy. It premiered a few days after Nodier's landmark essay in a much-publicized concert at the Salle du Conservatoire. The piece was not, of course, a response to the essay; it had been in gestation well before (its first performance was originally planned for May 1830), and yet it must have seemed to its first audience a triumphant ratification of Nodier's claim, proof that his prediction was quickly coming to fruition. The rhetoric of the *Revue* piece bled swiftly into its reception, establishing the symphony as a volatile work from the outset – threatening, promising, or inscrutable depending on which early account one reads. And, as in the literary and visual worlds, it led to a body of other *fantastique* works (symphonies, sonatas, operas, and ballets, so labeled by composers or publishers) and to a sustained discourse among music critics around the nature and meaning of fantastic sound. Hardly just a fashionable tag or buzzword, the rubric was, for Nodier and his contemporaries, a loaded one, the stuff of controversy and "modernity," of a world in the throes of change. Joseph D'Ortigue, in an 1834 review of Berlioz's first symphony, argued "that a great development has taken place in the realm of musical art in France, and that this revolution dates precisely to the *Symphonie fantastique*."[7] Here, I unpack

---

[5] Gautier, "Hoffmann," in Lovenjoul, *Histoire des oevures de Théophile Gautier*, I:11–16 (here, 11). Gautier's first *conte fantastique*, "La Cafetière," appeared in 1831, marking the start of a series of otherworldly tales stretching through "Spirite" (1856). Jules Janin's collection *Contes fantastiques et contes littérairies* (1832), which begins with the story "Kreyssler," led to a series of musico-fantastic stories published in the *Gazette musicale* through 1835–36 to which we shall return in Chapter 3. Nerval translated Hoffmann's work alongside Goethe's *Faust*, which together influenced his own fantastic stories including "Aurélia" (1855). Balzac's *La Peau de chagrin* (1831) and Sand's "Le Secrétaire intime" (1833) both betray a Hoffmannesque influence that persists in the otherworldly writing of these authors over the following decade. A number of Baudelaire's aesthetic essays, notably "L'Essence du rire," feature sustained close readings of Hoffmann.

[6] For a sense of fantasy's visual manifestations during this period, see the following exhibition catalogues: Sueur-Hermel, *Fantastique!*; and Farigoule et al., *Visages de l'Effroi*.

[7] "nous ne sommes plus le seul à affirmer … qu'un grand développement a eu lieu dans l'art musical en France et que cette révolution date précisément de la *Symphonie fantastique*." *La Quotidienne* (12 November 1834).

this claim, opening up a series of contexts (literary, philosophical, political, musical) against which to read fantasy. I am concerned with how and what the term meant in France and with the ways in which it reshaped conceptions of the otherworldly – read, seen, and heard.

Reading Hoffmann

[T]he fantastic ... is already a fixed genre, a genre with its contours, its requirements, its color, its disposition. Hoffmann created the genre. One recognizes it, one expects its particular manner and would not have it otherwise.

– Review of Jules Janin, *Contes fantastiques*[8]

The emergence of the fantastic as a literary and more broadly aesthetic category in France was tied, as the above critic claims, to the arrival of Hoffmann. He was not the "creator" of the idiom (as we shall see, its roots are long and rich), but his tales sparked the first sustained theorization of the mode in France, situating him as a crucial formal and stylistic template. Work by the German author began to filter into Paris in the two years preceding Nodier's essay and Berlioz's symphony, first as a series of excerpts appearing in literary and music journals and slightly later (beginning in November 1829) in a complete, multivolume translation by François Adolphe Loève-Veimars published under the title *Contes fantastiques*.[9] The Parisian public consumed this material with appetite, generating a popular as well as scholarly vogue for fantastic tales that rendered Hoffmann among the most-read and much-discussed authors

---

[8] "[L]e fantastique ... est déjà un genre arrêté; un genre qui a ses lignes, ses exigences, sa couleur, sa portée. Hoffmann a fait le genre. On le connaît, on l'exige selon sa manière, on n'en veut pas d'autre." "*Contes fantastiques*, par M. Jules Janin," *L'Artiste* (28 October 1832).

[9] The first Hoffmann translations included "Mademoiselle de Scudéry" and "Les Écarts d'un homme à l'imagination," published in the *Bibliothèque universelle de Genève* (January–February and March–April, 1828), and "L'Archet du Baron de B." in *Le Gymnase* (8 May 1828). Through 1829 and early 1830, his work appeared in the *Revue de Paris, Revue musicale, Mode, Mercure des salons*, and *Journal des débats*. The translations by Loève-Veimars appeared in two series. The first was titled *Contes fantastiques de E. T. A. Hoffmann, traduits de l'allemand par M. Loève-Veimars, traducteur de Van der Velde et de Zschokke, et précédés d'une notice historique sur Hoffmann par Walter Scott* (Paris: Renduel, 1830), Vols. I–XII. The second was a continuation of the first, published as *Oeuvres complètes de Hoffmann. Contes nocturnes de E. T. A. Hoffmann* (Paris: Renduel, 1830), Vols. XIII–XIX. A rival team of translators, Théodor Toussenel and R. A. Richard, launched its own complete translation in May 1830 under the title *Oeuvres complètes de E. T. A. Hoffmann, traduites de l'allemand par M. Théodore Toussenel et par le traducteur des romans de Veit-Wéber* (Paris: J. Lefebvre, 1830). For a full chronology of Hoffmann translations, see Teichmann, *La Fortune d'Hoffmann en France*, 237–257; also Hübener, *Kreisler in Frankreich*, 72–82.

of the moment. His fiction gave rise to a debate that endured through the remainder of the decade as well as a spate of imitations extending through the rest of the century. Enticing and in some quarters threatening, Hoffmann opened up what many described as a "new" or "unknown" world, a space of transformation. The German *conteur* was, as French readers noted, better known and more influential in France than in Germany, if less well understood.[10]

Among the earliest Hoffmann excerpts to appear was a piece from the novella-length work "The Golden Pot" ("Le Pot d'or"), published in the *Revue de Paris* in May 1829 in a translation by the young author-academic Saint-Marc Girardin. The tale, which became a favorite among Parisian readers, is set in modern-day Dresden, its opening section (the "First Vigil") taking place at a precisely described time and location: three o'clock on Ascension Day outside the Black Gate. A student, Anselmus, while racing to the pub, accidentally knocks over a market stall whose contents are scattered on the ground. Covered in embarrassment, he offers his purse to the old woman who owns the stall and, having thus given up all his cash, can no longer indulge in the revelry he had planned at a local pub (Linke's Inn, according to Hoffmann). Instead, he wanders down to the shore of the Elbe, where he ruminates on his misfortune and smokes. His world, as it is painted in the tale's opening pages, is that of prosaic reality: he fills his pipe with "health-tobacco" (*tabac de santé*), bemoans his shoddy clothes, and contemplates a job opportunity suggested to him by one Rector Paulmann. But as the tale proceeds, the familiar world is slowly compromised: Anselmus begins to hear voices emanating from the grasses around him and from the tree under which he sits. Three green-and-gold snakes slithering up and down the tree reach their necks out to him and, gazing at them, he finds himself looking into a pair of "sparkling azure eyes" (*deux yeux d'un bleu d'azur étincelant*) which produce in him a sense of inexpressible yearning. As the sun goes down, these visions fade, the lovely eyes vanish, and the snakes once again seem just to be snakes, which disappear into the river.[11]

As this, the first portion of the tale, draws to a close, readers are left wondering whether Anselmus simply imagined the encounter with the blue eyes and "speaking" breezes or if these events actually took place.

---

[10] References to Hoffmann's "monde nouveau" or "monde inconnu" are ubiquitous; see, for instance, "Contes fantastiques d'Hoffmann, traduction d'un extrait du 'Pot-d'or,'" *Revue de Paris* (May 1829); "Hoffmann," *L'Artiste* (4/11); "Oeuvres d'Hoffmann," *Le Figaro* (30 January 1830). Gautier's claim for Hoffmann's importance (and opacity) in France appears in his essay "Hoffmann," *Chronique de Paris* (14 August 1836).

[11] Girardin, "Contes fantastiques d'Hoffmann, traduction d'un extrait du Pot d'or," *Revue de Paris* (May 1829), 65–73.

The experience, as Tzvetan Todorov puts it, is one of hesitation, an uncertainty surrounding the relationship between reality and the unreal, waking and dreaming, that stands (according to his oft-quoted definition) at the core of romantic fantasy.[12] And it was precisely this sensation that Girardin himself described in a brief comment appended to his translation:

> He [Hoffmann] excels in painting the bourgeoisie, and when he describes family life, with its monotonous and routine tranquility (which is, of course, not without charm) in a tone full of malicious good humor, when he recounts the smallest details with a kind of ingenious wit, one hardly thinks of the marvelous, of spirits and phantoms. We do not suspect that this story, entirely concerned until now with trivial and familiar things, will suddenly change – that we will be diverted all at once from the affairs of domestic life toward the most fantastic creations, toward the most mysterious horrors... that we will be transported to an unknown world full of marvels... that we will be, from one moment to the next, dazzled, delighted, charmed, terrified, seized with a mysterious horror, unable to breath or stir until the end of the story. This is the great art of Hoffmann.[13]

In the face of such a striking and unfamiliar style, how, Girardin asked, was he to respond? Literary analyses (*réflexions littéraires*) seemed virtually impossible; instead, he insisted, the tale would have to serve as its own exegesis.

Girardin's perplexity quickly became endemic among Parisian critics, who perceived in many of Hoffmann's other tales the same liminality – a tendency toward narrative wavering. A reviewer for *Le Globe* observed that "the marvelous, for him [Hoffmann], is not simply a flight of fancy nor a theatrical trick but something real which has its root in the human spirit." His mingling of natural with otherworldly impulses generated a sense of vertigo that was both readerly and writerly. Rather than just a narrative ruse, in other words – a bit of smoke and mirrors – it derived from a new sense of ontological instability:

---

[12] Todorov, *The Fantastic*, especially chap. 2, "Definition of the Fantastic," 24–40.

[13] "Il excelle à peindre la bourgeoisie, et quand il décrit d'un ton plein de bonhomie malicieuse la vie de famille et sa tranquillité monotone et routinière, qui n'est pourtant pas sans charme, quand il raconte les plus petits détails avec une sorte de commérage ingénieux, vous ne pensez certes pas au merveilleux, aux esprits, aux fantômes; vous ne soupçonnez pas que tout à l'heure cette histoire, tout occupée jusqu'ici de choses triviales et familières, va changer brusquement, et que des affaires de ménage nous allons être tout-à coup détournés vers les créations les plus fantastiques, vers les plus mystérieuses horreurs... que nous allons être transportés dans un monde inconnu, plein de merveilles... que nous allons, en moins d'un moment, être tour à tour éblouis, enchantés, charmés, épouvantés, saisis d'une horreur mystérieuse, ne pouvant ni respirer ni remuer jusqu'à la fin de l'histoire. Tel est le grand art d'Hoffmann." Girardin, "Contes fantastiques d'Hoffmann," 60–61.

We read the *Thousand and One Nights* with avid appetite, with delight, but to move us truly deeply the *Thousand and One Nights* is too foreign to our beliefs, too estranged from our regular lives. And, as in fairy tales, the sense of fiction [it generates] persists from the first to the last line, as much in the characters themselves as in the events, and in every detail throughout. With Hoffmann, we doubt whether it [the narrative] is truth or fiction and, curiously, Hoffmann himself sometimes also doubted.[14]

The result of this vacillation was pathological self-splintering – mere madness – according to some, but to others it suggested increased awareness, acknowledgment of a higher reality uncontainable by either the marvelous or realist modes. A critic for the *Journal des débats* argued that Hoffmann had cultivated a kind of "double" vision prefigured by Jean Paul Richter and Goethe. Rather than confining himself to *le grand chemin d'en haut* (the ethereal realm) or to *la terre tout simplement* (the material realm), he attempted to embrace both worlds at once, exploring the subtle and pervasive interconnections between the two.[15] In so doing, he introduced a novel form of literary fantasy: what many critics referred to as the "real" or "true" supernatural (*le surnaturel vrai*). This was not, as Gautier explained, the make-believe world of the French *conte de fées* – the domain of castles, magical talismans, and spells – but a supernatural for the modern age rooted in "occult sympathies and antipathies, singular [types of] madness, visions, magnetism, mysterious influences," in vibrant sentiments "true to nature" and to "the physiognomy of things."[16]

If it blurred ontological boundaries, Hoffmannesque fantasy also, as Gautier pointed out, ruptured epistemological ones, allowing the rhetoric of science to intermingle with that of fiction, references to microscopy,

---

[14] "Le merveilleux, pour lui, n'est ni un jeu d'esprit, ni un jeu de théâtre, mais quelque chose de réel qui a sa racine dans l'esprit humain."; "On lit les Mille et une Nuits avec avidité, avec ravissement; mais pour émouvoir si profondément, les Mille et une Nuits sont trop étrangères à nos croyances, trop en dehors de nos habitudes. Et quant aux contes de fées, la fiction se fait sentir depuis la première jusqu'à la dernière ligne, aussi bien dans les caractères que dans les événements, dans chaque détail que dans l'ensemble. Avec Hoffmann, on doute si c'est vérité ou fiction; et, chose curieuse, Hoffmann lui-même en doutait quelquefois." *Le Globe* (26 December 1829).
[15] *Journal des débats* (22 May 1830).
[16] "Le merveilleux d'Hoffmann n'est pas le merveilleux des contes de fées; il a toujours un pied dans le monde reel. ... Les talismans et les baguettes des Mille et une Nuits ne lui sont d'aucun usage. Les sympathies et les antipathies occultes, les folies singulières, les visions, le magnétisme, les influences mystérieuses et malignes d'un mauvais principe qu'il ne désigne que vaguement, voilà les éléments surnaturels ou extraordinaires qu'emploie habituellement Hoffmann.... La rapidité du succès d'Hoffmann est ... dans le sentiment vif et vrai de la nature qui éclate à un si haut degré dans ses compositions les moins explicables." *Chronique de Paris* (14 August 1836).

chemistry, and geology to shade into anecdotes from legend and history. This universalist quality had been noted in the earliest reviews of the German author's *contes*, including a piece for *Le Figaro*, which claimed that "every branch of human knowledge" (*chaque branche des connaissances humaines*) was represented in Hoffmann's fantastic reveries – that they seemed to dissolve the partitions between disciplinary modes. He was (as another critic put it) "accustomed to confusing plant with man, sound with image, marble statue with living being, the brilliantly colored canvas with its model, thought with organic entity," drawing together heterogeneous collections of material into "strange arabesques, in which can sometimes be felt the fine and energetic quality of [Jacques] Callot and the verve of the Venetian [Carlo] Gozzi."[17] Even more unsettling (and especially significant here) was Hoffmann's perceived destabilization of language. His writing overstepped the boundaries of text, the literary spilling over into the musical, the semantic hovering on the edge of the purely sonorous. Hoffmann had not written but heard and composed his tales, according to some. "Le Pot d'or" was "a magnificent concert in which all the harmonies are confused," and Hoffmannesque drama more broadly was "born in some sense from the noise of a musical instrument."[18] Hoffmann the *conteur* was inextricable from Hoffmann the musician: he wore both hats at once. Not just generically and stylistically polymorphic, then, his work rested on a slippery relationship between language and sound. Could such work be translated? How and what did it mean? Where had it come from? And what might it do?

From the late 1820s onward, critics asked and – in partial, sometimes hazy terms – attempted to answer these questions. Nodier's *Revue* piece, the first effort to historicize and contextualize fantasy, shows us with special clarity the complexity of its provenance. His essay is replete with literary echoes: references to his own earlier writing on *mélodrame*, to Hugo's much-touted Preface to the drama *Cromwell*, and to Germaine de Staël's *De l'Allemagne*. For him, as we have seen, fantasy was the product of revolution, a mode shaped by violence and rupture, by the forceful dissolution of established social and aesthetic systems. But equally obviously, it was

[17] *Le Figaro* (9 December 1830) and *Journal des débats* (22 May 1830), the second of which referred to "cet homme accoutumé à confondre la plante avec l'homme, le son avec l'image, la statue de marbre avec l'être vivant, le canevas brillant de couleurs avec le modèle qui s'y trouve copié, la pensée avec l'être organique," drawing this material into "arabesques étranges, où on retrouve quelquefois la touche fine et énergique de Callot, et la verve du vénitien Gozzi."

[18] In *L'Artiste* (4/15), the "Pot d'or" is "un magnifique concert où toutes les harmonies sont confondues"; in *Le Temps* (28 February 1830), "Le drame d'Hoffmann est né en quelque sorte au bruit d'un instrument de musique." See also *Le Corsaire* (2 April 1830), where Hoffmann himself is "la harpe éolienne; elle retentit et chacun l'entend avec ses sensations intimes."

generated by new and especially Teutonic modes of revelation. Germany, he wrote, was home to "a particular system of moral organization lending its beliefs an imaginative fervor, a vivacity of sentiment, a doctrinal mysticism, [and] a universal penchant for idealism which are fundamental to fantastic poetry."[19] Nodier's twin explanation for fantasy – his sense of the mode as both philosophically foreign and politically radical – was echoed by a host of later commentators, among them Jules Janin, who, in an 1832 entry for the *Dictionnaire de la conversation et de la lecture*, began by situating not just the aesthetics of the fantastic, but the term *itself* as German. "Fantastique," he argued, was an entirely new rubric, "a word more German than French, and this is precisely why we have embraced it so eagerly." Its entry into Parisian vocabulary could be dated to "five or six years ago," when the *contes fantastiques* had arrived, sparking a literary and political sea change. According to Janin, the term "produced among us a revolution at least equal to the one set in motion by that other word, *romantique!*"[20]

Janin's etymological claim is interesting partly because it is inaccurate. *Fantastique* was not a new word at all, but one with an old French provenance; it had appeared in the first edition of the *Dictionnaire de l'Académie française* (1694), where it was described as "illusory, chimerical" (*visionnaire, chimérique*), associated with something or someone imaginary, lacking true form (*Qui n'a que l'apparence, & non pas l'estre véritable*). Similar definitions appeared through the eighteenth-century editions of the *Dictionnaire* and in other lexicons of the period, among them Jean-François Féraud's *Dictionnaire critique de la langue française* (1787–88), which gave *fantastique* as the adjectival form of *fantôme*, a term referring to a "specter" or "empty image" (*vain image*). Rather than a novel term, then, it was one whose meaning had shifted, at least in critical and scholarly circles (if not always in popular usage), around the time of Hoffmann's ascendancy.

This was precisely the argument made by Nodier's friend Léon Cailleux, who, in a lengthy 1848 essay on the fantastic, situated the word as both domestic and foreign. It was by no means unknown in France, Cailleux acknowledged, but had been diverted in the late eighteenth century from its traditional usage. Up until then it had referred to imaginary worlds, flights

---

[19] "C'est que l'Allemagne, favorisée d'un système particulier d'organisation morale, porte dans ses croyances une ferveur d'imagination, une vivacité de sentimens, une mysticité de doctrines, un penchant universel à l'idéalisme, qui sont essentiellement propres à la poétique fantastique." Nodier, "Du Fantastique," 221.

[20] "Fantastique: c'est un mot qui est plus allemand que français, et voilà justement pourquoi nous l'avons adopté avec tant d'empressement. ... Ce mot nouveau, *fantastique*, produisit chez nous une révolution égale pour le moins à la révolution opérée par cet autre mot, romantique!" Janin, "Fantastique," 299.

of whimsy, eccentric or bizarre fabrications, but under the influence of romantic philosophical and social impulses its signification had changed. No longer synonymous with fanciful supernaturalism, the *fantastique moderne* was instead molded by skepticism:

[O]ne must not confuse the fantastic here [in a modern context] with the supernatural: one is the prerogative of a young nation of believers, the other is typical of a century jaded and marked by unbelief; one is the cause, the other the effect. One does not know the fantastic when one believes in the supernatural; one no longer believes in the supernatural when one knows the fantastic.[21]

Cailleux's ideas resurfaced in later definitions, including a detailed entry for *fantastique* in Larousse's *Grand dictionnaire universel du XIXe siècle* (1866–76), which replaced the supernatural-fantastic binary with a new pairing – one that would endure through the twentieth century. Fantasy in the old sense of the word, according to Larousse, was productive of a "marvelous" magical tradition native to France while the Hoffmannesque fantastic was a foreign and dangerous mode. Here again, the latter term is distanced from the French language entirely:

The word "fantastique," more German than French, refers in general to modern modes of literary production. The marvelous, on the contrary, is our venerable [literary] ancestor whose exemplars stretch back to the earliest times. It feeds on all that is illusory, [on] poetic falsehood; it operates in the domain of popular ignorance and credulity. Of philosophical speculations it knows nothing. The [marvelous] apparitions which form the basis of the ancient legends, the visitations by mythological divinities, the supernatural incidents which form the stuff of the Italian epics, have nothing in common with the subtle, incoherent, and sinister art of Hoffmann who, upon his appearance among us, around 1830, provoked such vertiginous enthusiasm.[22]

---

[21] "[I]l ne faut pas confondre ici le fantastique avec le surnaturel: l'un est l'apanage d'une nation jeune et croyante, l'autre le type d'un siècle usé et incrédule, l'un est la cause, l'autre est l'effet; on ne connaît pas le fantastique quand on croit au surnaturel; on ne croit plus au surnaturel lorsqu'on connaît le fantastique." Cailleux, "Études: Sur le fantastique," 228. The term *fantastique moderne* had been introduced well before Cailleux, in Nodier's Preface to the second edition of the tale *Smarra, ou les démons de la nuit* (1832).

[22] "Le mot fantastique, mot plus allemand que français, exprime en général des procédés de fabrication littéraire tout modernes. Le merveilleux, au contraire, est pour nous un ancêtre vénérable dont les parchemins remontent aux premiers âges. Il s'alimente de tout ce qui est illusion, mensonge poétique; il a pour domaine l'ignorance des peuples et leur crédulité. Les spéculations philosophiques, il s'en éloigne. Ces apparitions, qui faisaient le fond des anciennes légendes, ces interventions de divinités mythologiques, ces incidents surnaturels dont sont faits les poétiques qui remplissent les épopées italiennes, n'ont rien de commun avec l'art subtil, incohérent et sinistre de cet Hoffmann, qui, à son apparition chez nous, vers 1830, provoqua un enthousiasme si vertigineux." Larousse, "Fantastique," 93.

Larousse, like his predecessors, understood fantasy as a product of (and vehicle for) German philosophy, especially idealist currents, which rendered it a genre "equally open to the ideal and the real" (*également ouvert à l'idéal et à la réalité*). Steeped in (in places inextricable from) metaphysical speculation, it was tiresome, full of "laborious lucubrations" (*laborieuses élucubrations*) and intellectual pedantry, and as such, fundamentally opposed to the French virtues of transparency, grace, and charm. But its roots could not be traced to philosophy alone nor to Germany, for fantasy was equally clearly the product of France's own revolutionary history. The mode, in Larousse's description, was a species of terror, the locus not just of metaphysical theory, but a form of monstrous realism: "in the fantasy writer, there is generally a violent realist" (*dans l'écrivain fantastique, il y a généralement un réaliste violent*). Rather than just a spinner of tales he was a promulgator of chaos, the author of a world in which ugliness, distortion, and incoherence had ruptured the realm of order. His work was the fruit of psychological and social terror – drunkenness, confusion, nightmare – as well as willful perversion, "a love of the grotesque," and "a love of the horrible."[23]

Unlike Nodier, Larousse is relentlessly negative (in his assessment, the fantastic is absurd, extravagant, incoherent), but he nevertheless confirms the mode as an aesthetic category of widespread significance – one that impacted all the arts, from theater and fiction to painting. But fantasy's most important influence historically, he argues, lies in the domains of text and sound; indeed, his entry is divided into sections on the literary and *musical* fantastic (we shall return to the latter presently). The two are intertwined, both emerging from the same twin social and philosophical impulses, which together generate their distinctive "hesitation" – the feature that separates fantasies from marvels, innocent imaginings from otherworldly realities. Larousse provides, for the first time, a clear set of distinctions among magical ontologies: "ancient" enchantment, French marvels, English Gothic traditions, and Hoffmannesque fantasies. Each, he argues, has its own characteristics, not to be confounded with its neighbors; indeed, for him, understanding fantasy means placing Hoffmann's mode against this wider history of supernaturalism. His parsing, echoed and amplified by later theorists from Freud to Todorov, gestures toward a deep backdrop for the fantastic that bears teasing out, albeit briefly, here. How are marvels different from fantasies? What preceded these magical modes and why the series of shifts? And, most importantly for our purposes, how is music implicated in Larousse's overlapping and evolving taxonomy of magical systems?

---

[23] Ibid., 94.

In the sections to follow, I address these queries, not by developing a singular theory of fantasy, but by examining what French critics understood as the intellectual and political impulses catalyzing Hoffmann's *surnaturel vrai*: the innovations of idealist metaphysics, which facilitated a convergence of natural and supernatural domains; and the shock of revolutionary violence, which collapsed rationalism with unreason. In tracing these events, I also begin to connect (and separate) fantasy from both the "ancient" magic of the sixteenth century and the Gothic impulses of the eighteenth. From there, I deal with the marvelous-fantastic distinction so central to Larousse's definition, outlining the nationalist impulses associated with this divide, in particular the ways in which the French "theater of marvels" was destabilized by the advent of German fantasy. Sound, as we shall see, runs as a crucial thread through this history, activating and deactivating enchantment, articulating the shifting boundaries between reason and imagination. In the final section of this chapter, I home in on its importance and impact, detailing the ways in which music, especially Berlioz's *Symphonie fantastique*, set the stage for French fantasy, ushering in not just new ways of writing, but modern forms of hearing and listening.

The Return of Divinity *or* The Metaphysics of Fantasy

That French critics understood romantic fantasy in part as a Teutonic invention, a product of shifting eighteenth-century philosophical currents, is by no means surprising, for it was in German aesthetic discourse of the 1790s that the first sustained theorization of the "real" fantastic was to be found. Its tenets are described most clearly by Friedrich Schlegel, who, from the outset, figured the mode as both literary and sounding, both visceral and imaginary, marked by hesitations of various sorts. His remarks on the subject are to be found in the "Letter about the Novel" (1799), which begins by linking the fantastic to the romantic in a famously enigmatic claim: "The Romantic is a sentimental theme in a fantastic form." This form, as Schlegel outlines it, is synonymous with the one French Hoffmann critics describe: all-inclusive, transhistorical, and cross-disciplinary, uniting imaginary realms (the "world of the knights") with "things of the past," fairytales with "true histories," fiction with autobiography and science in an arabesque-like "mixture of storytelling, song and other forms."[24] Eliminating all

---

[24] Schlegel, "Letter about the Novel" ("Brief über den Roman"), in *Classic and Romantic German Aesthetics*, 287–96 (here, 293–94).

boundaries and classifications, it allows poets to capture the "sentimental," which, as Schlegel tells us, is really the "spiritual":

What then is this sentimental? It is that which appeals to us, where feeling prevails, and to be sure, not a sensual but a spiritual feeling. The source and soul of all these emotions is love, and the spirit of love must hover everywhere invisibly visible in romantic poetry. That is what is meant by this definition.[25]

The spiritual love that permeates the romantic is itself at the heart of the fantastic; indeed, it is "the source of the fantastic in the form of all poetic representation," the shaper of a new kind of supernaturalism. No longer purely elusive or immaterial, it is, in Schlegel's telling, visceral and immanent, a magic contained within and apprehended via the actual and, more pointedly, the natural world: "The imagination strives with all its might to express itself, but the divine can communicate and express itself only indirectly in the sphere of nature."[26] Romantic fantasy, he argues, articulates the supernatural through the sensible world.

This reconceptualization of spirituality, and therefore also of fantasy, was rooted (as French critics were well aware) in the idealist philosophy of the young German romantics centered in Jena and Berlin in the last decade of the eighteenth century, among them Friedrich Schlegel, his brother August Wilhelm, Georg Phillip Friedrich von Hardenberg (Novalis), Friedrich Hölderlin, Friedrich Schelling, and (somewhat later) Friedrich Schleiermacher. The innovations of this group were rooted, in part, in a rethinking of Kant's "transcendental" idealism, whose aim had been a reconciliation of the old tensions between rationalism and empiricism. Though it had succeeded in bridging this divide, Kant's critical philosophy had, in so doing, generated what his younger contemporaries regarded as a new and equally problematic division between understanding and sensibility, materiality and mysticism – a tendency to isolate reason from the rest of human experience. The new "romantic" idealism of Schlegel's circle was in part an attempt to solve this difficulty – to generate a philosophical model eliminating (or at least minimizing) dualism, drawing together the real and ideal, natural and supernatural into a logical whole. It did this in part by expanding the entrenched theological positions of the time, theism and atheism, to include a third way, a pantheistic stance rooted in the ideas of seventeenth-century philosopher Baruch Spinoza.[27]

---

[25] Ibid., 291.   [26] Ibid., 292.
[27] For a thorough treatment of romantic idealism (including its intersection with Spinozism), see Beiser, *German Idealism*. A more succinct overview is provided by Guyer in *The Cambridge Companion to German Idealism*, 37–56. And for a focused consideration of idealism's intersection with pantheism, see Lamm, "Romanticism and Pantheism."

Building on Spinoza's ideas (communicated largely via Gottfried Herder), the German *Frühromantiker* eliminated the idea of a personal God, a distinct, removed deity, replacing it with the notion of the divine as an organic force, an animator of the natural world at every level, from that of fundamental chemical reactions to growth, fruition, and decay. Their work combined Spinoza's monism – the notion of God as an abstract underlying Substance – with the tenets of vital materialism to produce a dynamic deity, "the infinite, substantial force ... that underlies all finite, organic forces." The result was an integration of spirituality and materiality, imaginary and actual worlds, which were subsumed into "an organic whole, where the identity of each part depends on every other, [where] the subject and object ... are interdependent aspects of a single living force."[28] Recast in this form, God (and enchantment more broadly) became compatible not just with the material but the empirical; indeed, magic was made accessible to (or at least could be intuited via) science, including the disciplines of chemistry, biology, geology, and botany. Schleiermacher encouraged his friends "to penetrate into nature's interior," arguing that "its chemical power, the eternal laws according to which bodies themselves are formed and destroyed, these are the phenomena in which we intuit the universe most clearly and in a most holy manner."[29] What emerged was, in the simplest terms, the notion of God-through-nature or, to return to the formulations we have already encountered, the idea of a "real," "natural," or "scientific" supernatural: the essence of metaphysical fantasy.[30]

Capturing and representing this new aesthetic, according to Schlegel, required human imagination and intuition – art – but not all arts were equally capable of the task. Neither literature nor visual media was best; instead, *music* was most apt:

> Painting is no longer as fantastic.... Modern music, on the other hand, as far as the ruling power of man in it is concerned, has remained true on the whole to its character, so that I would dare to call it without reservation a sentimental art.... [The spiritual] is the sacred breath which, in the tones of music, moves us. It cannot be grasped forcibly and comprehended mechanically, but it can be amiably lured by mortal beauty and veiled in it. The magic words of poetry can be infused with and inspired by its power.

Poetry, then, is fantastic only if it is animated by sentimental (spiritual) sound: language and music are yoked together at the heart of Schlegel's

---

[28] Lamm, "Romanticism and Pantheism," 172; and Beiser, *German Idealism*, 372.
[29] Lamm, "Romanticism and Pantheism," 176.
[30] The idea that "romantic" or "absolute" idealism departed from Kant's "critical" idealism by virtue of a greater degree of emphasis on realism and naturalism is at the core of Beiser's account; for a summary, see *German Idealism*, 349–74.

theory of romantic fantasy in an inextricable pairing. In tandem, they provide an intimation of true magic, "something higher, the infinite, a hieroglyph of the one eternal love and the sacred fullness of life of creative nature."[31]

As M. H. Abrams has taught us, Schlegel's fantastic was not an entirely new aesthetic but a recuperated one, an ontology (as Schlegel himself put it) "tending toward antiquity in spirit and in kind."[32] It represented a partial return to an earlier musico-magical domain, that of the Neoplatonic Renaissance (Larousse's "ancient" magic), in which visible and invisible, material and ethereal realms were bound together in a resonant whole. Schlegel described this as a "mystical" place in which Pythagorean ideas and Classical philosophy mingled with Christian tenets to generate an all-encompassing magic. Here, God was the source of all enchantment, the shaper of pure Platonic ideas that permeated everything from planetary bodies to human, animal, and vegetable life and even the raw elements themselves. According to Renaissance cosmologists, His divine enchantment flowed downward through all planes of being – intellectual, celestial, and mundane – in the form of harmonic concordances. They imagined these emanating from a taut string, a monochord vibrating along its length according to a sacred musico-mathematical logic. Every facet of the created universe was animated by its sound, connected to every other via resonant sympathies. The result was a single organism, an organic whole bound together via ubiquitous musical magic. Magician-philosophers harnessed its power by penetrating the secrets of the universal sympathies, the mathematical connections between macrocosm and microcosm. Hearing the *discordia concors* of the world, they were invested with Orphic sway, translating magical resonance into composed sound, which, vibrating within material bodies, brought them into (or out of) tune with the surrounding universe. Poets did much the same; indeed, spoken language shared the properties of sound, deriving meaning and efficacy from its imitation of divine harmony. As Gary Tomlinson puts it, "the magical forces of words and music were ... indistinguishable, since both were sounding number," both were human echoes of cosmic enchantment.[33]

This world, and the intellectual-magical unity on which it rested, exercised a persistent hold over Schlegel's generation. To them it seemed a lost utopia, a space of magic that had dissipated through the seventeenth and

---

[31] Schlegel, "Letter about the Novel," in *Classic and Romantic German Aesthetics*, 291.
[32] See Abrams, *Natural Supernaturalism*. Schlegel's remark can be found in *Classic and Romantic German Aesthetics*, 293.
[33] Tomlinson, *Music and Renaissance Magic*, 62–63. For a broader sense of the magical ontology I outline here, a classic starting point is Yates, *Giordano Bruno and the Hermetic Tradition*. More recent studies useful for their overviews of the scholarly literature on Renaissance magic include Kieckhefer, *Magic in the Middle Ages*; Copenhaver, *Magic in Western Culture*; and Gouk, *Music, Science, and Natural Magic*.

eighteenth centuries, disrupted by the burgeoning impulses of rationalism – the "enlightened" scientific and social forces that had repressed magic, exiling it to the intellectual peripheries. Indeed, the philosophical monism pursued by the post-Kantian idealists was propelled in part by a sense of loss and longing, an attempt to reanimate direct human access to divinity, grace, and spiritual experience, to re-forge the living connections between macro- and microcosm. Of course, their ideas did not restore sixteenth-century Neoplatonism (the intellectual legacy of the Enlightenment made such a thing impossible), but instead refashioned it along new lines. Their God was no longer a tuner of the universe, the head of a cosmic-sonic hierarchy, but a force implicit within it, synonymous with the natural world itself. Once again, the spiritual was accessible to reason, though not now through astronomy and occult mathematics (the disciplines that had laid bare the Pythagorean world), but instead through the emerging natural sciences (those able to penetrate the new organic universe). Perceiving God again meant looking at and especially listening to his physical creation, the voice of nature itself, whose sound – now audible rather than simply mathematical – was re-empowered, uniting all creatures in sympathy or concordance.

The speaking breezes and magical natural creatures of fantastic tales – those of Hoffmann and, later, of his French champions – were in large part products of idealism's recuperated enchantment, symbols of a renewed allegiance between materiality and spirituality. "Le Pot d'or" is a case in point (indeed, a *locus classicus* of the new natural enchantment), a story in which divinity is accessed through the organic world, especially through sounding nature. Anselmus's first inkling of enchantment arrives in the form of "crystalline" tones emanating from the earth around him, which alert him to the presence of the elemental being Serpentina (the green snake with whom he falls in love). Later, the rustling of the tree in which she hides divulges secrets of her magical world, and the myriad sounds of songbirds, buzzing insects, rushing streams, and roaring cataracts in her father's (Prince Phosphorous's) laboratory convey to him the truths of a higher world, a sonorous trace contained within the domain of the actual. The tale is in large part about his burgeoning awareness of this aural environment, which stimulates a spiritual and intellectual insight unavailable to others.[34]

But of course this sort of enchantment, seen and heard, was not the only magic reanimated in *contes fantastiques*. If Hoffmann's new mode rematerialized divinity, it also recalled darker forces: specters, ghouls, and vampires.

---

[34] Commentaries on this tale and its philosophical resonances are voluminous; see, as starting points, Brown, *E. T. A. Hoffmann and the Serapiontic Principle*; Bergström, *Between Real and Unreal*; Negus, "E. T. A. Hoffmann's *Der goldene Topf*"; idem, *E. T. A. Hoffmann's Other World*; and Bollnow, "Der 'goldene Topf.'"

And these creatures were not the product of idealist metaphysics, but, as Nodier and his contemporaries understood, of revolutionary terror.

The Return of Unreason *or* The Politics of Fantasy

Fantastic tales – both Hoffmann's and, even more persistently, those of his French champions – are replete with ominous figures. Among them, we might count the German author's Coppelia, the malevolent alchemist in "The Sandman"; Giulia, the temptress of "A New Year's Eve Adventure"; and Torbern, the black shadow in "The Mines of Falun." These are figures of nightmare although they are also tied to the waking world: Giulia is also the young girl Julietta, Coppelia is the merchant Coppola, and Torbern is the old miner of Göteborg. Together, such characters form unresolved doubles, floating between reverie and reality, sanity and insanity. In French fantastic tales, similar horrors are to be found: Gautier's "La Morte amoureuse" features a beloved woman who is also a corpse, Mérimée's "La Vénus d'Ille" a statue who doubles as a succubus, and Dumas's "La Femme au collier de velours" a socialite who is revealed as a dead guillotine victim. These emblems of darkness hover, like Schlegel's new organic divinity, in an ambiguous space between materiality and the imaginary, generating an uncomfortable sense of wavering: Are they actual monsters? Specters of the unconscious? Shadowy other selves? All of these at once?

Horrors of this sort are indebted to the Gothic literary tradition of the previous generation, inaugurated by Horace Walpole's *The Castle of Otranto* (1764) and extended through the popular novels of Ann Radcliffe and Matthew Lewis. Here, monsters – symbols of violence, sadism, and unsavory appetite – are already worryingly close, hovering on the peripheries of the known world in medieval castles, underground caverns, and foreign haunts. From these outposts they terrorize the realm of reason (that of sanity, logic, and modernity), suggesting encroaching dissolution and disaster. But Gothic specters differ from their fantastic counterparts, as Larousse understood, for in the final hour they are almost always neutralized, supernaturalism revealed as illusion or misconception, magic explained away and order restored. The pattern is linked, in modern literary criticism, to the sense of a world teetering on the edge of collapse, a last-ditch attempt to shore up the crumbling rationalist episteme and the social world that sustained it.[35] As the eighteenth century drew to a close, Gothic

---

[35] This idea is fleshed out in Hogle, ed., *The Cambridge Companion to Gothic Fiction*; also in Gamer, *Romanticism and the Gothic*.

containment eroded and gradually, rather than hovering on the margins, monsters began to infiltrate the center, crowding into the domain of the real, emancipating themselves from distant or underground hiding places to wander the urban landscape and the space of domestic reality. No longer explained, they were left radically unresolved – and it was this release that marked the shift from a Gothic to a fantastic tradition. Pinpointing the moment of change is difficult (and unfruitful) in part because so many images, characters, and thematic tropes are shared between the two modes. Fantasy did not replace the Gothic, it simply eliminated its crucial rationalization, allowing specters to operate unchecked in the domain of the real.[36]

It was not, of course, nostalgia or spiritual alienation that propelled this shift, but, as cultural historians have argued, social and political marginalization, the existence of an unrepresented (indigent, poor, disenfranchised) majority, which, suppressed through much of the century, grew increasingly visible and audible as it drew to a close. Borrowing from Foucault, José Monleón identifies the French Revolution as a crucial break point, the end of unreason's "confinement" and the birth of fantasy, the moment in which rationalism's dark fringes collapsed into its carefully protected heart. Those who had been exiled to the peripheries came flooding back, crowding the streets of "enlightened" Paris, demanding recognition and representation. Not just members of a social and economic underclass, they were specters of a superstitious past, part of the eighteenth century's repressed unconscious rejoined, by force, with its rational conscious. They brought with them all the vague terrors, irrational beliefs, and delusions of uneducated minds – specters that had, until then, been constrained and disciplined by reason. What resulted was a newly fractured whole, a mingling of archaic and modern, real and unreal that ushered in a modern imaginative mode. As Monleón puts it:

The specter of revolution ... seems to be at the base of this reappearance of unreason in general, and of the fantastic in particular. ... The storming of La Bastille on July 14, 1789 ... marked the end of tyranny and the beginning of liberty. It was not the beheading of Louis XVI that tradition recorded as the gesture of liberation, but rather the demolition of a castle, of a prison which, as is well known,

---

[36] Todorov marks Jacques Cazotte's story "Le Diable amoureux" as the rough starting point of the literary fantastic and Maupassant's tales as the endpoint (*The Fantastic*, 166). Monleón, responding to Walter Scott, argues for "the end of the 1700s" as the moment of shift in his *A Specter is Haunting Europe*, 6. Jackson, in *Fantasy*, suggests that "from Gothic fiction onwards, there is a gradual transition from the marvelous to the uncanny," with the fantastic existing in a window in between: "During the nineteenth century ... the fantastic began to hollow out the 'real' world, making it strange, without providing any explanation for the strangeness" (24–25).

contained few prisoners. The demolition of confinement was an act that, if on the one hand, it liquidated the obsolete premises of the medieval world, on the other hand it served to unleash unreason.[37]

Other critics, notably H. L. Malchow, have modulated this claim, pointing out that while the dark margins of Europe were collapsing inward, they also began to extend outward. The revolutionary forces that released unreason into France's cultural center were mirrored by burgeoning imperialist impulses absorbing irrationality through its outer borders. Beginning with Napoleon, France began a long series of colonial expansions, first on the continent, then (in the wake of Bonaparte's fall) in more far-flung places. Foreign – incoherent, threatening, dark – bodies were increasingly wedded to light/enlightened Metropolitan ones, the "civilized" self to an imperial shadow. The result was a sense of rupture and burgeoning disquiet. Tales of the colonies from the 1790s onward read much like popular horror stories, featuring incidents of savagery, violence, and hysteria. They generated both titillation and fear, intimations of a world under threat not just by ill and mad specters on the edges of cities, but by monsters in more remote places that, once distant and separate, had become increasingly real and proximate.[38]

It was in part, then, political collapse and convergence – a sense of eroding boundaries – that shaped the fantastic worlds of the early nineteenth century, fueling their characteristic wavering between supernatural and rational, exotic and domestic domains. Together, revolutionary and imperialist incursion gave fantasy's demons a body, a reality, and a voice: the roaring of "savages," the shouting of the revolutionary mob, the cabbalistic incantations of the superstitious. These sounds, along with the bodies producing them, began to invade realist fiction: tales of waking life were infiltrated by the echoes of dream; nightmarish cackling became audible in the landscapes of the everyday; foreign babbling penetrated legible spaces. Such moments of intrusion were signals of a newly liminal ontology, what Nodier refers to as a violent synthesis, an enjambing of enchantment and disenchantment, mysticism and skepticism. More recent critics have echoed this description: Rosemary Jackson theorizes fantasy in terms of oxymoron, as a world that "holds together contradictions and sustains them in an impossible unity," and Monleón describes it as a form of paradox, the "simultaneous representation of two incompatible systems in one single sign."[39] Fantasists themselves, from Hoffmann through Gautier and

---

[37] Monleón, *A Specter is Haunting Europe*, 38–39. For Foucault's discussion of unreason's "confinement," see *Folie et déraison*.
[38] Malchow, *Gothic Images of Race*. Malchow relies in part on Brantlinger's notion of "imperial gothic" as fleshed out in *Rule of Darkness*.
[39] Jackson, *Fantasy*, 12. Monleón, *A Specter is Haunting Europe*, 40.

Baudelaire, have tied their own work to the idea of uncomfortable union – to the hybrid figures of a grotesque world, a place slipping between the recognizable and imaginary, often demonstrating the features of both. Callot's perplexed animal-vegetable forms, Delacroix's urban Mephistopheles, Goya's human-monster conflations: for many, these are key symbols of fantasy's Janus-faced orientation. What they suggest is not just a conflation, but a new *allegiance* between reason and the irrational.[40] Science, in the age of fantasy, was not just enjambed with, but increasingly inextricable from magic. In Mary Shelley, medicine generated monsters; in George Sand, microscopes revealed fairies; in Balzac, sober observation bled into superstition; in Schlegel (as we have already seen), the rhetoric of science recalled the natural magic at the heart of idealist enchantment.

Revolution and idealist revelation – the two tropes central to French criticism of the fantastic – were not, as Nodier and his contemporaries understood, separate; indeed, the events of 1789 hovered behind the resistant reconciliation brokered by the German romantic philosophers as a vital precondition. For Schlegel, as for Nodier, idealist magic was partly the product of a new political reality: the collapse of old social hegemonies and rigid thought systems in the wake of the revolution, whose upheaval he regarded as among "the greatest tendencies of the age."[41] The fluidity of the late eighteenth-century world allowed for the central hesitations of metaphysical fantasy, its simultaneous embrace of the "ideality of the real" and the "reality of the ideal," its precarious balance between subject and object, Fichte and Spinoza.[42] But the same forces, as I have just argued, released and reanimated monsters. As fantasy recalled the divine, it also, inevitably, readmitted the demonic. This double menace was clearly intuited by Hoffmann's French readers, who sensed in the mode both a philosophical challenge (a threat to Catholic orthodoxy) as well as a re-invocation of revolutionary madness (an unsettling of the precarious order of the Restoration). Hoffmann's mode suggested a new and potentially dangerous kind of power, social as well as metaphysical. At the same time – and here is the final piece of our puzzle – its danger was ontological. It threatened to unseat France's "native" magical world, that of the marvelous, and along with it, a long-standing tradition of literary unreality.

---

[40] See Kayser, *The Grotesque in Art and Literature*; Harpham, *On the Grotesque*; and Sanyal, *The Violence of Modernity*. Key primary sources on fantasy's grotesque orientation include Hoffmann's essay on Jacques Callot at the outset of the *Fantasiestücke* and Baudelaire's piece "De l'Essence du rire."
[41] The others were Fichte's *Wissenschaftslehre* and Goethe's *Wilhelm Meister*. See Athenaeum Fragment No. 216 in *Classic and Romantic German Aesthetics*, 251.
[42] Beiser, *German Idealism*, 458.

Of (French) Marvels and (German) Fantasies

In contemporary theoretical writing on the fantastic – the work of Jackson, Armitt, Cornwell, and others – tales in Hoffmann's vein are routinely distinguished from, even defined against, the literature of the marvelous (that of the purely imaginary). Echoing Todorov, these theorists separate *contes fantastiques* from fairy or ghost stories that operate in a removed supernatural world – one that never asks us to believe in genies or gnomes, and therefore "provoke[s] no particular reaction either in the characters or in the implicit reader"; in other words, never generates the hesitation so central to modern fantasy.[43] What such critics tend not to point out, but their nineteenth-century counterparts were well aware of, was that the domain of marvels was in large part a French place, conceived and perpetuated during the so-called Age of Reason. It was constructed as the impulses of rationalism – ideas bound up, famously, with the *philosophes* from Voltaire onward – began to gather power, disrupting the (already unraveling) ontology of natural magic associated with the Renaissance. This was a slow process, unfolding over the course of the seventeenth century and certainly in place by the early eighteenth, when the occult ideas of an earlier magical world (those that would later appeal so strongly to Schlegel's generation) had been discredited or gone underground. By this point, as Penelope Gouk argues, interest in alchemy and astrology was by no means extinguished, but had been marginalized: "natural magic was not associated openly with the places where reliable philosophical and scientific knowledge was produced and legitimated"; instead, "a new form of scientific discourse was to be forged, one which avoided the veiled and hidden symbolism of the occult and its reliance on 'false' correspondences between the macrocosm and the microcosm."[44] Experimental philosophy supplanted natural magic, skepticism, induction, and the privileging of physical data replacing the idea of secret concordances and cosmic revelation. Enchantment ceased to be "real," emerging instead as imaginary, the stuff of childish imagination, fraud, or mere entertainment.

---

[43] Todorov, *The Fantastic*, 54. See Todorov's elaborate, multipartite system of distinction between marvelous and fantastic modes (44) and Jackson's echo (*Fantasy*, 32). Ever finer systems of delineation, often building on the work of these scholars, continue to appear.

[44] Gouk, *Music, Science, and Natural Magic*, 261–62. For more on the suppression (and clandestine continuation) of occult beliefs and practices over the course of the eighteenth century, see Hollander, *The Untuning of the Sky*; and Fara, "Marginalized Practices." The contingent relationship between rationalism and its magical "other" in the eighteenth century is explored, famously, by Horkheimer and Adorno in *Dialectic of Enlightenment*; see also Jacob, *The Radical Enlightenment*; and Castle, *The Female Thermometer*.

Among the key literary signals of this shift – the move from "ancient" magic to eighteenth-century marvels – was an outpouring of otherworldly literature (*contes de fées* and *contes orientales*) beginning in the decade before 1700, generated largely in France and then exported across Europe. This body of work was ushered in by Jean de la Fontaine's *Fables choisies* (1688), the Comtesse d'Aulnoy's *Les Contes de fées* (1696), and Charles Perrault's *Contes de ma mère l'Oye* (1697). Soon thereafter came Antoine Galland's free translation of Arabic stories, *Les Mille et une nuits* (1704), and François Pétis de la Croix's adaptation of Persian tales, *Les Mille et un jours* (1710). Full of fabulous incidents and exotic creatures, these fictions relocated enchantment to make-believe, distant, and "uncivilized" places, rendering it the stuff of illusion rather than real knowledge, of allegory rather than reality. *Contes de fées* demoted spirits and genies (old harbingers of occult magic) to the status of literary symbols, often in the interest of social satire or moral instruction aimed at women and children. As Lewis C. Seifert puts it, French marvelous literature represented "a retreat from the constraints of the real or the present ... an alternate plane onto which the real can be transposed and imagined."[45]

Widely read though also controversial, tales of marvels emerged as key to a new conception of French literary style, championed by the "moderns" (of the *Querelle des anciens et des modernes*) as a vibrant repository of Gallic history, sensibility, and morality, resisted by the "ancients" as a signal of decline. Their success inside and outside of France sparked a second wave of fairy tale production beginning around 1730, and now, even more obviously than during the first, stories of the supernatural were associated with pleasure and unreality. They spread throughout Western Europe, where they were widely imitated, their templates adapted to other languages and literary traditions.[46] What such tales disseminated was not just a new storytelling model, but an "enlightened" form of illusory magic meant to confine and constrain old forms of enchantment, to provide a rationalist bulwark against antiquated (but still latent) forms of superstition. Both their pedagogical utility and their capacity for political critique lay in their estrangement from perceived actuality. Marvelous tales represented the other against which reason was constructed and from which it was necessarily separated.[47]

---

[45] Seifert, "Marvelous Realities," 131.

[46] Grätz points out that the literary fairy tale in both Germany and England relied on French models; see his *Das Märchen in der deutschen Aufklärung*. Bottigheimer argues along similar lines, locating the origins of the European fairy tale not in ancient oral traditions, but in French literary templates in "The Ultimate Fairy Tale."

[47] Seifert, dealing with the moralizing tendency of *contes de fées*, argues in *Fairy Tales, Sexuality, and Gender in France*, that "its [the marvelous's] inherent rejection of empirical reality results in

As David J. Buch demonstrates, the transition from a magical to a marvelous paradigm – from widespread belief in the efficacy of enchantment to general acceptance of its status as illusion – influenced the theatrical world as clearly as the fictional; in particular, it altered the ways in which musical works were conceived and received. As the fairy tale vogue developed, operatic tales of exoticism and make-believe also proliferated (again, particularly in France), rendering the stage rather than the scientist's or philosopher's study the proper home of the supernatural. Music in these works was demoted along with magic, ceasing to be associated with mystical mathematics, occult power, or with any serious science but instead with the production of theatrical effects. Buch describes the shift as the moment when "composers, theorists, and critics could define music in purely rational terms," when sound was no longer inherently divine, but simply aesthetic. It was this, as he argues, which allowed "a distinct category for magical topics" to emerge: a sounding marvelous.[48] Encyclopedist Jean-François Marmontel identified *le théâtre du merveilleux* as a broad category of supernatural representation defined in contrast to "simple nature." And his compatriot Louis de Cahusac, in his article "Féerie," located it as a style of music marked by "an enchanting sound productive of illusion" (*un ton d'enchantement qui fait illusion*), a form of aural décor akin to the elaborate machinery that allowed fairies and genies to appear on stage.[49] The sounding "illusions" to which he referred were part of a new rhetoric of otherness, a collection of eighteenth-century musical topics carefully cordoned off from the realm of the real, designed to transport listeners to imaginary domains. Muted registers, modal harmonic sequences, and wind instruments, for instance, marked scenes of dream or sleep; diminished harmonies, low brass scoring, descending chromatic lines, and noisy orchestral effects were associated with the underworld; static harmony, open intervals, and unison scoring denoted oracle scenes; and "elegant," lightly orchestrated dance music conjured the realm of the elves. By mid-century, this constellation of effects had emerged as a stable language – one that defined as well as confined magic, denying it access to both reason and real-world efficacy.[50]

---

a reaffirmation, but also a questioning of dominant ethical and social codes, which are themselves encompassed by *vraisemblance*" (11). A discussion of the pedagogical and satirical implications of marvelous literature is to be found in Harries, *Twice Upon a Time*.

[48] Buch, *Magic Flutes and Enchanted Forests*, 74. Buch traces the French use of the term *marvelous* in both literary and operatic criticism, noting its application to "a new kind of story, based on fairy tales and legends, developed during the (early) eighteenth century" (ix), and its later application "about 1750" to a distinct operatic style (xi).

[49] Marmontel, "Merveilleux," 906; Cahusac, "Féerie." Buch remarks on these entries in *Magic Flutes and Enchanted Forests*, xii–xiii and 46.

[50] See Buch, *Magic Flutes and Enchanted Forests*, 47–49 and 74–76.

The Fantastique moderne

The tradition of marvelous evocation strengthened and solidified through the time of Gluck and Piccini – what André Grétry termed the "third age" of the marvelous[51] – and, as Buch suggests, carried through Mozart's late operas (*Die Zauberflöte* marks the endpoint of his study). Around this time, as we have seen, political and philosophical shifts began to destabilize the idea of illusory magic as well as the various forms of containment and repression on which it relied and, in so doing, disrupted a strongly nationalist strand of French literary-theatrical production. Vigorous attempts to shore up and recall the marvelous world were made in the years following the revolution – efforts to hold the burgeoning resurgence of "real" magic, demonic and divine, at bay. But intimations of the new ontology began to seep in nevertheless. Increasingly "real" demons reared their heads in early-nineteenth-century *romans noirs* and *romans frénétiques* (French variations on the English Gothic novel), signaling a world of reason under attack. And the idea of "natural supernaturalism," as Abrams terms it, inflected the writing of authors including Chateaubriand and Senacour, whose pastoral landscapes are shot through with intimations of otherworldliness.[52] By 1814, the philosophical underpinnings of the new material divinity had been framed (and to some degree explained) by Staël's *De l'Allemagne*, which imported German "romantic" literature and philosophy to France, introducing Schlegel and Schelling alongside Kant and Fichte. Slightly later, in the early–mid-1820s, Victor Cousin took up the ideas of these philosophers, folding them (along with other religious and philosophical impulses) into his "eclectic" philosophy.[53] These slow erosions of France's rationalist-marvelous world set the stage for Hoffmann, whose tales consolidated, cemented – and, most importantly, popularized – the new "real" magic of fantasy, invoking both the visceral horrors of the revolutionary world and the natural divinity bound up with post-Kantian German philosophy. His work spoke to a wide audience, disseminating the political, theological, and especially the sonorous tenets of the new *surnaturel vrai*.[54]

---

[51] Ibid., 58. [52] Abrams, *Natural Supernaturalism*, 65–70.
[53] Natural notions of divinity were explored in French philosophical writing both before and during Cousin's ascendancy; see, for instance, Fénelon, *Démonstration de l'existence de Dieu*; Butler, *L'Analogie de la religion naturelle*; and Stoeber, *Idées sur les rapports de Dieu à la nature*. Cousin's ties to pantheism were the subject of a series of essays through mid-century, including Maret, *Essai sur le panthéisme dans les sociétés modernes*; and Gioberti, *Le Panthéisme de M. Cousin exposé par lui-même*.
[54] Sound had already played a role in both Chateaubriand's and Senacour's pantheistic landscapes, which primed French audiences for Hoffmann's more specialized musico-philosophical writings; see Perot, *Discours sur la musique à l'époque de Chateaubriand*.

"Le Pot d'or" was, as I have already noted, a story in which Hoffmann showcased Schlegel's new metaphysics clearly, its enchantment rooted in natural-magical forms of listening, its sonorous landscapes alive with the potential for divine revelation. But the story of Anselmus was far from isolated; many other musical tales with similar tropes appeared among the early Hoffmann translations, some published in literary magazines, others in music journals. Among these were "Le Sanctus," "La Vie d'artiste," "Marino Falieri," "Le Majorat," "Don Juan," and "Le Violin de Crémone."[55] Often presented alongside the German *conteur*'s critical essays, these tales challenged the idea of music as merely aesthetic, elevating it once again to the level of the magical, the spiritual, the metaphysical. The most influential of Hoffmann's writings in this regard was the cycle *Kreisleriana* (Part 1 of the *Fantasiestücke in Callots Manier*, available in French by 1829), which Balzac and others hailed as key to the emergence of a new imaginative and artistic mode. Here, French readers encountered a mixture of music journalism, biography, anecdotal accounting, and literary invention, a quintessentially fantastic amalgam, and one that drew in obvious ways on both Schlegelian metaphysics and on the wider edifice of German *Naturphilosophie*. The cycle is significant in part because it so clearly connects fantasy with aurality and, more importantly, fictional listening with practical composition; it is, as David Charlton puts it, "Hoffmann's contribution to romantic musical aesthetics," a sonorous guide for the would-be fantasist.[56]

In *Kreisleriana*, the natural soundworld associated with Anselmus returns, weaving through a series of meditations on musical romanticism and artistic temperament. We encounter it first in the third fragment, "Thoughts on the Great Value of Music," where the new "world of fantasy" celebrated in *Kreisleriana* is described as synonymous with "the sublime sound of trees, flowers, animals, stones, water." But such sounds are heard and recognized only by the few. The point is made clear in a later essay, an ironic piece titled "The Music Hater," whose protagonist, a listener of refined sensibility, abjures the empty content of salon pieces and concert *études* in favor of "the rustling of oak-leaves above my head, or the splashing of streams below."[57] He is ridiculed for his preference, but, as Hoffmann insists, is not a misguided but a truly inspired figure; indeed, a model for the *conteur*'s own musical alter ego, the Kapellmeister Johannes Kreisler, who is invested with a similarly sensitive capacity for natural hearing.

---

[55] Teichmann notes the importance of Hoffmann's musical tales in *La Fortune d'Hoffmann en France*, 22–53; see also Hübener, *Kreisler in Frankreich*, 11–82.
[56] Charlton, *E. T. A. Hoffmann's Musical Writings*, 6. [57] Hoffmann, *Kreisleriana*, 94, 150.

This characterization of Kreisler is given in the final essay of the cycle, "Johannes Kreisler's Apprentice Letter," which marks the end of the Kapellmeister's training (and of ours), the moment when he/we have learned to listen to and interpret the voice of the created world. Here, Hoffmann places organic sound at the heart of romantic composition: "The audible sounds of nature, the sighing of the wind, the rushing of streams, and so on, are perceived by the musician first as individual chords and then as melodies with harmonic accompaniment." Music emerges as physically immanent within nature (the point has been noted by musicologists, including Charlton, as well as literary scholars as far back as Pauline Watts).[58] Speaking as/to Kreisler, Hoffmann writes, "you have sharpened your faculty of hearing to such an extent that now and then you perceive the voice of the poet hidden within you." This sound – the voice within – is synonymous with that of the created universe without, the mystical tones of the physical world. It is the job of the composer to capture these, in part by developing an occult relationship with nature, learning to vibrate "in sympathy" with its aural resonances and finally to "seize upon his inspirations with a special power of will" conjuring them into "signs and symbols."[59] The strains of sounding fantasy are reproduced, according to Hoffmann, via the technologies of nineteenth-century instrumental music – famously, by the innovations of the Beethovenian orchestra, which is uniquely equipped to capture and render audible the sounds of the magical real.[60] In the "Apprentice Letter," Hoffmann (echoing Schlegel) likens the spiritual music associated with Beethoven to "hieroglyphs," not straightforward instances of imitation, but only "a vague approximation of what we have distantly heard." The true musician understands and harnesses this hieroglyphic idiom, abandoning the empty domain of marvels (that of superficial or merely theatrical "effects") in favor of the Pythagorean power of fantasy, the "real" enchantment of "a remote and fabulous age."[61]

But doing so is dangerous; indeed, the price of metaphysical listening is high. Kreisler, like other Hoffmannesque artist-heroes, hears the divine only by slipping into spaces of madness. His experience of listening is quintessentially grotesque, magico-natural perception inextricable from hallucination, nightmare, and intoxication, revelatory hieroglyphs hovering

---

[58] Ibid., 164; see also Charlton's commentary on nature sounds in the "Apprentice Letter" in *E. T. A. Hoffmann's Musical Writings*, 13. Watts notes the importance of organic sound to Hoffmann in *Music*, 34–35.

[59] Hoffmann, *Kreisleriana*, 160–64.

[60] A revised version of Hoffmann's much-touted review of the Fifth Symphony stands at the heart of *Kreisleriana*, with the surrounding essays and fragments operating in many senses as a working out of the review's central premises.

[61] Hoffmann, *Kreisleriana*, 163.

constantly on the edge of mere gibberish. Developing access to the sonorous divine means, for him, becoming permeable to the demonic real, to the cacophony of madness, of a world and a mind unhinged. He is, as Hoffmann tells us in the introduction to *Kreisleriana*, a dysfunctional figure, an "error" of nature, fatally twisted and ill.[62] Kreisler is illuminated but also estranged, a symbol of fantasy's double origin and therefore its dangerous promise: that of idealist revelation inextricable from (even predicated on) mental and social dislocation. The idea was challenging and alluring for the first French consumers of Hoffmann's *contes fantastiques*; indeed, Kreisler emerged as a key shaper of both fantasists and fantasy itself in France. He ensured that the mode's new imaginative ontology was synonymous not just with novel literary forms and shapes (digressive structures, unresolved narrative threads, generic conflation), but with new auditory interfaces (mysterious, even spiritual forms of listening). The two were inextricable from the start: hearing fantastic narratives was synonymous with reading and seeing them.

The *Genre fantastique*

Listen to Hoffmann: in the midst of his tale he stops, he preludes, he sings, he acts as does Kreisler, abandoning himself utterly to harmony.
—Jules Janin, Preface to *Contes fantastiques*[63]

The earliest French *contes fantastiques* – those written in the wake of Hoffmann's arrival – were rooted explicitly in instrumental soundworlds. The core magical action of Gautier's 1831 tale "La Cafetière" – the animation of a coffeepot, an armchair, and a collection of characters from a painted wall-mural – is ushered in via the strains of an imaginary orchestra, which draws the living and inert alike into a wild dance, blurring the boundaries between organic and inorganic, dream and reality. Likewise, the hallucinatory events of Janin's "Kreyssler" (the first of his 1832 *Contes fantastiques et contes littéraires*) begins with a description of orchestral sound, an imaginary ensemble of clinking glasses and popping corks that sets the stage for a waking dream, a series of semi-illusory encounters with otherworldly and fictional characters. Nodier's *contes fantastiques* are shot through with melody from *Smarra* onward, as are Balzac's fantastic stories. And those of George Sand, beginning in 1832, return repeatedly to descriptions of instrumental sound, which spark transformation, revelation,

---

[62] Ibid., 79–80.
[63] "Ecoutez Hoffmann: au milieu de son récit il s'arrête, il prélude, il chante, il agit comme Kreyssler, s'abandonnant à toute harmonie." Janin, *Contes fantastiques et contes littéraires*, 22.

sometimes estrangement and madness (we shall examine some of these tales in later chapters).[64]

Behind these fictions and their newly "real" magic is Hoffmann's fantastic orchestra and Beethoven's real one. But just as clearly, such tales are responses to Berlioz, who had already wedded text and sound in his *Symphonie fantastique* (1830) and, in so doing, set the stage for the wave of French fantastic production that followed. The newly expanded, quasi-magical ensemble of the *Fantastique* was clearly in Gautier's mind when he composed the demonic dance scene of "La Cafetière"; it must also have been hovering in Janin's imagination when he described his protagonist's musico-magical search for the feminine ideal. The literary tradition of the *conte fantastique* emerged, in a sense, from *musique fantastique*, which was itself shaped by fictional (especially Hoffmannesque) theories of audition. Berlioz was central to this cross-disciplinary transference; indeed, he was the first of the major French fantasists, a composer whose literary-symphonic template proved central not just to the development of fantastic fiction (both he and Hoffmann appear repeatedly as characters in French otherworldly tales), but to a burgeoning field of fantastic *composition*. Music critics, as we shall see, identified the *Symphonie fantastique* as the template for a new brand of sounding supernaturalism, a Hoffmannesque impulse shaping not just Berlioz's own otherworldly works of the later 1830s and 1840s, but those of his musical contemporaries.

That Berlioz should have responded so quickly and keenly to fantastic writing is hardly surprising. He was a composer strongly attracted to romantic metaphysics, modern science, and revolutionary activism – to the impulses hovering around and behind Hoffmann's work (and behind modern fantasy at large). Unhappy with the restricted aesthetic world of the Conservatoire, he turned, famously, to external stimuli: to Beethoven, Shakespeare, Staël, and, in the late 1820s, to Hoffmann, who provided him with a fresh musical approach. In an 1829 letter to his sister Nanci, he described hearing Beethoven's quartets and, in the next paragraph, reading Hoffmann's tales: "Hoffmann's *Contes fantastiques* I have really enjoyed!" And a few days later, to his friend Humbert Ferrand, "Have you read Hoffmann's *Contes fantastiques*? They are very intriguing."[65] His first symphony, already in percolation, was a powerful response to the new

---

[64] For more on Gautier's musical prose, both in the *Contes fantastiques* and elsewhere, see Brunet, *Théophile Gautier et la musique*.

[65] "Hoffman [sic], ses *Contes fantastiques* m'ont beaucoup plu." *CG*, 1:148 (28 December 1829); "Avez-vous lu les *Contes fantastiques* d'Hoffmann? C'est fort curieux!" *CG*, 1:149 (2 January 1830). Richard, one of the translators of the German author's work, was among Berlioz's close friends in 1829–30.

aesthetics of fantasy, and one that articulated clearly the twin impulses at its heart. The piece united metaphysical longing (obsession with an "être idéal") with revolutionary imagery (marching feet, the guillotine, the specter of a hellish tribunal), the sounds of mystical love with those of musical terror, images of the waking world with those of dream and nightmare. From the outset, Berlioz's symphony made the promise and threat of Hoffmann's mode clear: access to the ideal was impossible without the admission of the monstrous; the newly "real" divinity was yoked to echoes of modern demonism.

As we might expect, the *Fantastique* was received from the start not just as a musical composition, but as a political and philosophical challenge. Its immediate appeal lay in its autobiographical content (its confessional account of Berlioz's own life and that of Harriet Smithson), but underlying this, critics intuited something more radical. Clearly, the work was not *fantastique* in the old sense of the word, the sense of the purely imaginative (the native marvelous); instead, it was oddly illegible, hovering between sound and text, imitation and expression, orchestral "science" and musical "art," threatening to undo entrenched and legitimately French modes of listening. It garnered more attention that a single piece by a relatively untested composer might normally have enjoyed; indeed, conversation surrounding the work grew more rather than less fraught as the decade proceeded, escalating into what one critic called a *querelle*.[66] Many of the same questions circled around Berlioz that had earlier been attached to Hoffmann – questions surrounding the relationship between language and music, the tensions between imagination and mimesis, and the place of metaphysics in musical aesthetics.

François Fétis, editor of the *Revue musicale* and one of Berlioz's most vocal detractors, was quick to dismiss the *Fantastique*, his review of the premiere styling it as an oddity appealing only to the musically uninitiated:

The concert given by M. Berlioz last Sunday in the great hall of the Conservatory attracted a large number of amateurs, artists, and the curious. This youthful musician, propelled by his instinct toward a new path, has numerous supporters among the young, who are always hungry for novelties.[67]

In 1832, when the symphony was extended by a sequel, *Le Retour à la vie* (which attacked the French Academy and, tacitly, Fétis himself), the Belgian critic's denunciations became harsher. He exiled Berlioz's symphony from the realm of legitimate composition entirely, arguing that it emerged from

---

[66] Blaze, "De l'École fantastique," 103.
[67] "Le concert que M. Berlioz a donné dimanche dernier dans la grande salle du Conservatoire, avait attiré grand nombre d'amateurs, d'artistes et de curieux. Ce jeune musicien, poussé par son instinct vers une route nouvelle, a de nombreux partisans parmi la jeunesse, toujours avide de nouveautés." *Revue musicale* (11 December 1830).

delusion and incompetence, that it was external to the "aims of art." Berlioz's supporters (like Berlioz himself), he contended, lacked proper musical training; rather than composers they were writers, painters, and poets, and as such were ill-equipped to assess the *Fantastique*'s merit. Placed before a knowledgeable audience, the symphony would surely be condemned: "It has always been my desire that M. Berlioz should be presented to a public composed, not of his friends and disciples, but of that enlightened segment of society that instinctively arrives at a sound verdict."[68]

Berlioz's advocates rebutted these attacks by arguing that the *Fantastique* had moved beyond conventional legibility, embracing a mode unmoored from "the established laws" and "the normal rules of art." It heralded a new age, a sea change in musical aesthetics and philosophy. Responding directly to Fétis in a piece for *La Quotidienne*, Joseph D'Ortigue situated the symphony as the mouthpiece of a modern public and a contemporary social reality:

The public, the *true public* according to us, is composed of intelligent men, musicians or non-musicians, endowed with a profound sentiment for art, who recognize in the harmonic language and external forms [of the symphony] a new kind of thought, of feeling, a novel and original conception in tune with current social needs.[69]

Echoes of both Nodier's *Revue* essay and of wider Hoffmann reception are transparent here, as they are in the responses of other Berlioz supporters, including Jules Janin, who scoffed at the notion of the composer as an incompetent, situating him instead as an agitator: Berlioz "knows how to write his music perfectly and correctly; one feels it, one sees it; but he turns up his nose at regulations and established rules, trampling them underfoot."[70] The idiom of the *Fantastique* was experimental but not unmusical. It held out the promise of rejuvenation, its "new paths" leading to a "new world."[71]

---

[68] "Ce que j'ai toujours désiré, c'est que les oeuvres de M. Berlioz fussent livrées au public, composé non d'amis et de gens endoctrinés, mais de cette portion éclairée de la société qui, d'instinct, finit par juger sainement des choses." *Gazette musicale* (1 February 1835).

[69] "Le public, le vénérable public pour nous, se compose de ces hommes intelligens, musiciens ou non musiciens, doués d'un profond sentiment de l'art, qui découvrent à travers le tissu des combinaisons harmoniques et des formes matérielles, un nouveau type de pensées, de sentimens, une conception neuve et originale, en harmonie avec les besoins sociaux actuels." *La Quotidienne* (10 May 1835).

[70] "Ce jeune homme . . . sait écrire sa musique parfaitement et correctement; on le sent, on le voit, il le prouve; mais il dédaigne et foule aux pieds les coordonnantes et les ordres prévus." *Journal des débats* (10 December 1832).

[71] This claim was ubiquitous; see, for instance, the review of the *Symphonie fantastique* and its sequel in *La Quotidienne* (10 December 1832), which embraced Berlioz's fantastic "voie nouvelle."

This world – Nodier's "monde intermédiaire" – proved a musically enticing one, despite the denunciations of some. By the late 1830s, even its opponents were forced to admit that fantastic soundscapes were proliferating. Among these was author-critic Ange-Henri Blaze (son of the better-known Castil-Blaze), who published a large-scale essay in the *Revue des deux mondes* titled "De L'École fantastique et de M. Berlioz" (1838). Heated and lengthy (extending to twenty-one pages), Blaze's piece was in many senses a negative version of Nodier's 1830 manifesto, an anti-fantastic diatribe in which he bemoaned the burgeoning power of Hoffmann's musical ideas and of Berlioz himself, who had emerged not as the isolated figure conservative critics had hoped, but instead as the leader of a "school" of fantastic composition. The essay appeared just after the premiere of *Benvenuto Cellini* and drew together the majority of Berlioz's major works, from the first symphony to *Harold en Italie* and the *Messe des morts* under the *fantastique* label. In all of these compositions, Blaze heard evidence of the same malignant influence – that of Hoffmann:

Detestable storyteller, it was you who introduced disorder and confusion among the best minds of our century. You did not imagine, sublime drunkard, when you dreamed away the night in your Berlin cellar, that these phantoms of your mind would one day lead an entire generation of young men astray; or perhaps, as I suppose, you foresaw it and laughed in advance at the great adventure. I, for my part, was never persuaded by that mask of beaming candor with which you so often cover the irony of your diabolic face.[72]

At the heart of the Hoffmann problem, in Blaze's telling, was a collection of "inadmissible theories" (*inadmissibles théories*). He pointed to "the ecstasies of Pythagoras" and "the hallucinations of Paracelsus," and later to the "impenetrable metaphysicians" lurking behind and within the *contes fantastiques*, including "Spinoza, Kant, Herder," whose ideas had "maddened the minds" of an entire musical generation. No one had been more affected than Berlioz, who, "for eight years" (i.e., since the *Symphonie fantastique*) had been estranged from the incontestable truths of art, caught instead in "the snares laid by Hoffmann for excitable heads."[73]

---

[72] "Détestable conteur, c'est toi qui as jeté le trouble et la confusion parmi les meilleurs esprits de notre siècle. Tu ne te doutais pas, ivrogne sublime, quand tu rêvais la nuit dans ta cave de Berlin, que ces fantômes de ton cerveau entraîneraient un jour à leur suite toute une génération de jeunes hommes égarés, ou plutôt tu le présentais et riais d'avance de la bonne aventure, je suppose; car je n'ai jamais cru, pour ma part, à ce masque de candeur épanouie dont tu couvres par momens l'ironie de ta face diabolique." Blaze, "De L'École fantastique," 120.

[73] "les extases de Phythagore ... les hallucinations de Paracelse"; "M. Berlioz nous semble avoir donné en plein dans les embûches qu'Hoffmann tend dans l'air aux cerveaux exaltés." According to Blaze, he numbers among the "généreux jeunes gens, dont le tort est d'avoir lu les

Berlioz, as Blaze claimed, had begun to think of music as symbolic rather than aesthetic, as an imprint of philosophical ideas, a kind of "algebra or metaphysics," rather than an articulation of human emotions: "From the beginning you misunderstood its [music's] nature, its goal, its essence. It quickly escaped you, fled from you, and more and more the din of your orchestra leads you away from it."[74] The composer of the *Fantastique* had lost sight of music's purpose and capabilities, abandoning the tenets of beauty and nobility in favor of a misguided mission:

> M. Berlioz insists on searching in music for effects which it is not capable of expressing, while on the other hand he seems to take pleasure in neglecting its most beautiful gifts. . . . For M. Berlioz music is . . . a mysterious Isis, austere, fatal, surrounded by impenetrable signs and dark superstition, of which he believes himself the hierophant and mystagogue.[75]

Kreisler too, in Hoffmann's writings, had been a student of Isis (the Greco-Roman nature deity), and this is surely why Blaze invokes her here. In *Kreisleriana*, we encounter her twice, first in "Thoughts on the Great Value of Music," where Hoffmann (in the voice of a layman) describes artists as "unhappy dreamers" in the grip of "mild insanity." These unfortunates believe that "art allows men to sense their higher destiny, and that it will lead them from the futile hurly-burly of everyday life into the Temple of Isis," where "nature will speak to them in sacred sounds unheard before yet immediately comprehensible." Later, at the close of "Johannes Kreisler's Certificate of Apprenticeship," he returns to the idea, now speaking in his own voice: "With these few words of wisdom I now deliver you, my dear Johannes, at the gates of the Temple of Isis, so that you might study diligently."[76] In both cases, Hoffmann is figuring musicians as disciples of an old natural magic – that of Isis herself – who promises to reveal to them the hidden enchantment of the visceral world and to stimulate the special perception that will render it accessible to mortal senses. But the entire

---

philosophes avec des têtes exaltées de musiciens! Spinosa, Kant, Herder, leur ont tourné l'esprit." Ibid., 100–04, 121.

[74] Dès le premier jour, vous vous êtes mépris sur sa nature, sa destination, son essence. Aussi elle vous a bientôt échappé, elle s'est enfuie de vous, et de plus en plus le torrent de vos orchestres vous entraîne loin d'elle." Ibid., 100.

[75] "M. Berlioz s'obstine à chercher dans la musique des effets qu'il n'est pas en elle d'exprimer, tandis qu'en revanche il semble prendre plaisir à négliger ses plus beaux dons. . . . Pour M. Berlioz, la musique [est] . . . une Isis mystérieuse, austère, fatale, entourée de signes impénétrables et de superstitions sombres, dont il se croit l'hiérophante et le mystagogue." Ibid., 103–04.

[76] Hoffmann, *Kreisleriana*, 95, 165. Behind Hoffmann's references to Isis lay Novalis's fragmentary novel, *Die Lehrlinge zu Sais* (1802), with its narrative of artistic pilgrimage and mystical self-discovery; see ibid., 27–32. Blaze would have been aware of Novalis's novel via Staël, who had described it in some detail in *De L'Allemagne* (1813).

premise of such an endeavor, Blaze argues, is false. Referring once again to Hoffmann, now to his theory of sounding fantasy itself, he insists that "the art of sounds is in no sense the art of hieroglyphs."[77]

And misguided metaphysics is not the only problem with *musique fantastique*, according to Blaze. For him, as for his literary compatriots, it is equally clearly bound up with politics – especially revolutionary violence. The two are musically inextricable, hieroglyphic effects linked to uncivilized sounds and, even more clearly, to incoherent musical structures and syntax. The newfangled sonorities at the heart of fantastic evocation eradicate the essence of music itself, eliminating its melodic and rhythmic logic, the laws that render it noble and *truly* spiritual. These are replaced by a new grammar rooted in ugliness and confusion, a mode in which antecedents lack consequents, dissonances are unprepared and unresolved, rhythms distorted, and periods lopsided. Fantastic language, Blaze argues, encodes and engenders disorder, appropriating the weapons of literary radicalism. It unites Hoffmannesque aesthetics with Hugo's new grotesque poetics, the foreign with the revolutionary. Wielding such a language, Berlioz is not just a metaphysician, but a Jacobin, a purveyor of musical terror – and his ideas are spreading. He is both a practitioner of the new fantastic mode and a promulgator (a "hierophant and mystagogue") whose own works are luring others into Hoffmannesque error:

Who would believe it? These insane dreams of the marvelous Berlin teller-of-tales, these creations, extravagant in essence, grotesque to the point of melancholy and madness, whispers of air and sound which reveal themselves only in clouds of tobacco smoke, in the froth of new wine, in the vapors of the teapot; one meets reasonable people who have taken them [these dreams] seriously, men of flesh and blood, who get it into their heads to shape their own personae along similar lines, sublime madmen who spend their days in digging with their fingernails for color and sound, in order in this manner to catch by surprise the Salvator Rosa or the Kreissler [sic] of a *conte fantastique*. In truth, Kreissler has already generated at least as many victims as Werther."[78]

---

[77] "l'art des sons n'est en aucune manière l'art des hiéroglyphes." Blaze, "De l'École fantastique," 102. The connections Blaze forges between Berlioz, Isis, and *fantastique* evocation resonate in interesting ways with links among Beethoven, the "veiled Isis," and "picturesque" aesthetics traced by Richards in *The Free Fantasia and the Musical Picturesque*, 183–231. We shall return to Berlioz's Beethovenian connections (and Beethoven's Berliozian ethos) in Chapter 3.

[78] "Qui le croirait? ces rêves insensés du merveilleux conteur de Berlin, ces créations extravagantes dans leur essence, grotesques à force de mélancolie et d'enthousiasme, soufflées d'air et de son, qui ne se meuvent que dans les nuages du tabac, l'écume du vin nouveau, les vapeurs de la théière, il s'est rencontré d'honnêtes gens qui les ont prises au sérieux, des hommes de chair et d'os qui se sont mis en tête de régler leur personnage sur de semblables patrons, des fous sublimes qui passent leur vie à creuser de leurs ongles la couleur et le son, pour y surprendre le

This complaint was echoed in another large-scale essay on Berlioz published in the same year by Joseph Mainzer, who lamented the fantastic "void" into which Berlioz had fallen and which was now consuming others, including Franz Liszt: "We regret to see Liszt, like Berlioz, be drawn down the path of the fantastic. It behooves those who are endowed with such power and talent to work more seriously, to awaken in us noble thoughts and deep feelings instead of giving themselves over to a genre that has little effect on either."[79] For Mainzer, fantasy was not just aesthetically empty, but unknowable, a dark spot for analysts and critics. It was rooted in a supernaturalism unmoored from faith, derived instead from bizarre metaphysics and cerebral "calculation." The mode manifested itself in overburdened orchestration, "imitation," bizarre or misshapen forms, and ugliness for its own sake.[80] These tenets, once the province of Berlioz, were now in evidence in Liszt, who (as Mainzer was clearly aware) had become bound up with the same kinds of arcane philosophical ideas and political impulses already associated with the composer of the *Fantastique*. The pianist had, beginning in 1834, produced a series of transcriptions of (and improvisations on) Berlioz, many marked with the *fantastique* rubric, and, hard on their heels, his own *Rondeau fantastique* (1836).[81] These pieces formed part of a tide of other fantastic works published in Paris and around the same time, and a body of French *contes fantastiques* on musical themes that championed and popularized the mode. Increasingly, fantasy emerged not just as a fringe impulse, but a concrete if controversial compositional category.

Entries for *fantastique* began to appear in music lexicons and encyclopedias as early as 1835 (largely as vehicles for conservative denunciation), becoming more frequent through the 1840s and 1850s. And by the 1860s, Blaze's idea of Berlioz as the head of a fantastic "school" of composition had concretized to the point where it was cited in general reference works. Larousse's *Grand dictionnaire*, as I noted at the outset of this chapter, includes an entry under *fantastique* divided into two sections – literary and musical – identifying Hoffmann as the primary champion of the former

---

Salvator Rosa ou le Kreissler du conte fantastique. En vérité, Kreissler a déjà fait au moins autant de victimes que Werther." Blaze, "De l'École fantastique," 98–99.

[79] "Nous regrettons de voir entrer Liszt comme Berlioz dans la voie du fantastique. C'est à ceux qui sont doués d'une telle force et d'un tel talent qu'il appartient de travailler plus solidement, d'éveiller en nous de nobles pensées et des sentiments profonds, au lieu de se vouer à un genre qui n'a d'action ni sur les uns ni sur les autres." Mainzer, *Chronique musicale de Paris*, 11–12.

[80] Ibid., 25–26.

[81] George Sand produced an elaborate program for the *Rondeau* (a "paraphrase fantastique") meditating on life, death, and the nature of the romantic self. See Brittan, "Liszt, Sand, García and the Contrebandier."

and Berlioz of the latter. Running to seven columns, the entry is a testament to the perceived significance of the mode for both text and sound. Its section on literature, which we have already encountered, is long and detailed, sketching out a history of the genre and quoting from a wide array of secondary sources, among them Nodier and Gautier. Fantastic literature is, for the most part, absurd and extravagant in Larousse's assessment, although he acknowledges that it has been wielded to powerful effect by some: Hoffmann, Achim von Arnim, Jean Paul Richter, Nodier, and Edgar Allan Poe.

The section on fantastic music is less focused and (as is true of many earlier accounts) less fully fleshed out than that on fantastic fiction; indeed, Larousse has difficulty articulating precisely how sound is *fantastique*, telling us at one point simply that the problems associated with *contes fantastiques* are reproduced in works of musical fantasy ("the adherents of fantastic music imitate all too well ... the adherents of fantastic literature").[82] His opening claim is characteristically vague: "The name *musique fantastique* is given to a genre of composition in which one encounters a great number of themes and ideas couched in new forms, with unusual [orchestral] combinations, and featuring a particular employment of instruments."[83] Precisely how orchestration constructs fantastic soundworlds or why its musical forms are unusual remains mysterious. Works of fantasy are unreadable, at once imitative (rooted in "natural" or "material" sound) and dreamlike (composed of incomprehensible sonorities). They resist coherent reading, smacking not just of aesthetic heterodoxy, but of danger. For Larousse, as for Blaze, their compositional tactics are tantamount to musical terrorism. In a passage of now-familiar complaint, he traces the roots of musical fantasy to foreign philosophy, social ills, and aesthetic radicalism. The mode "sacrifices almost completely the two constitutive elements of music: melody and rhythm," embracing "violent effects" (including "eplipectic phrases" and "broken rhythms") to the point of inflicting physical pain.[84] Its key features are its violence and incomprehensibility, its departure from established artistic laws, although Larousse admits that in music (as in fiction), fantasy has produced works of quality and lasting importance. Among these is Meyerbeer's *Robert le diable*,

---

[82] "les poursuivants du *fantastique* musical, imitant trop bien ... les poursuivants du *fantastique* littéraire." Larousse, "Fantastique," 94.

[83] "On a donné le nom de musique fantastique à un genre de composition où l'on trouve un grand nombre d'idées et de cantilènes présentées sous des formes nouvelles, avec des combinaisons inusitées, et où il est fait un emploi particulier des instruments." Ibid., 94.

[84] "On a reproché à ce système de sacrifier presque complètement les deux éléments constitutifs de la musique, la mélodie et le rythme, de violer de propos délibéré les lois de la composition." Ibid., 94–95.

"le chef-d'oeuvre de l'opéra fantastique," and, most recently, Wagner's *Tristan und Isolde* (an interesting claim to which we shall return). But the undisputed champion of fantastic music is Berlioz. In a list of representative works, Larousse begins by citing "Berlioz's *Symphonie fantastique*, the *Damnation de Faust*, and several [other] compositions by the same author."[85] His genealogy, like Blaze's, begins with the composer's first symphony, a piece whose importance lies less in its idiosyncrasy than in its connection to a wider repertory.

The idea is an important one – indeed, a partial justification for our repeated return, in what follows, to the *Fantastique*, which was connected not just to a perceived musical "revolution," but to a shift in the nature of musico-aesthetic criticism. Understanding how Berlioz embraced and transmitted the tenets of modern fantasy, how his early works established him as both a Hoffmannesque composer and Kreislerian listener, will be our task in the next chapters, where we turn our attention to the literary and musical construction of the *Fantastique* and *Le Retour à la vie*. We will be concerned with the philosophical and political content of these works and with their partisan reception – the ways in which they invited but also evaded musicological theorization, proving difficult to define and defend.

[85] "Nous citerons: la Symphonie fantastique de Berlioz, la Damnation de Faust, et plusiurs oeuvres du même auteur." Ibid., 95.

Épisode de la vie d'un artiste

2 ❖ Melancholy, Monomania, and the *Monde fantastique*

O all ye gods! All ye seven blessed heavens! A sweet voice said – no, sang! – no, breathed out the fragrance of love in musical sounds: "Oh Giglio, my Giglio!" And I beheld a being of such heavenly grace, such lofty charm, that the scorching sirocco of ardent love shot through all my veins and nerves, and the fiery stream turned into lava surging forth from the volcano of my flaming heart.[1]

This moment of infatuation stands at the heart of E. T. A. Hoffmann's 1820 tale "Princess Brambilla," which turns around the love-sickness of the young actor Giglio Fava. His attachment begins with a "fantastic dream" that reveals to him an image of the Princess – what he describes as a mirage of perfection, luminous and alluring, sparking in him an "endless yearning" (*unendlichen Sehnsucht*). The idea of the dream-woman, at first pleasant, quickly becomes disruptive, dominating Giglio's mind and appearing everywhere (through the window of a carriage, on the street, in a crowd), at once omnipresent and ever-elusive. She inspires not just amorous desire, but, as the story progresses, obsessive pathology, a "piercing agony" that takes "entire possession of his [Giglio's] mind." Consuming his every thought, the vision blurs reality and the unreal, waking and dreaming, driving him into a state of mental disorientation and then folly.[2]

A similar condition afflicts the character Elis Fröbom in another of Hoffmann's fantastic tales, "The Mines of Falun" (1816). Here, as in the case of Giglio, the young Elis becomes enraptured by a dream-vision that reveals to him the image of a beautiful woman (the queen of the mine). She exerts an irresistible attraction over him, which, over time, becomes a destructive force, a pathological longing marked by "an indescribable feeling of pain and rapture." The queen, like Giglio's Princess, proves elusive, dissolving around him, hovering in the shimmering air. He becomes fixated on her, roaming the streets of Göteborg, "constantly pursued by the strange figments of his dreams, constantly admonished by the unknown voice." His obsession leads to hallucination and derangement, luring him into "the jaws of hell" (the mine itself) and to his own death.[3]

---

[1] Hoffmann, "Princess Brambilla," 126. [2] Ibid., 125, 132, 140.
[3] Hoffmann, "The Mines of Falun," 155–57.

One final version of this love-pathology – and an especially interesting one in the context of this chapter – is to be found in Hoffmann's tale "Automata" (originally conceived as part of the 1814 *Fantasiestücke*, revised in 1819). As in the tales we have already encountered, it afflicts a young and artistic character, Ferdinand, who comes into contact with an ideal woman, a vision of perfection revealed to him in "a half-conscious state" brought on by alcohol and fatigue. In this case, the mysterious woman is yoked to a melody that reappears whenever she does, stimulating the now-familiar "endless longing":

> How can I ever hope to give you the faintest idea of the effect of those long-drawn swelling and dying notes upon me. I had never imagined anything approaching it. The melody was marvelous – quite unlike anything I had ever heard. It was itself the deep, tender sorrow of the most fervent love. As it rose in simple phrases ... a rapture which words cannot describe took possession of me – the pain of endless longing seized my heart like a spasm.[4]

Ferdinand becomes obsessed with the woman and her melody, the two inextricably conjoined as a musico-erotic fetish. Together, they begin to exert a hostile influence over his "whole existence," consuming his mind, causing him to give up "everybody and everything but the most eager search for the very slightest trace of [his] unknown love." As his infatuation deepens, it leads to bizarre imaginings, anguish, and alienation. In the end, Ferdinand is driven to madness – what Hoffmann calls "a distracted condition of the mind" – fleeing to a distant town and writing only that he might never return.[5]

These examples form an important backdrop for Berlioz's *Symphonie fantastique* of 1830, written at the beginning of the Hoffmann vogue in France, and drawing in obvious ways on tropes already established in the *Contes fantastiques*. Berlioz, too, describes a young man – now a *jeune musicien* – captivated by a dream-woman who seems to him to embody all the perfections of the ideal. And, like the fantastic heroes preceding him, his protagonist finds himself endlessly haunted by this image. It, like Ferdinand's vision, is tied to a musical melody that reappears whenever the beloved woman does, pursuing him through town and country, slowly eroding his sense of reality. It fills him with the same pathological longing described by Hoffmann, although now Berlioz refers to the condition as an *idée fixe*. Provoking the familiar hallucinations and mental convulsions, it eventually consumes the young musician, leading to opium-fueled despair, violence, (imagined) death, and a final hellish descent with echoes of Elis's

---

[4] Hoffmann, "Automata," 85. [5] Ibid., 87 and 100–01.

dark end. From the initial description of the fixation in Part I of the symphonic program:

Reveries – Passions
The author imagines that a young musician, afflicted with that moral disease that a well-known writer calls the *vague des passions*, sees for the first time a woman who embodies all the charms of the ideal being he has imagined in his dreams, and he falls desperately in love with her. Through an odd whim, whenever the beloved appears before the mind's eye of the artist it is linked with a musical thought whose character, passionate but at the same time noble and shy, he finds similar to the one he attributes to the beloved.

This melodic image and the model it reflects pursue him incessantly like a double *idée fixe*. That is the reason for the constant appearance, in every moment of the symphony, of the melody that begins the first Allegro. The passage from this state of melancholy reverie, interrupted by a few fits of groundless joy, to one of frenzied passion, with its movements of fury, jealousy, its return of tenderness, its tears, its religious consolations – this is the subject of the first movement.[6]

What all of these tales – those of Giglio, Elis, Ferdinand, and the *jeune musicien* – have in common is the conflation of ideal or fantastic vision and pathological absorption. To perceive the otherworldly, they suggest, is to give way to a deranged condition of the body and mind; celestial revelation (troped in both Hoffmann and Berlioz as the feminine ideal) is unavailable to the healthy mind. The idea was, as Hoffmann's work makes clear, in circulation in fantastic fiction well before the *Symphonie fantastique*. It was equally familiar to critical discourses; indeed, pathology had been central to definitions and descriptions of fantasy since Walter Scott's 1827 essay on Hoffmann, the first detailed English-language assessment of the author (and one in which Scott positions Hoffmann as the "inventor" of the mode). Here, Scott dwells at length on the diseased and mad characters of the *Fantasiestücke*, figuring them as symptoms of Hoffmann's own illness. Fictional and actual ailments are intertwined in his account, which suggests that the German author suffered from precisely the disorders he assigned to his own characters: "emotional exultation," "mental derangement," "moral palsy," and especially, unhealthy "absorption." Both Hoffmann and his tales are products of pathology, requiring "the assistance of medicine rather than of criticism."[7]

Scott's essay came to France in the late 1820s along with the first translations of Hoffmann's tales, and colored virtually all early Parisian writing on

---

[6] From the 1845 version of the program published with the score, trans. Cone, in *Berlioz: Fantastic Symphony*, 23.
[7] Scott, "On the Supernatural in Fictitious Compositions," 78, 97.

fantasy, including sketches of the *conteur* himself. Hoffmann emerged in the French press as a figure plagued, even defined by, illness. He was tied, in the *Revue de Paris*, to hallucination and nightmare, in *Le Figaro* to somnambulism, and in *L'Artiste* to both "mental extravagance" (*dévergondage mental*) and a "perpetual and voluntary unreason" (*déraison perpétuelle et voluntaire*).[8] But most clearly, as in Scott's assessment, he was linked to pathological absorption, or what the French, using their own term, described as *fixation* – an inability to separate the waking mind from the experience of dream or hallucination. We find the connection first in a review published in the *Revue des deux mondes* in October 1830 (two months before the premiere of the Fantastic Symphony), which promised to resolve once and for all the question of the *conteur*'s condition: "Today it has been proven that Hoffmann wrote under the continual influence of a nightmare, under the yoke of an *idée fixe*, and often without knowing what he was doing."[9]

Hoffmann's condition was not just fictional, then, but in some sense real. And so too was Berlioz's. The *idée fixe* afflicting his symphonic alter ego was a disease, which, well before the premiere of his first symphony, he had also assigned to himself. He invoked it in descriptions of his infatuation with Irish actress Harriet Smithson, a famously unrequited love that hovered like an autobiographical shadow behind his first symphony. Beginning as an experience of generalized yearning (what Berlioz called the *vague des passions*), it ossified over time into a more serious obsession, an illness inseparable from that of his symphonic alter ego and – as his letters of the period attest – from the production of the *Fantastique* itself. In a note to his friend Stéphen de La Madelaine (early February 1830), Berlioz yoked the two together, mapping the evolving idea of the symphony onto his own deepening pathology – emotional, psychological, and physical:

I was going to come and see you today, but the frightful state of nervous exaltation which I have been struggling against for the past few days is worse this morning and I am incapable of carrying on a conversation of any reasonableness. An *idée fixe* is killing me, all my muscles twitch like a dying man's.[10]

For Berlioz and Hoffmann (and for their readers), the conditions of longing, yearning, and fixating hovered in a curious place between fiction and reality, medicine and literary criticism. They were tropes of both invented characters and their producers, blurring the boundaries between actual and

---

[8] *Revue de Paris* (October 1829); *Le Figaro* (9 December 1830); *L'Artiste* (9 December 1830).
[9] "Aujourd'hui il demeure prouvé qu'Hoffmann écrivait sous l'influence continuelle d'un cauchemar, sous le joug d'une idée fixe, et souvent sans savoir ce qu'il voulait." *Revue des deux mondes* (October 1830).
[10] *CG*, I:153. Cairns also notes and discusses this letter in *Berlioz*, 1:357.

imagined selves, autobiographical and fanciful accounting. Here, I am interested in this wavering and, more pointedly, its relationship with the Berliozian imaginary. What was the *idée fixe*? How did it relate to the earlier *vague des passions*? To Hoffmann's "endless yearning"? To the act of fantastic invention? Answering these questions, as we shall see, means surveying both metaphysical and medical territory, histories of philosophy as well as those of science. It allows me to retrace and extend an argument I made some years ago, although now with a different goal. Then, as now, I take seriously Walter Scott's claim that fantasy was a fundamentally pathological mode in need of diagnosis as much as hermeneutic exegesis.[11]

I begin my exploration of fantastic disease by tracing Berlioz's own pathological self-accounting in the years around the *Fantastique*, noting the emergence and increasingly detailed description of his amorous obsession. From there, I turn to the overlapping histories of his pathology, both literary and psychiatric. The composer's obsession, as we shall see, owes something to the emotional, quasi-theological condition *Sehnsucht*, a term that surfaces in many of Hoffmann's fantastic narratives (including those I mention earlier) and in wider German romantic fiction. But even more clearly, his disorder is indebted to medical discourses, particularly French theories of monomania first described by psychiatrists in the early decades of the nineteenth century. The links between these ailments and their relationship with conceptions of genius occupies my attention in the following section, which traces the ways in which pathology became entangled with constructions of the romantic, and especially the fantastic imaginary. And finally, I contemplate interactions among metaphysical reflection, medical fixation, and artistic self-invention – the ways in which fantastic pathologies fractured, multiplied, and blurred identity, generating interpretive difficulty as well as promise. Philosophy and medicine were not, of course, estranged in the early part of the nineteenth century, although they sometimes existed in tension. Viewed along a single continuum, they show us something important about romantic selfhood and, most importantly, about the space Berlioz called his *monde fantastique*.

The Trope of Pathology in the "Fantastic" Letters

The year leading up to Berlioz's first symphony was one in which he wrote unceasingly about his health, physical and emotional. His correspondence is peppered with references to a planned instrumental composition of "immense" proportions inspired, so he claimed, by an unrequited passion

---

[11] See Brittan, "Berlioz and the Pathological Fantastic."

for Harriet Smithson. Fixated on the actress – a woman whose performances of Shakespeare had taken all of Paris by storm – he experienced a growing suite of symptoms, from anxiety to hallucinations and convulsions. These become inextricable, in his letters, from the artistic process itself, the two bound together in a feedback loop that Berlioz began to construct as early as winter 1829 in a series of letters to Edouard Rocher, Humbert Ferrand, and Albert du Boys.

Berlioz opened a missive to Rocher (January 11, 1829) with the melancholy notion that he could write only of "suffering," and of the "continuous alternation between hope and despair" provoked by his passion for Harriet. The composer's lovesick distress mingled with a gripping ambition to achieve "new things," propelling revolutionary musical innovation:

Oh, if only I did not suffer so much! . . . So many musical ideas are seething within me. [. . .] There are new things, many new things to be done, I feel it with an intense energy, and I shall do it, have no doubt, if I live. Oh, must my entire destiny be engulfed by this overpowering passion? . . . If on the other hand it turned out well, everything I've suffered would enhance my musical ideas. I would work non-stop . . . my powers would be tripled, a whole new world of music would spring fully armed from my brain or rather from my heart.[12]

In the months that followed, Berlioz's obsession intensified, his letters documenting a series of convoluted communications with friends and acquaintances of the actress through whom he hoped to reach her. Via the English impresario Turner, who chaperoned Smithson and her mother on their European travels, Berlioz relayed a series of love letters to Harriet, but they failed to elicit a response. Even a note in English proved unsuccessful and, after weeks of fruitless pursuit, Berlioz seemed reconciled with his amorous failure, declaring "everything over" in a miserable letter to Albert du Boys.[13] But only days later, he renewed his efforts, hatching a plot to communicate with Harriet through the *maître de la maison* at her Parisian

---

[12] *CG*, I:111, trans. Cairns in *Berlioz*, 1:355. Here and going forward, in quotations from Berlioz's letters, ellipses without brackets are the composer's; ellipses within brackets indicate omitted text. Berlioz's fixation on Smithson, which became intertwined with a Shakespearean obsession, had begun some time before. He first encountered both the actress and the English playwright in September 1827, when Harriet appeared as Ophelia in a production of *Hamlet* at the Odéon theatre. Berlioz recalls the overwhelming emotional and psychological effect of the experience in the *Memoirs*, couching his description in unmistakably pathological terms: "A feeling of intense, overpowering sadness came over me, accompanied by a nervous condition like a sickness, of which only a great writer on physiology could give any adequate idea. I lost my power of sleep and with it all my former animation, all taste for my favorite studies, all ability to work. I wandered aimlessly about the Paris streets and the neighboring plains." *Memoirs*, trans. Cairns, 95–99.

[13] *CG*, I:117. Berlioz's letter to Du Boys describes a series of events stretching over several weeks, from the failure of his English letter to Harriet, to his ill-fated interactions with her Parisian landlord and subsequent despair.

residence. The results were disastrous: Harriet was annoyed and frightened and, in reply to Berlioz's pleas, insisted brusquely that the composer's advances were unwanted, that she "absolutely could not share his sentiments," and indeed, that "nothing was more impossible." *Il n'y a rien de plus impossible*: the phrase reverberates through Berlioz's correspondence over the following months as the melancholic leitmotif of his *idée fixe*, and yet even in the face of Harriet's explicit rejection he continued to refer to her as his darling, to speak of her love, and to anticipate their union.

Letters of the period seldom refer to Harriet by name; instead, Berlioz called her Ophélie, a reference to the Shakespearian guise in which he first encountered her. He had, in fact, never exchanged a word with the actress; the heroine of *Hamlet* was more immediate than the woman herself. She wavered between the fictional and actual, her theatrical personas accruing substance and agency in Berlioz's letters. At times, he imagined her as a conflation of literary characters: "Oh Juliet, Ophelia, Belvidera, Jane Shore, names which Hell repeats unceasingly."[14] Unattainable and uncontainable, she represented an imaginary perfection that, like the poetic vision of the symphony itself, was as yet agonizingly beyond his reach. As time wore on, Berlioz associated his romantic fetish ever more intimately with the symphony-in-progress, his letters figuring disease as a central impetus in the production of the *Fantastique*. He wrote to Ferrand that "this passion will kill me," although, only a few letters earlier, he had assured his friend that "Ophelia's love has increased my powers a hundredfold."[15] The symphony was not just generated by Berlioz's obsession, but promised to perpetuate it. Again, to Ferrand: "When I have written an immense instrumental composition on which I am meditating [...] I will achieve a brilliant success in *her* eyes."[16]

The longer Berlioz contemplated his fixation, the more specific his accounting of its symptoms became. In the 2 March letter to Albert du Boys, he was already reporting intense misery and alienation from the "physical and intellectual" worlds. Elaborating on this in a later note, he described a feeling of utter isolation in which, bereft of his rational faculties, he was abandoned to the realm of memory, unable to order his thoughts:

[I]t is as though I am at the center of a circle whose circumference is continuously enlarging; the physical and intellectual world appear placed on this unceasingly expanding circumference, and I remain alone with my memory and a sense of isolation which is always intensifying. In the morning when I wake from the

---

[14] *CG*, I:156 (3 March 1830). All, of course, roles in which Smithson appeared on the Parisian stage at the height of her fame. For more on her career, and on the wider impact of Shakespeare in France, see Pemble, *Shakespeare Goes to Paris*.
[15] *CG*, I:126 (3 June 1829) and I:114 (18 February 1829), respectively.   [16] *CG*, I:126.

nothingness wherein I am plunged during sleep, my spirit – which was so easily accustomed to the ideas of happiness – awakes smiling; [but] this brief illusion is soon replaced by the atrocious idea of reality which overwhelms me with all its weight and freezes my entire being with a mortal shudder. I have great trouble gathering my thoughts. [...] I have been forced to recommence this letter many times in order arrive at this point.[17]

By June, Berlioz was desperate enough to consult a doctor, who diagnosed a nervous disorder brought on by emotional strain:

[M]y life is so painful to me that I cannot help but regard death as a deliverance. In the past days, I have gone out very little, I could not abide it; my strength disappears with an alarming rapidity. A doctor, whom I consulted the day before yesterday, attributed the symptoms to fatigue of the nervous system caused by an excess of emotion. He could also have added, by a sorrow that is destroying me.[18]

The baths and solitary rest the physician prescribed provided only temporary relief. A few days later, in a missive of melodramatic pitch, Berlioz complained of "anguish" and "terrible despair" sparked by Harriet's departure for London, linking the return of his physical suffering to a familiar sense of isolation now coupled with a convulsive impulse:

Now she's left! ... London! ... Enormous success! ... While I am alone ... wandering through the streets at night, with a poignant misery which obsesses me like a red-hot iron on my chest. I feel like rolling on the ground to try to alleviate it! ... Going out into society doesn't help; I keep myself busy all day long but I can't take my mind off her. I haven't seen her for four months now. [...]You talk to me of my parents, all I can do for them is to stay alive; and I'm the only person in the world who knows the courage I need in order to do this.[19]

February 1830 found the composer in "a frightful state of nervous exaltation" accompanied by muscle tremors. The cause of his misery was the ailment that Berlioz now identified specifically as an *idée fixe*.[20]

Plans for the *Fantastique* continued to progress, despite (or perhaps because of) Berlioz's distress. As early as 6 February, he informed Ferrand that "the whole thing is in my head," although he had not been able to write it down. The symphony was to trace the course of his "infernal passion" – not simply his infatuation with Harriet, but the obsessive illness that had resulted. Nervous overstimulation, trembling, and a painful sensitivity were now

---

[17] CG, I:117. For an earlier contemplation of Berlioz's malaise drawing in this and several surrounding letters, see Ironfield, "Creative Developments of the 'Mal de l'Isolement' in Berlioz."
[18] CG, I:127 (14 June 1829) to Edouard Rocher.
[19] CG, I:129 (25 June 1829) to Rocher, trans. Nichols in *Selected Letters of Berlioz*, 55–56.
[20] CG, I:153 (early February 1830).

among the problems he documented: "I listen to the beating of my heart, its pulsations shake me like the pounding pistons of a steam engine. Every muscle in my body quivers with pain ... Futile! ... Horrible!" At times he seemed to lapse into a semi-delirious state, writing of "clouds charged with lightning" that "rumbled" in his head.[21] A longer and more detailed letter to his father followed several weeks later (19 February), in which Berlioz interrogated not only the immediate symptoms of his illness, but also its preconditions. As he implied in a later missive to Rocher, he was reluctant to reveal to his father that Harriet was the focus of his "cruel *maladie morale*," omitting mention of the actress in the description of his affliction he sent to Papa.[22]

Here, in the most diagnostic letter yet, Berlioz suggested that anxiety and emotional excess were fundamental aspects of his character – they "come from the way I am made" – and have tormented him since early youth. His tendency toward melancholy, he explained, was fueled by an imagination so vivid that he experienced "extraordinary impressions" akin to opium hallucinations. And this *fantastique* world had only grown in breadth and power as he aged, exerting increasing influence over his rational faculties. A source of inspiration, it was also the cause of crippling pain:

I wish I could also find a remedy to calm the feverish excitement that so often torments me; but I shall never find it, it comes from the way I am made. In addition, the habit I have got into of constantly observing myself means that no sensation escapes me, and reflection doubles it – I see myself in a mirror. Often I experience the most extraordinary impressions, of which nothing can give an idea; nervous exaltation is no doubt the cause, but the effect is like opium intoxication.

Well, this fantastic world (*ce monde fantastique*) is still part of me, and has grown by the addition of all the new impressions I experience as my life goes on; it's become a real illness (*c'est devenu une véritable maladie*). Sometimes I can scarcely endure this mental or physical pain (I can't separate the two), especially on fine summer days when I'm in an open space like the Tuileries Garden, alone. Oh then (as M. Azaïs rightly says) I could well believe there is a violent *expansive force* within me. I see that wide horizon and the sun, and I suffer so much, so much, that if I did not take a grip of myself I should shout and roll on the ground. I have found only one way of completely satisfying this immense *appetite for emotion*, and that is music. Without it I am certain I could not go on living.[23]

---

[21] *CG*, I:152 (6 February 1830).

[22] *CG*, I:165 (5 June 1830). Berlioz reminds Edouard Rocher that his father must know nothing of his attachment to Harriet: "Mais que mon père n'apprenne rien de ma cruelle maladie morale pour H. Smithson: c'est inutile."

[23] *CG*, I:155 (19 February 1830), trans. adapted from Cairns, *Berlioz*, 1:357–58. Pierre-Hyacinthe Azaïs (1766–1845) was a philosopher best known for his *Traité des compensations* (1809) in which he proposed that all experience could be understood in terms of an interaction between expansive and compressive forces.

Reports of anguished hallucination followed: Berlioz told Hiller that he "saw Ophelia" shedding tears and "heard her tragic voice," going on to describe a series of odd imaginings in which Beethoven "looked at him severely" and Weber "whispered in [his] ear like a familiar spirit." Suddenly breaking off, he acknowledged that his behavior was bordering on madness: "All this is crazy . . . completely crazy, for a man who plays dominoes in the Café de Régence or for a member of the Institut . . . No, I want to live . . . once more." The letter dissolves into near-incoherence as Berlioz returns again to his *idée fixe*: "I'm beside myself, quite incapable of saying anything . . . reasonable . . . Today it is a year since I saw HER for the last time . . . Unhappy woman, how I loved you! *I love you*, and I shudder as I write the words." A desperate attempt to locate his obsession in the past tense fails, the fixation quickly reasserting itself in the present. As the letter draws to a close, Berlioz seems to sink into despondency: "I am a miserably unhappy man, a being almost isolated from the world, an animal burdened with an imagination that he cannot endure, devoured by a boundless love which is rewarded only by indifference and contempt."[24]

Desperate for a reprieve from his pathology, Berlioz suddenly received it: slanderous reports of Harriet's moral character reached the composer in March 1830, apparently jolting him from solipsistic despair into compositional action. He poured out the tale of his suffering and obsession in musico-literary form, describing an amorous illness with clear autobiographical resonances. The *jeune musicien* of his symphonic program suffers from an affliction much like Berlioz's: an amorous longing that ossifies into fixation. Of course, his hero also departs from lived experience, taking an opium overdose, committing (imagined) murder, and succumbing to a hellish dream sequence. Fact and fiction are blurred in the *Fantastique*'s program, which is not just a record of Berlioz's own experience, but a carefully controlled document of self-construction allowing illnesses of various sorts to overlap and intersect: romantic yearning, medical fixation, and homicidal alienation. In its first form, as we shall see, what we encounter in the *Fantastique* is a philosophical problem, a disorder linking Berlioz to a series of earlier literary protagonists and their creators.

Metaphysical Longing

The ailment initially afflicting Berlioz (and his fantastic "other") is one the composer identifies by name in the opening portion of his symphonic program: "that moral disease which a well-known writer calls the *vague*

---

[24] *CG*, I:156 (3 March 1830).

des passions." The author is Chateaubriand and the disease is defined in his much-touted 1805 novel *René* as follows:

> a state which precedes the development of the passions, when our faculties, young, active, fully formed but confined, are exercised only on themselves, without aim or object.... [When] the imagination is rich, abundant, full of marvels, existence poor, dry, disenchanted. One inhabits, with a full heart, an empty world.[25]

This was the condition of Chateaubriand's title character (based loosely on the author himself), whose restless longing and eventual suicidal despair provided the template for an ailment so widespread the French labeled it the *mal de siècle*. Berlioz associated it not just with his symphonic alter ego, but with himself and many of his artistic contemporaries. In a note of October 1830 to Humbert Ferrand written at the height of his own emotional distress, he sympathized with his friend's melancholy by writing, "I expect you're eating your heart out because of miseries that affect you only in your imagination. There are so many that beset us at close quarters [...] Why!, O why! ... I understand it better than you think; it's your way of life, your poetry, *your chateaubrianisme*."[26]

The author of *René* was not, of course, the first to describe such a malaise; well before 1805, the German romantics had identified his languishing as *Sehnsucht*, the desire for an unattainable perfection, a lost plenitude. It was a malady dictated in part by idealist philosophy, which situated it as a state of spiritual seeking, the yearning for a sense of completion (knowledge of the ideal) always just outside the grasp of reason and reality. Goethe's Werther (another quasi-autobiographical hero) was among its first and most famous victims, his proto-idealist longing projected onto a woman whose inaccessibility leads to despair and finally death. Perennially unavailable, she is a symbol of the protagonist's own lack, an emblem of his better or larger self. Goethe's hero provided the template for a series of similar (and similarly autobiographical) characters generated by Jean Paul Richter, Friedrich Schlegel, Byron, Benjamin Constant, and (as we have seen) Hoffmann: characters in endless pursuit of imagined perfection.

That Berlioz's passion has the same self-absorbed flavor is clear. The *être idéal* that held him in thrall was, as his symphonic program indicates, an invention of his own fantasy: his *jeune musicien* "sees for the first time a woman who unites all the charms of the ideal being *his imagination was dreaming of*, and falls desperately in love with her." The same is true of

---

[25] Chateaubriand, *Génie du Christianisme*, 159. The novel *René* appeared originally as part of *Génie*; it was detached and published separately in 1805.

[26] *CG*, I:182.

Hoffmann's Ferdinand, who, upon encountering the mysterious lady, recognizes "with unspeakable rapture, that she was the beloved of my soul, *whose image had been enshrined in my heart since childhood.*"[27] What both men were suffering from was an obsession with a self-generated or intuited idea – and in Berlioz's case, the condition was apparently chronic. Years after the *Fantastique*, in a late-life confession to Pauline Viardot, he admitted that "my whole life has been one ardent pursuit of an ideal formed in my own imagination":

> Whenever I found a single one of the qualities, of the graces that define this ideal, my heart, avid for love, fixed on it – and alas, disillusionment soon followed to show me how mistaken I had been. All my life has passed like that, and now at the moment when I feel it to be near its end this same ideal, which I had given up as the fantastic creation of a deranged imagination, appears suddenly before my dying heart! How can you expect me not to adore it![28]

This condition of utopian yearning was that of all thinking beings (or at least those endowed with spiritual awareness), according to the early German romantics. It was a state of worship, of deep desire to experience the perfection of divinity itself. Friedrich Schlegel argued that "there is nothing higher in humanity" than the "longing for the infinite," and Jean Paul situated such yearning as the ultimate source of self-knowledge.[29] It was, as they confirmed, an essentially self-reflexive desire, an attempt on the part of the rational mind to know the irrational domain of soul or, to put it differently, for the subject to experience itself. But how to achieve such a thing? Schleiermacher famously argued that meditative self-scrutiny, a kind of self-splitting, was the only way. He advised his readers, "Observe yourself with unceasing effort. Detach all that is not yourself, always proceed with ever-sharper sense, and the more you fade from yourself, the clearer will the universe stand forth before you, the more splendidly you will be recompensed for the horror of self-annihilation through the feeling of the infinite in you."[30] What he was describing was a form of controlled alienation, an experience hovering on the edge of (but not quite tipping over into) madness. The idea became inextricable, in early nineteenth-century aesthetic and literary discourses, from conceptions of inspiration. This is especially true in Hoffmann, where obsessive focus on dreamed or intuited perfection is a key trope of characters with access to otherworldly illumination. We have already seen how *Sehnsucht*

---

[27] Hoffmann, "Automata," 86.
[28] As reported by Viardot in a letter to Julius Rietz (22 September 1859), trans. Cairns, *Berlioz*, 1:524.
[29] Bonds, *Music as Thought*, 47 and 55.
[30] Schleiermacher, *On Religion*, 68. This quotation, and the implications of *Sehnsucht* for Hoffmann's aesthetics, are dealt with in Chantler, *E. T. A. Hoffmann's Musical Aesthetics*, 1–32. For a discussion of *Sehnsucht*'s broader relationship with musical romanticism, see Wurth, *Musically Sublime*, 47–71; also Bonds, *Music as Thought*, 44–62.

allows the characters Elis, Giglio, and Ferdinand to perceive (see, hear) the domain of spirit, and to these figures we could add Kreisler, Abraham, and others, all of whom suffer from what Hoffmann calls "chronic dualism."[31] It is their compulsive reflection that generates their fantastic hesitation, their ability to bridge the waking/dreaming, soul/body divide.

That Berlioz thought of his own *fantastique* illness in this metaphysical sense, at least some of the time, is made clear in the weighty letter to his father written just as the first symphony was coming to fruition. Here, as I have already noted, he described himself locked in a state of self-reflection, "constantly observing myself" as though "in a mirror." It was this species of absorption, he implied, that gave him access to otherworldly perfection – that generated his *monde fantastique*, and by extension, the *Symphonie fantastique*. His obsession, like René's and Ferdinand's, was in a fundamental sense with himself, his own yearning, which, by intimating an absence, gestured toward the presence of the unattainable object. As Julian Rushton has pointed out, the musical *idée fixe* suggests just this: rather than a portrait of the beloved (who is not just unattainable but also unrepresentable), it is an imprint of Berlioz's own desire. Replete with heaving and falling lines, chromaticism, sigh motives, and urgent sequential extensions, the melody is a virtual catalogue of the topics of longing, and one Berlioz had already used elsewhere (his early cantata *Herminie*) to evoke the idea of impossible love.[32]

But metaphysics alone is not enough to explain either the rhetoric of the program or the pathology at its heart. If Berlioz's musical *idée fixe* is an idealist symbol, it is also a medical one, a melody with clear physiological resonances. Its rapid undergirding heartbeat (the pulsing figures in the low strings) and jerky treble syncopations evoke a body convulsed with nervous energy, in the grip of physical distress. And the language of the program bears this out, drawing not just on literary tropes, but on the more positivist rhetoric of French medicine. Berlioz's protagonist not only pines, he also fixates; if his problem is the stuff of romantic philosophy, it is equally clearly derived from modern psychiatry.

The Monomania Diagnosis

The rhetoric of fixation on which Berlioz drew in his letters and program was that of an emerging *médecine des aliénés* (mental medicine) that took

---

[31] The term appears in "Princess Brambilla," 224. It is discussed in detail in Brown, *The Shape of German Romanticism*. See also Webber, "Hoffmann's Chronic Dualisms," in *The Doppelgänger*, 133–94.

[32] Rushton, *The Music of Berlioz*, 84. Bloom also draws attention to self-scrutiny as a key element of Berlioz's poetic self-construction in "A Return to Berlioz's 'Retour à la vie.'"

shape in France around 1800. Rooted in the work of the Idéologues, it drew together philosophical method and sensationalist psychology, the domain of *le morale* with that of *le physique*, bringing clinical method to bear on questions of mental illness. Its roots were laid by P.-J.-G. Cabanis and Philippe Pinel, who proposed a complex symbiosis between "internal impressions" of the imagination and physical sensations transmitted via the nervous system. The result, as scholars including Jan Goldstein, Ian R. Dowbiggin, and Elizabeth A. Williams have shown, was an emerging "medicine of the imagination" that rendered intellectual functions and even the mechanisms of sentiment accessible to rational inquiry, laying the foundation for the first generation of psychiatrists.[33] Mental and emotional disorders (*maladies morales*) began to be described and defined with a new body of clinical language; references to *hystérie, hallucination,* and *idées fixes* permeated medical and legal texts and quickly filtered into popular discourse. Through the early 1800s, psychiatry evolved as an autonomous and increasingly important medical field in France, and the new *médecin-aliéniste* as a powerful figure in both the scientific and the public realms.

Foremost among doctors of the new school was Jean-Etienne-Dominique Esquirol, a student of the revered Pinel, who devoted his long career exclusively to the study and classification of madness, becoming the principal psychiatrist of the first half of the century. Among Esquirol's chief contributions was the theorization of a mental malady called "monomania," which he first identified around 1810 and later defined and classified in an 1819 paper published in the *Dictionaire des sciences médicales*.[34] Here, as Goldstein explains, Esquirol situated *monomanie* as a circumscribed type of mania involving a "partial deliria" or localized "disorder of the understanding." Classing it as an ailment of the nervous system, he identified its primary symptom as the pathological fixation on a single idea: an *idée fixe*.[35] Monomaniacs were consumed by one thought, idea, or plan of action,

---

[33] The origins of French psychiatry are traced in Goldstein, *Console and Classify*, where she notes that the terms *le morale* and *le physique* were first paired in Pierre-Jean-George Cabanis's 1802 treatise *Rapports du physique et du moral de l'homme*; also, that "medicine of the imagination" was a broad designation applied both to speculative practices including mesmerism and to the newly rigorous and "scientific" field of French psychiatry (54, 78–79). During the early nineteenth century, similar developments in "imaginative" medicine were under way in Germany and England, although French physicians played a central role in establishing the new science. Sources that have underpinned my work in this chapter include (in addition to Goldstein), Williams, *The Physical and the Moral*; and Dowbiggin, *Inheriting Madness*.

[34] Goldstein, *Console and Classify*, 155–56.

[35] Esquirol, "Monomania," *Dictionaire des sciences médicales*, 34:117–22, qtd. in Goldstein, *Console and Classify*, 156–57. The terms *monomanie* and *idée fixe* were coined well before 1819. *Monomanie* appears in Esquirol's early writings, ca. 1810; *idée fixe* dates from the same period in both Esquirol and in Gall and Spurzheim's commentary on Esquirol given in their 1812 treatise on phrenology, *Anatomie et physiologie du système nerveux*.

a state of obsession producing an "energetic" effect while also causing "nervous exaltation," "illusions," feverish thought patterns, and – in advanced cases – hallucinations, convulsions, and disturbing dreams.[36]

According to Esquirol's later treatise on insanity, *Des Maladies mentales: considérées sous les rapports médical, hygiénique et médico-légal* (1838), monomaniacs were those who "appear[ed] to enjoy the use of their reason, and whose affective functions alone seem[ed] to be in the wrong."[37] In all areas outside of their fixation, they reasoned logically; indeed, Esquirol argued that the minds most susceptible to *idées fixes* were those endowed with marked intelligence, sensitivity, and vivid imagination. Such persons were given to ambitious or "exaggerated" projects and fantastic imaginings, often allowing setbacks and frustrations to drive them to mental instability:

Sanguine and nervous-sanguine temperaments, and persons endowed with a brilliant, warm and vivid imagination; minds of a meditative and exclusive cast, which seem to be susceptible only of a series of thoughts and emotions; individuals who, through self-love, vanity, pride, and ambition, abandon themselves to their reflections, to exaggerated projects and unwarrantable pretensions, are especially disposed to monomania.[38]

Esquirol's 1838 treatise not only synthesized his earlier writing on monomania, but also described certain subclassifications of mental fixation in greater detail. Drawing on a series of case studies, he detailed the symptoms and effects of theomania, incendiary monomania, monomania from drunkenness, and – most important here – erotic monomania.[39] Erotic fixation was a species of obsession characterized by an "overabundance of passion" (*un amour excessif*) in which "the affections take on the character of monomania; that is to say, they are fixed and concentrated upon a single object."[40] Esquirol reported that some men were seized with monomaniacal passion for mythical characters, imaginary creatures, or women they had never met but to whom they assigned all manner of physical and moral perfections. Such patients were "pursued both night and day by the same thoughts and affections," although their sentiments were directed toward an unattainable object:

[36] These symptoms are described in Esquirol's later treatise, *Des Maladies mentales*, 2:1–4, in which he consolidated his earlier writings on monomania, detailing case studies gathered over several decades of work in Parisian asylums and hospitals. My quotations from this source are given in translations adapted from those of Raymond de Saussure, in *Mental Maladies*.
[37] *Des Maladies mentales*, 1:94.   [38] Ibid., I:29.
[39] Not all of these subtypes of monomania were new to Esquirol's diagnosis, but they were presented in 1838 with fresh evidence. Goldstein draws our attention to the "specific forms of monomania," including its erotic manifestation (*Console and Classify*, 171), although she does not explore *monomanie érotique* in any detail.
[40] Esquirol, *Des Maladies mentales*, 1:47.

While contemplating its often imaginary perfections, they are thrown into ecstasies. Despairing in its absence, the look of this class of patients is dejected; their complexion becomes pale; their features change, sleep and appetite are lost: these unfortunates are restless, thoughtful, greatly depressed in mind, agitated, irritable and passionate, etc.[41]

The link to earlier forms of yearning – the stuff of Werther and René – is strong, but now the metaphysical implications of *Sehnsucht* have been replaced by a constellation of bodily symptoms. Esquirol described the "expansive" and frenetically lively temperaments of erotomanics, whose constant emotional unrest resulted in nervous pains, fever, convulsions, and "irrational conversation." "Fear, hope, jealousy, joy, fury, seem unitedly to concur, or in turn, to render more cruel the torment of these wretched beings," he wrote, who are "capable of the most extraordinary, difficult, painful and strange actions."[42] As with monomania in general, the personalities most likely to be afflicted were those with an intense emotional capacity, whose natural passions were exaggerated to the point of delirium and, eventually, suicidal despondency.

This is, surely, the species of fixation Berlioz had in mind when he diagnosed himself and his symphonic protagonist with an *idée fixe*. It was a logical medical extension of his "Chateaubriandism," complete with the panoply of indicators Esquirol enumerated: nervous excitability, mood swings, suicidal imaginings, and convulsions brought on by obsession with an imaginary perfection.[43] The link between his own condition and that of the erotomaniac is clinched by one of Esquirol's case studies, which recounts the story of a young man "of nervous temperament and melancholy character" (*d'un tempérament nerveux, d'un caractère mélancolique*) who moves to Paris in the hopes of advancing his career. While in the capital, he "goes to the theatre, and conceives a passion for one of the most beautiful actresses of [the Théâtre] Feydeau, and believes that his sentiments are reciprocated. From this period he makes every possible attempt to reach the object of his passion."[44] The young man talks constantly of his beloved, imagines their blissful union, and devotes himself fully to the pursuit of his *idée fixe*. He waits for the actress at her dressing room, goes to her lodgings, and attends her performances assiduously: "Whenever Mad. ... appears

---

[41] Ibid., I:33–34.   [42] Ibid., I:34.

[43] Berlioz's relationship with the monomania diagnosis is also noted, in passing, by Goldstein in *Console and Classify*, 155, n. 21; also by Meyer in "Marschner's Villains," 115, n. 15, where he identifies the *Symphonie fantastique* as "the most famous musical expression" of "fixed delusion." See, too, Van Zuylen, who notes in the introduction to her study *Monomania* that Berlioz "was the first artist to make music and monomania coincide" (9–10).

[44] Esquirol, *Des Maladies mentales*, I:37.

upon the stage, M. . . . attends the theatre, places himself on the fourth tier of seats opposite the stage, and when this actress appears, waves a white handkerchief to attract her attention."[45] The actress rebuffs his advances, refuses to acknowledge his letters and visits, and expresses her annoyance with his constant attentions. Nevertheless, the young man insists that she loves him, that her rough treatment is only a ruse to deceive others, and that they will soon be united. Eventually, he begins to experience hallucinations, believing that he hears the voice of his beloved and imagining that she is in the house. Esquirol reported that his obsession intensified over time, becoming a consuming and dangerous fixation despite the fact that he reasoned logically on all other subjects.

So close is this scenario to Berlioz's own, that one wonders whether Esquirol was aware of the composer's story. What is more certain is that Berlioz knew of Esquirol's disease. Once a medical student, he had more than a passing interest in psychiatric theory, and a network of connections (some of them familial) in the scientific community. Even without these, he could hardly have escaped knowledge of the monomania diagnosis. It created a major stir in both medical and lay circles, catapulting Esquirol and his system of classifications for *aliénation mentale* to the forefront of the psychiatric field. Teachers of *médecine mentale* in Paris focused heavily on the concept of monomania, and a spate of supporting research began to appear in the early 1820s. By 1826, monomania "was the single most frequent diagnosis made of patients entering Charenton," becoming a virtual epidemic that dominated medical debate and captured the imagination of the public at large.[46] In Parisian salons, mental illness and psychiatric theory were fashionable concerns, and references to monomaniacal fixation began to surface in journalism, fiction, and even visual culture (notably, in the series of "monomaniac" portraits painted by Géricault in the early 1820s).[47]

Not just the symptoms of monomania but also its remedies became topics of public interest and knowledge. These included a collection of "moral treatments" or *doux remèdes*, which Esquirol (like Pinel before him) preferred to older physical cures such as purging and bleeding. Among them was a palliative referred to as "religious consolation"

---

[45] Ibid., I:38. [46] Goldstein, *Console and Classify*, 153–54.

[47] Goldstein lists a series of articles on monomania published in leading French journals through the mid to late 1820s, including pieces in the *Globe*, *Journal des débats*, *Figaro*, and *Mercure de France aux XIX siècle* (see 184, nn. 114–16). To these, I can add two slightly later articles: "Les Monomanies," *Figaro*, 13 October 1833, and "Monomania," *Figaro*, 13 September 1834.
On Géricault's portraits of monomaniacs, see Miller, "Géricault's Paintings of the Insane." Goldstein reproduces one of these portraits, *The Physiognomy of Monomania* (ca. 1822) on plate 3, p. 223.

Figure 2.1 Théodore Géricault, *Monomanie du vol* (*The Kleptomaniac*), ca. 1820–24. Oil on canvas, 61.2 cm × 50.1 cm. Museum voor Schone Kunsten, Gent, Belgium. Photo: Scala/Art Resource, NY.

spearheaded by spiritual practitioners active in Parisian hospitals through the middle decades of the century. Relying on what they termed "sweet" and courteous treatment of lunatics, they encouraged such patients to "return to themselves," coaxing them back to reason. The method proved considerably successful and was taken up by medical personnel as well as clergy in and outside of Paris.[48] It was likely this that Berlioz was referencing when, in Part I of his symphonic program, he referred to *consolations religieuses*, an indication mirrored musically by the *religioso* section at the close of the *Fantastique*'s first movement. Here, we encounter a period of calm on the heels of the "melancholy reverie" and "frenzied passions" of the work's

---

[48] See Goldstein, *Console and Classify*, 197–225 (here, 200–02), where she points to a substantial body of nineteenth-century literature on "religious consolation"; also Dowbiggen, "François Leurent and Medical Opposition to Moral Treatment," in *Inheriting Madness*, 38–53.

opening – a short lived promise of relief.[49] It has no obvious connection to Berlioz's lived experience; indeed, in letters to Rocher and Ferrand describing instructions from his own doctor, he notes only remedies of the old physical type, namely, purifying baths and quiet rest. Even more clearly than the composer himself, then, Berlioz's hero was shaped by the symptoms and remedies associated with "scientific" yearning.

The erotic disease Berlioz invokes was relatively benign, but, according to contemporary medical theory, it could lead to more dangerous forms of fixation, including the violent "homicidal monomania." This disorder, identified in 1825 by a student of Esquirol's, Etienne-Jean Georget, was characterized as a "lesion of the will" (rather than simply an error of the imagination). It resulted in temporary madness, driving otherwise sane persons to commit murderous crimes. Homicidal monomaniacs were, according to Georget, often "compelled to kill the persons they loved the most"; indeed, his case studies (some borrowed from Pinel) record children killing their siblings, mothers their children, and husbands their wives.[50] Such murderers, he argued, were neither monsters nor criminals, but victims of a terrible mental affliction who could neither prevent nor explain their actions. Georget's diagnosis began to feature regularly as a defense in criminal trials from the mid-1820s onward, sparking widespread debate surrounding the legal, medical, and social ramifications of the disease.[51] Crowds gathered to witness court proceedings, consuming each new tale of "fixated" murder with greater relish and lending homicidal monomania a fashionable gloss that, according to Esquirol, encouraged a spate of imitative murders: "A woman cuts off the head of a child whom she scarcely knew, and is brought to trial for it. The trial is very extensively published, and produces, from the effects of imitation, many cases of homicidal monomania without delirium."[52] Self-perpetuating and increasingly rampant, homicidal madness held the public in a state of horrified suspense as they waited for the next monomaniac to strike.

It was hardly surprising, then, that the disease found its way into Berlioz's program, which cast the *jeune musicien* not only as an erotomaniacal fixator, but (at least in the realm of imagination) as a sufferer from Georget's more violent disorder. Under the influence of an opium overdose, the symphony's hero imagines he has killed the beloved, been sentenced to

---

[49] This portion of the program, as well as the corresponding *religioso* section of the first movement of the symphony, were added during Berlioz's time in Italy in 1831.
[50] Georget, *Examen médical*, 94.
[51] See Goldstein, *Console and Classify*, 165–66, where she details the sensational 1826 trial of Henriette Cornier, the first in which Georget's *monomanie-homicide* diagnosis was invoked as a legal defense.
[52] Esquirol, *Des Maladies mentales*, 2:101–02.

death by guillotine, and come before a hellish tribunal. The plot twist – a clear deviation from Berliozian "fact" – was obviously sensational, catering to public appetite for tales of violent crime. But it was also symbolic, a way of underscoring the extremity of the artist's desire. Not just infatuated with his dream woman, Berlioz's alter ego was drastically absorbed, his fixation accelerating to the point of violent alienation and criminal action. The composer's eagerness to deepen his relationship with pathology – to portray his hero (and himself) along homicidal lines – is revealing. It speaks not just to the popularization of monomania over the early decades of the nineteenth century, but also to its aestheticization.

As with the earlier and related *Sehnsucht* or *vague des passions*, fixation became bound up with creative insight in French circles, associated with special access to other, higher, or richer realms of experience. It too posited a mind hovering between reason and unreason, although no longer as the product of metaphysical alienation, but now of Esquirol's "partial lesion." The shift, as we shall see, was crucial, for it updated the idea of Hoffmannesque hesitation, rendering monomania the primary symptom of modern creative fantasy, and science itself the key explicator of inspiration.

The Fixated Fantasist

When I am dead,
Reflect betimes and mourn my dreadful doom;
Let thy angelic orisons be said,
Above thy sire's – the monomaniac's tomb!
           –Joseph P. Robson, "The Monomaniac" (1848)

By the time Berlioz interpolated an *idée fixe* into the literary program of his symphony, the term had already been absorbed into popular French discourse. Benjamin Constant was among the first to use it, referring to a "fixed idea" in his *Cours de Politique Constitutionnelle* as a "sentiment habitué."[53] A few years later, statesman-philosopher Pierre Maine de Biran described his own obsessions (and those of his friends and colleagues) as fixations, writing in his *Journal intime*, "The solitary man who nourishes an unhealthy passion, or some *idée fixe* relative to the exterior world, may be said to devour himself."[54] By the early 1820s, fixation had emerged, not just as

---

[53] The term appears in his essay "De l'Esprit de conquête"; see *Cours de Politique Constitutionnelle*, 2:252.
[54] "L'homme solitaire qui nourrit une passion malheureuse ou telle idée fixe relative au monde extérieur, peut être dit se *dévorer lui-même*." Biran, *Journal intime*, 2:209. Biran's diaries from

a mark of intellectualism or introversion, but, more importantly, as a French explanation for idealist longing ("self-devouring"). Claire de Duras, in her 1825 novel *Édouard*, applied it in precisely this way, as a modern diagnosis for an old form of yearning. Her protagonist, the young Édouard, is a character akin to René and Werther, a man in love with an unavailable woman (Natalie Nevers) who seems to embody biblical and fictional perfections: "the beauty and modesty of Milton's Eve, the tenderness of Juliette, and the devotedness of Emma." Édouard's mind becomes trained on the ideal Natalie, producing the familiar Goethian problem, "a state between despair and madness," which stimulates his imagination while casting him into delirium. But Duras now refers to his condition neither as *Sehnsucht* nor the *vague des passions*, but as a "fixed idea": "consumed by an *idée fixe*, I saw Madame de Nevers ceaselessly; she pursued me during my sleep, I rushed forth to seize her in my arms, but an abyss opened suddenly between us."[55] Édouard's obsessive love has become medical rather than metaphysical, attended by a host of familiar physical symptoms: hallucinations, nervous excitement, palpitations. He is a clinical Werther, a character mapping the artistic benefits of longing onto those of Esquirolian obsession.

When Hoffmann arrived in the late 1820s, the yearning characters of his *contes fantastiques* – Kreisler, Giglio, and others – were also diagnosed as monomaniacs. And, more tellingly, as I noted at the outset of this chapter, Hoffmann himself was pegged with the disease, his status as a monomaniac apparently "proven" by French medical science. The *conteur*'s hesitation, the wavering at the heart of his fantastic mode became, over the following several years, increasingly bound up with Esquirol's pathology, signaling part of a broader medicalizing of genius – what Frederick Burwick describes as a shift in "the concept of the *furor poeticus*" such that it "could no longer be described simply as a moment of inspiration [but] . . . must bear the burden of psychiatric scrutiny."[56] Hoffmann's own work reflects such a change; from the late 1810s onward, his tales began to absorb psychiatric terminology, including the fashionable French *idée fixe*, which he assigned to characters of sensitive or insightful temperament. The otherworldly vision of his character Adelgunda, for instance (a peripheral figure in the revised 1819 version of "Automata"), is generated, so Hoffmann claims, via fixation. Breaking down normal barriers between reason and imagination, her *idée fixe* causes her to see a ghost – the White Lady – who becomes visible to her every evening when the clock strikes nine, although it is imperceptible to others. Around the same

1816 onward contain numerous references to *idées fixes*; some are trivial fetishes while others escalate "to the point of near madness" (see, for example, ibid., I:109 and 186).
[55] Duras, *Édouard*, 124, 131.   [56] Burwick, *Poetic Madness and the Romantic Imagination*, 12.

time, in *The Serapion Brethren*, Hoffmann also assigned an *idée fixe* to the protagonist, Count P., whose obsession (like Adelgunda's) becomes inextricable from his spiritual vision. The Count is entranced with – indeed, believes himself to *be* – the third-century Christian martyr Serapion (yet another symbol of elusive perfection), fixating on this delusion despite all attempts to convince him of its fallacy. Hoffmann's description of Count P.'s condition borrows transparently from Esquirol's work, describing the familiar problem of circumscribed madness:

> In all that did not touch the idea that he [the Count] was the hermit Serapion ... his mind was completely unaffected. He could carry on the most intellectual conversation, and often showed traces of the brilliant humor and charming individuality of character for which he had been remarkable in his former life. The ... doctor declared him to be completely incurable, and strongly deprecated all attempts to restore him to the world and to his former pursuits and duties.

Hardly a handicap, the Count's *idée fixe* is presented in Hoffmann's tale as an asset, a pathology lending him spiritual and historical insight and therefore "extraordinary poetic genius" and "higher knowledge."[57]

In France, the idea of the inspired or heroic monomaniac became entrenched through the 1830s, giving rise to a spate of works with fixated protagonists: Charles Honoré Rémy's humorous *Bonardin dans la lune, ou La Monomanie astronomique*, Eugène Sue's *Atar-Gull*, Honoré de Balzac's *Gobseck*, Charles Nodier's *La Fée aux miettes*, and Victor Hugo's *Notre-Dame de Paris*, among others.[58] Balzac, more so than any other author, embraced the new psychiatric discourse, making it a key feature of the artistic mind. His *conte fantastique La Peau de chagrin* (1831) is a case in point. Here, the protagonist Raphael is associated both with a mysterious power (that of the sinister shagreen skin) and a curious absorption. The two begin to overlap as the tale unfolds, Raphael's insistence on solitude and peculiar rituals of etiquette rumored to be monomania and linked to the intense intellectual focus demonstrated by writers and philosophers. An old professor who comes to visit assumes that Raphael is hard at work on a poem or "something very important," explaining that "when he is engaged

---

[57] Hoffmann, *The Serapion Brethren*, 1:12; I:19–20.
[58] A complete list of the fictional works featuring monomaniacal fixations published in the 1830s is too extensive to give in full; in addition to those just mentioned, it includes Musset's *Lorenzaccio*, Saint-Beuve's *Volupté*, Scribe's *Une Monomanie*, Hugo's *Le Dernier jour d'un condamné*, Vigny's *Chatterton*, Stendhal's *Vie de Henri Brulard*, Barbey d'Aurevilly's *Memorandum*, Duveyrier's *Le Monomane*, and many works by Balzac, who had a voracious interest in the new psychiatric medicine; see, for instance, his *La Peau de chagrin* (1831), *Eugénie Grandet* (1834), *Le Lys dans la vallée* (1836), and *Histoire de la grandeur et de la décadence de César Birotteau* (1837).

in intellectual endeavors, a genius forgets everything else."[59] Eugène Scribe's play *Une Monomanie*, given at the Théâtre du gymnase dramatique the following year (August 1832), emphasized, even parodied, the link between fixation and genius. In order to prove himself an artist of substance, the impressionable hero Émile must not only suffer from melancholy and *ennui*, he must develop an *idée fixe* and, succumbing to delirium, drown himself. Émile writes his own obituary, sends his final verses ("Mes Adieux à la vie") to a fellow writer, and throws himself in the river. He is rescued, but his status as a modern artist – a creator of "pathological temperament" – is ensured, and eager publishers snatch up his work. When Émile's uncle demands an explanation for the young man's attempted suicide, his nephew replies only, "What can I say? I have but one excuse! One justification: it was stronger than I, it was an *idée fixe*, a monomania."[60]

The figure of the monomaniacal genius was further solidified by a collection of essays edited by Renault in 1835 and published as *Les Fous célèbres; Histoire des hommes qui se sont le plus singularisés par leur monomanie, leur originalité et leurs extravagances* (*Famous madmen: A history of the men who have most distinguished themselves by virtue of their monomania, their originality, and their extravagances*). Here, Renault stoked public appetite for monomaniacal eccentricities in a series of biographical sketches describing famously (and infamously) mad characters including the Marquis de Sade, the murderer Papavoine, and the violinist Pugnani. In these accounts, as in Scribe's play, monomania ceases to be an affliction and becomes a mark of illumination. It is precisely Pugnani's "bizarrerie de son esprit," his fixations and quirks, that mark him as a musical genius: "Pugnani was, as is well known, a madman of rare intelligence; his madness itself made him a famous man: it is true that, in his brain, it [madness] was akin to genius, and that genius and madness are two things often confounded."[61] A similar series of essays published through the 1830s and 1840s in the *Revue et Gazette musicale*, *Le Ménestrel*, and *La France musicale* detailed the "Monomanies des compositeurs," retroactively assigning the disorder to a variety of musical figures from Haydn and Gluck to Salieri and Paisiello.[62]

---

[59] Balzac, *La Peau de chagrin*, 260. The true cause of Raphael's odd behavior is the skin itself, which shrinks with each wish he makes and will eventually claim his soul in fulfillment of the Faustian bargain made at the beginning of the tale.

[60] Scribe, "Une Monomanie," 167. Overnight, Émile becomes a desirable man in the eyes of both Henriette Maugiron and her aunt, Mademoiselle Palmyre Maugiron, who regard the young stranger rescued from the river as a man of appealingly "pathological" personality; Henriette remarks that he has "an exquisite sensibility, a profound melancholy, and a bitter disgust for life" (171).

[61] Renault, *Les Fous célèbres*, 180.

[62] The following articles appeared in the *Revue et Gazette musicale:* "Monomanies de compositeurs," [Anon.] (3 January 1836) and Henri Blanchard, "Les Monomanies artistiques" (3 May 1840). Two separate essays, both titled "Monomanie de quelques compositeurs,"

Suddenly, everyone with creative pretensions was a monomaniac, a figure like Hoffmann's Serapion or Scribe's Émile, whose pursuit of imaginary (transcendental, otherworldly) revelation was tied to psychiatric alienation. Berlioz was among the first, but hardly the only, artist to cast himself in these terms. His fixated *jeune musicien* was preceded and followed by a series of other, clearly resonant, monomaniacal alter egos projected by artists including Jules Janin (a friend and fellow fantasist) and Alfred de Musset. Janin's self-telling (titled simply *La Confession*, 1830) paints its author as a melancholic figure (Anatole) afflicted with youthful *ennui*, unable to find meaning or satisfaction in daily life. His mother chooses him a bride – the lovely and naïve Anna – who embodies all that is fresh and beautiful, holding out the promise of moral rejuvenation and vision. Seeing in her the promise of the ideal, Janin/Anatole finds himself increasingly fixated, "estranged from himself" (*étranger à lui-même*), as he puts it. But his desire is inextricable from a sense of impending loss. Already, at their wedding ball, Anna's promised perfection seems to retreat, Anatole imagining her as an old woman, sunken and hideous. And finally, in their wedding chamber, it dissolves entirely, proving unattainable: she becomes a "sweaty," "white," and "repugnant" figure. The change provokes first a violent despair, then an attack of homicidal madness. Gripped by "apoplexy" (what Georget would have termed a "lesion of the will"), Anatole strangles her.[63]

A few years later, Musset's *La Confession d'un enfant du siècle* (1836) conjured a similarly deranged artistic self: the figure Octave. As with both Berlioz's and Janin's alter egos, Octave's life is dominated by the search for spiritual insight and creative impetus; he is unsettled, melancholy, suffering

---

appeared in *Le Ménestrel* (17 January 1836 and 7 July 1839), as well as several pieces featuring a newly invented type of monomaniac, the *mélomane*, defined in the *Dictionnaire de L'Académie française* (1832–35) as "Celui, celle qui aime la musique à l'excès, avec passion." Publications exploring the figure of the *mélomane* included "Tablettes d'un Mélomane" (10 August 1835) and "Du Mélomane Autrichien" (14 June 1835), as well as a *Romance* titled "Le Mélomane moderne: Bêtise en 3 ou 4 Couplets" by Ruotte, which tells the story of a man "crazy" for modern music and especially for the loud, newfangled instruments of the orchestra (one wonders, of course, whether the author had Berlioz in mind). *La France musicale* ran a series of articles through the early 1840s titled *Caprices, manies, excentricités d'artistes*, detailing the odd quirks and fixations of well-known composers. Outside of France, obvious spin-offs on the French articles appeared, including one by Piazza, titled "Monomanie di alcuni maestri di musica [Abitudini di Haydn, Gluck, Sarti, Zingarelli, Salieri, Paër, Paisiello]," *Gazzetta musicale di Milano* (21 February 1847), 57–58.

[63] Anna becomes "une figure blanche et fatigue ... [ses] bras pleins de sueur" (Janin, *La Confession*, 52). Her murder is described on pp. 56–57. As Janet Levin points out in *The Romantic Art of Confession*, Janin's work was spurred in part by a youthful and tempestuous love affair with George Sand, serving both as a fashionably pathological self-profile and as a piece of social critique (120–30).

from a *maladie morale*. Eventually, he retreats to the town of his birth, where he seems to find the muse he seeks in the form of the lovely Brigitte, another symbol of perfection – a "saint," an "angel," even "la fée Mab," a window onto another, better world. Predictably, she draws him into a state of fixation, a desire that "devours and destroys" even as it enlivens and inspires. But access to utopian vision proves fleeting and perilous. All too soon, having conquered his ideal Brigitte, Musset/Octave becomes convinced of her infidelity, sure that her transcendental promise has dissolved. Desperate and enraged, he too finds himself on the brink of homicidal violence, stopping short of murder only in the final second.[64]

These kinds of self-constructions show us how central erotomaniacal and even homicidal madness had become to the persona of the modern artist. Fixation on the ideal was the source of fantastic inspiration – a condition inextricable from artistic pursuit – but it was also dangerous and potentially fatal. All too easily absorption could become violent passion, the inevitable elusiveness of divine vision driving creative minds to frenzy. This possibility, and other threats posed by the medicalizing of inspiration, became subjects of discussion not just for French artists, but also for doctors. A spate of articles on the dangers of modern fantasy began to emerge, including an 1832 piece in the *Gazette médicale* titled "De l'Influence hygiénique du fantastique en littérature," which opened with the bold claim: "Every century has its intellectual abnormality.... The middle ages had its cabbalists and astrology; the eighteenth century, mesmerism and convulsives; the nineteenth, the one in which we have the pleasure of living, has the fantastic."[65] Fantasy, according to the author, had become a medical category, a "veritable moral epidemic" (*une véritable épidémie morale*) producing a slew of monomaniacs suffering from somnambulism, hypochondria, fixation, and "deregulation of the nervous system" (*dérangement du système nerveux*). Luring artists into spaces of chimerical perfection or seducing them with phantoms, fantasy produced hallucinatory stories and selves, worlds rupturing "the laws of hygiene" and those of "moral order." What was necessary was immediate action; indeed, the author called for clinical investigation, observation, and even dissection, arguing that fantasy's roots and influences must be treated as "among the most grave concerns of the modern doctor."[66]

---

[64] Musset describes his love as "un fatal amour, qui me dévore et qui me tue" (*La Confession d'un enfant du siècle*, 178). The account of his near-murder of Brigitte is given on pp. 306–07. Levin notes that Musset, too, was motivated in part by a failed love affair with George Sand (*The Romantic Art of Confession*, 42–60).

[65] "Chaque siècle a quelque anomalie intellectuelle.... Le moyen âge a eu sa cabalistique et son astrologie; le dix-huitième siècle, le mesmérisme et les convulsionnaires, le dix-neuvième, qui est celui où nous avons le bonheur de vivre, a le fantastique." *Gazette médicale* (27 October 1832).

[66] "un des plus graves sujets de méditation pour le médecin philosophe." Ibid.

If the medicalizing of fantasy generated anxiety in some quarters, it raised critical suspicion in others. Around the time of the *Gazette médicale* article, literary critic St. Chéron published a piece in *L'Artiste* meditating on the same questions of artistic vision and self-construction. He opened by echoing the complaints of doctors, arguing that virtually all young artists had developed deranged (melancholic, fixated, suicidal) selves modeled on the "fantastic and unregulated" heroes of contemporary fiction. But these personas were hardly all to be taken seriously; rather than real, they were in most cases simply delusional or invented, the stuff of calculated construction. Such selves emerged from what St. Chéron described as a false form of self-doubling dividing the "exterior, public" identity from the "interior, private" one, the real self from the *fantasque*.[67] He distinguished "he who lives as we all do, subject to all the whims of fate, to all the emotions of private life, he who smokes his cigar, who drinks a cup of coffee at Tortoni's, who controls himself – the man," from "he who has somber or fairy visions, whose imagination perceives divine sounds, sees magic colors, is gripped by bizarre or charming forms, he who takes up his pen, his brush or his chisel and who creates – the artist."[68] The bifurcation was symptomatic, for St. Chéron, of an erosion of artistic integrity. How could the pathological second self be authentic? Sincere? Surely it was either deranged or simply performative, a signal of estrangement from truth? As he put it, "it is this false opposition, this abstraction of the individuality of the painter, musician, or poet which, to my mind, explains the absence of spontaneity, inspiration, truth, and naiveté characterizing the majority of the artworks of our time."[69] Art, according to St. Chéron, came from a whole self, a single mind. The doubled artist was unresolvable and therefore unbelievable – not just a danger to health, but an elaborate ruse.

This idea intensified through the 1830s, the clinical artist emerging as a dubious character as well as an interpretive problem. By 1840, Henri Blanchard, writing for the *Revue et Gazette musicale*, could dub the young composers and poets of the day "a crowd of monomaniacs" (*une foule de*

---

[67] St. Chéron, "Philosophie de l'art: La vie poétique et la vie privée," *L'Artiste* 1/4/24 (1832), 269–71 (here, 269).

[68] "En effet, ne voyez-vous pas deux êtres entièrement distincts dans la personne de nos artistes. Celui qui vit comme nous tous, soumis à toutes les chances de la fortune, à toutes les émotions de la vie individuelle, celui qui fume son cigare, qui prend sa tasse de café chez Tortoni, qui montre sa garde, l'homme; puis celui qui a de sombres ou gracieuses visions, dont l'imagination entend des sons divins, voit des couleurs magiques, saisit des formes bizarres ou charmantes, celui qui prend sa plume, son pinceau ou son ciseau, et qui crée, l'artiste." Ibid., 269–70.

[69] "C'est cette opposition contradictoire, c'est cette abstraction de l'individualité du peintre, du musicien ou du poète, qui m'expliquent cette absence de spontanéité, d'inspiration, de vérité, de naiveté, qui caractérise la plupart des oeuvres d'art de nos jours." Ibid., 270.

monomanes) whose psychiatric selves he now considered "peu naturel," difficult to regard as logical or authentic.[70] His skepticism was rooted partly in the erosion of Esquirol's diagnosis, the central "condition" of the modern creator, which had begun to come under professional scrutiny. Monomania, according to younger doctors, was not the product of serious science, but instead a strange mixture of clinical and fanciful anecdotes. They pointed to Esquirol's case studies as evidence, claiming that many borrowed the language and even narrative arcs of sentimental novels. His fixators were, in some cases, not medical specimens at all, but historical figures (Esquirol identified both Nina and Lucretia as sufferers from erotic monomania) and quasi-dramatic heroes. The case of a "young lady of Lyons" was one such example, in which a girl prevented from marrying the suitor of her choice fell victim, according to Esquirol, to erotomaniacal despair. But rather than physiological details of her condition, he provided only a fanciful description: she "says nothing, confines herself to her bed," and "refuses all nourishment," and finally, when her lover is called, she "dies in his arms," in a scene of melodramatic pathos.[71] For younger psychiatrists, such a "case study" was inadmissible; Esquirol's medicine, inextricable from fiction, seemed constantly to slip back into it, too imaginative, too unscientific to appeal to a new generation. More importantly, the "partial lesion" at the center of his diagnosis was increasingly seen as flawed. Doctors with wider clinical data began to claim that subjects could not be partially mad; instead, local obsessions were signals of more global mental illness that had simply gone unrecognized. Criticism of this sort accelerated through the 1840s, leading to a total breakdown of the idea of monomaniacal or circumscribed madness by the early 1850s – and with it the defining feature of Hoffmann's mode.[72]

As the verity of the monomaniac was called into question, so too was the validity of the fantasist (it is no accident that Hoffmann's star, already dwindling, finally fell around the same time as Esquirol's). Was he a real figure? An imaginary construct? How were critics to reconcile his conjunction of sane and insane, realist and imaginative modes? What logic might be brought to bear to explain fantasy's trademark duality, its mental (autobiographical, ontological) doubling? Precisely this set of questions hovered around Berlioz himself, whose alter ego generated increasing controversy through the 1830s and 1840s. Mendelssohn, on meeting the composer at the French Academy in Rome in 1831, could already denounce him as a fake:

---

[70] Blanchard, "Les Monomanies artistiques," *Revue et Gazette musicale* (3 May 1840).
[71] Esquirol, *Des Maladies mentales*, 1:48. For a similar case study, see 42ff.
[72] Goldstein gives an account of the discrediting and final rejection of the monomania diagnosis in *Console and Classify*, 189–96.

[He] is actually worse than the others because he is more affected in his behavior. Once and for all, I cannot endure these blatantly extrovert passions, these affectations of despair for the benefit of the ladies, this genius proclaimed in gothic lettering, black on white.[73]

Even Ernest Legouvé, one of Berlioz's literary collaborators and closest friends, acknowledged his reputation as "an eccentric who gloried in his own eccentricity," a man generally regarded as a "poseur." But if the composer's behavior bordered on hyperbole, Legouvé insisted, it was not born of deception:

I seem to see before me once again that touching, extravagant, ingenuous creature, violent, scatterbrained, vulnerable, but above all sincere. It has been said that he was a *poseur*. But to pose, that is to conceal what you really are and show the world what you are not, to pretend, to calculate, to be master of yourself. And where would he have found the strength to act such a role, this being who lived at the mercy of his nerves, who was the slave of every new impression, who dashed precipitately from one emotion to another, who winced, turned pale, wept in spite of himself, and could no more control his words than the muscles of his face?[74]

Berlioz's artistic self was, as Legouvé suggested, a representation of the "real" inner man acted out involuntarily on the body itself. His performance was not an act of concealment or even calculation, in other words, but of revelation.

Modern critics have found themselves as torn as their nineteenth-century counterparts, some embracing Berlioz's erotomaniacal (homicidal, opium-fueled) self as a form of genuine self-representation (a "distillation of real life" or a "quasi-autobiography") while others, pointing to an obvious slippage between "truth" and "imagination" in the composer's narrative, dismiss it as mere fiction.[75] Of course, both positions are valid; indeed, it is their coexistence or, to put it differently, the *hesitation* between them that

---

[73] In a letter to his family (29 March 1831), trans. Rose, Berlioz Remembered, 46.

[74] Legouvé, "Hector Berlioz," in *Soixante ans de souvenirs*, 1:299, trans. Rose, *Berlioz Remembered*, 67. Legouvé's memoir is not always a reliable source of factual information (his dates and places are sometimes misremembered), but his character sketches of Berlioz are written with care and reveal an intimate knowledge of the composer.

[75] Barzun unequivocally dismisses the program as a life account on the grounds that it fails to document verifiable historical events; see his *Berlioz and the Romantic Century*, 1:157. Cone describes the symphony as an expression of the "leading motives" of Berlioz's life while calling for clear "separation" between composer and persona in *Berlioz: Fantastic Symphony*, 5; and *The Composer's Voice*, 84–85 and 92–93. Both Holoman, in *The Nineteenth-Century Symphony*, and Macdonald, in *Berlioz*, acknowledge the autobiographical implications of the program with less reservation (see pp. 114 and 18 respectively), while Rushton regards it as both "quasi-autobiography" and "fiction" in *The Music of Berlioz*, 29 and 159. More recently, Cairns has described the composer's narrative as an emotional "distillation," a repository of Berlioz's "entire imaginative existence," and a work in which "autobiography was absorbed into art" (*Berlioz*, 1:365–67).

stands at the heart of fantasy. But resolving the two – generating a logic for St. Chéron divided self – proved possible only once the genre's metaphysical dimensions were reunited with its clinical ones, once monomania's "partial lesion" was brought back into contact with *Sehnsucht*'s more symbolic "partial alienation." The merger did happen in Berlioz's lifetime, as we shall see, in the form of one final version of the monomania diagnosis, a clinical-philosophical rationale with pointedly Berliozian resonances.

Doubled Selves

The divided self that posed a problem for certain nineteenth-century critics is a familiar one to modern literary theorists, who have long recognized the Doppelgänger as a central trope of the fantastic mode. From Hoffmann onward, tales of fantasy have been replete with doubles: imagined, reflected, or hallucinated others seen in pools of water, portraits, shadows, or mirrors, pursuing or pursued by "real" selves, constantly emerging from or collapsing into the domain of the unreal. In many senses, these twinned figures represent the primary goal of fantasy itself: a reunification of imaginative and rational worlds, a bridging of the dualisms resonating back to Descartes and carried forward in new ways through Kant. They are symbols of madness but, equally clearly, of revelation, figures whose gesture toward completeness is also a threat to subjectivity and aesthetic integrity, striking "at the very core of narrative life and life-likeness."[76] As Marina Warner puts it, doubles hold out the threat of "possession ... and estrangement," but also "a possible becoming different while remaining the same person, of escaping the bounds of self." They "relate to your innermost, secret self, and act epiphanically to unveil you to the world – and to yourself."[77]

Doubles point back to (indeed, are in many senses products of) fantasy's first pathology, *Sehnsucht*, whose catastrophic yearning was also understood, as we have seen, as a form of self-twinning. The act of ideal longing, to return to Schleiermacher, was also one of self-reflection, the acute focusing of the rational mind on its own irrational other – the soul, spirit, or unconscious. What emerged was not a separate self but a contingent one, an imaginative, cosmic, sometimes frightening shadow glimpsed in moments of temporary estrangement ("self-annihilation") or in the semiconscious conditions of dream and hallucination. Such figures play a key role in Hoffmann's work (and surrounding fiction), some contained within the literary frame (Coppelius and Coppola in "The Sandman," the Archivist and

---

[76] Webber, *The Doppelgänger*, 60.   [77] Warner, *Fantastic Metamorphoses*, 164–65.

Prince Phosphorous in "The Golden Pot," etc.), others crossing the boundaries between "reality" and "fiction" operating as alter egos of fantasists themselves.[78]

In the latter category is Hoffmann's own double, the musician Johannes Kreisler, whose relationship with the *conteur* is famously ambiguous, wavering in and out of the autobiographical mode throughout *Kreisleriana* and the later novel *Kater Murr*. Factual as well as imaginary, Kreisler absorbs elements of Hoffmann's lived experience – his musical interests, legal knowledge, artistic philosophies, romantic encounters – while also departing from "reality," introducing imaginary personages, nonexistent geographies, dreamed or imagined events. In descriptions of him, Hoffmann allows his pronouns to waver: Kreisler is "he" as well as "I," subject as well as object, a figure both foreign to and synonymous with his factual self. In the final fragment of *Kreisleriana*, the *conteur* dramatizes this tension clearly, speaking directly to Kreisler as a figure "in the mirror," a "you" who is also "me." "Who knows you better than I?," he asks. "Who has looked within you – in fact, who has looked out *from* within you – except myself?" Kreisler is both a burden, a symbol of his own madness, and a gift, a harbinger of spiritual revelation whom Hoffmann tries, unsuccessfully, to lay to rest at the close of the cycle.[79] His relationship with the Kapellmeister is echoed in the alter egos constructed by many of his literary contemporaries; Wackenroder, for instance, painted himself as the mad artist Berlinger and Jean Paul, in his *Selberlebensbeschreibung*, simply as a dimly seen "other." These second selves have similar flavors; they are hazy or hallucinatory twins, not the stuff of external reality or lived experience, but of internal, unconscious truths, identities glimpsed out of the corner of the eye. They are, as romantic literary theorists put it, both I and not-I, irrational shadows yoked to rational centers as the necessary, terrifying partners in the creative process, without whom there could be no access to the domains of imagination or revelation.

The idea was not just Teutonic, but, conceived slightly differently, also English. Thomas De Quincey's Opium Eater (of the *Confessions of an English Opium Eater*, a text well-known to Berlioz) was, like Kreisler, a mad, visionary persona at once synonymous with and separate from the author himself. Born of drug-induced delusion, he was both destructive and productive, ushering De Quincey into spaces inaccessible to his waking mind and in so doing providing the stuff of creative work. Charles Lamb

---

[78] Hoffmann's tale "The Doubles" ("Die Doppelgänger," 1821) is a classic locus of this trope, which also became central to French *contes fantastiques*, as in Gautier's tale "Le Chevalier double" (1840).

[79] Hoffmann, *Kreisleriana*, 159–68.

constructed a similar (and similarly addicted) alter ego in his *Confessions of a Drunkard* and, in the wake of De Quincey, the brilliant madman James Hogg sketched an "inner" self in his *The Private Memoirs and Confessions of a Justified Sinner*. Fantasized or quasi-autobiographical artistic personas also have a French history; indeed the "confessions" of English authors take their cue from Rousseau's prototypical *Les Confessions*, a work of creative self-construction wavering between fact and fiction, projecting an interior (spiritual, emotional) landscape as much as an exterior one.[80] Rousseau, prefiguring Schleiermacher, ascribed his confession to precisely the kind of self-scrutiny that would later become key to the early German romantics. As he put it, "no longer was experiencing oneself as an 'other' outside of myself to be cured, but now to be encouraged!"[81] This idea persisted in French criticism through the early decades of the nineteenth century, both Renault and Balzac citing self-observation as key to the artistic temperament. It produced the "confessed" selves of Musset and Janin and, as Berlioz's references to self-scrutiny make clear, also the *jeune musicien* of the Fantastic Symphony. But, crucially, these artistic projections (at least those of Berlioz's circle) ceased to be understood in terms of *Sehnsucht*'s reflexive philosophy; instead they were bound up with monomaniacal insanity – what I have situated here as fantasy's clinical pathology.

The shift was important, since it meant that readers and critics began to understand artistic "others" not as authentic selves, but as delusional or outlandish personas, the stuff of unreality rather than alternative reality. St. Chéron's difficulty reconciling *fantasques* with their producers was due in part, I suggest, to the estrangement of Esquirol's disease from its metaphysical forerunner. As philosophical longing gave way to medical fixation, the original implications of the fantastic self, the Doppelgänger, became opaque. No longer revelatory, a symbol reuniting reason and spirit, the "other" emerged as purely pathological or simply performative. And it *was*, as we have seen, both of these things. In Berlioz's case, it is difficult to argue that the *fantasque* was not to some degree staged. A sense of theater – extravagant typography, melodramatic description, emotional hyperbole – runs through both his symphonic program and the surrounding letters. But equally unconvincing is the argument that this was the whole truth, that his artistic persona had no life or larger import. Berlioz himself suggested a middle ground, referring to the program of the *Fantastique* as both "my novel" (*mon*

---

[80] For more on English and French confessions, including those by the authors discussed here, see Levin, *The Romantic Art of Confession*; also, the final portion of my own article "Berlioz and the Pathological Fantastic," which situates Berlioz within this tradition in a more localized manner (233–39).

[81] Qtd. in Goldstein, *The Post-Revolutionary Self*, 98.

roman) and "my history" (*mon histoire*).[82] It was the product not just of fiction or projection, but also, as his letters confirmed, of *reflection*. Like Hoffmann's double, Berlioz's *jeune musicien* was both "I" and "he," an imaginative truth at once inextricable and separate from verifiable reality.

But this idea – that of the "real" or authentic twin – became available in France only once psychiatry and philosophy were reunited. This involved one final diagnosis of fantasy that was itself a reconciliation (or moment of hesitation), a merger of the metaphysics of the Doppelgänger with the physiological science of the fixator. It emerged not in the medical, but in the literary domain (where it remained) in the writing of Charles Nodier, long an explicator and champion of the fantastic. Nodier situated his theory as a corrective, the most accurate and modern explanation for fantasy, which promised to resolve both confusion and negative criticism. He laid it out in an essay titled "Piranèse: Contes psychologiques, à propos de la monomanie reflective" (1836), whose purpose was to clarify the nature (or "psychology") of artistic fixation, which he claimed had not been fully understood either by doctors or lawyers. Monomania, as he argued, was indeed central to the temperament of the romantic creator, although it was not simply a medical disorder, but also a spiritual condition. In its artistic form, Nodier termed the disease, tellingly, "reflective monomania," characterizing it as a form of radical introversion, a fixation on the innermost domains of being: those of spirit, imagination, and dream. The ailment was native to poetic types, who, in order to experience transcendence, allowed the mind to foray beyond the limits of the rational. Entranced by the promise of revelation and driven by an impulse toward ever-greater spiritual "expansion," they became absorbed in spaces of ideal reflection. Taken to extremes, this resulted in an urge to dissolve entirely into the realm of spirit. As Nodier put it, the reflective monomaniac, drawn irresistibly toward "the principal of all creation," preferred to "float among the atoms in a ray of [God's] light rather than live out life in a world animated with [his own] will."[83] Attempting to straddle the material and ethereal worlds, he became painfully divided – melancholy, convulsive, withdrawn, incoherent. His body broke down as well as his mind. And finally, convinced that "his soul and corpus cannot exist together without strife and violence," he embraced total self-annihilation.[84]

---

[82] In a letter to Ferrand containing the first known draft of the symphonic program, *CG*, I:158 (16 April 1830).

[83] In the voice of the monomaniac: "J'aimerions mieux flotter avec les atomes dans un rayon de votre lumière, que de vivre toute la vie d'un monde et de l'animer de ma volonté!" Nodier, "Piranèse," 203. Van Zuylen also deals with this essay (largely in the context of Nodier's wider output) in *Monomania*, 62–81.

[84] "son âme et son corps ne pouvoient plus exister ensemble sans lutte et sans déchirements." Nodier, "Piranèse," 177.

What Nodier was describing was, of course, a version of the old *Sehnsucht* or *vague des passions*, now integrated with the newer monomania diagnosis. His "reflective" fixator comes close to Schleiermacher's obsessive self-scrutinizer, combining the physical symptoms of monomania with the solipsistic impulse of the romantic yearner. Among the results of this union was that the "other" worlds/selves of the monomaniac could again be understood as parts of a single subject. Nodier's essay was a defense of the *fantasque*, an attempt to rescue artistic alienation from the charges either of insincerity or lunacy by repositioning it as a form of daring (and dangerous) self-knowing. He fleshed out his thesis in a series of case studies including some focused on historical characters, others on clinical patients, and one on himself. In his own youth, he admitted, he suffered from a mild form of reflective fixation, which began as an obsession with the wonders of the natural world. An avid botanist and entomologist, he dreamed of finding ever rarer and more beautiful specimens. To capture these, he felt, would be to understand the nature of creation and therefore of the soul itself. His fixation on transcendental (natural, spiritual) knowledge became overmastering, leading to ever-more precarious expeditions taking him onto peaks and precipices. He describes an inclination not just to explore, but to become one with nature, to experience his own "other" or spiritual self by dissolving into the vital energy of the universe itself. He was, as he put it, poised to die in order to understand the nature of life.[85]

More serious – indeed, fatal – was the case of the Italian artist Piranesi, who spent his life pursuing (and pursued by) a vision of perfection. He externalized it as the image of an endless stair, an architectural impossibility that, as his obsession grew, became increasingly real. At first confined to his imagination, the stair soon began appearing before his eyes constantly, with "a cruel obstinacy." He found himself torn between the soul-world for which he yearned and the limited consciousness to which he was confined – a twinned self. Eventually the tension became unsupportable, deregulating both his body and mind, and he succumbed, disappearing entirely into the inner realm. But the torture was not in vain, according to Nodier, for it produced "fantastic and marvelous" artworks, glimpses of another, higher world (that of the second identity) translated by the rational consciousness (the first).[86]

Links between these case studies and Berlioz's pathology are not hard to make: Piranesi's obsessively recurring image and uncontainable imagination, as well as Nodier's experience of an "expansive force" and a slow nervous collapse resonate easily with the composer's self-described

---

[85] For this case study, see ibid., 186–87.   [86] The Piranesi material can be found in ibid., 187–97.

emotional and physical condition. If he was an erotomaniac à la Esquirol (and an imagined homicidal maniac in the manner of Georget), he was equally clearly a victim of Nodier's "spiritual" monomania. And Nodier himself suggested as much; indeed, the relationship between his "reflective" disease and Berlioz's illness was one toward which he had already gestured. Well before the 1836 essay, with its formal delineation of the new monomania diagnosis, Nodier had produced a preliminary sketch of his "reflective" sufferer. It took the form of a *conte fantastique* and focused not on a painter or author, but instead on a fantastic *listener* (it was later published alongside the Piranesi essay in the first edition of Nodier's collected works). The tale appeared in 1831 soon after the premiere of Berlioz's first symphony, and seems in many senses a response to the work. It offers us a glimpse of how one of Berlioz's own artistic contemporaries (and a fellow fantasist) might have understood the composer's fixation; indeed, it suggests that the composer of the *Fantastique* was the prototypical "reflective monomaniac," a figure who stimulated Nodier's ruminations on spiritual obsession and twinned self-construction.

Entitled "Jean-François les bas-bleus," Nodier's story opens with a familiar defense of the fantastic, in which he argues that it is not a silly nor merely a make-believe idiom, but a vessel for higher or occult truths as yet opaque to science. True fantasy, he insists – including the tale he is about to tell – is rooted in "real" events, to which he has not added "anything of mine."[87] The narrative that follows revolves around a young man, Jean-François Touvent, a promising student whose work is derailed when he falls in love with the daughter of his wealthy benefactress. Enraptured from the start, he "could not see her without loving her"; the girl appears to him as the image of perfection.[88] But marriage is impossible given the difference in their social ranks and, in the face of this, Jean-François goes mad, becoming "a monomaniac, a madman" (*un monomane, un fou*). He fixates on the unattainable perfection his beloved represents – on "visions of an exalted spiritualism" (*visions d'un spiritualisme exalté*) – slowly becoming estranged from himself and from the domain of reality. The result is a doubled identity: he is, as Nodier's narrator tells us, a man "with two souls, one belonged to the gross world in which we live, the other was purged in the subtle space he believed to have penetrated with his thought."[89] His first self

---

[87] "Après cela, madame, je suis prêt, si cela vous convient le moins du monde, à vous raconter une histoire fantastique où je vous promets de ne rien mettre du mien." Nodier, "Jean-François les bas-bleus," 142.

[88] Ibid., 163.

[89] "Jean-François eût deux âmes, l'une qui appartenoit au monde grossier où nous vivons, et l'autre qui s'épuroit dans le subtil espace où il croyait pénétrer par la pensée." Ibid., 152–53. For reference to the "spiritual visions" produced by Jean-François's monomania, see 142–43 and 163.

operates in the physical realm, allowing him to hear and respond to passers-by. But his second self, freed from the limitations of his own subjectivity, soars into the realm of the cosmic, letting him perceive the sound of an ideal world – that of all creation, the entirety of nature itself.

This panoptic or, to use Nodier's term, "pantheistic" listening gives him access to truths unavailable to others. He *hears* the sound of divine perfection – an aural imprint of the beloved herself – which is also that of his own soul and all others. In listening continuously to its/her resonance, he becomes increasingly absorbed into its magical sound, attuned to musical perfection; he is afflicted with an aural form of what Nodier would later term *reflective monomania*. Among the results is a familiar physical breakdown: convulsions, epilepsy, even somnambulism – nervous disturbances seemingly brought on by his contact with the ideal, which slowly erode his body, transmuting him into his ethereal "second" self. Unsurprisingly, his illness is also the source of his creative illumination, giving rise to special aesthetic and scientific insight. Translating the truths revealed by his soul-self into the language of the physical world, he is able to speak brilliantly on all manner of subjects from aesthetics and astronomy to botany and theology. He is also gifted with immediate knowledge of distant events, "hearing" (or feeling) as vibrations in the universal soundworld all the physical activities of the earth. When his beloved dies, he perceives her passing and, at the same instant, is himself dissolved completely into the universal totality of which she was also a part. Ideal love (and aesthetic perfection) the tale suggests, is unavailable to the singular mind, proving available only in states of mental alienation and, ultimately, death – in the case of Jean-François, a kind of proto-Wagnerian Liebestod.

Jean-Francois's aural-erotic fixation resonates in obvious ways with Berlioz's symphonic tale; indeed, it is difficult to believe that Nodier and his readers were not imagining the *Symphonie fantastique* while writing/reading about Jean-François. We might even situate the tale as a diagnosis of the *jeune musicien* and, by extension, of Berlioz himself. It gives us a sense of how Nodier conceived of both the composer's twinned self-construction and its relationship with medical fixation. Berlioz was, Nodier's tale implies, a figure at once singular and double. His "other" self was not simply the product of lunacy but of self-scrutiny; it was the essential spiritual half of a genius self, the product of metaphysical reflection as much as external fixation. Together, medicine and philosophy produced and explained the fantasist, who for Nodier, was a figure defined by suffering (emotional and physical) and self-fracturing – as Berlioz would later put it, condemned to spend his whole life "in pursuit of an ideal formed only in my own imagination."[90]

[90] See note 28.

Nodier's tale is an answer (in advance) to the skepticism of St. Chéron and like-minded critics, a theory of fantastic identity drawing together medical and philosophical theory to show how clinical notions of alienation might be rendered compatible with metaphysical reflection. Berlioz was, the story invites us to consider, neither a sentimental yearner nor a monomaniacal madman, but (as his own symphonic program suggests) both. It was in the combination of the two pathologies, the *vague des passions* and the *idée fixe*, spiritual longing and nervous exultation, that he and his fellow French fantasists located their own condition, and in so doing provide a vehicle for historical interpretation/explanation. Nodier's diagnosis, fully fleshed out in 1836, was the last in a long line of psychiatric meditations on the subject of fantastic selfhood, and one that allows us, among other things, to lay to rest the divide between both philosophical/physiological readings of fantastic pathology and fictional/actual interpretations of Berlioz's symphony, locating the composer and his illness midway between both modes at the tipping point between French science and German metaphysics.

And, of course, Nodier's prototypical tale also does much more; it is not just about twinned subjectivity, but also about a kind of doubled hearing. Its musical implications are as significant for Berlioz as its medico-philosophical claims, although the connection between Jean-François's "pantheistic" or "cosmic" listening and the soundworld of Berliozian fantasy is not immediately apparent, having little obvious connection with the *Symphonie fantastique*. It becomes clear only when we follow the tale of the *jeune musicien* to its end – when we connect Berlioz's first symphony to its lesser-known sequel, *Le Retour à la vie*. This is the project of the next chapter, which brings us back through Nodier and Hoffmann and forward through to the second part of the two-part tale of Berlioz's "other" self. The *Fantastique* was in large part a work of self-situating, a place in which Berlioz yoked himself to the two central pathologies of fantasy, generating a Hoffmannesque identity imbued with modern French resonances. In its sequel, he shows us how that self hears and listens, forging connections between the twinned self and the twinned ear, between fantastic fixation and musical production.

3 ❦ *Le Retour à la vie*: Natural Magic and the Ideal Orchestra

Let's return for a moment to Hoffmann's Ferdinand. As we have seen, his is a tale of metaphysical longing or what French critics might have diagnosed as proto-Berliozian fixation. But it is also, as Emily Dolan has pointed out, a meditation on the nature of ideal listening.[1] Hoffmann brings the two strands together at the heart of the tale "Automata," making spiritual-erotic obsession central to a theory of musical perception/production. Ferdinand and his friend Lewis, in pursuit of the elusive beloved and her otherworldly melody, have been to the workshop of the sinister Professor X, an inventor of clockwork instruments. Put off by his "soulless" mechanical contraptions, they embark on a discussion of the "higher mechanics of music," which Lewis (in a typically fantastic digression) describes as the attempt to understand and capture the sounds of creation: the "music of the air" or of Mother Nature herself. Such tones cannot be elicited by musical automata, he argues, but only by instruments vibrating in accordance with the divine world – those calling sound from metal, glass, or marble, activated by human breath, or (in the case of string instruments) set in motion by the activity of the wind itself. These instruments reveal "the marvelous acoustical secrets which lie hidden all around us in nature," and are thus sources of power and revelation, echoes of a prelapsarian world – of Eden, pure love, spirit itself.[2] Among these Lewis singles out the glass harmonica and Ferdinand the aeolian harp, both with special access to "higher" sound. As their conversation draws to a conclusion, Hoffmann brings us back to their central romantic quest – the search for Ferdinand's beloved – by entwining it with their organological discussion, the two coming suddenly and climactically together:

Just at this moment there suddenly came floating through the air an extraordinary sound, which, as it swelled and became more distinguishable, seemed to resemble the tone of a glass harmonica. Lewis and Ferdinand stood rooted to the spot in amazement, not unmixed with awe; the tones took the form of a profoundly sorrowful melody sung by a female voice. Ferdinand grasped

---

[1] Dolan, "Hoffmann and the Ethereal Technologies of Nature Music."
[2] Hoffmann, "Automata," 96–98.

Lewis by the hand, while the latter whispered the words, "Mio ben, ricordati, s'avvien ch'io mora."[3]

Here, the sound/song of the dream woman – Ferdinand's musical *idée fixe* – is revealed as precisely the natural sound about which the two friends have been speaking. The feminine ideal is also the natural *real*, an intimation of divine creation itself and in this sense of Ferdinand's own soul. A little girl playing in the grass near them remarks revealingly, "Oh, how beautifully my sister is singing again!" At the same time the two friends see Professor X, no longer repulsive but transformed: "his gaze was fixed upon the heavens, as if he were contemplating that world beyond the skies, of which those marvelous tones, floating in the air like the breath of a zephyr, were telling." And not only the Professor himself but everything around him seems to waken to sonorous life in the presence of the airy voice: "In every direction crystal tones came scintillating out of the dark bushes and trees, and, streaming through the air like flame, united in a wondrous concert, penetrating the inmost heart, and waking in the soul the most rapturous emotions of a higher world."[4]

This sequence of events is not confined to Ferdinand's tale, but echoes through other Hoffmann (and Hoffmannesque) scenarios. In the fragmentary novel *Kater Murr*, Abraham perceives the unattainable Chiara via the strains of an aeolian harp. Elsewhere, Kreisler compares the voice of the transcendent Miss Amalie to "long-held, welling armonica-notes" that "transport me into heaven." And, as we saw at the close of the previous chapter, Nodier's Jean-François "hears" his ideal beloved through a similar form of cosmic or pantheistic listening giving him access to sonorous nature in its entirety.[5] In all such cases, real and imaginary soundworlds become synonymous; sensitive perception of the natural opens a window onto the supernatural, evoking the domain of fantastic perfection or idealist self-completion (Dolan makes this point clearly: ideal sound in Hoffmann, as she argues, is not divorced but inextricable from that of material reality). Hoffmann spells out the connection more fully in *Kreisleriana*, where he conflates the sonorous "world of fantasy" with the sounds of the natural

---

[3] Ibid., 99. The Italian Ferdinand whispers is the first line of the song sung by his elusive beloved: "Darling! remember well, / When I have passed away, / How this unchanging soul / Loves you forever / Though my poor ashes rest / Deep in my silent grave, / Even in the urn of Death / You I adore!" (85).

[4] Ibid., 99–100.

[5] For the reference to Miss Amalie, see Hoffmann, *Kreisleriana*, 87. For the *Kater Murr* passage, see idem, *The Life and Opinions of the Tomcat Murr*, 285–86. The "pantheistic" listening assigned to Jean-François in Nodier's *conte fantastique* rubs off on the tale's young narrator, who begins to hear spiritual messages in the murmuring water of a fountain, the whispering of trees, and the intimations of distant thunder; see "Jean-François les bas-bleus," 139–66.

world: "trees, flowers, animals, stones, water," and later "the rustling of oak-leaves above my head, or the splashing of streams below."[6] To truly listen to such sounds is to perceive the divine, to gain access to a form of revelation – the world of "spirit." As such it is the goal of the yearning artist, including (and most obviously) Hoffmann's own alter ego, Kreisler, who devotes his studenthood to searching for the natural sound invoked by Amalie: that of pantheistic magic itself.

In the final essay of the cycle, Hoffmann confirms that Kreisler has achieved his aim: he has begun to hear "the whole of nature" and, in so doing, gained access to the beloved voice he seeks and also to his own poetic voice: "You have sharpened your faculty of hearing to such an extent that now and then you perceive the voice of the poet hidden within you." Not only has Kreisler begun to hear nature, he has been drawn into "sympathy" with its mysterious resonances and learned to manipulate them:

> As his recognition grows, so does his personal will, and may not the musician then behave towards the natural world surrounding him like the mesmerist towards his patient, since his active will is the question which nature never leaves unanswered?[7]

Having "mesmerized" nature, Kreisler must then translate its power into composed sound. The wind harp and glass harmonica – instruments famously associated with otherworldly as well as nervous power – play a key role in this process, but the most important of the new instruments, for Hoffmann, is the orchestra. This is among the points made in his essay on Beethoven – the centerpiece of *Kreisleriana* – which situates the composer's instrumental music, especially the Fifth Symphony, as the first signal of a new kind of fantastic listening. Beethoven's music, he argues, is rooted in and productive of the same "endless yearning" motivating Kreisler and Ferdinand and captures, for the first time, the object of such yearning: Schlegel's "spirit" realm. It operates neither in the "human" domain of Haydn nor in the "supernatural" world of Mozart, but instead straddles both, vibrating across the boundaries of the physical and otherworldly, reactivating an old form of magic: that of Orpheus's lyre. The technologies of the Beethovenian orchestra are akin to those of Ferdinand's nature instruments; indeed, more sophisticated, capturing with even greater sensitivity the intimations of "spiritual" sound. Their effect is that of sublime elevation as well as physical transformation: "lightning flashes" that "burst our hearts," "constrict our breast," producing "intimations ... of annihilation." Beethoven's fantastic world is a dangerous

---

[6] Hoffmann, *Kreisleriana*, 94, 150. For further detail, see Chapter 1, pp. 39–41.
[7] Ibid., 160–64.

as well as an exhilarating place – and an elusive one. Its ideal sound, like the ideal love from which it is inextricable, can never be fully realized or represented, only intimated; to record it is to recall the enchantment of a long-forgotten age, to write in "hieroglyphs" or "Sanskrit." But, as Hoffmann argues, even these distant or mysterious resonances contain power – enough, in any case, to stoke the artist's own yearning (the prerequisite, as we have seen, for fantastic revelation).[8]

Hoffmann's connections in *Kreisleriana*, "Automata," and elsewhere – his yoking of actual and supernatural sound, erotic fixation with pantheistic (and even mesmeric) revelation – did much to shape Berlioz's own symphonic story and its musical working-out. Indeed, if we follow the tale of his young hero, the *jeune musicien*, to its end, through the Fantastic Symphony and on into its lesser-known sequel *Le Retour à la vie*, we find that his own dream sound is also, like Ferdinand's, a natural one, perceived via a form of elemental listening. Berlioz's rendering of it calls on precisely the organological innovations hailed by Ferdinand and Lewis, and the "spiritual" orchestral language associated with Beethoven. His *monde fantastique*, as I suggest here, is a place defined in part by Hoffmannesque pantheism or what we might think of as a form of transcendental realism – a space of revelatory audition made available via instrumental innovation.

The Return to Life

Berlioz began work on *Le Retour à la vie* in the early summer of 1831 on the way back to Rome, where, as a Prix-de-Rome laureate, he was in residence at the French Academy. Among the stipulations of the prize was that candidates remain in the country, presumably hard at work on a *chef d'oeuvre*. But Berlioz, in flagrant disregard of this, had gone on a mad dash to Nice with every intention of continuing to Paris. News of his dissolved engagement to Camille Moke (the woman who had replaced Harriet as his "beloved" and to whom he had become engaged) was the motivation. As he learned in a curt note from her mother, Camille had abandoned him for a more promising prospect: piano-builder Ignaz Pleyel. The news was not entirely unexpected; having had no letters from his bride-to-be, Berlioz had already begun to suffer anxiety, but confirmation of her betrayal sparked blind despair and rage. Yet again, the ideal woman had proved unattainable and perhaps would remain so forever. Berlioz concocted a mad plan to murder Camille, her mother, and Pleyel, pursuing it through Genoa

---

[8] Ibid., 96–102.

(where, in a moment of desperation, he threw himself in the sea), and on to Nice.[9] But there his fires cooled; he realized the fruitlessness of the journey and the jeopardy in which he had placed his stipend. He began, as his letters of the period attest, to ruminate on the mercurial events of the previous two years: his fixation on Harriet (so easily transferred to Camille), and its relationship to his aesthetic and compositional world. All of this converged in a sequel to the *Fantastique* dwelling on the nature of his own obsession, its origins and meaning, and its musical implications – a piece born of contemplation as well as aesthetic transfiguration, sketched as he trudged a weary path back to Rome.

Le Retour is not a well-known work today; indeed, it has in large part disappeared from the concert repertory and, in scholarly writing, tends to be glossed over either as a collage of pre-composed work or as a melodramatic oddity.[10] And it is in many senses an unusual piece, a series of musical numbers interleaved with spoken text to which Berlioz referred first as a "mélologue" and later a "monodrama." Some of its music did come from earlier works, including the 1828 and 1829 Prix de Rome cantatas, the *Ouverture de la tempête*, and a (now lost) setting of Hugo's *Chanson des pirates*. But it was by no means, in Berlioz's eyes, an inconsequential composition; instead, it was the final installment of his *Épisode de la vie d'un artiste*, "la fin et le complément" of his *Symphonie fantastique*.[11] As Peter Bloom points out, Berlioz's sense of its significance can be inferred from the booklet disseminated at the work's premiere in December 1832 (a thirty-page affair providing the *Fantastique* program and *Le Retour*'s libretto), which listed the *mélologue* before the symphony: "Le Retour à la vie, Mélologue, faisant suite à la Symphonie fantastique intitulée Épisode de la vie d'un artiste."[12] Excerpts from the piece appeared on Berlioz's concert programs over 1833–34, followed by a second full performance (with the symphony) in 1835. Twenty years later, he was still interested enough in *Le Retour* to revise it for a concert in Weimar. He referred repeatedly to the piece in the Orchestration Treatise and, in 1857, published it in full score.

The forces for *Le Retour* include an orchestra of more than 100 musicians, "invisible" male and female choruses, and a speaking role for the *jeune musicien* – now called L'Artiste – who, emerging from the third-person narrative of the symphony, becomes a visible presence in its sequel. Among

---

[9] The details of this escapade are described in Berlioz, *Memoirs*, trans. Cairns, 152.

[10] An important exception is the work of Bloom, which has long drawn attention to the importance of *Le Retour*. See his "Orpheus' Lyre Resurrected"; and "A Return to Berlioz's 'Retour à la vie.'"

[11] As described in the libretto printed for the 1832 premiere; see *NBE*, 7:viii.

[12] See Bloom's introduction to the work in ibid, viii–xxxix, where he also notes that the premiere was well-attended by Parisian notables, among them Liszt, Cherubini, Pleyel, Habeneck, Hugo, Dumas, and Janin.

the extraordinary features of the work is Berlioz's suggestion (though not requirement) that it be performed "dramatically," by which he meant that the orchestra and the invisible choruses must be placed on the stage, behind the curtain. The actor speaks and acts only on the apron. At the end of the final monologue, he exits, and the curtain, lifting, reveals all the players for the finale.[13]

The goal of this was to dramatize the interiority of the *mélologue*, making clear to the audience that it was being ushered into the unseen space of imagination, the composer's *monde fantastique* itself, from whence the mental convulsion and musical inspiration of the opening symphony had emerged. *Le Retour* was conceived in part as an explanatory work, a meditation on the nature of "his art," as Berlioz put it – on the musical, literary and more broadly aesthetic impulses underpinning his Fantastic Symphony. Thomas Moore's *mélologue* was among its templates (Moore introduced Berlioz to the title term itself and the idea of interleaved music and discourse), but the work's curious conflation of autobiographical, literary, and critical writing, and its tendency toward narrative fragmentation, point equally clearly to Hoffmann – especially *Kreisleriana*. At the center of *Le Retour* (as with the *Fantastique*) is the composer's lovesickness and the musical impulse to which it was attached. Berlioz contemplates the terrible power of his *idée fixe*, its origins, its metaphysical and physical dimensions, and, in the end, its artistic potential, giving us a philosophical and critical context in which to hear/read his first symphony. In so doing, as we shall see, he begins to situate his famous melody not just as a symptom of pathological yearning, but a signal of fantastic *listening*.

Le Retour begins at the moment when Berlioz has awoken, alive, from the opium hallucination described in the fifth movement of the *Fantastique*. Still hazy, he recalls the horror of witnessing his degraded beloved and the depths to which his own fixation has driven him: "Again her, always her, with her inscrutable smile."[14] Surely, he speculates, his friend Horatio heard his cries during the night of terror – and yet perhaps not, for the suicide note he left remains unopened. As the Artist wonders aloud, he hears the sound of a piano and realizes it is Horatio himself playing the opening measures of a ballad. According to Berlioz's instructions for "dramatic" staging, the performance is unseen, emanating from behind the curtain (or, as we are meant to understand, from the mind of the Artist himself). As it unfolds, it emerges as a commentary on the *idée fixe*, an initial situating of its sources

---

[13] In a note attached to the score; see *NBE*, 7:232. The subject of visuality in "dramatic" performances of the *Épisode* is explored in Van Rij, *The Other Worlds of Hector Berlioz*, 127–92.

[14] The libretto of *Le Retour*, given in this chapter in my translations, is laid out in both the 1832 and 1855 versions in *NBE*, 7:232–40 (here, 233).

and meaning. The piece is a setting of Goethe's poem "Der Fischer" (in Albert Du Boys's French translation), which tells the tale of a young fisherman on the bank of a lake whose waters exercise a curious fascination. He "guides his line errantly on the waves," hardly seeing what he is doing, and suddenly, a spirit appears – "la nymphe des eaux." In a tender voice, she sings of the wonders of her watery kingdom, a place where the sunlight is more brilliant, the mirrored sky more blue, and existence more alluring than the fisherman can imagine. "If you knew the sweet life / of the happy subjects under my sway / Their destiny would arouse your envy / You would wish to live with me." The nymph entices him not just with pleasure and magic (the goddess Phoebe glitters in her waves), but with his own image, "which smiles at you from the watery depths." Finally, her voice proves too enticing to resist, and, as waves wet the fisherman's feet, he succumbs: "Unwittingly, unable to help himself, / He follows the nymph ... he disappears."[15]

The connection between Berlioz's beloved melody and the siren song is, of course, transparent – and is made all the more so in his 1855 revision of the piece where, after the second verse, Berlioz interrupts the poem with a partial statement of the *idée fixe*, temporarily replacing the voice/piano texture with solo violins (Example 3.1). The Artist's own dream melody is now made implicitly synonymous with the one heard by Goethe's protagonist and, to cement the connection, Berlioz has his Artist-hero cry, as the *idée fixe* unfolds, "Siren! Siren! God, my heart is breaking!" As the third phrase of the "fixated" tune begins, it dissolves back into the ballad, Horatio taking over fluidly where the violins leave off. From there, in the 1855 version, Berlioz jumps directly to Goethe's final stanza of capitulation and watery descent. And while Horatio sings of the siren's irresistible song, the Artist, speaking overtop, confirms, "Yes, yes, I have heard it all too often."

From the outset of *Le Retour*, then, Berlioz situates his *être idéal* as a symbol of nature who is, at the same time, an echo/reflection of his own sound/image. The ballad is an important choice as an opening gesture, in part because it situates the *mélologue* so clearly in the domain of German musical aesthetics but, more pointedly, because "Der Fischer" was a work that would already have been known to Berlioz's contemporaries. It was one of the few ballads singled out for commentary in Germaine de Staël's *De l'Allemagne*, the panoramic 1813 text offering French readers their first sustained theorization of Teutonic "romantic" literature and philosophy,

---

[15] *NBE*, 7:241. Berlioz remarked on his choice of Goethe's ballad in a letter to Du Boys of 4 or 5 March 1832 (*CG*, I:264): "Do you remember the ballad of "Le Pêcheur," by Goethe, for which you sent me a translation? I have *seized upon* it for a work whose words and music I have written here. Since the subject of your little poem was compatible with my own I included it, indicating of course that the verses were not composed by me."

Example 3.1 Berlioz, "Le Pêcheur" with *idée fixe* interpolation (1855), mm. 58–79

and as such, already freighted with meaning. Staël, in her chapter on poetry, had marked the ballad as a prototypical evocation of natural supernaturalism, the pantheistic magic she would later connect with Schlegel's and Schelling's idealism. Goethe's poem was first and foremost, she claimed, a dramatization of "the mysterious power which may proceed from the phenomena of nature." Drawing together the physical and moral worlds, it emblematized their interdependence and indeed, the "miraculous sympathies" between man and divine creation. To attend carefully to the sounds/forms of "air, water, flowers, and trees" was to gain access to an all-encompassing magic – to succumb to a thirst for divine access that was also a desire for self-knowledge. As Staël put it, "there is no one who has not felt the indefinable attraction which we experience when looking on the waves of the sea"; such natural phenomena contained echoes of infinite love as well as the "sensations and occult powers" of the observer himself, intimating "the secret alliance of our being with the wonders of the universe."[16] Few of Berlioz's literate contemporaries were unfamiliar with Staël's text; indeed, Berlioz, in offering his own reading of Goethe's ballad, also implicitly invoked hers.[17] The erotic sound he pursued, and that pursued him, he suggested, was bound up with the siren-voice of nature itself.

The second and third pieces of the *mélologue* move away, temporarily, from a contemplation of the beloved, meditating on mortality (a *Choeur d'ombres*) and vitality (a *Chanson des brigands*) – on the mercurial extremes of Berlioz's own temperament (we shall return to these pieces later, in other contexts). In the intervening monologues, the composer waxes rhapsodic over Shakespeare, brigands, and especially Beethoven, a composer whose instrumental soundworld, with its "sublime meditations," provides the foundation for his own. Gathering brigand-like energy, he rails against the composer's detractors who, knowing nothing of his true nature, denigrate him and even dare to "correct" his work (the target of this diatribe is, quite clearly, critic François Fétis). But quickly, Berlioz's ire cools and he is drawn back into the "heavenly" realm he imagines Beethoven to inhabit: that of his own longed-for perfection. The Artist of *Le Retour* gains access to this world via what he terms an "ideal orchestra" (*orchestre idéal*), an internal instrument giving voice to domains glimpsed only in moments of transcendence: "What, then, is this remarkable faculty that substitutes imagination for reality?" the Artist wonders, "What is this ideal orchestra that sings inside me?"[18] In listening to its soul-sound, he begins to perceive more clearly the source of his power and longing: the voice of the beloved herself. And now the connection between his sonorous fantasy and that of Hoffmann's Ferdinand comes more sharply into focus. The Artist imagines himself, in the fourth monologue, standing under a night sky studded with stars. His suffering alleviated, he is "crowned with love" and, as he listens, he hears wafting toward him on the air the melody for which he longs:

[A] harmonious breeze carries distant harmonies, which seem to me a mysterious echo of the beloved voice; tears of tenderness come finally to refresh my eyelids still burning with tears of rage and despair. I am happy, and my angel smiles on, admiring her work; her noble and pure spirit sparkles under long black eyelashes modestly lowered; with one of her hands in mine, I sing, and with her other hand, wandering over the strings of the harp, she languidly accompanies my hymn of joy.[19]

[16] Staël, *De l'Allemagne*, trans. Wight, 1:231–32.
[17] French commentaries on Staël also drew attention to Goethe's ballad; see, for instance, Nodier's "*De l'Allemagne*, par Madame de Staël," *Mélanges de littérature et de critique*, 2:325–52 (at 347).
[18] *NBE*, 7:234–35.   [19] Ibid., 237.

Épisode de la vie d'un artiste

Example 3.2 Berlioz, "Chant de bonheur," mm. 1–19

As in the case of Ferdinand's musical *idée fixe*, Berlioz's beloved melody is revealed here as an elemental sound, a melody carried on the breeze. (In the *Memoirs*, Berlioz recalls the moment of the tune's "arrival": "it came to me one day as I lay on the flat top of the thick clipped box hedge in our formal Academy garden, lulled by the soft, insidious airs of my enemy the south wind."[20]) It seems, at least in the realm of his fancy, to materialize the woman herself (the *rêveuse aimante*) who has now transformed from a water spirit into a creature of air drawing wandering chords from a harp. As he listens to her orchestral song, the Artist hears his own voice – an unconscious, imaginative self – sing a "Chant de bonheur" (a tenor performing behind the curtain).[21] Natural and supernatural, subjective and objective worlds converge, ushering us into the wavering space of the *monde fantastique*, a sonorous universe behind/within the domain of the physical.

The sound of this world is a distant, pastoral one evoked, at first, by strings alone playing in a *ppp* register, their shimmering effect partly the result of a *divisi* texture (Example 3.2). Their melody is composed of a series of sighs – the whispering of the breeze – which, as the first musical

---

[20] Berlioz, *Memoirs*, trans. Cairns, 187. The composer's reference is to the garden of the French Academy, at the Villa de Medici in Rome.

[21] Berlioz's note in the score: "Il vaut mieux pour ce morceau avoir un autre ténor que lui qui a chanté la Ballade, Lélio étant censé entendre sa propre voix." *NBE*, 7:58.

Le Retour à la vie: *Natural Magic and the Ideal Orchestra*

Example 3.2 (cont.)

period comes to a close, are echoed in the flutes and clarinets. As their exchanges grow more frequent, the sigh gesture becomes a dotted figure, an intimation of birdsong. The Artist's "inner" voice enters on the same figure seemingly as an extension of the orchestra's elemental soundworld, and when it does, the strings and winds are replaced by the airy strumming of the harp, a signal of old Orphic magic. Two-note sighs in the voice rise in a climactic line mirrored in the text by an image of cosmic expansion: what the Artist has found, he tells us, is not just "my happiness," but "my life, my entire being, my God, my universe!"[22] The song of his own bliss is also, as the title of the piece makes clear, a "hymn," a moment of erotic-sacred union that is at the same time one of self-realization. The beloved voice is both his own soul-voice and that of the natural universe itself. As the piece closes, the harp fades into crystalline harmonics, ascending via an upward arpeggio into near-inaudibility.

This gesture ushers us into *Le Retour*'s most extraordinary piece, entitled "Les Derniers soupirs de la harpe" (in 1855, "La Harpe aeolienne"). Here, the sound of Berlioz's dream woman has become the sonorous whisper of a wind harp – as we have seen, among the instruments linked by Ferdinand and Lewis with "higher" sound and, by extension, the elusive beloved. The piece is preceded, in the fourth monologue, by an anguished cry: "Oh! if I could only find her, this Juliette, this Ophelia, whom my heart calls."[23] The union the Artist seeks does, at last, become available in the aeolian world, where his own song of happiness, distant and fragmented, is absorbed into the wind-sound of the beloved herself: that of unmediated nature. But the price of this is death, a final and fatal dissolution of subjectivity into the natural totality. The Artist imagines himself expired, buried alongside his beloved in a grave under an oak tree from whose branches an "orphan harp" whispers. He has been drawn entirely into the sonorous world of longing, a victim of what Nodier (coming back to the previous chapter) diagnosed as the final stage of "reflective monomania" and Schleiermacher situated as a form of idealist self-annihilation. The dissipation of self is articulated expertly in the elliptical end of the pre-aeolian monologue, which tracks a slow unraveling: "thoughts of time ... space ... love ... oblivion ... " Unable to keep one foot in the realm of actuality, lured by the siren voice of creation itself, the Artist "expands" into dissolution, giving way to the fatal *Liebestod* of Goethe's fisherman and Nodier's monomaniacal Jean-François.

No longer able to describe the sound of the *idée fixe* himself, the Artist conveys it to us second hand: it is Horatio who listens while sitting on his friend's grave. What he hears is a distant echo of elemental perfection, a *pianissimo* world barely audible to the living. Gusts of sound shiver in the strings, fading in and out of the range of audition, while fragments of the "Chant de bonheur" still reverberate, conjured by a clarinet muted in a leather bag. The fragmentation of consciousness is also, Berlioz suggests, a dissipation of composerly subjectivity. "Music" is replaced by sound – by a composition that comes close to a transcendental transcription – or to what Hoffmann (and before him, Schlegel) termed a "hieroglyph,"

---

[22] Ibid., 238.   [23] Ibid., 238.

Le Retour à la vie: *Natural Magic and the Ideal Orchestra*

Example 3.3 Berlioz, "La Harpe éolienne," mm. 1–12

a moment in which soul-perception has been rendered, via strange characters, into artistic representation. There is no text in the aeolian evocation; it alone, of the pieces making up *Le Retour*, lacks voices. Its natural sound is renderable only via the "higher mechanics" of instruments, a sonorous intuition partially preserved via ingenious orchestration (Example 3.3).

According to Hoffmann, it is hieroglyphic sound of this sort, an echo of creation itself, that lies behind Beethoven's spiritual instrumental music and Kreisler's *fantastique* orchestration. The idea also appears in Goethe; indeed, in penning the aeolian piece, Berlioz might well have had in mind the Dedication to Part 1 of *Faust* (among the works he most revered and that was much in his mind during composition of the *Épisode*), where Goethe draws together, much as Hoffmann would later do, notions of yearning, aeolian listening, and "spirit" revelation.[24] From the final stanza:

And I am seized by a long unwonted yearning
For that still, solemn spirit-realm which then
Was mine; these hovering lisping tones returning
Sigh as from some Aeolian harp, as when
I sang them first; I tremble, and my burning
Tears flow, my stern heart melts to love again.
All that I now possess seems far away
And vanished worlds are real to me today.[25]

The "vanished worlds" revealed to Goethe via aeolian resonances are those of a lost Orphic magic, a natural enchantment recoverable only via the longing of the true fantasist. That Berlioz tied his own fixation to this kind of spiritual nostalgia – a yearning for the sound of natural divinity itself – is suggested by the history of his aeolian piece. "Les Derniers soupirs" is taken, virtually unaltered, from the final pages of his early cantata *La Mort d'Orphée*. Here, Orpheus is gone, having met his end at the hands of the Bacchantes. His lyre too is half-destroyed, sighing mournfully in the wind while, in the distance, echoes of his love song to Euridice still resound. Importing this music directly into the *mélologue*, Berlioz situates his own fantastic orchestra as an instrument akin to Orpheus's harp and his own longing as an echo of the Greek hero's lament (for his beloved, for his musical magic, for his own sonorous divinity). In a sense, he makes concrete Hoffmann's metaphorical claim that a "yearning" instrumental soundworld (that of Beethoven and Kreisler) might open onto a domain of lost power: "Orpheus's lyre unlocks the gates of Orcus."[26] The sound of the beloved is that of both an external/natural and internal/spiritual enchantment, a power only distantly intuited by the waking mind.

As we have seen, the price of its reactivation – the reunion with Berlioz's symbolic beloved – was violence. Longing for (and listening to) the ideal

---

[24] Goethe played a key role in Berlioz's early development and in the writing of the first symphony; indeed, a letter to Ferrand written in early 1829 suggests that the *Fantastique* might have begun as a Faust symphony (*CG*, I:113).
[25] Goethe, *Faust*, Part 1, trans. Luke, 3.   [26] Hoffmann, *Kreisleriana*, 96.

meant hovering constantly on the edge of nonexistence, grappling with what Berlioz himself described both in the *fantastique* letters and elsewhere as an impulse to transcend the limitations of individual experience and even sentience. From a passage in the *Memoirs*:

> On one of those dark days towards the end of the year, made more dismal still by the blasts of a chill north wind, try listening, while you read your Ossian, to the fantastic harmonies of the aeolian harp hung from the top of a leafless tree, and you will experience a feeling of infinite yearning, a vague but overmastering desire for another existence and a disgust with this one, in short a powerful access of spleen combined with an inclination to suicide.[27]

And the dangers of the aeolian world were not just psychological, but, as Carmel Raz has pointed out (and Hoffmann himself suggested), physical. Raz traces a link between the wind harp and nineteenth-century notions of nervous disorder, demonstrating that the instrument was thought to transmit the electrical energy of nature itself. Exposed to its sound, listeners were infused with "ethereal" vibration stimulating both revelation and, in some cases, physiological breakdown.[28] Her work elucidates further the connection between metaphysical illumination and nervous disturbance we encountered in the previous chapter – Berlioz's repeated references, in descriptions of his fixation, to both convulsion and physical exaltation. Fantastic perception, we are invited to conclude, was also a kind of electrical overstimulation, a moment of direct contact with the (divine) energy of the living world. The idea is shored up in Berlioz's 1855 revision of the aeolian monologue, where he tells us that his orchestral wind harp produced not just the condition of "spleen," but of nervous shock: "an unknown shiver through his [Horatio's] veins." The description recalls the "electric spark" he first felt on seeing Estelle Duboeuf, his earliest "ideal" love, and the convulsive impact of Harriet herself.[29]

As the aeolian music comes to an end, and *Le Retour* reaches its culminating musical movement, the Artist draws himself out of this damaging world – the domain of psychiatric dissolution and nervous fritz-out. "But

---

[27] Berlioz, *Memoirs*, trans. Cairns, 184.

[28] Raz, "The Expressive Organ within Us." See also Hankins and Silverman, "The Aeolian Harp and the Romantic Quest of Nature," in *Instruments and the Imagination*, 86–112; and Trower, *Senses of Vibration*, 19–26, 32–36.

[29] *NBE*, 7:238. In recalling his first encounter with Estelle Duboeuf, the girl with whom he fell in love at age twelve: "The moment I set eyes on her I felt an electric shock; in fact, I fell in love with her, desperately, hopelessly. I had no wishes, no hopes, I had no idea what was the matter with me, but I suffered acutely and spent my nights in sleepless anguish." Translation adapted from that of Cairns in Berlioz, *Memoirs*, 37.

why abandon myself to these poetic illusions?" he asks; and (more tellingly), "Why *reflect*? (*Pourquoi réfléchir*?) I have no more deadly enemy than reflection (*la réflexion*); I must distance myself from it."[30] In ending his own obsessive self-scrutiny, he hopes to avoid both Ferdinand's alienation and Jean-François's monomaniacal absorption (his *monomanie reflective*), instead converting the spiritual-electric ravages of the aeolian world into the stuff of creative work. His orchestra, he announces in the final monologue, will be an instrument of electric power – an *ensemble nerveux* – holding sway over the elements themselves. If Beethoven was a "Nouveau Colomb," he will be a "Nouveau Faust," a musical leader wielding the powers of the *fantastique* orchestra like a Renaissance magus or (as he paints himself in the final piece), a modern musical Prospero, "a magician who riles and sooths the elements at will." Now *he* will control the natural forces, the Paracelsian "spirits of the air," on which he had been fixated, emerging as a manipulator of pantheistic soul-sounds, an orchestral metaphysician.[31] He figures himself as one who has, as Hoffmann said of Kreisler, "found the voice within," which is also the sound without.

At the close of this triumphant declaration, the *orchestre idéal* becomes an *orchestre réel*; the curtain comes up to reveal a large-scale ensemble poised to perform a Fantasy on Shakespeare's *Tempest* conducted by the hero himself as proof of his own dominion over the *monde fantastique*.[32] The piece opens onto much the same muted, pastoral terrain we encountered in "Le Chant de bonheur" and "Les Derniers soupirs," although now the Artist is in control, at least temporarily, of the natural soundworld he associates with his *idée fixe*. The ideal feminine is under his command; indeed, the Fantasy begins with yet another representation of her: an Invocation to Miranda (entirely interchangeable, for Berlioz, with Ophelia, Juliet, Harriet, Camille...) by a Chorus of Spirits of the Air. And here, returning to our organological discussion, we find that the status of the beloved as a Hoffmannesque "elemental" sound is confirmed once again. Miranda is conjured in the final Fantasy not by the strains of water or wind, but by the sound of the glass harmonica (another instrument famously caught up with nervous overstimulation and otherworldly "vibration," as Heather Hadlock and others have shown).[33] Berlioz does not call for the glass instrument itself (apparently he did not have access to a playable exemplar), but its sonority is approximated by two pianos both employing a *pédale céleste*. This device, which modified sound by inserting

---

[30] *NBE*, 7:239. [31] Ibid.
[32] This work, *Ouverture de la tempête*, had already been written and was originally to have been performed in autumn 1830 at the Théâtre Italien.
[33] Hadlock, "Sonorous Bodies." See also Kennaway, *Bad Vibrations*, 23–53.

a cloth damper between hammers and strings, produced a muted shimmering effect – one that, especially in combination with the sustain pedal, had been identified by Louis Adam in his 1804 *Méthode nouvelle pour le piano* as akin to that of the glass harmonica.[34] What the two piano-cum-harmonicas play is a series of rising arpeggios echoing the harp music of the *Chant de bonheur*, each culminating in a trilled bird call. The keyboard part is embedded in a wider and now-familiar collection of muted, pastoral sonorities drawn from the "ideal" soundworlds we have already heard: gusts of arpeggiated breeze in the upper winds, a series of pulsing sixteenth-note figures heard *piano* in the middle strings, and shimmering sustained chords, *ppp*, in the first violins. When it enters, the spirit choir sighs Miranda's name, echoing the two-note figures of both "Bonheur" and "Le Dernier Soupir." Quickly, their sighs become gasps (a bit of heavy breathing) as the choir invites Miranda to meet her "destined spouse" and to "know love." And finally, welcoming her to her "new life," we hear the magical string/harmonica tremolo of the aeolian world (Example 3.4).

Having conjured the airy spirit domain – a place of benign pantheistic power – the conductor-magician goes on, in a second section of the Fantasy, to invoke a storm (as Prospero does in Shakespeare's play). And now a different set of natural tropes emerges in the orchestra, from rolling thunder in the timpani to lashing winds in the strings and winds, and bolts of lightning. But at the height of the noise, Berlioz's spirit choir calls for Miranda, and her birdcalls and celestial breezes return, stilling the storm. The third section, "L'Action," outlines the play's major events and characters, including the antics of Caliban and Ariel, but it too begins and ends with Miranda's pastoral music. As it comes to a close, the choir bids her farewell: "O Miranda, you are leaving, he is taking you away, we shall see you no more. From the open air, our homeland, we shall seek in vain the brilliant and graceful flower whom we admire on earth. O Miranda, we shall see you no more. Farewell, farewell, Miranda!"[35] A musical *denouement* follows – the final orchestral windup with a rousing tutti finish. The sense one gets is that Berlioz has at last bidden farewell

---

[34] Later, Berlioz added to the "celestial" piano music a part for harmonica-glockenspiel, although he eventually removed it, likely because the instrument was not widely available (see *NBE*, 7: xvi–xvii). Berlioz's own description of the harmonica-glockenspiel, given in the Orchestration Treatise, is telling: "This is an instrument of the same type as the glockenspiel, except that the hammers strike plates of glass. Its tone is incomparably delicate and voluptuous and can often be used for the most poetic effects. Like the steel-bar keyboard which I have just described, its tone is extremely soft, which must be borne in mind when using it with other orchestral instruments. . . . It is normally piano manufacturers who undertake to build this lovely and too little known instrument." A part for the glass instrument also appeared in the *Concert de sylphes*, in the *Huit scènes de Faust*. See Berlioz, *Orchestration Treatise*, trans. Macdonald, 278.

[35] *NBE*, 7:240.

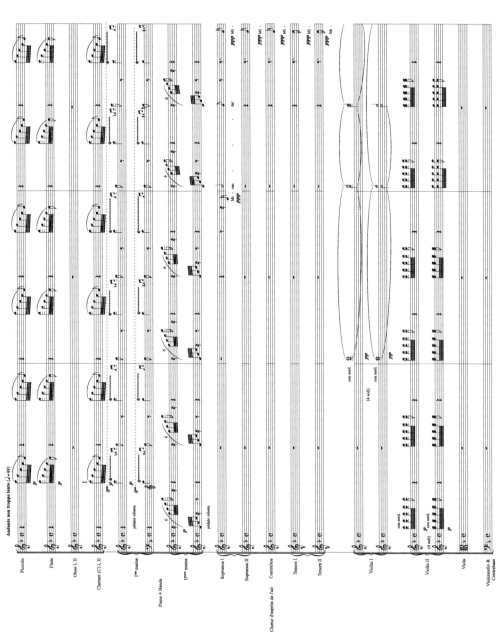

Example 3.4 Berlioz, "Fantaisie sur la tempête de Shakespeare," mm. 1–6

Example 3.4 (cont.)

to his fixation. Longing has been transmuted into art, fantastic listening into inspired composition.

And this is where he leaves things in the 1832 version of the *mélologue*. But events unfold differently in *Le Retour*'s 1855 revision, perhaps because Berlioz realized that he had not – indeed, could not – put his obsession to rest. Here, after commending his orchestra, the Artist bids the musicians farewell: "Goodbye, my friends, I am suffering; leave me alone."[36] Most of the instrumentalists and the choir exit, leaving Berlioz's protagonist isolated once more on the apron. He, and we, are cast back into the domain of the imaginary – that of the *orchestre idéal* – and of pathology. Out of silence, the *idée fixe* emerges one last time, *pianissimo*. It unfolds through the opening five measures, only to hang incomplete on the sixth scale degree, which Berlioz elongates over a fermata. The rest of the melody goes unsung. Instead (as in the opening ballad), it dissolves back into a natural soundworld: the familiar *pianissimo* tremolo associated with the aeolian harp. It is from this pantheistic, nervously overcharged space, Berlioz suggests, that his yearning takes him and to which he must return. "Again?" his Artist asks as the melody begins. "Again, and forever," he confirms, as the *mélologue* comes to a close (Example 3.5).[37]

The moment represents a drawing together and summation of the *Symphonie fantastique* and its sequel; a place in which Berlioz underscores the link between fantastic fixation and musico-idealist revelation. Pathology – nervous, psychiatric, spiritual – is both the precondition for, and the result of, hearing the ideal within the real. It facilitates a twinned form of listening, a suspension between physical and metaphysical, natural and supernatural domains, in what Nodier called the "intermediate world" of modern fantasy. Berlioz's ties to the psychological and aural landscapes of this place seem transparent now, but, as we shall see, they were difficult to make for his first listeners; indeed, critics seemed unable – in some cases unwilling – to hear in the double manner Berlioz described (and Hoffmann prescribed). Early responses to the *Symphonie fantastique* and its sequel outline the critical and conceptual roadblocks as well as the philosophical impediments that stood in the way of a clear exegesis of Berlioz's work. They show us, in microcosm, how sounding fantasy will be received through the remainder of the century, explaining to some degree why it never emerged in France with the same clarity (and eventually, legitimacy) as its literary counterpart.

---

[36] Ibid.   [37] Ibid.

Example 3.5 Berlioz, "Fantaisie sur la tempête de Shakespeare," coda

Listening to Hesitation

A rhetoric of novelty and unintelligibility runs through early reception of the two-part *Épisode dans la vie d'un artiste*, many claiming that it opened up a "new" or "unknown world," a musical landscape "unlike anything one has ever heard" (the rhetoric resonates clearly with early Hoffmann reception).[38] These sorts of claims were yoked to perceived innovations in

---

[38] See, for instance, reviews in *La Quotidienne* (10 December 1832) and *Le Journal des débats* (10 December 1832), where the phrases "monde inconnu," "monde nouveau," "sans nom, sans analogie," and "si nouveau et si bizarre" are to be found.

harmony and form, but above all, to Berlioz's novel orchestration. References to new effects and "marvelous sounds" abound in descriptions of the *Épisode*, in many cases linked to Hoffmannesque aesthetics. Typical is this description in *Le Temps*:

> M. Berlioz is gifted with a rich, varied, and vigorous imagination, and the orchestra, whose resources he has studied rigorously, obeys his most capricious fantasies with marvelous docility. Few composers have mastered to his degree the science of effects, and there is something in his manner [of orchestrating], something unexpected, brusque, fantastic that responds perfectly to the demands of his favored inspirations. I imagine that M. Berlioz must love Hoffmann passionately, that he read the *Thousand and One Nights* often, and that in his childhood he was lulled to sleep by ghost stories.[39]

Supporters and detractors alike agreed that orchestral "science" was key to the new fantastic soundworld, although they disagreed about how and what Berlioz's orchestral language meant. Seemingly irreconcilable ways of hearing the *Épisode* played out in criticism over the course of the early 1830s, becoming central to broader debates surrounding the work's legitimacy and the nature of sounding fantasy itself.

The Belgian critic Fétis, who had been among the targets of Berlioz's ire in *Le Retour*, published a damning review of the work and its symphonic prequel in the widely read *Revue musicale* (1832), in which he claimed that it confirmed all his worst fears about Berlioz. Rather than correcting the problems of the *Symphonie fantastique*, Berlioz's *mélologue* deepened them. It was malformed and noisy and Berlioz himself was an ill-trained composer who had failed to absorb the fundamentals of composition: those of melody, harmony, and form. His only strength lay in the domain of orchestration, and yet he employed his "effects" only in the interest of bombast, novelty for its own sake, and worse yet, physical imitation:

> What, then, does he [Berlioz] do, and in what manner is it different from other composers? Here is the answer: nature has obviously endowed him with an instinct for instrumental effects; however, he almost always conceives these effects as the representation of something physical or material. It is a storm, the wind stirring in

---

[39] "M. Berlioz est doué d'une imagination riche, variée, vigoureuse, et l'orchestre, dont il a profondément étudié les ressources, obéit avec une docilité merveilleuse à ses plus capricieuses fantaisies. Peu de compositeurs ont eu autant que lui la science des effets, et il y a dans sa manière quelque chose d'inattendu, de brusque, de fantasque qui répond parfaitement aux besoins de ses inspirations préférées. Je suppose que M. Berlioz doit aimer passionnément Hoffmann, qu'il a lu souvent les Mille et une Nuits, et que dans son enfance il aura été bercé avec des contes de revenant." *Le Temps* (27 November 1834). See also *Le Figaro* (4 December 1830), which describes Berlioz's "fantastique" orchestration and later in the same journal, "les merveilles de l'orchestre" (11 December 1832).

the leaves, the breeze caressing the strings of a harp, the hasty footfalls of a disorderly crowd, or something similar. To produce these effects, he requires in some cases six- or eight-part violins, in others multiple timpanis, pianos, harp, a blending of voices with instruments, and who knows what else?[40]

Fétis had already linked overcharged orchestration (along with melodic deficiency, harmonic abstrusity, and "bizarre" musical construction) to Beethoven; indeed, he had tried to correct the composer's work – the behavior so roundly condemned in *Le Retour*. Berlioz, Fétis suggested, had embraced many of these Beethovenian errors, particularly a tendency toward orchestral excess, with poor results. His "fantastic" mode was both self-consciously modern and oddly regressive, akin to the old *genre imitatif*. "Berlioz wishes to be dramatic," Fétis concluded, "but nothing is less dramatic than material imitation."[41]

This way of hearing the *Épisode* proved influential, leading to a slew of related critical attacks (some borrowing directly from Fétis) and, later, a collection of parodies – faux *fantastique* programs lampooning the "material" language of the symphony and *mélologue*. These were humorous affairs, among which numbered Etienne Arnal's send-up titled "Episode in the Life of a Gambler" (*Épisode de la vie d'un joueur*) performed at the first of the 1835 opera balls, which recast Berlioz's tale of yearning and revelation as an account of stock-market speculation. Set to music by Adolphe Adam, it claimed to "paint," by way of orchestral effects, every detail of a session at the market, from the color of the traders' coats, to the size of their wagers, the mathematical odds of the day, and even the contents of a telegraphic dispatch. Rather than an otherworldly medium, it suggested, Berlioz's orchestral fantasy was an exercise in silly tone-painting.[42] Other similar satires followed, including one in *Le Corsaire*, which rewrote the two-part *Épisode* as a weather report, a refreshment list, and a series of

---

[40] "Que fait-il donc, et en quoi diffère-t-il des autres compositeurs? Le voici. La nature l'a évidemment pourvu d'un instinct des effets de l'instrumentation. Or, ces effets il les conçoit presque toujours comme la réalisation de quelque chose de physique ou de matériel. C'est un orage, le vent qui agite le feuillage, le zéphir qui caresse les cordes d'une harpe, les pas précipités d'une foule désordonnée, ou quelque chose de semblable. Pour produire ces effets, il a besoin tantôt de six ou huit parties de violon différentes, tantôt de plusieurs timbales, de pianos, de harpe, de mélange de voix parmi les instruments, que sais-je? (15 December 1832).

[41] "M. Berlioz veut être dramatique ... mais rien n'est moins dramatique que l'imitation matérielle." Ibid. For more on Fétis's remarks on Beethoven, see Ellis, *Music Criticism in Nineteenth-Century France*, 101–26; Wallace, *Beethoven's Critics*, 105–25; Bloom, "François-Joseph Fétis," 92–207.

[42] See the full description of the program in *La Quotidienne* (13 January 1835).

animal encounters. Again, the idea was that Berlioz was indulging in empty orchestral entertainment, his music nothing but physical description.[43] The composer emerged from these kinds of accounts as an unambiguous imitator, the promulgator of a style rooted in cheap musical tricks. Fétis, the first to include the term *fantastique* in a musical lexicon (*La Musique mise à la portée de tout la monde*, 1835), consolidated this line of criticism in a single-line entry: "Fantastic music is composed of instrumental effects lacking melodic organization and with incorrect harmony."[44]

Faced with these sorts of attacks, Berlioz's proponents began to resist and even reverse the claims of conservative critics, positioning the language of the *Épisode* as that of the mind and soul rather than the body. Jules Janin, in his own 1832 review of the premiere, figured its soundworld as an echo of "the beating of his [Berlioz's] heart" and of his most private dreams – "dreams of the night, dreams of day, fevered dreams, dreams of spring, winter dreams, dreams of the mountains."[45] And Joseph D'Ortigue, writing shortly thereafter, challenged Fétis directly, arguing that Berlioz's fantastic language was not physical, but "ineffable," not an imitative, but an "elevated" mode along Beethovenian lines, capturing "dreams, despair, consolations, meditations, prayers, history and analysis of the heart."[46] If Berlioz was "more direct" than Beethoven, it was in the interest of philosophical communication rather than mere tone-painting: "There is in this work," D'Ortigue admitted, "a philosophical aspect to which the purely musical one is subordinated." But this hardly meant that the *Épisode* was "coldly literal" (*froidement littérale*); indeed, the work dealt mainly in the metaphysical. D'Ortigue's own reading defended the idea repeatedly, downplaying the Berliozian "real" in favor of the ideal. In the *Scène aux champs*, he argued, the composer was not producing pastoral description so much as inspired contemplation: "And what accents! Has the heart ever spoken a language more ineffable, more rapturous, more intimate? ... One expects a pastoral scene. But this is not that at

---

[43] In a piece titled "La musique de M. Berlioz exécutée par les virtuoses du *Journal des débats*," *Le Corsaire* (22 November 1838).

[44] "La musique fantastique est composée d'effets d'instrumentation sans dessin mélodique et avec une harmonie incorrecte." In a list of musical terms included with the second edition of *La musique mise à la portée de tout la monde*. The line of criticism denouncing Berlioz as a mere purveyor of orchestral novelties or, worse, an abuser of effects, is traced in part in Dolan, *The Orchestral Revolution*, 211–57.

[45] "rêves de la nuit, rêves du jour, rêves de la fièvre, rêves du printemps, rêves de l'hiver, rêves des montagnes, rêves italien et allemand, pensé et exécuté en italien et en allemand, une véritable fièvre sans relâche et sans repos." *Journal des débats* (10 December 1832).

[46] "rêveries, désespoir, consolations, méditations, prières, histoire et analyse du coeur." *La Quotidienne* (4 January 1833).

all: it is a passionate reverie, a melancholy plaint addressed by a lover to the totality of nature."[47] Likewise, in the *Bal*, the second movement, he insisted that the "rich and piquant instrumentation" produced not the image of a dance, but instead a sort of "sad and fearful pleasure," which was not a representation of happiness, but only "the *dream* of happiness" (*seulement le rêve du bonheur*). If Berlioz's orchestra "painted," it was an inner landscape, that of his "rich and brilliant imagination." His effects were less material than ethereal, especially in *Le Retour*, where, in the final three movements (the "Chant de bonheur," "Dernier soupirs," and "Fantaisie sur la Tempête"), Berlioz's orchestration drew listeners upward into an imaginative realm, his instruments themselves achieving incorporeality. In the concluding Fantasy, D'Ortigue heard "airy choirs, an accompaniment whose undulations appeared to hover in space, [and] intangible instruments seemly moved by the breeze and zephyr."[48]

But D'Ortigue's attempt to defend Berlioz along these lines did little to stem the tide of critical attacks, in large part because "real" sound *was* clearly represented in Berlioz's work. Claims that the music of the *Épisode* was purely ineffable were as unconvincing as those situating it as merely material. Both registers were invoked. Physical soundworlds (natural, domestic, urban) were consciously ruptured by those of imagination (reverie, nightmare, dream) in the *Fantastique*. And in *Le Retour*, as we have just seen, the two became synonymous, natural sound revealed as the source of ideal melody. Of course, it was precisely this twinning that rendered Berlioz's work novel, Hoffmannesque, *fantastique* in the new sense of the word. His *Épisode* hovered in an uncertain place between this world and the next, suggesting not just an intersection, but a connection between the two domains. The idea had, since Hoffmann's arrival, been available in literary circles. As we have already seen, early French readers of *contes fantastiques* had remarked repeatedly on the intertwining of reality and the unreal in Hoffmann's writing, whose key aesthetic was that of disorientation or *hesitation*. But the concept seemed to elude listeners; indeed, it took a literary critic to point out the fundamental liminality of Berlioz's *Épisode*. A piece in *La France littéraire* described the two-part work as "a vast subject, incorporating *both the imaginary and the real*, in which there is blood, tears, cries of love, cries of rage, where a lofty moral sentiment

---

[47] "Il y a dans cette oeuvre une partie philosophique à laquelle la partie purement musicale est subordonnée"; "Et quels accens! le coeur a-t-il jamais parlé une langue plus ineffable, plus délirante, plus intime? ... On s'attend à une scène pastorale. Point du tout: c'est une rêverie passionnée, une plainte mélancolique adressée par un amant à toute la nature." Ibid.

[48] "Des choeurs aériens, un accompagnement dont les ondulations semblent se balancer dans l'espace, des instrumens incorporels qu'on dirait mûs par la brise et le zéphire." Ibid.

dominates a mixture of episodes of passion, sarcasm, [and] sensuality, which intersect, intertwine, and press against one another."[49] So why was it that musicians seemed unable to make the same observation? Why was it so difficult, in other words, to *hear* hesitation?

Part of an explanation lies in a limitation in the available frameworks for listening (or, more pointedly, a bias against "imitative" sound). James H. Johnson's now-classic *Listening in Paris* traces the emergence of this bias, a hardening of the so-called imitation-expression binary in France through the 1810s and 1820s, which formed part of a perceived modernizing of musical hearing. Over the course of the early nineteenth century, as he reminds us, the old tenets of mimesis – those calling on music to depict concrete ideas or images – gave way to the notion that it should do precisely the opposite. The doctrine of representation was replaced by a philosophy of "higher" evocation, which emancipated music from the confines of language, casting it as the voice of a new metaphysics, a vehicle for intimate or infinite expression. As this idea took root, imitation was increasingly distanced from expression, perceived as a facile mode and a perversion of music's true purpose. Given this, it is hardly surprising that on hearing Berlioz's *Épisode*, his detractors hastened to place it in the category of imitation while his supporters insisted on expression. There was no clear category in which the real could also be perceived as the ideal or, to return to the parlance of the previous chapter, in which subject could be understood simultaneously as object.[50]

It was precisely this problem that made Beethoven's Pastoral Symphony a difficult sell. Fétis famously condemned it, calling it "a sad parody" in which Beethoven "prostituted his pen in the imitation of farmyard birds."[51] The piece presented a challenge even for Beethoven's advocates, who either avoided it or placed its representational mode in a third category: imitation of the *sentiments* invoked by nature rather than of nature itself – in other words, really a form of expression. Among the only enthusiastic advocates of the symphony was Berlioz, whose defense of it – in particular, his

---

[49] "un sujet vaste, plein à la fois de fantastique et de réel, où il y ait du sang, des larmes, des cris d'amour, des cris de rage, où une grande pensée morale domine une foule d'épisodes de passions, de sarcasme, de volupté, qui se croisent, se pressent et s'entrelacent." *La France littéraire* (December 1832).

[50] Johnson, *Listening in Paris*, esp. chap. 15, "Beethoven Triumphant" (257–69) and chap. 16, "The Musical Experience of Romanticism" (270–80).

[51] As Johnson notes in *Listening in Paris* (271 and 344, n. 7), Fétis had begun polemicizing against the Pastoral Symphony as early as 1829 (see his articles in the *Revue musicale* between February and July), as had his like-minded contemporaries (see the *Journal des débats* of 24 March 1829). The remark about farmyard birds, which clearly extends this line of attack, is to be found in Fétis's essay "De la musique pittoresque et des symphonies de Beethoven," *La France musicale* (7 January 1838).

willingness to see it as aligned with, rather than separate from, the wider project of instrumental metaphysics – provides us with a sense of how he regarded his own "natural" evocation in the *Épisode*, particularly in *Le Retour*. His first essay on the Pastoral Symphony appeared in March 1834, and contained a constellation of ideas to which he returned repeatedly through the later 1830s. Here, he made clear that he regarded the work neither as a mere reproduction of natural sound nor an invocation of an idealized pastoral world (it had nothing to do, he argued, with the sentimental nature invoked in Florian's novels or in the operas of Lebrun and Rousseau). Instead, it was a capturing of "true nature" (*la nature vraie*) – sublime, unknown, magical.[52] This was achieved not via distance (either physical or emotional), but, on the contrary, via *proximity*: acute attention to the domain of the real. Berlioz imagines Beethoven composing from the countryside itself, eyes and ears attuned to the details of the landscape. In a passage on the second movement:

> No doubt the author created this admirable adagio while reclining on the grass, his eyes turned toward the sky, his ear attuned to the wind, fascinated by the surrounding soft reflections of both light and sound, at one and the same time looking at, and listening to, the tiny white waves as they sparkled along and, with a slight murmur, broke upon the pebbles of the brink. It is beautiful.[53]

Physicality, the experience of hearing and seeing the natural world (the two seemingly interchangeable), is at the heart of Beethovenian sublimity for Berlioz; indeed, he places the spiritual within the material. Inextricable from the Pastoral's evocation of an "unknown world" is an experience of the actual one communicated to the listener via what Berlioz calls a "material effect" (*effet matériel*), a bodily sensation. His translation of the title for Beethoven's first movement ("Empfindungen bei der Ankunft auf dem Lande") underscores the idea: "*Sensations* douces qu'inspire l'aspect d'un riant paysage." The term implies not just emotions ("Empfindungen," as Beethoven put it), but also visceral experience. But only some listeners are able to receive the music's crucial sensation, according to Berlioz, and therefore hear the otherworldly within the physical; all others are immune.

---

[52] Berlioz, "Troisième Concert du Conservatoire: *Symphonie pastorale*," *Le Rénovateur* (2 March 1834), in *CM*, 1:181–86 (here, 183). Berlioz's references are to J.-P. Florian's pastoral novel *Estelle et Némorin* (1788), J.-J. Rousseau's opera *Le Devin du village* (1752), and Louis Sébastien Lebrun's pastoral comedy *Le Rossignol* (1816).

[53] *CM*, 1:183. The image of Beethoven composing his "Szene am Bach" from the banks of the brook had already been suggested in early German reviews of the Pastoral Symphony, including that of Friedrich Mosengeil and, more obviously, in a series of visual depictions of the composer in the journal *Cäcilia* (1833), the *Taschenbuch fur Freunde der Tonkunst* (1834), and the *Zurich Musikgesellschaft Almanac* (1834). Such images became, for some, as controversial as the symphony itself; see Alessandra Comini, *The Changing Image of Beethoven*, 85–157.

He returns to this idea again and again in his writing on the symphony, including in an 1838 extension of his original essay:

> If you are not ... moved, delighted, transported by the beauty of its (the music's) forms, the sympathetic emotion of its voice, the divine harmony of all its movements, then you lack enough sensibility to perceive *the material effect of the music (l'effet matériel de la musique)*, and also the imagination and intelligence to understand its rich language, which speaks only to the elect.[54]

Failure to perceive in a twinned manner results in a confusion concerning the nature of Beethovenian expression, namely, its rejection as imitation. Less gifted listeners, for Berlioz, are those "who cannot distinguish expressive music from that which is not" and therefore condemn the symphony as merely "programmatic." But in so doing, they reveal their own ignorance. Aping their position, Berlioz writes, "whenever you [Beethoven] speak that language in which you find so many charms but to which we have no access, our pride is bruised. Far from acknowledging our inability, we attack you, targeting your absurd and impertinent pretensions."[55]

This collection of ideas takes us back to Berlioz's own link, in *Le Retour*, between visceral and ideal registers, nervous *frisson* and pantheistic listening. What he describes in the Pastoral essays is a similar kind of bodily revelation, an experience in which the ineffable is made inextricable from (rather than incompatible with) the effable, and in this sense "expression" and "imitation" interlocked. The concept is tantalizing, though it is not fully fleshed out either in Berlioz's writing on the Pastoral or even in his 1837 essay on Imitation which, though it tries to expand the options for imitative registers, never quite explains his own ideas around expressive sensation.[56] French musico-critical language of the 1830s, still struggling to describe and define the impact of instrumental sound, seemed unable to provide a full explication for these concepts – in other words, to frame a theory of real or material supernaturalism.

As we have seen, Berlioz's own staunchest advocates found it difficult to defend his "mimetic" sounds, some (as with D'Ortigue) taking a defensive posture and others simply avoiding the topic entirely. Katharine Ellis points out that even the *Gazette musicale* – the mouthpiece of a burgeoning musical romanticism and a champion of Berlioz's work – never published a sustained review of the *Symphonie fantastique* or *Le Retour*. Berlioz's

---

[54] Berlioz, "Symphonies de Beethoven. Deuxième article," *Revue et gazette musicale de Paris* (4 February 1838), in *CM*, 3:383–88 (here, 387).
[55] *CM*, 3:384.
[56] Berlioz, "De l'imitation musicale," *Revue et gazette musicale de Paris* (1 and 8 January 1837), in *CM*, 3:1–8.

perceived leanings toward imitation, she suggests, were in the end simply too difficult to fruitfully position or explain, therefore these works were swept under the rug, cast as pieces of juvenilia.[57] The observation is a keen one, although here I want to argue along different lines – to suggest that Berlioz's two-part *Épisode* (and, more broadly, the fantastic mode it exemplified) *was* dealt with by reviewers, although not in the domain of conventional criticism, but instead that of fiction. Stymied by the limitations of existing musico-aesthetic discourse, Berlioz's proponents began to tease out the origins and implications of fantastic sound by drawing on Hoffmann's own medium: the *conte fantastique* itself. Fantastic tales emerged, through the mid-1830s, as key vehicles for Berlioz's defense, a framework in which to explore his newly powerful effects and to refute the claims of his detractors. They showed readers how to hear fantasy, allowing critics to conceptualize (sometimes in fanciful or occult language) Berlioz's (and Beethoven's) expressive imitation or musical hesitation. More broadly, they began to situate instrumentation and the orchestra itself as important vehicles for imaginative evocation – indeed, the key tools of the modern fantasist.

The Fantastic Orchestra

Works of fiction were central to the *Gazette musicale* from the year of its founding, 1834. Commissioned by the journal's editor, Maurice Schlesinger, their purpose was twofold: to diversify the readership of the *Gazette* and ensure its popularity, and to champion the tenets of the modern or "romantic" school. Written by the most prominent author-critics of the moment, the stories were cast in the form of *contes fantastiques*, each with a musical focus, and many riffing on, referencing, or borrowing directly from the works of Hoffmann. From the outset, they interfaced with criticism, drawing on and bleeding back into it, until they generated what Ellis describes as "a new closeness in French writing between fiction, the descriptive analysis of music, and even the writing of music history."[58] Among their key producers was Jules Janin, a Berlioz advocate and editor of the literary journal *L'Artiste* (which had, somewhat earlier, began to include pieces of fiction among its historical and critical essays). Janin published seven tales between 1834 and 1836, including the first of the *Gazette*'s *contes*

---

[57] Ellis, *Music Criticism in Nineteenth-Century France*, 221.
[58] Ellis, "The Uses of Fiction," 256. Ellis's readings of the *Gazette*'s musical *contes fantastiques* provide an important jumping-off point for my own; see also her helpful chronology of such tales in *Music Criticism in Nineteenth-Century France*, 262–65.

fantastiques, in which the Berliozian-Beethovenian orchestra is immediately made central.[59]

Janin's tale is titled "Le Dîner de Beethoven, conte fantastique" (January 1834), and is not an entirely new narrative, but one fed to the author by Schlesinger – although, as we shall see, it is crucially altered and extended.[60] It recounts a sighting of Beethoven in his late years, when he has fallen into deafness, irascibility, and obscurity. The narrator (Janin himself, as is implied by the first person) encounters the composer on the street, describing him from the first as a wild, disordered figure with one foot "outside the world of the real" (*hors du monde réel*). Following him to a music shop, Janin witnesses him compose a piece on the spot in order to earn enough money for lunch, after which he walks to a tavern. Links between Beethoven and Hoffmann, already implied at the beginning of the tale, now begin to multiply. The eating establishment the composer favors is the same the German author himself frequented (Le Chat qui file), and the barmaid, when asked to identify him, casts him as "a kind of musician, [an] eater and drinker, a friend of Hoffmann, another drunkard who is now dead. . . . I think his name is Beethoven."[61] Janin, chagrined to see her refuse the composer his meal, prevails upon her to sell him the roast meat and takes it to the composer's residence himself as an act of homage.[62]

Here ends the original version of the anecdote and the beginning of Janin's extension, which he uses both to diagnose Beethoven's condition more fully and to plumb the nature of his genius. He describes entering the composer's apartment and witnessing him tending flowers by his window in a state of melancholy. The reason for his angst, as Beethoven explains, is an estrangement from the sonorous world that once animated and enlivened him: that of nature itself. The sounds of water, wind, insects, animals, trees, and the elemental world at large – these were the sources of his inspiration, which he at one time heard and could also harness. He describes himself, in earlier days, at the head of a natural orchestra responsive to his every command, which furnished both his "poetry" and "harmony," connecting him to all things vital and living. But deafness has cut him off from this world, leaving him in silence:

---

[59] The orchestra also figures in Janin's earlier *Contes fantastiques et contes littéraires* (1832), including in the first story of this collection, "Kreyssler," which begins with an extended instrumental metaphor clearly riffing on Hoffmann's own orchestral rhetoric.

[60] Ellis notes Schlesinger's role in shaping Janin's tale in "The Uses of Fiction," 256.

[61] "c'est une espèce de musicien, mangeur et ivrogne, un ami d'Hoffmann, un autre ivrogne qui est mort. . . . Je crois qu'il s'appelle Beethoven." Janin, "Le Dîner de Beethoven, conte fantastique," pt. 1, *Gazette musicale* (5 January 1834).

[62] The Beethovenian "pilgrimage" was a known genre in which Janin was self-consciously participating; see Knittel, "Pilgrimages to Beethoven."

Le Retour à la vie: *Natural Magic and the Ideal Orchestra*

"Oh!" he said, with tears in his eyes, "It's just that I am so alone, completely alone; no one speaks to me; no one asks what has become of old Beethoven; as for me, I no longer know my name or who I am. Once I was master of the world; I was in command of the most powerful invisible orchestra which ever filled the air; I daily leant my ear to the most ravishing symphonies, of which I was at once the author, the orchestra, the singer, the judge, the king, the god! My life was a perpetual concert, a symphony without end; at this time what ravishing ecstasies! What lyric passion! What mysterious and saintly voices! What an immense bow left the earth to touch the sky! All this was an echo in my soul! Then my soul received the least sounds from the air or from the earth: the songs of birds, the noise of the wind, the murmur of the water, the sighs of the night breeze, the swaying of the poplar's branches, the gaiety of the sparrows, the buzzing of the bees, the plaintive murmur of the cricket on the hearth – all these were harmonies to me and I perceived them all in my soul, for I lived for noise, dreams, silence, sighs, ecstasies, friendship, loves, and poetry!"[63]

The ensemble Janin's Beethoven describes – the internal/external nature-orchestra – is, of course, reminiscent of the one Berlioz invoked in *Le Retour*; indeed, in writing this passage, Janin borrowed directly from his 1832 review of the *mélologue* in which he had waxed rhapsodic over Berlioz's own "invisible orchestra," the "dreams" it communicated, and its capacity to communicate the "entire life" or "soul" of its wielder.[64] For Berlioz, as we have seen, access to this world came only at the price of pathology, and Janin makes clear that Beethoven paid the same

---

[63] "Oh!" dit-il les larmes aux yeux, "c'est que je suis bien seul, tout seul; personne ne me parle, personne ne demande ce que devient le vieux Beethoven; moi-même je ne sais plus comment je m'appelle et qui je suis; autrefois j'étais le maître d'un monde, je commandais au plus puissant orchestre invisible qui ait jamais rempli les airs; je prêtais l'oreille nuit et jour à des ravissantes symphonies dont j'étais à la fois l'auteur, l'orchestre, le chanteur, le juge, le roi, le dieu! Ma vie était un concert perpétuel, une symphonie sans fin; en ce temps-là quelles ravissantes extases! Quel emportement lyrique! Quelles voix mystérieuses et saintes! Quel immense archet qui partait de la terre pour toucher le ciel! Tout cela avait un écho dans mon âme! Mon âme recevait alors les moindres sons venus de l'air ou de la terre, le chant des oiseaux, le bruit du vent, le murmure de l'eau, les soupirs de la bise dans la nuit, le balancement du peuplier dans le ciel, toute la gaieté du passereau, le bourdonnement des abeilles, le plaintif murmure du grillon au foyer domestique; c'était là autant d'harmonies pour moi, qui les recevais toutes dans mon coeur, dans mon âme, pour moi qui vivais de bruit, de rêves, de silence, de soupirs, d'extases, d'amitié, d'amours, de poésie!" Janin, "Le Dîner de Beethoven," pt. 2, *Gazette musicale* (12 January 1834).

[64] From Janin's review of *Le Retour* in *Journal des débats* (10 December 1832): "Berlioz se place en tête de tout ce monde musical; il le suppose invisible, lui tout seul présent. Soyez tranquilles! C'est lui seul qui va jouer tout son drame. Dans sa pensée, ces musiciens que vous voyez là assemblés n'existent pas; tout cet orchestre est un écho invisible qui va répéter les battemens de son coeur.... L'orchestre s'en va chantant au hasard, poussant de petits cris de joie qui entrecoupent cette rêverie mélancolique. Nous sommes donc au commencement de cette vie d'artiste." A host of other links appear between Janin's profile of Beethoven and his earlier description of Berlioz; for instance, Berlioz too (in the 1832 review) exists "hors du monde réel" in a space of Hoffmannesque otherworldliness.

price – indeed, suffered from the same ailment. As the tale draws to a close, he leaves his reader with a definitive assessment of the composer's condition, positioning him not just as a drunkard or a melancholic, but a monomaniac. He is, as Janin tells his reader, an artist who has lived in the thrall of an *idée fixe*, an obsessive focus whose eventual waning has led to his creative demise:

> Beethoven was one of those old men who have lived all their lives *under the influence of a single idea*, which is sufficient in great part for their existence. It absorbs them; it is all their joy, all their sorrow; it is all their past, all their present; it grows with them and weakens with them; and when it dies, they die.[65]

The idea on which Beethoven is fixated is, as Janin has already made clear, that of sonorous nature; indeed, he suffers from the same combination of idealist obsession and nervous oversensitivity already tied, in French circles, to both Berlioz's Artist and Nodier's Jean-François. The disorder is at once the root of his suffering and his creative insight, affording him special access to a form of cosmic perception – sonorous, visionary, poetic – and to the mystical organic orchestra itself, the source of his "spiritual" composition.

Janin accomplishes several crucial tasks in this inaugural tale: he not only yokes Berlioz with Beethoven, but brings both composers under the auspices of the fantastic. Together, they are animated by the same form of pantheistic listening, their work rooted in a "natural" symphonic sound-world that reveals to them "saintly" voices as well as an echo of their own souls. If Berlioz is a French Beethoven (an idea already in circulation) Beethoven emerges equally clearly here as a kind of German Berlioz, the two united and explained via fantasy's defining tenets of real, natural, and nervous supernaturalism.

Ruminations on the fantastic orchestra return in Janin's next tale, titled simply "Hoffman [*sic*], conte fantastique," published two weeks later. This narrative is a clear adaptation of one of Hoffmann's own stories, the late "Zufällige Gedanken bei dem Erscheinen dieser Blätter" ("Casual Reflections on the Appearance of This Journal," 1820), which Janin uses as a vehicle to underscore the Berlioz–Beethoven connection he had begun (tacitly) to forge in his first tale and to undercut critics who denounced the orchestral language of these composers as empty bombast.[66] Hoffmann's

---

[65] "Beethoven était un de ces vieillards qui ont vécu toute leur vie d'une seule idée; une grande idée suffit à l'existence de ces hommes à part, elle les absorbe, elle est toute leur joie; elle est tout leur chagrin, elle est tout leur passé, tout leur présent; elle grandit avec eux, elle s'affaiblit avec eux, et quand l'idée est épuisée, l'homme meurt." Janin, "Le Dîner de Beethoven," pt. 1, *Gazette musicale* (5 January 1834).

[66] See Ellis's commentary on this tale in "The Uses of Fiction," 258–62, where she also discusses Janin's travesty of Hoffmann's "Zufällige Gedanken," pointing out its implicit denunciation of

original story had opened by lauding music critics, positioning them as "allied spirits" who approached great works with empathy and insight. Animated by a mysterious magic, they allowed such works to be fully understood, producing analyses that could "lead people to listen well."[67] But in Janin's version of the tale (cast as a dialogue between himself and the German *conteur*), precisely the opposite is true. His rewritten version has Hoffmann denounce music critics as the enemy, casting them as "venomous snakes" (*serpents venimeux*) rather than enlightened facilitators. Instead of showing the public how to navigate the wondrous musical "edifice" (*merveilleux édifice*) of the inspired composer, they destroy "your fantastic castle" (*ton château fantastique*) or dissect it by tearing it to pieces. Hardly models of sensitive listening, such men (i.e., those of Fétis's ilk rather than Janin's) are simply philistines who cannot understand how it (the musical work) "could have prospered so wonderfully."[68]

Having reversed Hoffmann's opening claim, Janin goes on to borrow more straightforwardly from the last half of the *conteur*'s original tale, which takes up questions surrounding instrumental music and orchestration. Here, he differentiates between the empty and inspired effects to be found in the works of modern orchestral composers, arguing that it is one of the tasks of the good listener/reviewer to know the difference. But few are able to make the distinction, either in Hoffmann's or in Janin's version of the tale; indeed, the inability to do so is what renders so many French critics deficient. Since they themselves are unable to hear orchestration with a true ear, they are hardly in a position to instruct others. Speaking as/through Hoffmann in a long passage taken virtually verbatim from the *conteur*'s original tale, Janin acknowledges that gratuitous orchestration – the kind Hoffmann had denounced nearly a decade earlier in *Kreisleriana* – is all too common in modern compositions. "It is certain," he argues, "that all the arsenal of woodwind and brass instruments is tested today in the fire and water of good taste," and that, as a result, "a great many scores nowadays are so covered with notes that a flea of little daring could do whatever he wanted

---

conservative French critics. As she argues, the tale allowed Janin to underscore the idea that "only the creative had the right to judge creativity or to explain its inner workings" (258).
[67] Hoffmann, "Casual Reflections on the Appearance of This Journal," 426.
[68] Janin, "Hoffmann, conte fantastique," *Gazette musicale* (30 March and 4 April 1834).
The quotations are taken from pt. 2 (4 April) in a passage on musical form lauding a composer who "abandoned [himself] to dramatic passion," pouring forth "all that was in you of pity, terror, voluptuousness," articulating "love, tenderness, the desires of all men, hatred, the transports of delight, [and] despair." The link to Berlioz (which will become stronger presently) is already clear, as is Janin's invocation of Hoffmann's organicist rhetoric, which is – so he implies – at the root of "fantastic" form.

without being noticed."[69] But not all modern scores fall into this category, nor are all orchestrators so talentless.

Sensitive physiognomy, as Janin argues (echoing Hoffmann), is necessary both to produce and truly *hear* inspired effects: "the talent to produce an effect is truly one of the marvelous secrets of the art of composition because the human organization on which it acts is also the most marvelous of all secrets."[70] In the absence of this physical receptivity, many effects strike the ear simply as empty or material sounds. Frederick II, for instance, heard in Gluck's "marvelous" orchestration only a confused racket. And many modern critics are equally deaf. Hoffmann, in his original tale, lampooned the demands of these unfortunates by parodying them: "'Go back to the simplicity of the early masters,' I hear you cry, my dear old composers, to your young followers. 'No more of this jangle and clatter, forget all your modern music, forget Mozart and Beethoven, the sooner the better.'"[71] Riffing on this line, in his reworked version of the tale, Janin extends Hoffmann's remark pointedly: "Return to the simplicity of the ancients, you cry, old masters, to our young men; down with all this noise and clatter; forget all modern music; forget Mozart, and Beethoven, *and especially* –."[72] Here, his manipulation of Hoffmann's story comes to a head; we are clearly meant to insert Berlioz's name in the blank space at the end of his elongated Hoffmann quote, Berlioz being, of course, the composer whom French readers would have been thinking of, the "young man" most viciously denounced for noisy, senseless orchestration. But this assessment, as Janin's story insisted, was the stuff of ignorance. His tale foreshadows Berlioz's own claim, in the 1838 Pastoral essay, that only audiences lacking in sensitivity heard in Beethoven's work mere imitation or noise. Instead, as Janin had already suggested in "Le Dîner de Beethoven," they should have heard the wondrous nature-orchestra. And this same ensemble, he now implies, was also at the root of Berlioz's soundworld; indeed, he situates the

---

[69] "Il est bien positif que tout l'arsenal des armes en bois et en cuivre, entre aujourd'hui dans les épreuves de l'eau et du feu du bon goût." ... Il est également vrai de dire que mainte partition de nos jours est tellement noircie de notes, qu'une puce un peu hardie pourrait y faire ses incongruités sans que cela fût remarqué." Ibid.

[70] " le talent de produire de l'effet est réellement un des plus merveilleux secrets de l'art de la composition, car la raison que l'organisation humaine sur laquelle il est question d'agir, est aussi de tous les secrets le plus merveilleux." Ibid.

[71] Hoffmann, "Casual Reflections," 428–29.

[72] "Retournez à la simplicité des *anciens*, t'écries-tu, toi, vieux maître; en t'adressant à nos jeunes gens; à bas toute cette sonnerie et tout ce cliquetis; oubliez toute musique moderne; oubliez Mozart et Beethoven, *et surtout* — " Janin, "Hoffmann, conte fantastique," pt. 2 (4 April 1834).

composer of the *Épisode* as the logical inheritor of Beethoven, a figure associated not with the empty effects of lesser composers, but with the otherworldly orchestration of truly visionary ones. He also elevates himself to a position among the critical elite, a listener cast in Hoffmann's own mold, unique in his ability to perceive and explain the mysteries of fantastic sound.

But in what sense were the effects of Janin's "true" orchestrator magical? How did they exert the mysterious physical influence that both he and Berlioz (drawing on Hoffmann) ascribed to them? These questions, too, began to be answered in the *Gazette*'s *contes fantastiques*, which circled back repeatedly to issues surrounding orchestral sound, musical enchantment, and fantastic listening. This was true of Janin's later contributions ("Le Concert dans la maison" and "L'Homme vert") as with those of other authors, including Joseph Méry and Frédéric Mab. Mab's work, especially his tale "Les Cignes chantent en mourant" (spring 1835), is especially interesting for our purposes since it brings back the nature-orchestra originally introduced by Janin, now in a richer and more revealing context. Mab, like his fellow fantasists, casts his story as a refashioning of Hoffmann's own work, drawing most obviously on "Le Pot d'or," but also on "Le Violon de Crémone" and parts of *Kreisleriana*. And, as with Janin's alteration of "Zufällige Gedanken," he extends and alters his models in critically strategic ways.

Mab's tale features a young girl, Lucinde, who is intent on becoming a musician in order to win over her beloved, the artist Wilhelm. She comes unwittingly under the influence of the alchemist Coppelius, who facilitates her training, using his influence to guide her through a magical greenhouse in her parents' house to a hidden piano. Finally, at the climax of the tale, he appears to her in a dream-sequence (an embedded story) as she seeks out the ultimately beautiful voice. Entering an alternative reality or *monde nouveau* – though one clearly related to the real flower conservatory in which she has been practicing – she finds herself in Coppelius's laboratory, which is an enchanted garden. Mab elaborately describes its sights and sounds:

[A]n immense garden entirely filled with luminous foliage and sonorous branches. Lilies over six feet high trembled in the night breeze, their amorous, crystalline voices singing the most charming Italian sonnets on wonderful melodies. ... The prairie resonated with soft and fluted sounds; the woods with muted murmurs, and the waterfall, gushing, communicated metallic vibrations through the air in forms which one might compare to the most inspired *roulades* of Italian singers. It was, in truth, a magnificent symphony composed of a hundred different voices each performing a different part, though – what a miracle! – never offending the ear.[73]

This place is "an Eden," a prelapsarian utopia (re)constructed by Coppelius, who is, in Mab's story, a figure akin to Faust. He is also clearly derived from Hoffmann's character Prince Phosphorus, the alchemist at the center of "Le Pot d'or." Indeed, Mab's description of Coppelius's laboratory-garden is taken almost verbatim from Hoffmann's own account of Phosphorus's magical-natural workshop.[74] In the narratives of both, the alchemist's world is alive with the sonorous energy of creation. Buzzing insects, whirring birds, singing flowers, and rustling trees produce magical "vibrations," transmitting sounds, light, colors, and perfumes in wondrous synesthetic unity, all separation between objects, senses, and inner and outer realities eradicated.

In Mab's tale, as in Hoffmann's, it is this natural world that is the source of magical-musical power. Both Phosphorous and Coppelius have special access to the properties of minerals, plants, and other living creatures, perceiving them as patterns of vibrating (visible, audible, metaphysical) energy that can be harnessed and directed. But Mab's alchemist differs crucially from Hoffmann's in that he is not just a "professor" or "natural philosopher," but a *conductor*, and his instrument is not just nature in general, but a natural orchestra. He leads the symphony of creation itself, composed of a vast array of "real" sounds united in marvelous accord:

It was truly an admirable orchestra, where each played according to his fantasy, and the musicians were marvelously unencumbered by score, instruments, or ebony baton. At times, Coppelius suspended his work and, with head lowered, listened with delight to this extraordinary music, beating time by striking his hands on his chest. Then the sound amplified in a strange fashion. To satisfy the least whim of

---

[73] "[U]n immense jardin tout rempli d'arbustes lumineux et de tiges sonnantes. Des lys hauts de six coudées tremblaient à la brise nocturne, et leurs voix amoureuses et cristallines chantaient sur des airs inouïs les plus charmans sonnets italicus. . . . La prairie avait des sons timides et flûtés; le bois de sourds murmures, et la cascade, en jaillissant, secouait dans les airs de métalliques vibrations, qu'on aurait pu comparer aux plus fraîches roulades des cantatrices italiennes. C'était, en vérité, une magnifique symphonie, où chantaient cent voix diverses qui ne s'accordaient nullement; et pourtant, ô miracle! l'oreille n'était blessée en aucun point." Frédéric Mab, "Les Cygnes chantent en mourant," *Gazette musicale* (8, 15, and 22 March and 5 April 1835); this quotation appears in pt. 4 (22 March).

[74] "a dazzling magical light was everywhere . . . Anselmus [the protagonist] saw the gleam of marble basins, from which wondrous figures rose and scattered crystal jets that fell splashing into the cups of luminous lilies; strange voices murmured and whistled amid the forest of wondrous plants, and glorious perfumes rose and descended." Hoffmann, "The Golden Pot," 37. See also the wider description of Phosphorus's laboratory given in the "Sixth Vigil" of this tale (36–42). The name Coppelius also has overtly Hoffmannesque implications, derived from another (though more malignant) alchemist in "The Sandman."

their master, all the little birds sang in full voice, and the corn-poppies and purple flowers waved in the depths of his green robe.[75]

To hold sway over this soundworld was to wield the power of divinity, a power that, as Mab tells us, waxes and wanes with the motions of the sun. What he describes is a modern music of the spheres controlled by a new kind of magus-philosopher – not the Renaissance magician influencing the silent music of a Pythagorean mathematical universe, but a modern metaphysician wielding the audible voices of a romantic-pantheistic one (a persona akin to the "nouveau Faust" or modern Prospero Berlioz had described in *Le Retour*). Transmitted by and in this sound is a mysterious energy. Mab calls it a "vital life force" and Hoffmann (in "Le Pot d'or") an "electric warmth," a power uniting all things in sonorous sympathy: animals, plants, humans, earth, and air. To truly capture it is not to imitate, but to animate, to convey the electro-cosmic energy of the universe itself and therefore an intimation or *sensation* of divinity. The experience of this is so powerful that when Lucinde first hears Coppelius's orchestra, she loses consciousness, the miraculous "vibrations" overwhelming her. It is their power that the alchemist proposes to give her, an orchestral nature-voice so mesmerizing that it will alter all those around her, placing Wilhelm under her sway. He bottles a liquid that will, he tells her, transform the "vital principal that warms your veins, illuminates your eyes in their orbits, and makes your heart beat" into a sonorous medium, a stream of "vivid and limpid vibrations." Bio-electric impulses will become sonorous waves. Lucinde will literally sing out her soul, activating the "orchestra in her breast" (*un orchestra ... dans sa poitrine*) – a microcosm of the cosmic nature-orchestra – and in so doing emanate the same energy she herself felt upon first hearing Coppelius's ensemble. But he warns her of the danger involved in this act of magic: to sing for too long will mean exhausting her own energy, dissipating back into the natural-electric totality from which she came (a version of the expansion into luminous "atoms" Nodier had described in connection with reflective fixation and the idealist short-out Berlioz had hinted at in his *mélologue*).[76]

---

[75] "C'était vraiment un admirable orchestre, ou chacun allait selon sa fantaisie, et dont les musiciens se passaient tous à merveille de papier réglé, d'instrumens, et du petit bâton d'ébène. Par instans, Coppelius suspendait son travail; et, renversé sur son front, écoutait avec ravissement cette musique singulière; et battait la mesure en se frappant le ventre avec ses mains. Alors le bruit augmentait d'une façon étrange: tous les petits oiseaux pour flatter les moindres fantaisies du maître, chantaient à plein gosier, et les coquelicots et les fleurs de pourpre, s'agitant sur le fond vert de sa robe de chambre." Mab, "Les Cygnes chantent en mourant," pt. 5 (5 April 1835).

[76] "Ecoute: au principe vital qui réchauffe tes veines, illumine tes yeux dans leur orbite, et fait battre ton coeur en ta poitrine, je vais faire subir une transformation sonore, afin que désormais, au lieu d'agir à l'intérieur et de se concentrer il s'exhale par ta bouche et se disperse en vibrations

Lucinde goes forward despite the potential peril, producing a sound "such as only Hoffmann has heard on this earth." Its vibrations shatter glass, cause crystal to vibrate, and enrapture Wilhelm, whose artistic makeup renders him more susceptible than any other to her natural enchantment. He is, as Mab puts it, "ahead of his fellow men in the arena of sensations," gifted with "a most exquisite sensibility."[77] But, having entranced him, Lucinde goes on to make precisely the mistake Coppelius had warned her of: she sings too long, exhaling all her vital current. In so doing, she ascends to the highest spiritual regions, but also destroys her own body. As she expires, dissolving into the natural-sonorous divine, she experiences a kind of nervous overload in the face of its all-powerful energy: "With the final measures of her song, Lucinde turned pale, her body failing, and seized by a convulsive agitation, quivered like the cords of a lyre long after the sound had stopped vibrating.... The warmth had retreated from her veins, the pulsation of her arteries had ceased. ... Mademoiselle Lucinde ... was dead."[78]

With this tale, the implications of the natural orchestra linked to both Beethoven and Berlioz come more sharply into focus, as do Berlioz's claims around sensational imitation and, in *Le Retour*, electrical overstimulation. Mab's story draws, in fanciful terms, on theories of vitalism resonating back to Newton and forward in various iterations through Mesmer and Schelling. At the heart of these theories is the concept of an all-encompassing energy resonating across the physical world, uniting and "vitalizing" all living beings. In some cases it was understood as a magical or divine force, in others an impersonal one. Toward the end of the eighteenth century, in the wake of a series of experiments by Alessandro Volta, Luigi Galvani, and Giovanni Aldini, it also began to be conceived as an electric and, crucially, a nervous impulse, an energy running through the external world as well as the human body. Some scientists of the period theorized it as a ubiquitous ether (Mab's "magical essence") composed of a combination of electric, luminous, caloric, magnetic, and *sonorous* fluids. It could, in other words, communicate heat, light, magnetism, electricity, and sound. These

éclatantes et limpides, comme un flot de cristal. Tu chanteras avec ta vie et non avec ta voix; et tu comprends à cette heure, ma fille, combien tu dois être avare de tes chanson, puisqu'à l'avenir, ce ne seront pas des notes qui jailliront de ton gosier, mais des gouttes de sang." Ibid.

[77] "Elle chanta. – C'était une voix incomparable et comme, depuis, Hofmann en a seul entendu sur la terre"; "Les hommes de la trempe de Wilhelm devancent toujours leurs frères dans l'ordre des sensations. . . . ce n'est point à eux qu'il faut s'en prendre, mais à la nature qui les a doués d'une sensibilité plus exquise." Ibid.

[78] "Sur les dernières mesures de son air, Lucinde avait pâli, son corps en défaillance et saisi d'un agitation convulsive, tressaillait comme les cordes d'une lyre longtemps après que le son a vibré. . . . La chaleur s'était retirée insensiblement de ses veines, la pulsation de ses artères avait cessé. . . . Mademoiselle Lucinde . . . était morte." Ibid.

properties were perceived as to some degree interchangeable and therefore productive of synesthetic experience: sound could be nervous or magnetic, light could be sonorous, visual landscapes could be perceived as aural, sonorous ones as more broadly sensible (hence Mab's "luminous foliage" and "sonorous branches").[79] It was this nexus of connections that laid the groundwork for Mesmer's musico-electric cures, his manipulation of human nervous energy or "animal magnetism" via specially calibrated sounds (including those of the aeolian harp and glass harmonica), which promised to bring bodies into sympathy with the vital resonances of creation. It also provided a starting point for Schelling's theory of an all-embracing *Weltseele*, an electric world soul locating all beings within the same energy network.[80]

These strands of vitalist theory, which hover clearly behind Hoffmann's musical writing are, in Mab's tale, translated and popularized for French audiences. Extending and literalizing Hoffmann, Mab harnesses the idea of sonorous current as a partial explanation for the power of modern instrumental sound. The fantastic natural orchestra manipulated by his alchemist is synonymous, he invites *Gazette* readers to assume, with the "invisible" elemental ensembles of Beethoven and Berlioz, which operate as vehicles carrying the sound (and through it, the animating spark) of the cosmos itself. The newfangled symphonic effects of these composer-magicians are calibrated not just to reproduce nature's sound, but to transmit its energy. They operate, in other words, like the aeolian harp or glass harmonica but much more powerfully, channeling the electric power of creation – at least to those listeners who, like Wilhelm, are sufficiently sensitive to receive it. The "material effect" Berlioz associates both with his own "ideal" orchestra and with Beethoven's Pastoral ensemble is, Mab's tale suggests, a vitalist one, a vehicle not of imitation, but of energetic transmission.

The idea of a material divinity and a nature orchestra able to capture and convey it was invoked repeatedly in the *Gazette*'s *contes fantastiques* around the time of Mab's tale. And in many cases it was tied directly to Berlioz, who emerged as a kind of modern Coppelius or Faust, a wielder of musico-natural magic. Méry's "La Fontaine d'ivoire" (to which we return in greater detail in Chapter 5) is a case in point, featuring another natural-supernatural

---

[79] For a history of music's interface with vitalist theory and ideas around nervous function, see as starting points: Gouk, *Music, Science, and Natural Magic*; idem, "Music and the Nervous System"; idem, "Music's Pathological and Therapeutic Effects on the Body Politic"; Kennaway, *Bad Vibrations*; Rousseau, *Nervous Acts*, esp. pt. 1 (3–80).

[80] Histories and theories of vitalism are too many and varied to summarize in full here. Starting points for a fuller contextualization of Mab's tale might include Gigante, *Life*; Mitchell, *Experimental Life*; Packham *Eighteenth-Century Vitalism*; and Reill, *Vitalizing Nature in the Enlightenment*.

landscape, this one sinister rather than utopian, which is described in close aural detail: "I found myself in a clump of spindly pines that appeared to have been plated in iron. ... A stream wept; the pine needles shivered; the saxifrage murmured with melancholy; the dry yellow leaves turned in the breeze; the cricket performed his nocturne; the mountain drew chords from all its caverns, the sea from all its reefs."[81] This place, a demonic soundscape perceived at night, is the flip side of Mab's magical daytime garden, and it too is capturable only via the modern, especially the Berliozian, orchestra. As Méry writes, "If I had the honor of being Berlioz, I would steal from nature the symphony that she performed for me, even were she to charge me with forgery." Only the "nature orchestra" wielded by the composer of the *Fantastique* could capture "the invisible waves of sounds and melodies" at the heart of Méry's otherworldly landscape, the "ravishing overture to the night drama" in which "there was not a single wrong note, not a chord that disobeyed the rules; not one error of composition."[82]

The image of both the orchestra as nature and nature as orchestral proliferated, as John Spitzer has shown, in wider French fictional writing over the following decades. Victor Hugo, in his 1842 travel account "Le Rhin," described the combined songs of the wood pigeon, goldfinch, and sparrow as an instrumental tutti and the whole wood as "an orchestra." Two years later, Heine, in his poem "Neuer Frühling," wrote of ringing trees and singing nests, asking, "who is the *Kapellmeister* / In this green forest orchestra?" And H.-F. Amiel in his *Journal de l'année* of 1866 described the coming of warm weather as a symphonic awakening led by the creator himself: "the orchestra of spring plays an overture to the great symphony of May, a winged, flowering, leafy symphony in praise of the master of life, the creator of the universe."[83] These descriptions frame Berlioz's account of his own ensemble in the Orchestration Treatise (first published 1844). Here, he gives specifications for an ideal festival orchestra (another imaginary ensemble) drawing together some 467 players including 120 violins, 45 cellos, 16 horns, 30 harps, and 30 pianos. He conceives of this group quite

---

[81] "Je me trouvai compromis dans un massif de pins grêles qui paraissaient avoir été écaillés par des doigts de fer. ... Un ruisseau pleurait; les aiguilles des pins frissonnaient, les saxifrages murmuraient avec mélancolie; les feuilles jaunes et sèches tourbillonnaient à la brise; le Grillon exécutait son nocturne; la montagne tirait des accords de toutes ses cavernes, la mer de tous ses écueils." Méry, "La Fontaine d'ivoire," *Gazette musicale* (25 January 1835).

[82] "Si j'avais l'honneur d'être Berlioz, je volerais à la nature la symphonie qu'elle exécutait alors pour moi, dût-elle m'attaquer en contrefaçon. ... Dans cette ravissante ouverture du drame de la nuit, il n'y avait pas une fausse note, pas un accords contre les règles; pas une erreur de composition." Ibid.

[83] Spitzer, "Metaphors of the Orchestra." For a discussion of the quotations from Hugo, Heine, and Amiel, see 249–50; for the excerpts themselves, in fuller form, see 259–60. Spitzer points out that natural metaphors for the orchestra have an older provenance in German and English writing.

Le Retour à la vie: Natural Magic and the Ideal Orchestra

clearly as a natural orchestra, a single transcendental instrument able to capture and transmit the sounds of the entirety of creation:

> In the thousand combinations possible with the giant orchestra described above, there would reside a wealth of harmonies, a variety of timbres, an abundance of contrasts surpassing anything previously achieved in music. ... Its calm would be as majestic as an ocean in repose, its outbursts would recall tropical typhoons, its explosive power the eruptions of volcanoes. In it could be heard the sighs, the murmurs and the mysterious sounds of the virgin forest. ... Its silence would inspire awe by its solemnity. And even the most recalcitrant of constitutions would shudder to see its crescendo grow, with a roar like a forest fire, immense and sublime.[84]

Were this group to be assembled, its power would overcome even the dull physiognomies (the "recalcitrant constitutions") of those who had misheard his own earlier music. It would cause audiences not just to listen, but to "shudder," their nervous systems bombarded with the vitalist power of creation itself. And the leader of the group, in Berlioz's telling, would operate as the controller and channeler of its power. In his essay on conducting (appended to an English version of the Orchestration Treatise in 1855), the composer suggested as much, describing the orchestral leader as an energy transmitter: "his inner flame will warm them, his electricity will charge them, his drive will propel them. He will radiate the vital spark of music." Here, Berlioz imagines himself doing for his audiences what Lucinde, via Coppelius's power, did for hers: transmitting and directing his own inner spark, which was also the animating energy of the natural world – the power that had galvanized him "back to life" in 1832.[85] What made his *mélologue* an important "explanatory" work and the Pastoral Symphony a crucial (rather than problematic) Beethovenian contribution, was the way in which these works exposed the source of such power – the underlying materiality or *vitality* of ideal sound, the "real" root, so to speak, of musical ineffability.

Berlioz's orchestral rhetoric, especially its magico-nervous language, was modeled in part on the fantastic tales of the 1830s, which explained as well as generating his soundworld, providing a vocabulary in which to describe and rationalize it. And quite quickly, this rhetoric was transferred, in *contes fantastiques* of the period, to other composers, among them Liszt, whose

---

[84] Translation adapted from that of Spitzer in "Metaphors of the Orchestra," 246. For the wider context, see Berlioz's essay "The Orchestra" given in the *Orchestration Treatise*, trans. Macdonald, 319–35.

[85] Berlioz, *Orchestration Treatise*, trans. Macdonald, 337. Winter, in *Mesmerized*, notes that this electric or mesmeric power was also assigned to (and claimed by) other conductors, notably Mendelssohn, Jullien, and Costa (309–20).

Berliozian tendencies were championed (also gently mocked) in Théophile Ferrière's story "Brand-Sachs" (*Gazette musicale*, 1836). Here, the title character, Wilhelm Brand-Sachs (a thinly disguised portrait of Liszt), is presented as an artist of the modern *fantastique* type, modeled on Kreisler and weaned on the writings of Hoffmann. Ferrière describes him as "a tale of Hoffmann made manifest," a musician of "galvanic and nervous sensibility" who understands art as "the mysterious link uniting the ideal with the real world."[86] Enraptured by the new possibilities of instrumental sound, he gives himself up to "the vibrations of the orchestra," producing a concerto in which "the instruments ... were combined such as to produce unknown effects." The overtly Kreislerian purpose of his work, as Ferrière explains, is to make "the whole of nature ... articulate," to achieve a "spiritualization of the material world." But pursuing this end drives Liszt/Brand-Sachs mad, leading to a fate that connects him unmistakably to Berlioz: he hears the *Dies irae*, ushered in by ophicleides, and then the "cursed violins" (*maudits violons*) of the infernal dance, which prefigure his death.[87]

Fictions of this sort – explanations and celebrations of the fantastic soundworld and the fantastic composer himself – proved increasingly alluring, spreading beyond the *Gazette* to other journals (*Le Ménestrel*, *La France musicale*) and, as we have seen, into the wider domain of French

---

[86] Samuel Bach (Théophile Ferrière), "Brand-Sachs," *Gazette musicale* (26 April and 1 May 1836). The premise for this story is a friendship between Hoffmann and Brand-Sach's father. The two agree to an experiment: they will raise their sons in accordance with their metaphysical and musical ideas. Hoffmann raises Kreisler and his friend raises Brand-Sachs (clearly Liszt's "double" in this tale), who spends his youth reading Hoffmann's work (especially the literary portraits of Kreisler). The result is the image of the artist I describe here. Brand-Sachs (Liszt) is "ce conte d'Hoffmann fait homme," a musician whose "sensibilité galvanique et nerveuse annonçait de belles choses pour l'avenir." He regards art "comme l'anneau mystérieux qui unit le monde idéal au monde réel." Earlier, we learn that "La vie était pour lui comme un conte de fées. Il la voyait entre les lignes d'un cahier de musique, en dièze ou en bémol, avec des paroles d'opéra, les ailes abandonnées aux vibrations de l'orchestre." Liszt's concerto "était fort travaillé dans le goût de l'école moderne. Les instrumens de l'orchestre étaient combinés de manière à produire des effets inconnus" (pt. 2, 1 May 1836). See Ellis's commentary on this tale in *The Cambridge Companion to Liszt*, 1–13, where she draws a series of connections among Liszt, Kreisler, Beethoven, and Berlioz.

[87] Brand-Sachs defines the artist (and the true artwork) as "la nature entière qui devient parole ... un commencement de spiritualization du monde matériel." His final, Berliozian madness is described thus: "Ha! Ha! entendez-vous? les ophyclëides ... comme dans l'église, au *dies irae*? ... ta, ta, ta, je veux danser aussi, moi! ... ah! les maudits, les maudits violons, violons ... que je suis bête!" "Brand-Sachs," pt. 2 (1 May 1836). Note that in this quotation, the suspension points are part of the original text. Liszt's connection to nervous "revelation" was not just orchestral, but, as Davies has argued, pianistic, bound up with a brand of "metapianism" in which his hands themselves were given over to "uncanny, occult" forces (perhaps divine, perhaps diabolical); see Davies, "Liszt, Metapianism, and the Cultural History of the Hand"; and for another investigation of Liszt's nervous virtuosity, see Thormählen, "Physical Distortion, Emotion and Subjectivity."

fiction. Together, they began to achieve a certain coherence, the beginnings of a theory of musical fantasy rooted in what we might term nervous idealism or physiological metaphysics – a theory already implicit in Hoffmann's own tales. But in the end, the quasi-scientific exegeses of the *contes fantastiques* did not persuade conservative critics. On the contrary, as the decade advanced, Berlioz's detractors became increasingly resistant to (and wary of) the lessons of these stories, whose soundworlds posed a clear challenge to existing authority. Allegedly written by "nature itself" (as Méry put it), they wandered outside aesthetic and institutional control, threatening to electrify, mesmerize, transform, or manipulate. Around 1838 – the year of Berlioz's *Benvenuto Cellini* – critical resistance came to a head, the composer's detractors launching a series of denunciations of both fantasy and the tales constructing it. These were no longer satires or brush-offs, but instead dissertation-like rebuttals that shut down the philosophical ideas and taxonomical blurrings of the *contes fantastiques* (natural/supernatural; imitation/expression; sound/sensation) and therefore the key tenets of musical fantasy, returning, now in more sustained fashion, to the denunciations of the early 1830s.

On Deaf Ears

Among the large-scale overviews of Berlioz to appear in 1838 were those of Joseph Mainzer, Joseph D'Ortigue, and Ange-Henri Blaze. These were motivated in part by the premiere of Berlioz's first opera (the moment when he became a composer of "serious" status), but equally so by the ongoing *querelle* over the Fantastic Symphony and its sequel, which had begun to shape Berlioz's reception/construction in a global sense. As I noted in Chapter 1, the most extensive of these was the twenty-one-page diatribe by Blaze written for the *Revue des deux mondes* and titled "De l'École fantastique et de M. Berlioz." The piece is couched as an overview of Berlioz's output to date (one in a series of profiles of "Musiciens français") and gives detailed commentary on his instrumental and dramatic works from the *Épisode de la vie d'artiste* onward. But even more clearly, it is a refutation of the ideas introduced in popular *contes fantastiques* (both imported and native), which, for Blaze, are inextricable from Berlioz's soundworld; indeed, have shaped *all* of his work from the *Épisode* onward. Musical fantasy, he argues, is a response to the false ideas promulgated by its literary counterpart, especially the tales of Hoffmann, who, in his account, is primarily responsible for the errors of both Berlioz and his "school." The *contes fantastiques* are purveyors of arcane and misguided philosophies;

Blaze refers to "the delusions of Pythagoras," the "dreams of Paracelsus," and later to the false ideas of "Kant, Spinoza, [and] Herder."[88]

Over the course of the essay, he denounces the ideas associated with these figures (lumped together as purveyors of "foreign" metaphysics) and the sonorous magic they propound as nonsensical and unmusical, productive of meaningless noise. And even more pointedly, he refutes the idea of artistic "correspondences" or vitalist "sympathies" underpinning the theory of fantastic expression suggested in tales like Mab's. Berliozian imitation, he argues, is simply imitation – not nervous transmission, not electric illumination. Objects, senses, and the arts at large do not, he insists, exist in some mysterious or synesthetic unity; indeed, he lampoons such a position: "the poet colors his verse, the musician paints a landscape. One does not sing an air, one speaks it.... Preposterous!"[89] For Blaze, color is not sound, material is not spiritual (inner is not outer, natural is not supernatural). These fallacies produce madmen after the manner of Kreisler, musicians steeped in melancholy, endlessly seeking a (nonexistent) melodic ideal in instrumental "vibrations." Describing these musical "phantoms":

> The expression on their face is sad to the last. Their foreheads bend like a reed under the fatal hand of genius, rising toward the heavens, eternal abode of the melody which they vainly seek here below ... and their divine mission consists in perpetually passing their soul through the guts of an instrument which palpitates, animates, shivers and leaps at their approach, which shares their profound melancholies, their vague uncertainties, their seraphic ecstasies ... and in the end, their entire life.[90]

The jab both at Berlioz's autobiographical *Épisode* with its "nervous" effects and, more broadly, the vitalist orchestra celebrated in tales by the *Gazette* authors is clear here. For Blaze, the result of such an approach is not nervous illumination, as fantasists claim, but simply pathology (the "bad vibrations" theorized recently by James Kennaway) and, worse yet, a kind of blasphemy.[91] The pantheism (in the form of vital materialism) propounded

---

[88] Blaze, "De l'École fantastique," 100–02.
[89] "La peinture, la musique, la poésie, désormais ne font plus qu'un seul art immense, universel, que les mêmes lois gouvernent, qui tend au même but par les mêmes moyens: le poète colore son vers, le musicien dessine un paysage. On ne chante plus un air, on le dit.... Insensés!" Ibid., 102.
[90] "L'expression de leur visage est triste jusqu'à la fin. Parfois leur front incline comme un roseau sous la main fatale du genie se relève vers le ciel, séjour éternel de la mélodie qu'ils cherchent vainement ici-bas ... et leur mission divine consiste à faire passer incessamment leur âme dans les entrailles d'un instrument qui palpite, s'anime, tressaille et bondit à leur approche; qui partage leurs douleurs profondes, leurs vagues incertitudes, leurs extases séraphiques ... et vit enfin de leur propre vie." Ibid., 104–05.
[91] See Kennaway, *Bad Vibrations*, 23–61, where he traces postrevolutionary links among musical sensuality, moral turpitude, and nervous pathology.

by Hoffmann is a form of atheism eradicating rather than illuminating truth, elevating the physical to the level of the spiritual and the composer himself to the status of a deity. Such a belief is not just aesthetically flawed, as Blaze argues, but theologically unsound and will inevitably be rejected by the French public:

Ah! If this [your metaphysical theory] is true, then you are God. Very well then, grow up to the heavens, take the skies, take the entire universe, fly at will on your wing of flame into the vapors of the infinite. But don't complain if the public disregards you and if, when you grasp at its most cherished idols, it denounces and mocks you.[92]

This mode of attack proved resonant in part because it was familiar, tapping into long-standing French suspicions around Germany's "natural supernaturalism," in particular the electric metaphysics posited by Schelling. Resistance to these ideas was not confined to aesthetic conservatives, but voiced even by proponents of romanticism, including Staël herself. In *De l'Allemagne* she had lauded Kant's dualistic transcendentalism and, in general terms, the sacralization of nature posited by Schlegel and his contemporaries. But the notion of a pantheistic God, a deity reinterpreted as vital energy, was less appealing. Such a philosophy, Staël argued, leeched religion of personal sentiment, feeling, and in the end, human morality:

Vague ideas of reunion with nature will . . . destroy the empire of religion over our souls; for religion is addressed to each of us individually. . . . Christianity is adapted to every mind, and sympathizes, like a confidential friend, with the wants of every heart. Pantheism, on the contrary, that is, nature deified, by inspiring religion for every thing, disperses it over the world instead of concentrating it in ourselves. . . . We think we shall succeed in comprehending the universe as space, by always removing barriers, and setting difficulties farther from us without resolving them; and yet we are no nearer to the infinite. Sentiment alone reveals it to us, without explaining it.[93]

Similar refutations wove through the writings of her contemporaries, including religious conservatives (Joseph de Maistre) and even proponents of Victor Cousin's more open-minded eclecticism. Staël's stance also seems to have affected Fétis, who, as Rosalie Schellhous has argued, was more receptive to Fichtean idealism (a form of radical subjectivism) than to the pantheist-inflected ideas of Fichte's younger compatriots. For Fétis, as she

---

[92] "Ah! s'il est ainsi, vous êtes dieu. Alors grandissez jusqu'au ciel; prenez l'espace, prenez l'univers tout entier, roulez-vous au caprice de votre aile de flamme dans les vapeurs de l'infini; mais ne vous plaignez pas si la multitude vous méconnaît, et si, quand vous portez la main sur ses idoles les plus chères, elle vous blasphème et vous raille." Blaze, "De l'École fantastique," 103.

[93] Staël, *De l'Allemagne*, trans. Wight, I:199.

points out, nature was not a source of music, but merely a collection of raw sounds to be shaped and elevated.[94] Music's purpose was to aspire to higher spheres, but not by sacralizing the physical; indeed, the spiritual and material domains were incompatible and therefore the "real" supernaturalism suggested in *Le Retour* was inadmissible (and inaudible).

It was not just rhetorical or conceptual limitation, then, (as I suggested earlier) that prevented Berliozian fantasy from emerging into clarity in mainstream criticism, but also philosophical resistance. And in the end, the resistance won out; criticism triumphed over fiction. In reviews of the mid-late nineteenth century, Berlioz was virtually always cast as an imitator, a composer whose style was rooted in clever onomatopoeia or startling physical effects. There is little sense that the materiality of his *Épisode* might also be ineffable, that the orchestral real might be compatible with the musical ideal. Instead, both the *Fantastique* and *Le Retour* (along with the *genre fantastique* more broadly) remained firmly in the category of the mimetic. Berlioz's proponents as far forward as Jacques Barzun continued to struggle against this assessment – to downplay Berlioz's imitative passages and even his programs themselves (especially those of the *Fantastique* and its sequel) – while his detractors drew attention to them. Neither group was able to forge a critical interface between the ineffable and the sensible, and therefore a compelling explanation for fantasy's *surnaturel vrai*. Berlioz's imaginative world (and Berlioz himself) remained hazy, unmanageable, the victim of persistent taxonomical rigidity.

And for many, the "imitative" tendency of Berliozian fantasy was a signal of something beyond aesthetic or philosophical error; it was a form of willful illegibility, a dismantling of coherent modes of hearing and understanding. In privileging "vital" sonority, it disrupted musical line and therefore entrenched conceptions of meaning and beauty. Both were bound up closely in French discourses with melody, which seemed in short supply in Berlioz. His fantastic style abandoned the rhetorical logic of the melodic, speaking instead in hieroglyphic sound-shapes, an idiom estranged from "the language of men" and therefore the world of order. This idea, familiar to wider discourses of anxiety around instrumental sound (in and outside of France), is given concrete form in Hoffmann's tales, including "Le Pot d'or." Here, when Anselmus is in the magical nature-laboratory, he not only feels and hears the strains of vital creation, but also *reads* them in the form of

---

[94] Schellhous, "Fétis's 'Tonality' as a Metaphysical Principle." For more on Fétis's philosophical orientation, including his adherence to certain strands of Cousinian philosophy, his resolute separation of the "ideal" and the "real," and his rejection of "the avant-garde of Romanticism," see Ellis, *Music Criticism in Nineteenth-Century France*, 33–45; also Bloom, "François-Joseph Fétis," 316–80.

mysterious symbols ("strangely intertwined characters") arising from the sounds, marked by "dots, strokes, dashes, and curlicues, which seemed by turns to represent plants, or mosses, or animal shapes," at first impossible to interpret but gradually more legible.[95] What he perceives is the language of nature itself – of intuition, old magic, and, as Hoffmann makes clear, of power. It was this power that Mainzer, Blaze, and other denouncers of fantasy feared and heard. They tied Berlioz's "natural" sound to a primitive idiom bound up with ungovernable energy and therefore with radical political potentiality. As Blaze put it, fantasy's "inadmissible theories" were wedded to "the turbulent spirit of conquest and invasion," and even to Jacobinism.[96] The connection is an intriguing one, borne out by Berlioz himself, whose first symphony yokes ideal sound with images of the guillotine. But how do the two go together? What was the perceived relationship between foreign metaphysics and revolutionary linguistics? Between sonorous vitalism and the politics of the Terror? Answers to these questions require different kinds of contexts, and it is to this task that we turn next.

[95] Hoffmann, "The Golden Pot," 51–52.   [96] Blaze, "De l'École fantastique," 100.

4 ✧ Grammatical Imaginaries

I saw that he [Berlioz] had no sense of melody and but a feeble notion of rhythm; that his harmony, composed of piles of notes which were often monstrous, was nevertheless flat and monotonous. In a word, I saw that he lacked melodic and harmonic ideas, and I came to the conclusion that he would always write in a barbarous manner.

–François Fétis, 1835[1]

Listen to me, sir, renounce your rough and ungainly effects, your musical antitheses, your disordered harmony, and your clumsy piling-up of notes; return to the common tongue, return to the positive, take up once again the yoke of rational music.

–Le Ménestrel, 1836[2]

The greatest reproach one could level at M. Berlioz is that he does not know how to treat a musical idea. He lacks order; his phrases succeed one another but they are not conjoined; there is no thread, no logical weave in the style.

–Joseph Mainzer, 1838[3]

In place of the idiom of art, the sacred language, he substitutes a polyglot vocabulary, for which only initiates possess the key. Harmonies are confused, continuities and affinities destroyed; it is chaos.

–François Clément, 1868[4]

---

[1] "Je vis que la mélodie lui était antipathique, qu'il n'avait qu'une faible notion du rythme; que son harmonie, formée d'agrégations souvent monstrueuses de notes, était néanmoins plate et monotone; en un mot je vis qu'il manquait d'idées mélodiques et harmoniques, et je jugeai qu'il écrirait toujours d'une manière barbare." *Gazette musicale* (1 February 1835).

[2] "Croyez-moi, Monsieur, renoncez à vos effets brusques et heurtés, à vos antithèses musicales, à vos accords désordonnés, à vos fougueux attroupemens de notes; rentrez dans la voie commune, revenez au positif, reprenez le joug de la musique rationnelle" *Le Ménestrel* (11 December 1836). Here, the references to "piled-up" notes and musical irrationalism are clear echoes of Fétis's 1835 review.

[3] "Le plus grand reproche qu'on puisse faire à M. Berlioz, c'est qu'il ne sait pas traiter une idée musicale. Il manque de suite; ses phrases se succèdent, mais elles ne sont point liées entre elles; il n'a pas de trame, de tissu dans le style." Mainzer, *Chronique musicale*, 34.

[4] "A l'idiome de l'art, à la langue sacrée se substitue un vocabulaire polyglotte, dont les initiés possèdent seuls la clef. Les tonalités sont décousues, les relations et les affinités détruites, c'est le chaos." Clément, *Musiciens célèbres*, 516–17.

From the beginning to the end of Berlioz's career, his music was characterized as disordered, violent, and incoherent. More pointedly, it was grammatically wrong, marked by syntactical disruption, rhythmic confusion, and melodic deficiency. Berlioz refused to observe the fundamentals of rhetorical logic, misordering his ideas, leaving them unresolved, or jamming them together without sufficient transition. In places, according to his detractors, he seemed to eradicate melody itself, collapsing into willful monstrosity. These kinds of complaints began in earnest with the reception of the *Symphonie fantastique* (although there are hints earlier) and resonated through the following years with increasing tenacity, emerging by the late 1830s as central features of Berliozian "style." The problem and promise of his work was caught up with issues of language and legibility, an unraveling of what Joseph Mainzer described as the warp and woof of musical poetics. His musical imaginary – what critics called his *fantastique* mode – was a space of grammatical deficiency estranged from reason, order, and the "common tongue."

For many, the composer's musico-linguistic idiosyncrasies were bound up with innovations in literary form, particularly those of Victor Hugo. The two men were joined in critical discourse as early as 1832, in Joseph D'Ortigue's biographical sketch for the *Revue de Paris*. Reviews over the following several years reinscribed the coupling persistently: in 1834, in *Le Temps*, Berlioz was a composer in "secret affinity" with Hugo, and five years later, in *Le Corsaire*, he was "following the same incomprehensible, dead-end path forged by Hugo." A reviewer for *Le Constitutionnel* in 1839 called him "the counterpart [*le pendant*] of M. Victor Hugo," and Théophile Gautier, in his *Histoire du romantisme*, argued that "what poets attempted in their verse, Berlioz applied to music with an energy, an audacity, and an originality that astonished as much as it failed to charm."[5] The reference was, of course, to the reforms piloted in Hugo's *Hernani* (1827) and theorized two years later in his much-read Preface to *Cromwell*, a manifesto in which the dramatist called for a dissolution of conventional generic and stylistic strictures in favor of a free conflation of forms, images, shapes, and sounds – a "grotesque" poetics. At its core was a rejection of beauty as the sole model for artistic production and a championing of

---

[5] See *La Revue de Paris* 45 (1832); *Le Temps* (27 November 1834); *Le Corsaire* (5 May 1835); and *Le Constitutionnel* (23 November 1839). Gautier's remark is to be found on p. 260 of the *Histoire du romantisme*: "Ce que les poètes essayaient dans leurs vers, Hector Berlioz le tenta dans la musique avec une énergie, une audace et une originalité qui étonnèrent alors plus qu'elles ne charmèrent." The link between Berlioz and Hugo continued to be underscored through the late nineteenth century. Ferdinand Hiller, for instance, in his *Künstlerleben* (Cologne, 1880), recalled that, from the 1830s onward, Berlioz had been regarded as "the Victor Hugo of music" (85).

ugliness, deformity, even vulgarity as legitimate subjects of literary depiction. It was no longer enough, as Hugo argued, to capture only the noble facets of human experience; instead, modern drama was to paint the light alongside the dark, the grotesque alongside the sublime, the physical alongside the spiritual, the "interior" alongside the "exterior." The old dualities would be dissolved in favor of unconditional inclusion, representation of and for all, a poetics of the imagination rooted in a new kind of realism whose only models were "truth" and "nature."[6]

Achieving this new totality meant expanding and loosening form. On the broadest level, Hugo called for a jettisoning of the Aristotelian unities – those of time, place, and action – which confined the drama to the space of a single day, a singular plotline, and a static locale. On a more local level, he advocated loosening the classical Alexandrine, the poetic formula dictating twelve-syllable lines and an immovable middle caesura. Grammar, he argued, was no longer to be repressive but expressive, no longer to hold the author in "leading strings," but itself to be put "on a leash" such that it could "venture anything ... create or invent its style."[7] And, on the most fundamental level, he championed a freeing of the French lexicon itself, which was to be released from the stranglehold of the Academy. No longer fixed, words, the basic building blocks of drama, must be liberated such that they could take new forms and operate in new ways. Hugo devoted a long and impassioned paragraph to this, the most crucial and basic of his poetic renovations, which is worth quoting in full:

For, whatever certain men may have said who did not think what they were saying ... the French tongue is not *fixed* and never will be. A language does not become fixed. The human intellect is always on the march, or, if you prefer, in motion, and languages with it. Things are made so. When the body changes, how could the coat not change? The French of the nineteenth century can no more be that of the eighteenth, than the French the eighteenth is that of the seventeenth, or the French of the seventeenth is that of the sixteenth. Montaigne's language is not Rabelais's, Pascal's is not Montaigne's, Montesquieu's is not Pascal's. Each of the four languages, taken by itself, is admirable because it is original. Every age has its own ideas; it must have also words adapted to those ideas. Languages are like the sea, they move to and fro incessantly. At certain times they leave one shore of the world of thought and overflow another. All that their waves thus abandon dries up and vanishes. It is in this manner that ideas vanish, that words disappear. It is the same with human tongues as with everything. Each age adds and takes away something. What can be done? It is the decree of fate. In vain, therefore, should we seek to petrify the mobile physiognomy of our idiom in a fixed form. In vain do our literary Joshuas cry out to the language to stand still; languages and the sun do not stand

---

[6] Hugo, *Preface*, trans. Eliot, 385–90.   [7] Ibid., 393.

still. The day when they become *fixed*, they are dead. That is why the French of a certain contemporary school is a dead language.[8]

Living language, a syntax infused with vital energy and with the rhythms of creation itself: this was to be the stuff of romantic expression. It was a heady claim, and its connection to Berlioz is confirmed not just in the composer's critical reception, but in his own aesthetic writing. As early as October 1830, in the "Aperçu sur la musique classique et la musique romantique" (and in many places thereafter), Berlioz proclaimed himself a linguistic free agent in Hugo's mold. Quoting from a later preface (*Les Orientales*), he embraced "free inspiration," a release from "handcuffs, leading-strings, and gags" and an entry into "the great garden of poetry wherein there is no forbidden fruit."[9] The sentiment is compelling, although it is not immediately clear how it shaped compositional practice. Musicologists have made sense of it, in part, by mapping Hugo's relaxed alexandrine onto Berlioz's loosened musical phraseology – his tendency to lengthen, truncate, or enjamb the line. More broadly, they have seen in his music a Hugolian tendency to jettison neoclassical formulas, including strictures surrounding genre, style, and "high" tone. The result, for modern readers, is the beginning of a sense of the relationship between the two, although, as I argue here, we need a considerably broader context in order to work out how Berlioz used and adapted Hugo's poetics and, more fundamentally, how grammatical disruption (new approaches to melody, phraseology, and rhythm) became so central to his imaginative world.

Hugo's program of reform was not just structural or aesthetic, but clearly political, aimed at democratizing words, grammar, and the dramatic project at large. Rather than being entirely new, the Preface to *Cromwell* built on and extended old debates surrounding language that had been ongoing since the revolution and developed new impetus in the years leading up to 1830. And it was into this struggle that Berlioz also inserted himself when he embraced Hugo: a war over syntax and lexicography that was also, crucially, a debate surrounding meaning, authority, and, in the broadest sense, ontology. This wider history is the subject of the present chapter, which aims not only to flesh out Berlioz's Hugolian tendencies, but to place both figures against the backdrop of French linguistic philosophy before and after the revolution. A wider focus – one that looks in greater detail at the history and politics of language in the late eighteenth and early nineteenth centuries – begins to show us how Berlioz's sounding poetics took shape, what was at stake in the formation/deformation of musical syntax, and why questions of

---

[8] Ibid., 394.   [9] *Le Correspondant* (22 October 1830), in *CM*, 1:63–68 (here, 66).

linguistic correctness emerged as keystones in his fantastic production/construction.

Histories of language, as cultural and literary theorists from Pierre Bourdieu to Julia Kristeva have pointed out, are histories of power – of institutional authority, political control, and the manipulation of meaning. They show us how speech can be amplified or muted, speakers moved to the center or margins of coherence, and "official" linguistic practices used as weapons to shore up social and economic capital.[10] But equally clearly, linguistic histories are histories of imagination and especially, in the nineteenth century, of fantasy. To invent words, alter their meanings, or put them together in new ways is to create new worlds. From the *contes fantastiques* of Hoffmann, Charles Nodier, and Honoré de Balzac to the tales of Lewis Carroll, Hans Christian Andersen, and J. R. R. Tolkien, neological experimentation has been inextricable from ontological invention. We enter fantastic spaces by generating languages in which to define and describe them; the point has been made by critics from Nodier himself to Tzvetan Todorov and Ursula Le Guin.[11] The two theoretical strands, political and literary, are obviously intertwined. Grammars of revolution are also those of imagination, projections of better, other, utopian, or make-believe spaces.

This is especially true in the case of Berlioz, whose work was connected to both the imaginative and political charge associated with lexical/grammatical improvisation. Complaints surrounding his grotesqueness or syntactical dysfunctionality were also acknowledgments of the radical visionary potential of his musical poetics. The *Symphonie fantastique* – the place in which Berlioz's linguistic disorder seemed most apparent to critics – is replete with revolutionary images (the guillotine, the intimation of marching troops, the specter of a hellish tribunal) and visuality, as Inge van Rij and others have pointed out, is crucial to the work.[12] But underneath the symphony's sensational display was a deeper threat. What was truly radical about the symphony, as I argue here, was its grammar – a form of linguistic resistance and remaking that was also a kind of fantastical imagining, which

---

[10] As starting points: Bourdieu, *Ce que parler veut dire*; and Kristeva, *La Révolution du langage poétique*.

[11] Nodier's *Dictionnaire raisonné des onomatopées françoises* (1808) makes an eloquent argument for the importance of onomatopoeic words to literatures of the imagination. A range of other commentaries (both historical and contemporary) on fantasy's linguistic dimensions is represented in Sandner, ed., *Fantastic Literature*; see also Gilman, "The Languages of the Fantastic," in *The Cambridge Companion to Fantasy Literature*, 134–46. Dictionaries of fantastic languages abound; an especially useful one is Conley and Cain, *Encyclopedia of Fictional and Fantastic Languages*, which also contains a foreword by Le Guin (xvii–xx).

[12] Van Rij, *The Other Worlds of Hector Berlioz*, 127–92.

bled outward from the *Fantastique* permeating Berlioz's oeuvre at large. As with Hugo's new poetics, Berlioz's syntax threatened to naturalize and materialize phantasmagorical realities, drawing them into being via the power of naming itself. To understand the political charge associated with his fantastic mode is to contemplate the history and philosophy of syntax, to trace the evolution of what French critics understood as a radical grammatical imaginary. As we do this, we begin to connect fantasy's natural soundscapes – its pantheistic magic – with a natural poetics, Hoffmann's revelatory hieroglyph with the tenets of French revolutionary linguistics.

The Revolutionary Lexicon

It is nothing to know how many violent days the Revolution had and how many funerals those days prepared; it is nothing to know the history of uprisings, insurrections, civil war; in all that, the Revolution in fact shows, so to speak, its natural and exterior parts; it is no longer anything but the drama of human passions. Those who wish to comprehend the Revolution, so as to feel it like its contemporaries themselves, must seek its terrors elsewhere. They are in the words the Revolution created or those to which it gave a new sense, in that language impossible to grasp if one forgets for an instant that it personifies everything it names.
 –Philippe-Joseph-Benjamin Buchez and Prosper-Charles Roux, 1834[13]

Hugo's attack on academic language – an attack that, as we have seen, Berlioz seconded – was volatile not because of its novelty, but, on the contrary, its familiarity. It echoed a similar clarion call issued a generation earlier on the eve of 1789: a demand for linguistic renovation that, as Bouchez and Roux suggest in this quotation, was inextricable from the impulse toward political transformation. Not just linked to language, as they argue, revolution was constructed by and through it. Semiotic and social shift were inextricable; indeed, words and grammar *produced* the Terror. The claim has been taken up by a host of modern historians from Ferdinand Brunot onward, who have examined the central role of lexical and grammatical reform in the political unfolding of the revolution and its aftermath: waves of neological innovation, shifts in theories of signs and signification, use and "abuse" of words that mirrored and generated republican as well as anti-republican action, setting the stage for (and the stakes

---

[13] In *Histoire parlementaire de la révolution française*, 24:420, trans. Petrey in *History in the Text*, 9.

of) linguistic transformation – both poetic and musical – in the decades to follow.[14]

French disputes around language did not, of course, originate with the uprisings of the late eighteenth century. A chafing against syntactical and lexical control had begun decades earlier, spearheaded by the so-called Moderns (of the *Querelle des anciens et des modernes*) who resisted monarchical dominion over language – the confining of legitimate forms of speech to the academies, the bar, and the pulpit – calling for a more mobile and modern tongue. Their project of linguistic reform resonated through mid-century, becoming so central to the project of the philosophes (including Denis Diderot and his fellow Encyclopedists) that they coined the term *grammarien-philosophe*, equating the work of the Enlightenment thinker with that of the modern lexicographer.[15] A sense of the gravity of words and their usage intensified through the 1780s, as did the notion that they were the bedrock on which political action was to rest. In order for any discussion of rights, liberty, truth, or justice to take place, grammar and words themselves had to be repurposed or remade; the creation of a new political order was predicated on the invention of a lexicon that could frame and name it. This was the claim made by François-Urbain Domergue, among the central figures in the percolating linguistic ferment of the 1780s. Founder of the *Journal de la langue française* and author of a series of progressive French grammars, he rallied a collection of leading political and philosophical thinkers, including members of active Jacobin clubs, around the project of lexical reform. The Abbé Sicard, the Marquis de Condorcet, Jacques-Pierre Brissot, Fabre d'Eglantine, and Maximilien Robespierre were all members of Domergue's Société des Amateurs de la Langue Française, whose primary goal was to establish a republican dictionary, a revolutionary alternative to the official lexicon of the Académie française. Nothing, the group believed, was more crucial to the realization of its political goals than the "regeneration" of language; indeed, Domergue, as its leader, was held up as a radical new incarnation of the *grammarien-philosophe*: the *grammarien-patriote*.[16]

---

[14] Brunot, *Histoire de la langue française des origines à 1900*. Other texts that have influenced my work here include Blakemore, *Burke and the Fall of Language*; Ricken, *Linguistics, Anthropology and Philosophy in the French Enlightenment*; Renwick, *Language and Rhetoric of the Revolution*; Rosenfeld, *A Revolution in Language*; and Hodson, *Language and Revolution in Burke, Wollstonecraft, Paine, and Godwin*.

[15] For an overview of French linguistic philosophies before the revolution, see Ricken, *Linguistics, Anthropology and Philosophy*; and Nye, *Literary and Linguistic Theories in Eighteenth-Century France*.

[16] For more on this terminology and on Domergue's project more broadly, see Ricken, *Linguistics, Anthropology and Philosophy*, 191–225 (here, 198); and Rosenfeld, *A Revolution in Language*, 123–80.

The dictionary that emerged from Domergue's linguistic efforts was to be a national monument providing "the first free people" with a language worthy of them, an idiom not just of aristocrats, priests, and scholars, but of the French population at large, "ordinary writers as well as academicians, foreigners and provincials as well as Parisians, woman ... as well as men."[17] New words (neologisms) were crucial – words to describe and define revolutionary ideas, processes, and events – but equally so was a renovated grammar. Domergue and his colleagues demoted the rationalist linguistic paradigm cherished by the Academy, which argued for an innate or God-given syntax and therefore a "fixed" word-order (subject-verb-object) in favor of a grammar rooted in the sensualist epistemology of Condillac. This newer model conceived of language not as *a priori* (divinely inculcated), but as a medium emerging from *sensation transformée*, the transmutation of sense impressions garnered from the natural world into ideas and signs. No longer static (grammatically fixed), language became organic, open to free reorganizations or "inversions." Nature itself became a watchword of revolutionary grammarians, who associated their evolving language with all that was vital, alive, and free, opposed to everything artificial, inert, and enchained. Their idiom was to embrace the spark of creation itself, operating, according to Domergue, as "an electric conductor of freedom, of equality, and of reason."[18]

Through the 1790s, the process of lexical reform escalated drastically, evolving into an open struggle for the control of language – for dominion over what nineteenth-century commentators described as the "empire of words" or "words that saved and words that killed."[19] These came in the form of new lexicons and grammars as well as revolutionary pamphlets, addresses, and newspaper articles, and included not just neological additions, but also subtractions: the erasure of words denoting nobility, privilege, and aristocratic authority (*roi, Dieu, prince*). In their place were freshly minted terms for political service, natural rights, and social liberties (*nation, constitution, régénération, vigilance*), as well as for months of the year and even weights and measures – terms that reinvented not just social organization, but time, commerce, morality, and reality. More than mere labels, they were incantations born of a heightened sense of the power of naming, a collapse of the perceived relationship between sign and signified such that words were endowed with Austin-esque powers of materialization.[20]

---

[17] Ibid., 155. [18] Qtd. in Ricken, *Linguistics, Anthropology and Philosophy*, 198.
[19] The language is that of Jules Michelet; see Roger, "The French Revolution as Logomachy," 9–12.
[20] My reference is to Austin, *How to Do Things with Words*. On the revolutionary relationship among signs, sounds, and signifieds, see Rosenfeld, *A Revolution in Language*, 123–80. For German and English perspectives on revolutionary and romantic speech acts, see Esterhammer, *The Romantic Performative*.

Nowhere was this clearer than in the work of Louis-Sébastien Mercier, who, having numbered among the original members of Domergue's Société, continued to produce lexicographical writings through the 1790s and early 1800s, extending what he perceived to be the "pure" linguistic goals of the republic. The most important of his efforts was the *Néologie*, a dictionary-manifesto combining elements of theosophical mysticism with those of linguistic sensualism and lexical activism.[21] Mercier's tone is militant, as are the goals of his dictionary: "I march with a phalanx of three thousand words, infantry, heavy and light cavalry; and if there are many wounded and dead in the combat, so be it! I have another army in reserve, and I march a second time." His enemy is the *langue monarchique* or *sorbonique* of the academicians and neoclassicists, as well as the linguistic rigidity and false taste it imposes. In its place he offers an idiom born of "free fantasy" (*la libre fantaisie*) and "the inspiration of the moment" (*l'inspiration du moment*), an ever-changing language infused not just with the vitality that Domergue had touted, but with inventive spontaneity.[22] Mercier resisted all forms of fixation, including the burgeoning impulse even among republican lexicographers toward institutionalization, insisting on the tenets of linguistic growth, democratization, and naturalism.

The organicist rhetoric that had long been a part of revolutionary lexicography is amplified in Mercier's dictionary; his words are cuttings (*boutures*) from the trees of the French-language forest, which will go on to produce new trunks. He describes an idiom that grows like plants or swells like a river: "Language is like a river that nothing stops, that grows along its way, that becomes larger and more majestic in the same measure as it grows distant from its source."[23] This language, inspired by the sounds of creation itself, might be sonorous in some instances, noisy, convulsive, bizarre, or even tormented in others, depending on the subject under description and the expressive needs of the moment. Mercier described it as the "resounding

---

[21] The philosophical and cognitive orientation of Mercier's linguistic approach is not easy to summarize; suffice it to say that he both extended and broke with the tenets of the first revolutionary linguists. He continued to regard language as a key vehicle for change, but objected to the efforts of some republican grammarians to institutionalize their new "liberated" grammars. He also turned away from purely sensualist/secular linguistic models (those emanating from Locke and Condillac), situating words as sounds inspired by the strains of natural divinity (a neo-Cratylist position). For more on Mercier's (sometimes muddled) philosophy of language, see Rosenberg, "Louis-Sébastien Mercier's New Words."

[22] "Je marche avec une phalange de trois mille mots, infanterie, cavalerie, hussards; et s'il y a beaucoup de morts et de blessés dans le combat, eh bien! j'ai une autre armée en réserve, je marche une seconde fois." Mercier, *Néologie*, xxiii–iv, n. 1, and xxxviii.

[23] "Il en est d'une langue comme d'un fleuve que rien n'arrête, qui s'accroît dans son cours, et qui devient plus large et plus majestueux, à mesure qu'il s'éloigne de sa source." *Néologie*, vii, translation adapted from that of Rosenberg in "Louis-Sébastien Mercier's New Words," 376.

voice of the universe" (*la voix éclatante de l'univers*), a collection of words that "causes an unknown string within you to vibrate" (*fait vibrer chez vous la fibre inconnue*).[24] His language embraced both new and foreign terms, those created by accident or in the heat of the moment, even those encountered in states of dream or reverie. These, he argued, were lexical gifts imbued with magic, poised to materialize the expansive and illuminated spaces from which they emanated.

And it was not new words alone that Mercier's dictionary championed, but, more importantly, a radically loosened syntax and grammar. His *Néologie* was to be the foundation for a second work, a *Traité sur les inversions*, which would represent his crowning achievement. Its goal was the emancipation of language from a collection of repressive syntactical regulations that he described in detail:

> We bring words together, we chain them one to the other, but we never group them; we do not construct them, we accumulate them; it is not given to us to arrange them such that they provide mutual strength and support; circular and oblique movement are also forbidden us, we traverse only the straight line. In the end we can only choose the words; in all other respects, their organization is almost always immovably fixed. Either our grammarians have not understood the advantages of inversion, or they fear to reveal them. It is inversion that allowed the ancients to vary in near-infinite ways the forms of their language.[25]

Syntactical variation – freely formed, circular, even serpentine sentences, each with its own cadence – were to be at the center of Mercier's republican idiom, which would abandon the static forms, the *pas symétrisé*, of neoclassical poetry in favor of a naturalized prose: "The prose writers are our true poets; if they have but courage, language takes on entirely new accents. Words and syllables themselves, might they not be put together such that they produce the most unexpected effect?"[26] It was just such expressive effects, Mercier insisted, and the neological and grammatical innovations that produced them, that characterized the work of the truly revolutionary

---

[24] Mercier, *Néologie*, lxxii, n. 1, and xi.

[25] "Nous rapprochons les mots, nous les enchaînons les uns aux autres, mais nous ne les groupons jamais; nous ne les construisons pas, nous les accumulons; nous ne saurions les disposer de manière à se prêter mutuellement de la force et de l'appui; les mouvemens circulaires et les mouvemens obliques nous sont également défendus, nous ne pouvons parcourir que la ligne droite; enfin nous n'avons que le choix des mots; du reste leur place est presque toujours invariablement fixée. Ou nos grammairiens n'ont pas assez senti les avantages de l'inversion, ou ils ont craint de les exposer. C'est l'inversion qui conduisit les anciens à varier presqu'à l'infini les formes de leur langage." Ibid., xli–xlii.

[26] "Les prosateurs sont nos vrais poètes; qu'ils osent, et la langue prendra des accens tout nouveaux: les mots, les syllabes mêmes ne peuvent-ils pas se placer de manière que leur concours produise l'effet le plus inattendu?" Ibid., xliv–xlv.

artist, who was first and foremost a neologian. His idiom was at once a political tool, the primary weapon in the republican arsenal, and "the true organ of the interior man" (*le véritable organe de l'homme intérieur*), a language born of imagination, innovation, and the vital magic of creation itself. If spoken, it would materialize the inner world of the poet as well as the free republic to which he belonged.[27]

Mercier never published his *Traité sur les inversions*, nor did his *Néologie* have a long career. As Napoleon rose to power at the turn of the century, neological activity was repressed and anti-revolutionary voices (those touting the ideas of Jean-François La Harpe, Antoine de Rivarol, and Maine de Biran among others) grew louder. Liberated language, as they argued, was an anti-language, a form of lexical monstrosity at the root of political unreality and unrest.[28] The emerging imperial government, well aware of the potential threat of words, began to take up these ideas, banning first the *Néologie* and then Mercier's more radical project, *Mon Dictionnaire*. This trend deepened with the dawn of the Restoration, which saw a ban on all neological and syntactical innovations. Official dictionaries, first and foremost those of the reinvigorated Académie française, were established as conservators of the French language, meant to protect it from the political disease and violence of revolutionary lexicography. They were linked to the recovery of order, nobility, and godly society, most notably in the writings of the Restoration's primary political architect, Louis Gabriel Ambroise de Bonald.

Bonald, like his eighteenth-century predecessors, placed language at the center of his political program, identifying it as the source from which political recovery was to emanate. From his early essay "De la langue de la politique" (1807) through the weightier publications of the 1810s and 1820s, he argued that the Jacobins (and then the Idéologues) had invented a jargonized idiom and a "barbaric sentence structure," which had infected not only scholarly writing, but journalism, creative production, and daily life. Taking up La Harpe's and Joseph de Maistre's tune, he pointed to sensationalist philosophy as the root of revolutionary error – a philosophy that had made language human, malleable, secular. Refuting its tenets, Bonald contended that something as sophisticated as language could hardly have been produced piecemeal, via physical processes of sense-acquisition,

---

[27] Ibid., lii.
[28] A crystallization of La Harpe's anti-revolutionary linguistic philosophy is to be found in his "Du Fanatisme dans la langue révolutionnaire" (1797). For helpful readings of this text, see Roger, "The French Revolution as Logomachy"; and Rosenfeld, *A Revolution in Language*, chap. 4 (123–80). The positions of Rivarol and Maine de Biran are outlined in Ricken, *Linguistics, Anthropology and Philosophy*, chap. 14 (191–225).

nor could it simply be invented in response to the sonorous experience of the natural world. Instead it was divine, innate, and therefore immutable. Truly "natural" language, according to Bonald, was not a medium in flux, subject to growth and decay, but invariable, established by God at the beginning of all things. To alter, invert, or fantasize it was to commit a blasphemy – to produce the *législations absurdes* of the revolutionary government and, taken to extremes, the violence of the Terror.[29] Central to his agenda was a reclaiming of the idea of naturalism, a crucially ambiguous term, bent this way and that, as historians of language have long recognized, to legitimize the dominant linguistic mode. Bonald not only reassigned it to the rationalist grammatical paradigm, but extended his regressive linguistic philosophy into a social grammar or "science of society." He equated the triadic organization power-minister-subject (the political hierarchy of the *ancien régime*) with the linguistic formula subject-verb-object. "Restored" order rested on moral order, itself inscribed in a "noble" grammar: the old fixed word order.[30]

Bonald's conservative linguistics were enforced by a wave of approved dictionaries and language treatises whose purpose was, in large part, to correct and ultimately eradicate revolutionary syntax.[31] The most influential of these was Pierre Girault-Duvivier's *Grammaire des grammaires*, which appeared in 1811 and was reedited systematically until 1886. Viewed by many as the ultimate authority in matters of language, it was sanctioned by the Institute and absorbed into school curricula. Positioning itself as a purveyor of both "universal grammar" and "universal truth," it promised to restore the French language to a prerevolutionary state, to purge it of "vicious inversions" and (re-)fix it at its highest point of achievement, as in the works of Bousset, Fénelon, Pascal, and Racine.[32] At its heart lay an elaborate set of regulations governing the proper naming, placement, and use of every part of speech from vowels and

---

[29] This argument emerges in several places in Bonald's writing, including his "Législation primitive" (here, at 1056). For an overview of Bonald's social and linguistic philosophy, see Klinck, *The French Counterrevolutionary Theorist Louis de Bonald*; and Reedy, "Language, Counter-Revolution and the 'Two Cultures.'"

[30] Explored in Klinck, *The French Counterrevolutionary Theorist Louis de Bonald*, chap. 4 (115–36).

[31] Saint-Gérand, in *Les Grammaires françaises 1800–1914*, notes the publication of some 125 dictionaries and 291 grammars between 1800 and 1823. Among these were P.C.V. Boiste's *Dictionnaire universelle de la langue française*, which went through fourteen editions before 1857, M. Noel and M. Chapsal's *Nouvelle grammaire*, which went through eighty editions, and the *Grammarie nationale* of the Bescherelle brothers, billed as "le code de la langue française," which was reissued fifteen times between 1834 and mid-century. Self-help or corrective books also abounded, many promising to counteract the language abuses, onomatopoeias, and "popularisms" generated by the revolution, others focused on eradicating unsavory, foreign, or neological vocabulary (*phrases vicieuses, cacologie,* and *cacographie*).

[32] Girault-Duvivier, *Grammaire des grammaires*, 1:iv, viii.

consonants to articles, pronouns, prepositions, verbs, punctuation, and finally, "members," phrases, and periods. Words were to be considered as sounds, according to Girault-Duvivier, which the author must bring together in clear, balanced units according to the regulations of grammar, such that the result was "la pureté, la netteté, la propriété," and later "la grâce, l'élégance, la noblesse ... la beauté ... la moralité."[33]

Proper syntax was not just a matter of semiotics, but of sonorous control, an audible imprint of "restored" morality and healthy social hierarchy. Essential was the avoidance of grammatical pitfalls that might generate obscurity or foster insurrection: *le barbarisme* (using a word not adopted by the Academy or changing the meaning or spelling of a word); *le solécisme* (using a word outside the fixed regulations of syntax); *la disconvenance grammaticale* (bringing together the "diverse members of a phrase or a period" in a manner generating grammatical discordance); *la phrase équivoque* or *la phrase amphibologique* (joining together words in a false or badly ordered manner such that they fail to demonstrate "the connection of ideas"). Committing these errors did violence to the *ordre naturel*, producing chaotic forms: "ambiguous turns, phrases which are too long, overloading the main idea with incidental or accessory ideas," winding ("errant") sentences, and imbalanced periods.[34] The "order" Girault-Duvivier has in mind is clearly a poetic (rather than prosodic) one. His grammatical regulations are followed by a series of literary excerpts from the French neoclassical dramatists, whose verses are dissected line by line, every word shown to be in its place, every phrase balanced, controlled, tasteful, and shapely.

In essence, what the *Grammaire des grammaires* prescribes is a reversal (suppression, negation) of the linguistic philosophy Mercier and his revolutionary predecessors expounded. Its grammar was enforced via a series of increasingly repressive censorship laws engineered in large part by Bonald, which restricted the content and dissemination of French journals and the expressive compass of artists themselves. Eventually, as is well known, there was a backlash: Stendhal's essay *Racine et Shakespeare* (1823) rejected grammatical restrictions in favor of the free-wheeling verse and fantastic plot elements of the English playwright; Alexandre Dumas's historical play *Henri III et sa cour* (1829) eschewed verse entirely, cast as a prose drama; Nodier and Balzac, through the 1820s and onward, launched a vigorous

---

[33] Ibid., 2:1147.
[34] "les tours ambigus, les phrases trop longues, trop chargées d'idées incidentes et accessoires à l'idée principale, les tours épigrammatiques, dont la multitude ne peut sentir la finesse." Ibid., 2:1140. See, more broadly, chap. 13, "Des Qualités qui contribuent à la perfection du langage" (1134–46) and chap. 14, "De la phrase, de la période, des membres qui entrent dans la composition d'une phrase, et de la manière de l'analyser" (1149–60).

campaign in defense of neologism, onomatopoeia, and lexical-sonorous invention; and of course Hugo produced the new prosodic verse of *Hernani* and *Cromwell*.[35] This brings us full circle, although now Hugo's "natural," "fluid," and "liberated" prose begins to seem less like a romantic innovation and more like a revolutionary reinvigoration – as Ulrich Ricken puts it, with Hugo "the primary concern of the Enlightenment was once again restated as that of recognizing the development of language as the condition for the progress of thought itself."[36] What Hugo was doing in the Preface to *Cromwell* was not just calling for an aesthetic shift, but taking a military stand, marshaling Mercier's lexical troops, reactivating the ideas of linguistic liberty and incantatory fantasy at the heart of the *Néologie*. Romanticism as much as the revolution was, to borrow Steven Blakemore's term, a "linguistic event."[37]

And this was as true in the musical as in the literary domain. Although the grammatical repression of the Restoration originated in the writerly sphere, it soon spread to other arenas, especially that of composition (not surprising, given the perceived intersections among sound, language, and power). A wave of musical grammars appeared at precisely the same time as the texts by Girault-Duvivier and his contemporaries, laying down laws of melodic purity, formal coherence, and rhythmic intelligibility. Resonating with (indeed in many cases responding directly to) their literary counterparts, they show us the kind of sounding grammar Berlioz inherited: that of the Restoration. His syntactical experiments were modeled not just on Hugo, but in opposition to these repressive texts, which drew music squarely into the ongoing political and philosophical battles over syntax.

Musical Grammar

French musical grammars, though hardly new to the early nineteenth century, enjoyed an explosion of popularity through the 1810s, becoming increasingly prevalent and prescriptive through the 1820s and 1830s. Organized along the same lines as their literary counterparts, they were meant to achieve similar ends: to reign in the chaotic, quasi-cabbalistic

---

[35] See Nodier, *Dictionnaire raisonné des onomatopées françoises*; and, on Balzac and neologism, see Tilby, "New Words or Old?"; and idem, "Neologism."

[36] Ricken, *Linguistics, Anthropology, and Philosophy*, 206. Links between Hugo's project and that of the revolutionary linguists have been made as far back as Patterson, in "New Light on Dark Genius."

[37] Blakemore, *Burke and the Fall of Language*, 1.

soundworld of revolution, to protect the newly restored but still precarious health of what Ingrid J. Sykes terms the "auditory body politic."[38] The torrent of words that had rained down during the 1780s and 1790s – what royalists rejected as linguistic "noise" – was also a torrent of sound: massed festivals, patriotic slogan-chanting, deafening public concerts, and the widespread cacophony of urban revolt. This sonorous power was contained and ordered through the early nineteenth century by the same grammatical forces that suppressed lexical innovation. Just as Girault-Duvivier had counseled that words were to be understood as sounds, musical grammars likened sounds to words, which were to be organized according to the regulations of syntax, kept in obeisance to reason, universal law, beauty, grace, and (Conservatory-sponsored) taste. To depart from these regulations was to descend into incoherence and impropriety, to wander outside the carefully policed "official" domain of music itself.

Many early- and mid-century musical grammars looked back to Anton (Antoine) Reicha's *Traité de mélodie* (1814), a work published in the year of Louis XVIII's installation, which situated itself as the first-ever treatise on melody (as opposed to harmony). Purporting to provide a newly "reasoned" model for melodic construction and analysis, it was embraced by the Paris Conservatory, emerging as a mainstay of institutional musical pedagogy.[39] In it, Reicha is concerned first and foremost with the correct formulation of the musical line, marginalizing all other elements of musical composition, including harmony and instrumentation. His mono-focus was characterized by certain later critics as inscrutable or problematic, and yet it was hardly surprising given the climate of the time. At the dawn of the Restoration, what could have seemed more important (or politically timely) than cementing a musical grammar? That this is Reicha's aim is made clear in the opening paragraph of the introduction, which claims that his treatise will lay out a "melodic syntax" (*la syntaxe mélodique*), demonstrating how sounds, like words (*comme le Discours*) are to be properly connected. The idea is clarified and repeated at regular intervals throughout the following chapters: "Melody is only a succession of tones. But if these tones were arranged by chance, they would not make sense, that is, they would

---

[38] Sykes, "Le corps sonore." Sykes does not mention grammar in her piece, but the sonorous control I describe here resonates easily with her argument around post-revolutionary anxiety, musical health, and political listening.

[39] Reicha was not, of course, French, but had moved to Paris in 1808, during precisely the period in which the grammatical activities of the Restoration were gathering speed.

not make a melody. The same would happen if words were not connected by syntax and rationally directed."[40]

The linguistic model from which Reicha is working is clearly that of neoclassical poetry; indeed, he directs his treatise *both* to composers and to "lyric poets" working in the style "of Metastasio and Quinault" (later, he mentions Voltaire and Racine). The same "law of rhythm" (*lois du rythme*) pertains both to the construction of noble verse and that of beautiful melody, and it is this rhythmic grammar that stands at the center of Reicha's method.[41] He builds up to it slowly, first introducing the fundamentals of musical syntax – notes, clefs, scales, strategies for modulation – then showing how they are used to construct musical ideas and phrases. Melodic "feet" (which he compares to poetic feet) are organized into regular phrases or "members" that are joined via musical "punctuation" (cadences) into balanced groups of antecedents and consequents. These units, when linked together, form musical "periods." From the smallest to the largest elements of construction, Reicha's process of melodic building is governed by the principle of symmetry, which is synonymous with the all-important "law of rhythm": "A good melody thus requires, 1) that it be divisible into equal and similar members; 2) that these members contain resting points of greater or lesser strength, these being found at equal intervals, that is, symmetrically placed." Without symmetrical members, the period cannot function, and without the balanced period, "it is impossible for a good melody to be created."[42]

The grammar of symmetry is immutable for Reicha. He, like Bonald, defends its fixity by making it *a priori*, giving it the status of natural law: "Nature has etched each one (measure and rhythm) firmly in our minds, which seem not to recognize what is beautiful in music (particularly in melody) unless both elements are perfectly apprehended." And later,

---

[40] "La Mélodie n'est autre chose qu'une suite de sons; mais si ces sons étaient placés au hasard, ils ne formeraient point de sens, c'est-à-dire point de Mélodie; il en est de même des mots qui ne seraient point liés par la syntaxe et dirigés par l'esprit." Reicha, *Traité de mélodie*, 2 and 76–77. This and subsequent translations of Reicha are adapted from those of Landey in *Treatise on Melody*.

[41] Reicha, *Traité de mélodie*, 3. It is worth noting that Reicha's approach to harmony and counterpoint was considerably more adventurous than his attitude toward melody. I highlight a conservative strand of his aesthetic here, but at the Conservatoire, he numbered among the more forward-thinking pedagogues.

[42] "Une bonne Mélodie exige par conséquent, 1. qu'elle soit divisée en membres égaux et semblables; que ces membres fassent des repos plus ou moins forts, lesquels repos se trouvent à des distances égales, c'est-à-dire symétriquement placés." Without these features, "il est impossible qu'une bonne Mélodie puisse avoir lieu." Ibid., 10, 12. Reicha's privileging of symmetry, though heavily emphasized in the *Traité*, is not entirely new; for a discussion of its role in eighteenth-century music theory, see Christensen, ed., *The Cambridge History of Western Music Theory*, esp. chaps. 20, 21, and 27; also Dill, "The Influence of Linguistics on Rameau's Theory of Modulation"; and idem, "Le Cerf, Language, and Music: Toward an Epistemology of Music in Early Modern France," unpublished manuscript.

"Nature dictates the principles." Without these principles – those of a fixed rhythmic order – music loses structural integrity: "Symmetry and balance are tangible things; without them, architecture would only be a mass of stones."[43] The collapse of grammatical logic is synonymous, according to Reicha, with a descent into chaos: "oddity, nonsense, foolishness, or absolute worthlessness" (*la bizarrerie, l'extravagance, la folie, ou une nullité absolue*). More importantly, it means that musical language lacks the two most crucial elements of good grammar: clarity and purity. In a passage eerily reminiscent of Girault-Duvivier, Reicha defends these qualities, arguing that "it is not only purity but particularly clarity, which must be recommended and prescribed for students. What is not clear in music (as in poetry and oratory) is badly conceived and badly written."[44]

Reicha's melodic syntax was taken up in a series of equally unyielding musical handbooks published over the following decades, which, capitalizing on the wave of anxiety surrounding grammatical order, promised to reveal to amateurs and aspiring composers alike the principles of correct musical usage. Among these was Mlle Lesne's *Grammaire musicale, basée sur les principes de la grammaire française* (late 1810s), which made the connection between musical and spoken syntax literal.[45] Adopting the layout and pedagogical approach of a school grammar primer, Lesne (a "professeur d'harmonie, de chant, et de piano") mapped the parts of speech directly onto elements of musical construction. Nouns, in her system, were likened to basic note-types (whole, half, quarter, etc.), articles to musical clefs, adjectives to accidentals, pronouns to rests, verbs to time signatures (controllers of "l'action"), gender to major/minor modes, punctuation to elements of musical rhythm, and so forth. Lesne's point of reference is clearly Girault-Duvivier's *Grammaire des grammaires*, which she cites in several places. Her opening line ("La Grammaire est l'Art de parler correctement, et au moyen de règles prescrites, d'exprimer ses pensées avec élégance et clarté") is an echo both of Girault-Duvivier's first sentence ("La Grammaire est l'art de parler et d'écrire correctement") and his guiding

---

[43] "La nature a gravé l'un et l'autre (la mesure et le rhythme) d'une manière imperturbable dans notre sentiment, et elle paraît n'adopter ce qui est beau en Musique (particulièrement dans la Mélodie), que lorsque ces deux conditions sont absolument observées." Ibid., 11, n. 2. "La nature prescrit les principes" (33–34). "La symétrie et les belles proportions sont quelque chose de positif; sans elles, l'architecture ne serait qu'un amas de pierres" (122, n. 1).

[44] "Ce n'est pas seulement la *pureté*, mais en même temps et spécialement la *clarté* qu'on doit recommander et prescrire aux élèves. Ce qui n'est pas clair en Musique (comme en Poésie et en Eloquence) est mal conçu et mal écrit." Ibid., 13, n. 1.

[45] This text was widely noted and reviewed, continuing to appear in lists of recommended musical handbooks through the last third of the century. See, for instance, the write-up in Escudier, *Dictionnaire de musique théorique et historique*, 5th edition (Paris: Dentu, 1872).

principles of taste, purity, and clarity. These terms and the conservative aesthetic they represent are underscored repeatedly, as is the link between proper spoken grammar and correct musical usage: "those who study according to this new method, are in a position to understand with purity the principles of musical grammar, based on those of French grammar."[46]

In speaking or playing aloud the series of fifteen exercises provided by Lesne, the student not only masters the lesson, but renders audible – conjures into being – the sound of an orderly grammatical world. And grammar is only the beginning. As her text draws to a close, Lesne promises several more advanced manuals, one of which will draw on neoclassical poetics to demonstrate how the parts of musical "speech" are to be correctly conjoined (for her, as for Reicha, prerevolutionary French drama is the model for legible musical construction). Beginning with "la syntaxe," she promises to end with a full musical guide to "versification française." Such a guide is necessary since, as Lesne argues, "to know a language, it is not sufficient simply to know the words that constitute it; it takes much tracing and writing to become familiar with its phrases and its periods," and to learn to link them "with grace and purity."[47]

Lesne's promised guide to musical versification never appeared, but her approach was carried through a series of later musical grammars, including that of the guitarist and composer P. L. Aubéry du Boulley, whose *Grammaire musicale ou Méthode analytique et raisonnée pour apprendre et enseigner la lecture de la musique* appeared in 1830. Here again, we encounter a correlation between words and sounds, and between phrases and musical sentences, which are to be organized according to what Aubéry du Boulley calls "a true grammar" (*une véritable grammaire*).[48] Echoing what had, by 1830, become received wisdom, he claims that music is the stuff of inspiration, emanating directly from the heart. But flashes of composerly genius must be organized according to the laws of taste and the regulations of syntax, thus ensuring clarity, beauty, and reason (a now-familiar collection of adjectives). These are taught in the opening section via a series of Socratic questions and answers meant, as with Lesne's grammar, to be spoken aloud. The second part gives examples of correct harmony and melody abounding with Reicha-like

---

[46] "les personnes qui apprennent avec cette nouvelle méthode, sont à même de connaître avec pureté les principes de la grammaire musicale, basés sur ceux de la grammaire française." Lesne, *Grammaire musicale*, 56.

[47] "On sait qu'il ne suffit pas seulement de connaître les mots qui composent une Langue pour la savoir, mais qu'il faut encore beaucoup lire et écrire pour se familiariser avec ses phrases et ses periods ... [et] que l'on pourra réussir à enchaîner avec grâce et pureté les phrases musicales." Ibid., 64.

[48] Aubéry du Boulley, *Grammaire Musicale*, 2.

symmetry. And the final section, echoing a host of contemporary literary grammars, is corrective, composed of "observations surrounding errors, prejudices, and false opinions regarding music" (*observations sur les erreurs, préjugés et fausses opinions concernant la musique*), which promise to purge the student of dangerous, newfangled, or gauche ideas and usages.

Aubéry du Boulley's notion of music (especially melody) as the product of inspiration subjected to grammatical regulation is prefigured in Adolphe Le Dhuy's *Grammaire musicale* (1829) and echoed in François Fétis's *La Musique mise à la portée de tout le monde* (1830). Le Dhuy's text promises to situate musical principles according to "un ordre rationnel" (again, a nod to the old rationalist linguistic paradigm) in a series of lessons working from the basics of note and clef names to the grammar of melodic construction. Reinscribing Reicha's notion of a poetic rhythmic order, he equates syntactical correctness with *symétrie parfaite*. Melody is defined, in Le Dhuy's "Vocabulaire de la langue musicale," as a pleasing and tasteful collection of pitches organized according to the laws of versification, which are synonymous with *les règles de l'art*.[49] A similar idea is found in Fétis's text, which introduces melody to aspiring students (and the general public) as "the fruit of imagination," which, though apparently free, is in fact submissive to the "rule of symmetry" without which musical meaning (*le sens mélodique*) cannot exist. Four-by-four (two-by-two or, less often, three-by-three) phraseology with regular antecedent-consequent (*commencement-complément*) pairs produces this symmetry, which Fétis refers to as *carrure*. For him, as for earlier musical grammarians, such syntax is innate and inviolable: "the musician conforms to the *carrure des phrases* as the poet to the measure of the verse, naturally and without thinking."[50]

The production of musical grammars continued unabated through the following years, becoming increasingly reiterative and strident. Georges Kastner, now known primarily for his treatise on orchestration, published a *Grammaire musicale* in 1837 ratified by (among others) Cherubini, Auber, Lesueur, and Berton, approved by the Academy, and adopted by the Conservatory. In his introduction, Kastner is still hailing Reicha as the ultimate arbiter of musical syntax, defending the law of rhythm as indispensable to order and meaning, and syntactical symmetry as fundamental. His grammar is a stripped-down version of Reicha's principles, which, so he claims, will prevent students from falling into "the gross errors of rhythm which are so common these days."[51] A similar tone prevails in the

---

[49] Le Dhuy [Ledhuy], *Nouveau manuel simplifié de musique*, 54, 58.
[50] "Le musicien se conforme à la carrure des phrases comme le poète à la mesure des vers, naturellement et sans y penser." Fétis, "De la mélodie," 64.
[51] "ces grossières fautes de rythme qui sont assez communes de nos jours." Kastner, *Grammaire musicale*, 4.

Grammaire musicale published the following year by B. Wilhem (director-inspector general of vocal pedagogy in Parisian schools), whose system of musical instruction unfolds in three stages, based on "reading, grammar, and rhetoric."[52] He too points back at Reicha (Lesne, Fétis, etc.), arguing that meaning, order, and the articulation of "noble and beautiful thoughts" in music are reliant on a thorough knowledge of literary grammar. Unsurprisingly, his text is centrally concerned with "the study of melodic and rhythmic forms" (*l'étude des formes mélodiques et rythmiques*), which are to be modeled after the "pure" forms of poetry, leading to properly organized phrases and, ultimately, their contrapuntal intertwining in "the classical forms of fugue, canon, etc."[53] By this point, Wilhelm could claim to be drawing together the best of an array of musical grammars (his was a kind of grammar of grammars, like Girault-Duvivier's), a musico-linguistic edifice that had become inextricable from institutional authority, political order, and official French standards of taste and reason.

Berlioz, Morphology, Monstrosity

It was at the height of this grammatical furor – literary and musical – that Berlioz came of age, and in opposition to the heavily policed soundworld protected by the likes of Lesne and Wilhelm that he constructed his own aesthetic. Indeed, Kastner's reference to the "errors of rhythm" committed by a young generation of composers was surely aimed in part at Berlioz who, from his earliest years as a critic and composer, had been engaged in an offensive against the laws of symmetry and rhythm, rejecting syntactical formulas of all kinds and, by extension, the politics they enforced. As I noted at the start of this chapter, his first serious aesthetic essay, the "Aperçu sur la musique classique et la musique romantique," already referenced Hugo directly, mapping the liberty of the new "romantic" musical school onto the formal and grammatical freedoms championed by the author of *Hernani* and the *Odes et ballades*. Berlioz's essay is itself conceived as a refutation of standard musical grammars, opening with a series of musical definitions: sound, tone, melody, rhythm, harmony, etc. The tactic seems odd in an essay on aesthetics until one realizes that Berlioz is echoing the format of

---

[52] Wilhelm's text was advertised and outlined in *La France littéraire* 2/7 (1838) under the title "Programme générale, Etudes musicales establissant trois degrés d'instruction qui se rapportent à la lecture, à la grammaire et à la rhétorique dans l'étude des langues." The quotations just cited are taken from this source.

[53] "C'est *la rhétorique musicale* qui, outre les applications de la science harmonique aux études du contrepoint et aux formes classiques de la fugue, du canon, etc. comprend la composition proprement dite et *la poétique musicale*." Wilhelm, given in *La France littéraire* 2/7 (1838).

popular musical primers – in order to rewrite them. Among his clearest targets is Fétis's *La musique mise à la portée de tout le monde*, whose first line he references directly and whose central claim – that composition has a fixed grammar masterable by *tout le monde* – is anathema to his sensibility. Music cannot be defined via a collection of *règles scolastiques*, Berlioz argues, and is therefore unteachable in the manner that Fétis suggests. Instead, it draws its laws from "natural" inspiration and from nature itself (now in Mercier's sense rather than Bonald's), which provides the only true grammar of the new, romantic age.[54]

The old poetic symmetries Fétis insisted on are to be replaced by the relaxed, freely evolving verse forms championed by Hugo – circuitous, asymmetrical, dynamic – the forms of revolution or, as Mercier put it, of the "true republican tongue." Berlioz sees a musical harbinger of these shapes in the works of Gluck, a composer who flaunted the rules when they ran contrary to his inspiration, embracing a kind of avant-garde syntactical freedom: "a great number of new rhythms" (*un grand nombre de rythmes nouveaux*). Indeed, what makes Gluck a proto-romantic composer is not the harmonic content of his work, which Berlioz dismisses as unremarkable, but its *melodic* flexibility and metrical experimentation, features that generate "a true, profound, and energetic language" (*un langage vrai, profond et énergique*).[55] In later writing, Berlioz expands on this idea, citing examples from both *Iphigénie en Tauride* and *Alceste*. From the former opera, he singles out Oreste's aria "Le calme rentre dans mon coeur," which shifts between two- and three-bar phrases, underpinned by "a rhythm mixing syncopated and detached notes" that "had never been heard before," and from the latter, Alceste's piece "Ove fuggo, ove m'ascondo," which eschews both the formal phraseology (*phrase formulée*) of the aria and the purely declamatory style of recitative, hovering in the expressively free middle ground of *chant récitatif*. In these places and elsewhere, part of what makes Gluck's orchestra speak so compellingly, what lends it imaginative vigor, is its quasi-Hugolian prosody.[56]

But it is not just Hugo's relaxed syntax (nor its musical prefiguring in Gluck) that provides a model for Berlioz. Equally clearly, he connects his rejection of "official" French melodic language to an embrace of foreign, allegedly more primitive grammars, especially German. Teutonic music, he

---

[54] *Le Correspondant* (6 October 1829), in *CM*, 1:63–68. [55] Ibid., in *CM*, 1:66–67.
[56] For Berlioz's remarks on *Iphigénie en Tauride*, see his four-part essay in the *Gazette musicale* (9, 16, 23 November and 7 December 1834) in *CM*, 1:441–50; 455–58; 469–72. He deals with *Alceste*'s rhythmic innovations in a two-part Gluck biography published in the same journal earlier that year (1 and 8 June 1834), as well as in a piece for the *Journal des débats* (20 February 1835); see *CM*, 1:245–52; 257–68 and *CM* 2:67–72.

argues, is more rich and alive than its French counterpart in large part because it embraces more varied phraseology. He first broaches this idea in the 1830 "Aperçu," where he holds up Beethoven and Weber as key models for the romantic melodist. Emancipated from both the limitations of the human voice and the regulations of rationalist grammar, these composers "can produce the most original, even bizarre, phrases," and, in so doing, generate "extraordinary effects, strange sensations, ineffable emotions," the stuff of sublime expression and even "a new world."[57] The idea carries forward through Berlioz's writings of the later 1830s, becoming increasingly central to his conception of romantic (and, as we shall see presently, fantastic) musical semiotics.

The essays on Beethoven's symphonies (1837–38), as Berlioz scholars have long noted, come back persistently to issues of melodic-rhythmic construction, highlighting extended or truncated phrases, moments of metrical dissonance, and breaks in rhythmic symmetry as central to the composer's expressive power and vision.[58] The scherzo of the Fourth Symphony, for instance, "consists almost entirely of duple-time phrases forced to operate in triple-time meter," a discordance resulting in a sense of nervous energy and a suspended metrical logic, which, when reinstated, is all the more satisfying. Describing the passage, Berlioz draws on a constellation of grammatical rhetoric:

This strategy, which Beethoven employed frequently, lends much energy to his style. Melodic inflections (*désinences mélodiques*) become, as a result, more pungent, more unexpected; moreover, these warring rhythms have in themselves a very real charm, though it is difficult to explain. One feels pleasure in seeing the measure, disrupted in this way, return intact at the end of each period, and the meaning (*le sens*) of the musical discourse, for a time suspended, arrive at a satisfactory conclusion, a complete close.[59]

The same temporary metrical dissonance is found in the trio of the Seventh Symphony, producing an "astonishing" effect. And in the Eighth Symphony, Berlioz highlights another moment in which symmetry is disrupted for the purposes of expressive evocation: here, in the Allegretto scherzando, "the principal phrase is composed of two members each of three measures, whose symmetrical organization (*disposition symétrique*) is

---

[57] *Le Correspondant* (6 October 1829), in *CM*, 1:67–68.
[58] For commentaries on Berlioz's rhythmic critique of Beethoven, see (as starting places), Cairns, *Berlioz*, 1:262–69; Comini, *The Changing Image of Beethoven*, 315–87; Ellis, *Music Criticism in Nineteenth-Century France*, 101–26; Holoman, *Berlioz*, 93–95; and Schrade, *Beethoven in France*, 39–110.
[59] "Symphonies de Beethoven, premier concert du Conservatoire," *Revue et gazette musicale* (28 January 1838), in *CM*, 3:373–82 (here, 377).

disrupted by a [measure of] silence." The purpose of this asymmetry, according to Berlioz, is to delay and therefore render more striking the emergence of a "fresh melody," which follows immediately afterward. Symmetrical musical passages, he suggests, mean more clearly, or at least impact the emotions more readily, when they are juxtaposed with asymmetry: "One sees again, in this example, that the 'law of the carrure' may in some cases be broken with happy results."[60]

Even more striking is the second movement of the Seventh Symphony, whose fluid poetic syntax is at the heart of its impact: "Rhythm, a simple rhythm ... is again the principal cause of the incredible effect produced by the Andante. It consists only of a dactyl followed by a spondee, invoked repeatedly, sometimes in three parts, sometimes in only one, then in the whole ensemble." Against this inexorable rhythmic backdrop emerges a "melodious lamentation" (*mélodieuse plainte*) with the character of a "convulsive shudder" (*gémissement convulsif*): "irreconcilable rhythms collide painfully one against the other; these are the tears, the sobs, the supplications; it is the expression of pain without bounds, of devouring suffering."[61] Here, rhythmic complexity – the varying and even jettisoning of musico-poetic regularity – allows for an emotional immediacy and physiological effect unavailable in the rigid world of *carrure*.

This idea emerges as central not just to the Beethoven essays, but to Berlioz's wider critical writing of the 1830s, including two pieces on the music of Johannes Strauss, which serve as the vehicle for a contemplation of "the future of rhythm" ("l'avenir du rythme," as Berlioz puts it in the title of the second essay) and its volatile political and aesthetic status. Strauss's famous dances (as performed by his well-trained orchestra) contain rhythmic devices that, according to Berlioz, are simply unknown or unavailable to his French contemporaries, hampered as they are by "incredible prejudices" and "narrow and routine opinions." The majority of his peers still recognize only those "regularly rhymed melodies" (*mélodies régulièrement rythmées*) adhering to *carrure*, that is to say, formed of four or eight measures and finishing on a downbeat."[62] Other kinds of rhythmic organizations,

---

[60] "Symphonies de Beethoven, Quatrième article," *Revue et gazette musicale* (18 February 1838), in *CM*, 3:399–402.

[61] "Symphonies de Beethoven, Troisième article," *Revue et gazette musicale* (11 February 1838), in *CM*, 3:391–96 (here, 393). Though he refers to the "Andante," Berlioz is clearly describing the Allegretto.

[62] The remarks on "incroyable préjugés" and "opinions étroites et routinières" appear in the first of the Strauss essays, "Gymnase-musical: soirée de valses de [Johann] Strauss," *Revue et gazette musicale* (5 November 1837), in *CM*, 3:327–28. Berlioz expands these into more pointed complaints around *carrure* in the second piece, "Strauss: son orchestre, ses valses – De l'avenir du rythme," *Journal des débats* (10 November 1837), in *CM*, 3:329–36.

including the syntactical and metrical disruptions employed by Strauss, remained forbidden and in large part unplayable; indeed, "the cleverest of our virtuosos realize only with great difficulty the cross rhythms and syncopations that Strauss's musicians play with ease."[63] Not just a matter of narrow education, the problem was rooted, as Berlioz made clear, in a perceived link between rhythmic innovation and social disorder:

> I know many listeners among the French, and the Italians especially, accustomed as they are to rhythms that we will compare for their simplicity and their lack of variety to the unison and the octave in harmony, who see in these new forms only disorder and anarchy.[64]

The supposed dangers associated with rhythmic novelty produce fanatical resistance, a conservative school with self-appointed "protectors and priests" (*les défenseurs et les prêtres*). These figures, with their adherence to grammatical scholasticism, relegate composers and players to a state of "the most pitiable incapacity either to discover new rhythmic forms or to realize in performance those which Germany has sent us."[65] They are responsible for suppressing a raft of vital possible effects – those resulting not just from strategic asymmetries, but other forms of rhythmic nuance including the following:

> From accenting weak beats at the expense of strong; from the more or less rapid succession of alternating triple and duple groups; from the simultaneity of different meters whose lesser divisions are irreconcilable and which have no other point of contact than the first beat; from the occasional appearance of a melody in triple time introduced into a quadruple meter, and vice versa; or finally from the intermittent use of certain sounds independent of the principal melody and of the accompanimental rhythm, and separated from each other by expanding or contracting intervals in proportions which it is impossible to predict.[66]

The quashing of these devices was also, in Berlioz's account, a choking off of true musical poetry and therefore imaginative evocation. Coming back once again to examples from Gluck and Weber, he argues that Teutonic rhythmic flexibility is at the core of truthful and vibrant musical language. The truncated periods at the height of Gluck's *Orphée* ("J'ai perdu mon Eurydice") and Weber's *Der Freischütz* ("le grand monologue d'Agathe") follow "the impulsion of nature itself" (*l'impulsion de la nature même*) to communicate in raw terms the experiences of suffering and joy. Rather than

---

[63] "Gymnase-musical: soirée de valses de [Johann] Strauss," in *CM*, 3:328.
[64] "Strauss: son orchestre, ses valses," in *CM*, 3:334. Earlier in this piece, Berlioz notes that Strauss's rhythms were also received in France in terms of "le désordre et la barbarie" (331).
[65] Ibid., in *CM*, 3:333.
[66] Ibid., in *CM*, 3:333–34, trans. Rushton in *The Musical Language of Berlioz*, 128.

being imposed from without, they – and the collection of other rhythmic effects tied to Beethoven and Strauss – emerge from within, the stuff of a freely evolving syntax. And it was this that Berlioz claimed for the new generation of French composers, who were to "emancipate" rhythm, replacing French grammatical orthodoxy with German fluidity.[67]

In framing musical romanticism in these terms – as an embrace of Teutonic syntactical expressivity over French rigidity – Berlioz was responding to (and extending into the musical sphere) a strand of grammatical theory that had been in circulation since the eighteenth century. As Harold Mah demonstrates, connections between German syntax and notions of emotional immediacy date back to Condillac, whose sensualist psychology began to reverse entrenched ideas surrounding the innateness or fundamental humanness of French grammar (in particular its fixed word order: subject-verb-object), suggesting instead that German inverted constructions were closer to the original process of human language acquisition and therefore to "natural" perception. Objects, as he admitted in the *Essay on the Origin of Human Knowledge* (1746), would likely have been processed first by the awakening mind, rather than subjects or verbs; thus, French linear grammar was not the transparent, emotive vehicle linguists had long though it to be, but instead a syntax once-removed from visceral experience, a second-order mode. On the other hand, German, usually dismissed as barbaric and disorganized, was now cast as a language of direct emotional transference, an imprint of consciousness itself.[68]

Teutonic linguists from Herder onward began to use Condillac's evidence to demote French and promote German, casting the former language as artificial, rigid, and emotionally distant and the latter as spiritually alive, uniting originary sense perception with the faculties of reason, natural vitality with human creativity. From Mah: "Herder calls the consciousness that thinks without inversions, that thinks in French, mere 'Verstand' or abstract reasoning, which he says 'has nothing to do with the eye and ear.' The Germans, on the other hand, thinking and speaking in inversions, maintaining an unbroken relationship to direct experience, have earned for their language the title . . . of higher reason, of 'Vernunft.'" This idea was carried forward through the writing of the idealist philosophers, including Fichte and Hegel, both of whom equated French linear grammar with empty elegance and mere surface while situating the inverted, circuitous,

---

[67] Ibid., in *CM*, 3:333–34.
[68] Mah, "The Epistemology of the Sentence." See also Thomas, *Music and the Origins of Language*, 77–81, for more on Condillac's positioning of eighteenth-century French as a language of reason (a *langue des calculs*) rather than one of passion (a *langage d'action*).

even grotesque constructions of German as evidence of complexity and profundity. The Teutonic language was animated by the spark of nature itself and, so they claimed, that of "German freedom."[69]

This nexus of ideas began to bleed back into French linguistic theory around the time of the revolution, impacting Domergue's and especially Mercier's "republican" tongue, which embraced the inverted, serpentine sentence constructions associated with German. The language of emancipation, then, was modeled not just on new French words or relaxed neoclassical poetics, but on "free" Teutonic syntax. Later, the romantics, especially Hugo, made the same connection. The fluid French celebrated in the Preface to *Cromwell* was also, famously, a grotesque grammar, an idiom of organically evolving, "characteristic" forms, which, by 1827, had long since been associated not just with German linguistics, but also with romantic theories of imagination. Beginning with Justus Möser and Christoph Martin Wieland, writing in the 1760s and 1770s, grotesque shapes (among them, grammatical inversions) had been held up by German aesthetic theorists as necessary counterbalances to beautiful ones, forms capturing the evolution of the creative process and of variegated nature itself. Combining recognizable with unrecognizable shapes, symmetrical with asymmetrical, even legible with illegible, they jettisoned linear logic in favor of emancipated, sometimes monstrous metamorphoses. For Goethe, Friedrich Schlegel, and Jean Paul Richter (among others), such shapes became crucial emblems of romantic creativity – especially emerging notions of fantasy. The revolutionary creator, the fantasist, was an artist unmoored from the conventional (French) strictures of elegance and pleasantry, free to trace the digressive, semirational forms of the psyche, soul, or intuition (those of "higher reason").[70]

The link between unregulated grammar and modern fantasy was inherited and underscored by E. T. A. Hoffmann, whose *Fantasiestücke* (Part 1 of Kreisleriana) began with a paean to grotesque painter Jacques Callot, celebrating his bulbous, neological, often frightening figures. In a gloss on *The Temptation of St. Anthony* (the painting reproduced at the outset of his Fantasy Pieces), Hoffmann praised forms released from the strictures of "proper grouping" and "the rules of painting" – those in flux, shifting dynamically among animal, vegetable, and

---

[69] Mah, "The Epistemology of the Sentence, 74–77.

[70] Justus Möser, in *Harlekin oder Vertheidigung des Groteske-Komischen* (1761) and Christoph Martin Wieland in *Conversation between W** and the Parson of **** (1775) were among the first to frame the grotesque as a literary and more broadly aesthetic (proto-romantic) category. Their ideas were taken up and extended by, among others, Goethe, Denis Diderot, F. Schlegel, and Jean Paul Richter. See Harpham, *On the Grotesque*; and Kayser, *The Grotesque in Art and Literature*.

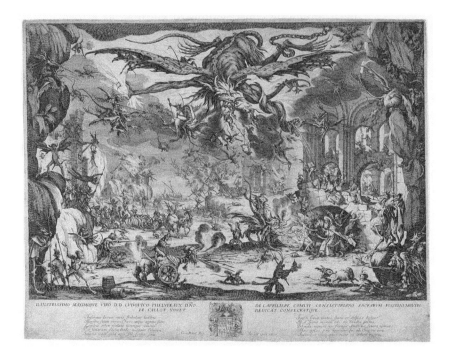

Figure 4.1 Jacques Callot, *The Temptation of St. Anthony*, 1635. Etching; third state of five (Lieure). Sheet: 36.1 cm × 47 cm. The Metropolitan Museum of Art, Bequest of Edwin De T. Bechtel, 1957. www.metmuseum.org

mineral, layered one on top of the other in complex and rich abundance (Figure 4.1). It was this grotesque grammar, infused with vital energy, according to Hoffmann, that allowed Callot to reach below the surface of things, to "reveal to the serious, deeper-seeing observer all the hidden meanings that lie beneath the cloak of absurdity."[71] Callot's visual grotesques furnished the models for his own fantastic literary pieces, which, echoing *The Temptation*, eschewed the linear and transparent in favor of the lopsided, embedded, and fragmented. A few years later, Hugo, in his Preface, made a similar argument, himself holding up Callot ("the burlesque Michelangelo") as a model for works of modern fantasy. The painter's bizarre forms, he argued, were vessels for truthful representation, refusing conformity, following the contours of the mind, mixing regularity and irregularity, sacred and secular. Callot's grammar of juxtaposition or "invasion" underpinned modern artistic production for Hugo, generating a new kind of organic

---

[71] Hoffmann, *Kreisleriana*, 76–77. The lauding of artistic depth in Callot is part of a broader rhetorical pattern in Hoffmann's aesthetic and critical writing, as Watkins points out in *Metaphors of Depth in German Musical Thought*.

imaginary central not just to romantic poetry, but to painting, novels, and architecture.[72]

Hugo makes no mention of music, but Hoffmann, in *Kreisleriana*, had already mapped the new grotesque syntax onto composition: Beethoven's "strange shapes," forming and unforming, seemingly alive with imaginative growth, were part of what drew his work into the domain of fantastic sublimity. And Berlioz, as we have just seen, reiterated this idea, hearing in Beethoven (alongside Gluck and Weber) a new kind of anti-grammatical energy – a tendency toward monstrous, even impenetrable constructions.[73] Repeatedly, echoing both Hoffmann and Hugo, he tied these not just to deeper expression, but to an explicitly fantastic form of invention. The connection emerges as early as the Gluck essays ("what could be more terrible ... more fantastic (*plus fantastique*) than the measured recitative [of *Alceste*], *Ove fuggo, ove m'ascondo*) and continues through his writing on Weber. *Der Freischütz* is a *fantastique* opera in part because of its *phraséologie nouvelle*, a language of bulges, asymmetries, and unexpected turns that calls into being the work's dark *monde nouveau*. And the same is true, even more transparently, of *Oberon*. At the heart of Weber's fairy opera (another *opéra fantastique*, according to Berlioz) is a fluid melodic language allowing shapes to grow into and out of one another seemingly spontaneously: "A phrase whose beginning has escaped the listener takes possession of his mind before he is aware that it exists. Another, which has vanished without his noticing, continues to absorb him for some time after he has ceased to hear it."[74]

This tendency toward grotesque transformation – a hesitation between shape and shapelessness – is yoked, for Berlioz, to the broader ontological blurring of fantasy, its convergence of recognizable and imaginary registers. In *Oberon*, he argues, "the supernatural is so well blended with the real world that it is hard to tell exactly where one ends and the other begins." The work's liminality is generated in part via syntactical flexibility; indeed, only "natural" grammar renders available the natural supernaturalism

---

[72] Hugo, Preface, trans. Eliot, 365. See also the links Nodier made between poetic fantasy and the German language in his two-part review of Staël's *De l'Allemagne* for the *Journal des débats* (February 1817).

[73] Berlioz was not alone in framing Beethoven in these terms; references to the impenetrable, laborious, and grotesque abound in the composer's French reception, the last of these terms applied sometimes as a pejorative, sometimes as a compliment. See Prod-homme, "Les Débuts de Beethoven à Paris"; idem, "Beethoven en France"; Schrade, *Beethoven in France*; Wallace, *Beethoven's Critics*; Johnson, "Beethoven and the Birth of Romantic Musical Experience"; and idem, *Listening in Paris*.

[74] For the remarks on *Alceste*, see the *Journal des débats* (20 February 1835), in *CM*, 2:69. For those on *Der Freischütz* and *Oberon*, see *À Travers chants*, trans. Csicsery-Rónay as *The Art of Music and Other Essays*, 242–43.

associated with Weber's (and Hoffmann's) mode. And accessing this language means engaging in a kind of insurgence, a revolutionary rejection of French regulation:

> Weber believes in absolute freedom for rhythmic patterns. Nobody else is so free from the tyranny of what is called *carrure*, that symmetry based on an equal number of measures in successive phrases which, when used exclusively, leads not just to painful monotony but the sure production of platitudes.[75]

The modern imaginary is, for Berlioz (as for Hugo), then, generated via both politico-linguistic radicalism and "foreign" syntactical organicism. The two are inextricable, Callot-esque monstrosity collapsing into revolutionary neology. Fantasy can be articulated only by escaping the tyranny of grammatical order and, in so doing, jettisoning the neoclassical stranglehold of beauty itself.

This collection of ideas emerges as pivotal to Berlioz's criticism, but was by no means confined to it. Links among free phraseology, political emancipation, and grotesque (German) naturalism emerge in other places as key to the conception of musico-fantastic evocation – especially (and unsurprisingly) in the series of *contes fantastiques* Schlesinger published in the *Gazette musicale* through the mid-1830s. Consider, for instance, the story "Brand-Sachs," which we encountered in the previous chapter. Here, Franz Liszt is cast by Théophile Ferrière as a semi-mad modern Kreisler, a figure steeped in pantheistic "vibrations" and Hoffmannesque imaginings who speaks for the modern musical school. At the heart of the story, Brand-Sachs/Liszt wanders into the house of a stranger and is invited to play the piano. Rifling through the available sheet music, he discovers the overture to *Der Freischütz* and falls on it rapturously. Explaining why it is such an important work, the pianist turns immediately to a discussion of its grammar:

> Weber, he cried with enthusiasm, you like Weber? Oh! say you like him, because you see, these are not the banal phrases pillaged from here and there, lined up symmetrically four measures by four measures like the forces of the Landwehr [the Austrian military], mere scraps thrown or sewn together, stitched and restitched in caprices and fantasies [in this sense, improvisations], chords deduced logically like mathematical theorems . . . Oh no! this is not that . . . instead it is [music] of the soul, of the heart, of love, of night, indeed of nights passed in tears, of days dashed on the sharp points of rocks and pummeled by tempestuous waves, of all that enlarges thought, all that elevates it, all that makes man not a singular entity but [a part of] all

---

[75] *À Travers chants* (author's translation), 243.

men, of all the world, of God, passion, misery, despair, vision, ecstasy, earth, hell, heaven, call it quits and die at age twenty-six – this is Weber, this is the poet![76]

As Brand-Sachs/Liszt plays the overture, his listeners are animated by the electric spark of nature itself, a "magnetic influence" that sends a "prodigious vibration" through their souls, transporting them into an untethered space, a fantastic world between heaven and earth, physical reality and the spiritual imaginary. Transcendent vision, true expression, and artistic liberation revolve, for (Ferrière's) Liszt as for Berlioz, around syntactical emancipation.

Fantastic Syntax

We encounter flashes of Berlioz's new grammatical world from the beginning of his output. His first overture, "Waverley" (1827–28), is dominated by rhythmic play, its phrases punched this way and that by fortissimo syncopation. And the *Huit scènes de Faust*, written around the same time, contain various sorts of syntactical experiments, including moments of duple-triple superimposition and metrical stretching (what Julian Rushton calls "sprung rhythm"), especially in Méphistophélès's solos and Brander's drinking song. Slightly later, in the *Neuf mélodies* (1829), we encounter collections of irregularly grouped phrases and playful offbeat accents (see "Hélène" and "La Belle voyageuse"). Berlioz was a student of Reicha during these early years and, as David Cairns notes, spoke of him respectfully, although in practice he was clearly distancing himself from the melodic grammar his teacher espoused. The composer was more forthright in his resistance to Cherubini's rule-bound pedagogy, particularly the notion that contrapuntal procedures (especially fugue) should be understood as the foundation of musical composition.[77]

---

[76] "Weber, s'écria-t-il avec enthousiasme, vous aimez Weber? Oh! dites, vous l'aimez, car, voyez-vous ce ne sont pas de ces phrases banales qu'on pille à droite, à gauche, et que l'on range symétriquement quatre mesures par quatre mesures, comme des compagnies de la Landwehr, de ces lambeaux que l'on jette, que l'on ramasse, que l'on décout et recout en caprices et fantaisies, de ces accords déduits logiquement comme des théorèmes d'arithmétique ... Oh! non, ce n'est pas cela! ... mais de l'âme, mais du coeur, mais de l'amour, mais des nuits, bien des nuits passées dans les larmes; des jours déchirés par les pointes des rochers et battus par les flots des tempêtes, tout ce qui élargit la pensée, tout ce qui l'élève, tout ce qui fait qu'un homme n'est plus homme, mais tous les hommes, mais le monde, mais Dieu, passion, malheur, désespoir, vision, extases, la terre, l'enfer, le ciel, appeler cela sa vie et mourir à trente-six ans, voilà Weber, voilà le poète!" Samuel Bach (Théophile de Ferrière), "Brand-Sachs," pt. 2, *Gazette musicale* (1 May 1836).

[77] For a discussion of Berlioz's rhythmic approach in these works, see Rushton, *The Musical Language of Berlioz*, 127–43; and *The Music of Berlioz*, 98–107. Cairns discusses Berlioz's time at the Conservatory under Reicha and Cherubini in *Berlioz*, 1:213–25.

His defiance crystallized in the *Symphonie fantastique* and its sequel, which showcased in more overt and sustained form the free syntax and "emancipated" rhythm he had begun to champion in his critical writing. Examples of grammatical rule-breaking in the symphony are numerous: elongating and truncating of phrases, moments of metrical dislocation or blurring, syncopated disruptions and interjections, irregularly repeating rhythmic figures, and sections of overtly amelodic and aharmonic material in which rhythm and texture themselves emerge as the dominant elements. These moments are made all the more radical by virtue of their intermingling with rhythmically conventional passages, the result being a sense of constant slippage, a hovering disorder that escalates to a fearsome degree as the piece progresses. A slip between melodic shape and shapelessness can be felt as early as the meditative opening of the symphony ("Rêveries, Passions"), where syntactically regular phrases are atomized via prolonged intervening rests, each leaving us hanging on an open-ended harmony. Eventually these multiplied antecedents trail off, never quite finding a melodic consequent (mm. 3–16). The same dissolution is reenacted a few systems later, Berlioz's phrase-ending sigh left hanging, unraveling into a chromatic descent in the low strings and then a prolonged A-flat pedal during which melodic contours grow hazy (mm. 43ff).

All of this could be chalked up to the kind of melodic nascence one expects of a slow introduction – a period of formation out of which more regular material emerges. But of course this is not what happens as Berlioz's movement arrives at the Allegro. Instead, we encounter the work's most famous example of grammatical heterodoxy: the lopsided *idée fixe*. Berlioz's theme begins as an eight-measure phrase tracing a predictable route from I to V, but it is followed by a truncated, seven-measure consequent whose trajectory back to I is disrupted by an out-of-place tonic in the low strings. Not just harmonically at odds, the bass figures have a lurching feeling, interjecting intermittently and at unpredictable intervals (one of the rhythmic effects the composer would later champion in his Strauss essays). Rather than accompanying in any conventional sense, they pursue their own (sometimes dislocated) harmonic and rhythmic course; indeed, the *idée fixe*, as has often been pointed out, is essentially unaccompanied. Berlioz's focus is on melody alone, whose asymmetry he lays bare, stripping it (like Reicha's treatise) of harmonic and orchestrational clothing in part to underscore its grammatical refusal.

What follows the opening antecedent-consequent pair is not the expected sixteen-bar answer – the second half of a balanced period – but a "spun-out, overweight consequent."[78] It begins as a four-measure sequence, but goes on

---

[78] Holoman, *Berlioz*, 103.

too long, perpetuated by escalating desire through a series of chromatic upshifts until it reaches an apex on which it lingers, finally descending, *ritenuto*, through a last sequential leg stretching out to five measures. An eight-measure phrase completes the period, but rather than regaining syntactical composure, it jolts us through syncopated upbeat figures and then a chromatic/erotic swoop over an offbeat *sforzando* before arriving at a cadence. In all, twenty-four measures, against the initial sixteen. This is far from the balanced poetics Restoration grammarians prescribed, the symmetrical unfolding of reason, purity, and order. Instead, it is an exuberant rejection of such language, a disfigurement not only of the balanced period, but what Charles Rosen calls the underlying four-bar musical "grid" (the metrical half-line). The *idée fixe* remains a melody divisible by four (it totals forty measures), but its contours are bent out of shape, stretched and contracted by the intensity of longing itself. Berlioz is doing in music what Hugo had already achieved in verse, opening up and rendering malleable the poetic form – breaking the caesura, truncating and enjambing the line – in the interest of expressive "truth" and "naturalness." The result is not just surface asymmetry, as Rosen claims, but something much more significant: a renovated musical poetics, a kind of self-generating dynamism. As we have seen, Berlioz understood it, in part, as a grammar of liberated feeling, the kind of bizarre or bulbous melodicism he praised in Beethoven and Weber.[79]

The grammatical stability of the *idée fixe* – its relationship with Conservatory-sponsored metrical-poetic rhetoric – grows even murkier (or less compliant) over the course of its next two appearances. Look, for instance, at its unfolding at m. 150, a moment sometimes identified as the "second theme," although it is clearly an iteration of the first. Here, it is presented in three overlapping phrases of five, seven, and seven measures, the second of these involving a melodic sequence with jolting weak-beat *sforzandi* that return (marked as crescendi) in the final phrase. It is more difficult, in this case, to talk simply about the deformation of a pre-established symmetrical "grid"; instead, one has the sense of a line never quite logically contained. This feeling of a freely evolving poetics is amplified as we arrive at the next solo iteration of the melody (mm. 232ff), which, emerging out of a lengthy passage of sliding chromaticism (a kind of

---

[79] Rosen's notion of a series of displaced phrases (four bar units starting "too early" beginning at m. 87, but recovering their rightful metrical place at m. 104) seems roughly right, although the score on which he relies (Liszt's transcription) makes this reading easier by adding accents on the downbeats of mm. 88, 92, and 96. These markings, which show the "rightful" beginning of each phrase according to Rosen's argument, do not appear in the final printed score of the symphony, whose "underlying symmetry" is therefore less apparent than its overt rhythmical dislocation. See *The Romantic Generation*, 546–50.

Example 4.1 Berlioz, *Symphonie fantastique* I, thematic emergence, mm. 232–41

harmonic-melodic void[80]), seems to grow into being via a process of generation. On the heels of a three-measure silence, Berlioz offers us a single note in the horns (d″). From this pitch, sustained for two measures, emerges a rising fourth in the second violins (a′-d″), which begins on the weak second beat and is heard five times before evolving into a second fourth building atop the previous one (d″-g″). Out of this amplifying melodic compass the *idée fixe* arises by a process of expansion: its opening fourth is an augmentation of the d″-g″ figure we have just heard (and a mirror of the falling fourth in the bass) and the rising interval at the start of its second, seven-measure phrase an outgrowth of the initial a′-d″ gesture (Example 4.1).

---

[80] On the significance of this passage to the overall shape and program of the movement, see Rodgers, *Form, Program, and Metaphor in the Music of Berlioz*, 85–106.

Nothing could be further from the idea of a melody pre-shaped via rhythmic "law" or immutable syntax; instead, Berlioz offers us a musical language evolving from formlessness, slowly animating or emerging into being. Rather than the linear grammar (subject-verb-object) Restoration linguists valorized, this is something akin to Mercier's and Hugo's "inverted" linguistic world: one in which raw sense impressions come first (the "naming" of tones, their expansion into intervals), leading only later to fully formed melodic thoughts (phrases with clear harmonic "subjects" and "verbs"). Each step builds on the previous as if via a process of unfolding cognitive development that, coming back to the claims made by German linguists, links "originary" sense impression, the raw sound of tone itself, with "higher understanding." The result is what Berlioz situated as a syntax of emancipated imagination and *fantastic* production. Recall for a moment his remarks on Weber's *Oberon*: "A phrase whose beginning has escaped the listener takes possession of his mind before he is aware that it exists. Another, which has vanished without his noticing, continues to absorb him for some time after he has ceased to hear it." The evolving *idée fixe* beginning in m. 234 could hardly come closer to this kind of syntax – a grammar of grotesque metamorphosis whose power lies both in its freedom from constraint and, equally importantly, its ties to long-forgotten "beginnings," the first impressions of an awakening mind still attuned to the sounds of creation. Schumann, in his 1835 review of the *Fantastique*, suggests precisely this in a passage crediting Berlioz with injecting a new kind of rhythmic "consciousness" into music:

The music of our day can offer no example in which meter and rhythm are more freely set to work in symmetrical and asymmetrical combinations than in this one. . . . It seems that in the present instance music is trying to *return to its origins*, when it was not yet bound by the law of the downbeat, and to achieve on its own a prose style or a higher poetic articulation.[81]

The domain of modern fantasy, so reliant (as we saw in the previous chapter) on a form of sacralized realism, was conjured into being via this syntactical freedom. Pantheistic revelation, in other words, was inextricable from grammatical revolution, magical sound from a newly organic grammar. If, as I have already argued, the *idée fixe* was a marker of fantastic selfhood (a symptom of psychiatric modernity), as well as a symbol of philosophical yearning, it was also clearly an emblem of semiotic resistance. What it represents – what pursues Berlioz (and us) through every movement of the first symphony – is at once the fantasy of idealist perfection and

---

[81] Schumann, "A Symphony by Berlioz," *Neue Zeitschrift für Musik* (July-August 1835), trans. Cone in *Berlioz: Fantastic Symphony*, 231–32.

the specter/promise of lexical revolution. The two are interlaced, Berlioz's grammatical loosening promising to materialize a new philosophical and political reality. The connection is made even more explicit in the sequel to the *Fantastique*, which returns to a contemplation of the musical beloved, finally giving her – and her melody – a voice: the sound of the natural world itself and, by extension, the divine totality (the better, larger, unconstrained self) for which Berlioz yearns.[82] The place in which we first encounter her directly, the "Chant de bonheur," is framed as both a moment of rapturous union and a site of syntactical innovation. Berlioz's original (1832) title reads, "Le Chant de bonheur. L'Artiste chant. Prose cadencée." The importance of modern language – the "cadenced prose" (or prosodic verse) of Hugo and Dumas – is underscored not just in the title, but in the libretto, where the text for the song is set off from the rest in special script: "O my happiness, my life! my entire being! my god! my universe!"[83]

Unsurprisingly, there is little sense of grammatically constrained phraseology here; the prosodic nature of the text provides the model for its musical setting, which wavers between song and recitative in the free (Gluckian) space of *chant récitatif*. An instrumental introduction unfolds through three phrases (6+4+4) full of sigh-gestures familiar from the *idée fixe*. As the voice enters, the orchestra drops out; again, Berlioz highlights melody itself, accompanied only by a harp played (so he imagines) by the wind-magic of the elusive beloved. His reduced texture allows for flexibility in the opening phrase, whose short, declamatory gestures gather impetus toward a climax ("mon univers") extended by a harp arpeggio ascending to a high C, which suspends us via a fermata in celestial regions. The second ten-measure phrase shifts into a songlike register, a variation of the opening instrumental melody, although now with an improvisatory feel, the harp once again lengthening the phrase in a three-measure arpeggiated flight ("les cieux me sont ouverts!") (Example 4.2). In the last period, we return to a loose, recitative-like line now with a series of chromatic inflections and syncopations, then another iteration of the lyrical theme unfolding as an asymmetrical phrase pair (6+8), which is "wafted" toward Berlioz's protagonist "on a harmonious breeze." "Natural" revelation is bound up in obvious ways, here, with republican neologism; or to put it differently, the

---

[82] See Chapter 3.
[83] The previous piece, the "Chanson de brigands" was also written in *prose cadencée* and marked as such, providing another indication of the link between idealist imagining and revolutionary activism. Berlioz drew attention to the feature in a letter to Thomas Gounet of 14 June 1831: "For the verses, I didn't rack my brain dreaming up rhymes; I simply wrote rhythmic, measured prose which sometimes happens to rhythm: this is all that is needed for musical setting." *CG*, I:231, trans. Bloom in "A Return to Berlioz's 'Retour à la vie,'" 357.

Example 4.2 Berlioz, "Chant de bonheur," mm. 14–31 (the strings reenter at mm. 28–29, but are omitted here)

siren call of ideal sound – an echo of nature itself – is inextricable from the syntactical promise of a new social order.

We might trace this connection right back to Berlioz's "Élégie en prose," the ninth and most striking of the *Neuf mélodies*. Composed in 1829 while the *Symphonie fantastique* was in gestation, it was the fruit of one of Berlioz's lovesick treks across the countryside during which he brooded on his ideal love and all it represented. The Élégie was his first attempt at a musical encapsulation of his obsession, which he cast as a setting of Thomas Moore's poem "When he who adores thee." It is, tellingly, the only song in the collection for which Berlioz used Louise Belloc's prose translation of Moore (rather than Thomas Gounet's poetic one), and the choice is reflected clearly in his music, which hovers in the same emancipated space between song and recitative that he will later invoke in the "Chant de bonheur." The first edition of the piece bears the dedication F. H. S. ("For Harriet Smithson"), as well as a familiar epigraph: "He died: his lyre was placed on his tomb. On stormy nights the wind drew forth harmonious wailing from it, with which his last vain lament still seemed to mingle."[84] This is, of course, almost identical to the epigraph (in the form of a spoken introduction) preceding "La Harpe aeolienne" in *Le Retour*, a place in which Berlioz purports to reveal most fully the sound of the beloved: that of the north wind, intermingled with airy, prosodic strains recalled from the "Chant de bonheur." In the Élégie, we hear foreshadowed the *fantastique* sound-shapes of this orchestral aeolian music, including gusting tremolos in the strings, swells from *pianissimo* to *forte*, and sudden *sforzandi*, which pull the vocal line this way and that according to the grammar of the breeze itself rather than any textbook syntactical formula.

Much has been written on the unusual phraseology of Berlioz's song; Rushton, among others, notes its interleaving of five-, six-, and thirteen-bar phrases, some ending "in mid-air."[85] Rhythmic tensions are also rampant, often associated with emotionally climactic moments, as in mm. 12–15, where Berlioz sets the vocal line in 4/4 against 3/4 harmonic changes in the keyboard. Here, over the emotionally laden text "wilt thou weep, when they darken the fame / Of a life that for thee was resign'd," the voice breaks temporarily free of its metrical frame, rupturing the phrasing of Moore's sentence and leading (as in the third phrase of the *idée fixe*) to a final measure stretched out over a *ritenuto*, with every note accented (Example 4.3). Effects of this sort – what we might think of as affective dislocations of rhythm – happen throughout, sometimes accompanied by stylistic shifts, including abrupt transitions from declamatory to lyrical

---

[84] "Il mourut: sa lyre fut placée sur sa tombe. Pendant les nuits orageuses, les vents en apportaient d'harmonieux gémissements, auxquels semblait se mêler encore sa dernière et inutile plainte." For details surrounding the literary affiliations and evolution of the Élégie, see *NBE*, 15:xii. In 1847–48, during Berlioz's London visit, he learned of the link between Moore's poem and the activities of Irish revolutionary Robert Emmet. In response, he added a new dedication, "In memory of the unfortunate Emmet," to the second edition (published as *Irlande*) and a portion of Emmet's speech (in an elaborate preface) to the third edition. In so doing, he underscored the connections among ideal love, emancipated language, and revolutionary politics for which I have been arguing here.

[85] Rushton, *The Music of Berlioz*, 178.

Example 4.3 Berlioz, "Élégie en prose," mm. 1–17

setting and even passages of chant-like monotone. The result is a heterogeneous piece in which shape and line are molded by the shifting intensities of the text itself or perhaps driven by the waxing and waning of sound produced by the wind-activated lyre. In his *Memoirs*, Berlioz wrote that the Élégie was an articulation of "endless and inextinguishable passion," marking the sole occasion in his early years "when I was able to express a feeling of this sort directly in music while still under its active influence."[86] The song offers us an early example of the convergence of idealist yearning, natural sound, and "liberated" syntax that, as I have already argued, played such an important role in the first symphony and its sequel.

---

[86] Berlioz, *Memoirs*, trans. Cairns, 96.

It was this nexus of associations that made the Élégie – and, more obviously, the *Fantastique* – such a threat, giving rise to a flood of conservative complaints around Berliozian grammar: charges of "broken" rhythm, disordered phraseology, and "vicious" syntax. I opened this chapter with a handful of examples, but dozens more exist – a fact that now seems unsurprising given the political-linguistic backdrop we have been exploring here. Among the inaugurators of this critical tradition was François Fétis, who made issues of language central to his early writing on the *Fantastique* and surrounding works. His 1832 review of the symphony homes in on syntactical errors in terms familiar from Reicha's treatise and its literary counterparts:

His [Berlioz's] melodic phrasing ... is poorly fashioned, awkward, wanting in balance, and to make matters worse, he almost always ends with a note that eradicates the sense, having no logical connection with what has gone before. His harmony is incorrect, composed of chords which are not properly related to each other or are badly arranged; at the same time, it is destitute of novelty. One might say that when it is not monstrous it is common. Shall I speak of [phrase] rhythm? It [the symphony] contains some remarkable peculiarities, but this is either because of a deficient or superabundant phrase-count. To innovate in rhythm is to discover new symmetrical combinations, but this is not what M. Berlioz has done.[87]

These charges continue through Fétis's later assessments, including an 1835 review, which deals in greater specifics:

He does not know what a musical period is, except, as I have just said, when he writes a vulgar one. Search all the movements of the symphony, and you will see that something is missing from either the antecedent or the consequent of each period, so that the phrase rhythm is constantly halting or crude. ... In short, the second phrase of a period is hardly ever an answer to the first.[88]

Without symmetrical phraseology (*carrure*) there could be no melody, hence Fétis's repeated claim (taken up by a host of others) that Berlioz's

---

[87] "Sa phrase de mélodie ... est mal faite, gauche, manquant de nombre, et pour comble de mal elle se termine presque toujours par une note qui forme un contresens parce qu'elle n'a nul rapporte logique avec ce qui précède. Son harmonie est incorrecte; les accords ne se lient point entre eux ou s'agencent mal; cependant elle est dépourvue de nouveauté: on peut même dire que lorsqu'elle n'est pas monstrueuse elle est commune. Parlerai-je du rythme? Il offre quelquefois des singularités remarquables, mais c'est parce qu'il lui manque du nombre ou parce que celui-ci est surabondant. Innover dans le rythme, ce serait trouver des nouvelles combinaisons cadencées; mais ce n'est pas ce que fait M. Berlioz." *Gazette musicale* (15 December 1832).

[88] "il ne sait ce que c'est que la phrase, à moins, comme je viens de le dire, qu'il ne fasse du commun. Examinez tous les morceaux de sa symphonie, et vous verrez qu'il manque toujours quelque chose dans l'un ou l'autre des membres de la phrase, en sorte que le rythme périodique est constamment boiteux ou insensible. ... Presque jamais, enfin, la seconde partie d'une phrase n'est la réponse de la première." *Gazette musicale* (1 February 1835).

music was untuneful. Of the instrumental works in general, he wrote, "le génie de la mélodie y était étranger."[89] And in the absence of melody, there could be no beauty, which remained for Fétis and many of his contemporaries the primary mark of the successful artwork. Instead, there was a disfiguring of shape and meaning ("innumerable digressions," "obscurity of thought") and, more worryingly, a willful descent into vulgarity and monstrosity. Neither the *Fantastique* nor the works surrounding it qualified, in Fétis's assessment, as music at all; their syntactical disorder rendered them illegible, vessels of primitive or unschooled sound. And here, his complaints surrounding grammatical failure begin to mesh with those surrounding musical imitation we encountered in the previous chapter. Fétis echoed conservative literary critics in suggesting that Berlioz's allegedly organic language was a mere copy of sounding nature, a form of empty replication or onomatopoeia divorced from (rather than linked with) the expressive depth or higher reason the German romantics and their French proponents claimed for it.[90] The result of this degradation – a confusion of musical composition with the raw transcription of sense-impression – was a collapse into materialism, a disintegration of the moral and social order. At the center of Berlioz's music, according to Fétis, was "barbarity and irrationality," an impulse born and generative of "violent passions."[91] This link between syntactical and social violence had already, as we have seen, been forged in the slew of conservative literary and musical grammars published during in the 1810s. Here, violating the laws of rational (pre-1789) syntax was not just an aesthetic mistake, but an act of aggression, a violation likely to catapult the world back into a state of political disorder. And Berlioz's symphony, written on the edge of the July Revolution, did indeed seem bound up with social tumult, inextricable from the dismantling of the Restoration and the birth of a new political era. The idea proved resonant among Berlioz's reviewers, voiced directly or indirectly in many of the denunciations of the *Fantastique* (and surrounding works) published over the following several years. These came back repeatedly to issues of phraseology and rhythm, their rejections of Berlioz clearly a response to the political and aesthetic threat associated with linguistic heterodoxy.

In the *Ménestrel*, for instance, the *Fantastique* was a work of terror and rupture, its faults lying in large part in its "bizarre syntax." This assessment applied most obviously to the first, third, and fifth movements, since they were the least grammatical, marred by "halting" and "clumsy" rhythm.

---

[89] Fétis, "Berlioz," in *Biographie universelle*, 1:151.
[90] *Gazette musicale* (1 February 1835). For a literary essay making this argument that Fétis is likely to have read, see "Les Romantiques et les Classiques," *La Quotidienne* (4 April 1830).
[91] *Gazette musicale* (1 February 1835).

The second and fourth could be praised to some degree, since their syntax was correct, producing "beautiful and pleasing melody, clean cut, in balanced rhythmic units (*carrure*)." The reviewer pointed out that these were the portions of the symphony least obviously connected to the ethos of the fantastic, which relied for its existence on a malicious language. He closed by summing up the features of this idiom, urging Berlioz to abandon "your incongruous and violent effects, your musical antitheses, your disordered harmonies," and return to "the common tongue," and "the yoke of rational music."[92]

Slightly later, in Joseph Mainzer's large-scale essay on Berlioz (1838), the same ideas surfaced. Among the most pressing problems with both the first symphony and the early works at large, according to Mainzer, was an absence of coherence; Berlioz's phrases succeeded one another and yet lacked a sense of logical connection (*elles ne sont point liées entre elles*). This opacity was the result of syntactical revolt, a "revolution in rhythm," which led to linguistic failure and structural collapse. In describing the problem, he reached back to Reicha's architectural metaphor:

Berliozian rhythm is nothing more than irregularity, disorder in the proportions of a piece. This revolution in rhythm seems as ridiculous to us as if a student of architecture proposed a total upheaval of what is commonly called symmetry. If you deprive music of rhythm, you remove its greatest charm; if you deprive architecture of symmetry, you destroy all beauty of form.

Not just a matter of ill training, Berlioz's formlessness was rooted in a flaunting of established taste and authority: "all that is bizarre and grotesque, all that rails against the established rules provokes the admiration of M. Berlioz."[93]

---

[92] "la deuxième et la quatrième partie de sa symphonie fantastique (le Bal et la Marche au supplice) possèdent seules un mérite musical réel, en ce qu'ils s'y révèle un enchaînement logique de suaves mélodies, soutenues par une instrumentation vigoureuse et suivie." *Le Ménestrel* (16 November 1834). Two years later, in the same journal, the same claim: "dans l'Episode de la Vie d'un Artiste, il n'y a que le Bal et le Marche du supplice, qu'on puisse applaudir en toute sûreté de conscience. Et notez bien, M. Berlioz, que ces trois fragmens qui plaisent à la foule, à juste titre sans doute, sont précisément ceux qui n'appartiennent pas au *genre fantastique*. . . . Croyez-moi, Monsieur, renoncez à vos effets brusques et heurtés, à vos antithèses musicales, à vos accords désordonnés, à vos fougueux attroupemens de notes; rentrez dans la voie commune, revenez au positif, reprenez le joug de la musique rationnelle." *Le Ménestrel* (11 December 1836). A similar singling out of the Ball and March happens in Blaze's essay "De L'École fantastique," 111–12.

[93] "Le rythme Berlioz n'est autre chose que l'irrégularité, le désordre dans les proportions d'un ouvrage. Cette révolution du rythme nous paraît aussi ridicule que si un élève en architecture proposait un bouleversement total de ce qu'on appelle vulgairement la symétrie. Si vous ôtez à la musique son rythme, vous lui enlevez son plus grand charme; si vous ôtez la symétrie à l'architecture, vous détruisez toute beauté de la forme." Joseph Mainzer, *Chronique musicale*, 46–47. "Tout ce qui est bizarre et grotesque, tout ce qui jure contre les règles adoptées provoque l'admiration de M. Berlioz." Ibid., 78.

Even more alarmist was Ange-Henri Blaze's denunciation of the composer, which was once again couched in large part in grammatical and political terms, drawing in obvious ways on the arguments of the counterrevolutionary (and anti-romantic) linguists. Berlioz was, in Blaze's estimation, a composer of "impetuous and militant imagination" (*une imagination fougueuse et militante*) who had, since the outset, approached his work "with the ferocious tactics of a Jacobin" (*avec les allures farouches d'un Jacobin*). His fantastic aesthetic was rooted in a "revolution in form," which threatened to eradicate not just coherent syntax, but melody itself (the Italian "soul" of music). As Blaze develops this idea, he draws increasingly on the rhetoric of violence, figuring Berlioz as a kind of guerilla composer:

As for melody, the majority of the time it escapes him and if, by chance, he grasps it in his hands, it is to torture it in the pincers of an iron rhythm with the barbarous joy of a child plucking a bird. As with all disruptive characters, M. Berlioz has a genius for destruction; he finds a way to destroy in one fell swoop both melody and rhythm, annihilating one with the other and thus the two essential elements of all music.[94]

Blaze charges Berlioz with an "abuse" of sound akin to the old "abuse of words" royalists associated with Domergue and his circle (*les plus nobles qualités périssent par l'abus*). Confused and serpentine, his language generates confusion rather than clarity, nervous discomfort rather than pleasure. Its faults can be traced both to an absorption of "foreign" influences (*une sorte d'infusion d'élémens étrangers*) and a tendency toward neologism. Idiosyncratic sound-shapes – moments of musico-linguistic invention – are especially evident in the *Fantastique*, according to Blaze. Here, he hears Berlioz doing what Mercier had attempted in the *Néologie* (or the more radical *Mon Dictionnaire*): unmooring himself from the common tongue and even from a shared lexicon, embracing a fantastic idiolect. This is clearest in the symphony's latter half, where, as he claims:

one encounters an isolated sensibility given over to its own enthusiasm, in the grip of personal inspiration, struggling, swept up and lost in an ocean of confused notes that ascend and descend, enliven or irritate, seemingly uncontrolled and

---

[94] "Pour la mélodie, la plupart du temps elle lui échappe, et, si d'aventure il la tient dans ses mains, c'est pour la torturer sous les tenailles d'un rhythme de fer, avec la joie barbare d'un enfant qui plume un oiseau. Comme tous les caractères désorganisateurs, M. Berlioz a le génie de la destruction; il trouve moyen d'en finir en une fois avec la mélodie et le rhythme, et d'anéantir l'un par l'autre ces deux élémens essentiels de toute musique." Blaze, "De l'École fantastique," 100.

uninfluenced by any higher power, proceeding at will, outside all the strictures of rhythm, all the laws of meter, all human traditions, [all] taste and common sense.[95]

Berlioz's neological impulse is rooted in self-absorption (*le soi seul*) and narcissism (*l'amour propre*), according to Blaze. Rather than emerging from creative originality, as Mercier had argued, it emanates from self-interested individualism and therefore social unraveling, a violation of the collective lexical/moral contract. Blaze links Berlioz's rhythmic innovation with an "immoderate desire for a life apart" (*ce besoin immodéré d'une vie excentrique*) and an "absolute despotism of thought" (*despotisme absolu de la pensée*), both of which fly in the face of true genius.[96] The argument is a transparent echo of Bonald, who had claimed a decade earlier, as part of his campaign against both linguistic and artistic individualism, that artists should speak in a collective and institutionally ratified voice. Art existed not for its own sake (as Berlioz would later argue), but for the state's sake, as a medium that reinforced lawful thought and behavior. Lexical/sonorous invention or manipulation of grammar was the stuff of individual despotism, a form of selfishness that placed the rights of "l'homme de soi" (the man as individual person) over those of "l'homme de tous" (the man as social being). The result of this was a collapse of orderly hierarchy, "social grammar" itself, and therefore a descent into cacophony, amorality, and political chaos.[97] Clearly, for Blaze and others, it was precisely this that Berlioz's idiosyncratic language, especially in the *Fantastique*, was poised to perpetuate. His music was invested with the same power of invention, erasure, and cabbalistic invocation associated with revolutionary dictionaries and, later, romantic prefaces. Berlioz, too, as Blaze put it, "wanted to write a Preface to *Cromwell*" – to replace legible discourse with "modern" and overtly radical syntax.[98] For Blaze, as for many others, the composer's *fantastique* mode was in large part *about* melodic grammar – its deconstruction, pollution, and reinvention.

This idea emerges clearly in reviews, but it was showcased even more transparently (and rather humorously) in one of the slew of parodies of the *Fantastique* published in the middle 1830s (another along the lines of those

---

[95] "Tout à l'heure, dans les morceaux suivans, vous allez le voir seul, livré à son propre enthousiasme, en proie à ses inspirations personnelles, se débattre, s'emporter et se perdre sous un océan de notes confuses, qui montent ou descendent, s'apaisent ou s'irritent, sans que nulle volonté supérieure semble les contenir ou les pousser, et vont à leur gré, en dehors de toutes les convenances du rythme, de toutes les lois de la mesure, de toutes les traditions humaines, du goût et du sens commun." Ibid., 104.

[96] Ibid., 120. Eccentricity was a term applied routinely to Berlioz through the 1830s and beyond, often to denote willful isolation or self-absorption.

[97] See Klinck, *The French Counterrevolutionary Theorist Louis de Bonald*, 161.

[98] "M. Berlioz, lui aussi, voulut faire sa préface de Cromwell." Blaze, "De l'école fantastique," 100.

we encountered in the previous chapter). Cast as a satire of the work's program, it was titled "Episode in the Life of a Grammarian" and situated the symphony as a kind of grammatical anti-primer, a handbook of linguistic perversion (Table 4.1). The program begins by echoing the first line of the now-familiar text by Girault-Duvivier: "Grammar is the art of speaking and writing correctly," imagining this as the literary program for the opening movement. But it soon becomes clear that Berlioz's grammar has little in common with Girault-Duvivier's; indeed, is a rejection of it. The second movement, an *Adagio onctueux*, translates "the nine parts of speech" into a series of bizarre orchestral and harmonic effects: a cello solo represents the Noun, a viola/clarinet duo the Adjective, a violin/oboe motive the Article, and so forth. And in the third and fourth parts (a *Menuet compliqué* and a *Stretta très animé*), the regulations of usage are laid out – the Treatise of Participles and the Rules of Syntax – but rather than producing legible musical discourse, they result only in confusion and noise. In the third, "one notices a succession of motives that interlace, collide, and destroy one another," and in the fourth, melody and musical meaning collapse completely into "a mixture of fugues, of syncopations, of timpani and triangle blows, of *pavillon chinois*, of piston trumpet, of piccolo and bagpipe, of sixteenth notes, of sharps, flats and naturals, of thirty-second notes, of detached notes, of tied notes, of dissonances and of consonances." This is Berlioz's version of grammar ("syntax, with all its rules and all its exceptions"), a terrible undoing of "noble" language and melodic "purity," which have been replaced by a conglomeration of foreign and empty sounds.

The parody is a funny one (and it takes us back nicely to conservative musical grammars published by the likes of Lesne, which do, of course, adhere to Girault-Duvivier's template), but lurking beneath it is a familiar anxiety: the sense that Berliozian syntax is undermining order, returning the world to a state of neological and syntactical free-for-all and, in so doing, conjuring into being a world of (politically) radical fantasy. This kind of return was, of course, precisely what conservatives most feared, and what Berlioz, Hugo, Dumas, and the other members of the emerging "romantic" school hailed as necessary and liberating. Joseph D'Ortigue, among others, embraced in "the harmonic language and external forms" of the symphony "a new kind of thought, of feeling, a novel and original conception *in tune with current social needs.*"[99]

However flippant, the trajectory traced in the Grammarian parody is essentially accurate. The symphony does indeed move toward revolution,

---

[99] "à travers le tissu des combinaisons harmoniques et des formes matérielles, un nouveau type de pensées, de sentimens, une conception neuve et originale, en harmonie avec les besoins sociaux actuels." *Gazette musicale* (10 May 1835).

Table 4.1. Symphonie fantastique en 4 parties. – *Épisode de la vie d'un grammairien.* Parodic symphonic program printed in *Le Ménestrel* (May 8, 1836)

Première partie. – *Allegro limpide* exprimant ces mots: "LA GRAMMAIRE est l'art de parler et d'écrire correctement."	First Part: *Limpid Allegro* expressing these words: "Grammar is the art of speaking and writing correctly."
Deuxième partie. – *Adagio onctueux,* composé de neuf périodes, et représentant les neuf parties du discours. L'adagio commence par un solo de violoncelle figurant le SUBSTANTIF; de là, par une heureuse transition opérée par l'alto et la clarinette, il entre dans l'ADJECTIF.	Second Part: *Unctuous Adagio*, composed of nine sentences, and representing the nine parts of discourse. The *adagio* begins with a cello solo representing the NOUN; from there, by a happy transition brought about by the viola and the clarinet, it enters into the ADJECTIVE.
Une savante dissonance effectuée par le violon et le hautbois, prépare l'ARTICLE. Douze coups d'archet détachés, démonstratifs et monosyllabiques amènent le PRONOM. Le VERBE s'annonce bientôt par une série de motifs à deux temps, à trois temps et à quatre temps, qui passent successivement par différens modes.	A learned dissonance effected by the violin and the oboe prepares the ARTICLE. Twelve detached bow strokes, demonstrative and monosyllabic, introduce the PRONOUN. Soon the VERB announces itself via a serious of motives in double time, in triple time and in quadruple time, which pass successively through different keys.
Un solo de flûte exprime ensuite la gracieuse PRÉPOSITION; quelques suaves triolets représentent l'ADVERBE et la CONJUNCTION, et disposent agréablement l'auditeur à la violente INTERJECTION qui s'annonce par un coup de tamtam, suivi d'un point d'orgue.	Thereafter, a flute solo articulates the gracious PREPOSITION; some suave triplets represent the ADVERB and the CONJUNCTION, and render the listener receptive to the violent INTERJECTION that announces itself by a stroke of the gong, followed by a pedal point.
Troisième partie. – *Menuet compliqué,* figurant le TRAITÉ DES PARTICIPES. On remarque une succession de motifs qui s'entrelacent, s'entrechoquent et s'entredétruisent, et dont quelques accords sont frappés à contretemps pour exprimer les difficultés de l'accord du *participe passé*, précédé de son *régime direct.*	Third Part: *Complicated Minuet*, representing the TREATISE OF PARTICIPLES. One notices a succession of motives that interlace, collide, and destroy one another, in which some syncopated chords are struck to represent the difficulties in agreement created by a past participle, preceded by its object.
Quatrième partie. – *Stretta* très animée, mêlée de fugues, de syncopes, de coups de timbales et de triangle, de pavillon chinois, de trompette à piston, de petite flûte et de cornemuse, de dièzes, de bémols et de béquarres, de triples croches, de notes détachées, de notes coulées, de dissonances et de consonances, représentant la *Syntaxe* avec toutes ses règles et avec toutes ses exceptions, les traditions du langage avec tout ses caprices, les exigeances de l'orthographe avec toutes ses bizarreries."	Fourth Part: *Stretta très animé*, mixture of fugues, of syncopations, of timpani and triangle blows, of *pavillon chinois*, of piston trumpet, of piccolo and of bagpipe, of sixteenth notes, of sharps, flats, and naturals, of thirty-second notes, of detached notes, of tied notes, of dissonances and of consonances, representing *Syntax* with all its rules and all its exceptions, the traditions of language with all its caprices, the exigencies of orthography with all its oddities.

not just programmatically – references to the guillotine, the marching horde, and the hellish tribunal appear in the fourth and fifth movements – but, more importantly, *syntactically*. It was not, first and foremost, the work's imagery that reviewers found threatening (specters of the Terror had long since been absorbed into popular French melodrama and by 1830 had lost much of their charge), but the deeper and more real danger concealed beneath these images: that of escalating linguistic chaos. By the time we arrive at the Fifth Movement, the potential for grammatical collapse (one that hovered around the edges of all four preceding movements) has been fully realized. As Rushton points out, there is hardly a symmetrical phrase or period to be found in Berlioz's finale; here, musical forms (both local and large-scale) break free of all established strictures. The *Larghetto* opening is, of course, almost completely amorphous, sound collections replacing concrete melodic shapes, which emerge only sporadically and divorced from any clear sense of meter or pulse ("distant cries which other cries seem to answer"). Even once the *Allegro* has begun, Berlioz remains completely untethered from periodicity, seven-, nine-, eleven-, and thirteen-measure phrases abounding.[100] Consider, for instance, the opening 8+11 statement (shrieking *idée fixe* and infernal "reply"), as well as the twenty-five-bar expansion of the main theme that follows. Large portions of the movement resist parsing in any meaningful sense, melodic question-and-answer formulas no longer in play, or actively parodied (as in the odd call-and-response patterns beginning at m. 305, which consist of two-measure brass fanfares followed by three-measure stretches of chromatic drooping in the upper strings and winds – Reicha's worst nightmare). In other places, Berlioz gives us openly amelodic material, as in the passage beginning at m. 65, composed of seven measures of fixated swirling and static tremolo (the effect is that of a skipping record, a disruption not just of melody, but of the temporal progress it marks) followed by another seven of chromatic rising and falling.

And it is not just a matter of jettisoned melodic symmetry, but of constant rhythmic disruption and experimentation. The Fifth Movement crams together many of the devices Berlioz would later describe in his Strauss essays, including irregularly recurring rhythmic patterns, passages of conflicting meter, and instances of extended syncopation or metrical displacement – the signals of an emancipated rhythmic "future." Among the most famous of these are the bells beginning at m. 102, their three strokes (sustained for eight measures) returning at intervals, which, in Berlioz's words, "are impossible to predict."[101] Following two back-to-back

---

[100] See Rushton's chart of phrase lengths in the Fifth Movement in *The Music of Berlioz*, 255.
[101] "Strauss: son orchestre, ses valses," in *CM*, 3:334.

initial statements, they return separated by spaces of three, five, four, and eight measures, dislocated from their wider rhythmic environment, sometimes coinciding with our sense of the downbeat, at other times giving the impression of syncopation. Overlaid onto them are expanding and contracting phrases of the *Dies irae* chant, each of which is echoed via diminution (in the brass) and then double-diminution (in the flippant upper strings and winds). And to complicate things still further, Berlioz adds a low-string/bass-drum figure to the final phrase of the chant, which causes each measure to lurch heavily forward as if with a limp. The result of all this is a passage of striking rhythmic complexity as well as outright irreverence.

The sense of willful rhetorical demolition and disobedience (Blaze's "impulse toward destruction") is even more apparent in the "Ronde du sabbat" that follows. Berlioz casts it as a fugue with asymmetrical (seven-measure) subject entries, its lines further distorted via offbeat *sforzandi* and trills. Eventually, fugal development peters out, giving way to the bizarre anti-melodic "dialogue" between brass and strings at m. 305, only to be resurrected in even more twisted form at m. 364. Now Berlioz's subject is a contorted, chromatic line that enters not at static intervals, but instead at ever-expanding ones: the second voice enters after five measures, the third after six, the fourth after seven. The result is both rhythmically disorienting and oddly organic, as though the fugue grows with each subject-statement through a process of incremental expansion rather than according to any symmetrical formula. But its energy becomes uncontainable, even monstrous, rising upward through a crescendo and finally exploding out of the bounds of counterpoint itself into a series of *fortissimo* overlapping hemiolas, a terrifyingly dissonant, rhythmically dislocated blasting that goes on for eight measures, extinguishing form, texture, and melody itself in an explosion of sheer noise. Berlioz, quite literally, sends Cherubini's beloved fugue – the paragon of "rational" musical discourse – to hell, incinerating it with a blast of syncopated flame.

Later, and famously, he commits other rhetorical crimes, including fusing sacred and blasphemous themes – the Dies Irae and the Witches' Dance – into an incongruous whole. The passage is important enough to be underlined in both the program and the score (*Dies irae et Ronde du Sabbat ensemble*), marking the only moment in which structural detail achieves programmatic status. It unfolds as a climatic, *fortissimo* collision, a jamming together of the A-minor chant and the G-major dance, which is also a conflation of high and low, human and supernatural, church and theater – a radical, even frightening instance of rupture. Berlioz was clearly interested, in the finale, not just in dissolving old syntactical formulas, but in destabilizing entrenched stylistic and formal grammars, exploring a grotesque aesthetics. It is easy to tie his thematic fusion to the registral intermixtures championed in the Preface to *Cromwell*, where Hugo had argued that modern poetry should do "as nature does, mingling in its creations – but without confounding them – darkness and light, the grotesque and the sublime ... the body and the soul, the beast and the intellect." Only this kind of taxonomical teardown, this elimination of generic distinction and entrenched dualisms, could produce a vital and relevant artistic form – one rooted in a new kind of aesthetic and political unity, excluding nothing and no one, acknowledging the base, marginal and carnal alongside the elevated, central, and spiritual. "A true poetry, a complete poetry," Hugo argued, "consists in the harmony of contrasts."[102]

As we have seen, Hoffmann (alongside Jean Paul, Goethe, and Schlegel) had already embraced Hugo's heterogeneous ideal, hailing grotesque forms as models for a new, liberated imaginary: that of modern fantasy. And Berlioz was surely responding to this model as well; indeed, if his wild conflations are a musical articulation of Hugo's aims, they are equally clearly an echo of Callot, the visual template for Hoffmann's *Fantasiestücke*. The finale of Berlioz's *Fantastique* is the sounding equivalent of the *Temptation of St. Anthony*: an explosion of neological, uncontainable shapes drawn together in an infernal setting. We might compare his sacred witches' dance to Callot's dragon-headed wheelcart, lobster-tailed human, or various vegetable-mineral conflations – places in which violations of formal grammar challenge received ontology, suggesting a new and disorientingly uncontainable reality. Reason collapses into unreason, the domain of dream into that of wakefulness, the irrational intellectual margins into the "enlightened" center. The result is a dissolution of all known categories and classes of being into a newly comingled whole, a postrevolutionary world of liberation, danger, and promise.

Rushton, among others, reads this moment as the lowest point in the symphony's descending narrative arc – the point of utter formal disintegration. He makes sense of the trajectory of the *Fantastique* in part by positioning it as a negative version of the Beethovenian *per ardua ad astra* trajectory, the narrative of struggle and triumph traced in the Third, Fifth, Sixth, and Ninth Symphonies. Berlioz perverts this teleology, Rushton argues, leading not toward "pious thanksgiving" or thematic unity, but "religious alienation," a reflection of his disillusioned and melancholy state.[103] Here I want to suggest something different: read syntactically, the finale of the

---

[102] Hugo, Preface, trans. Eliot, 263, 270.   [103] Rushton, *The Music of Berlioz*, 253.

Fantastique emerges not as a descent into structural collapse, but an emergence into the space of revolutionary neologism, a celebration of "natural" human rights and the fluid grammar that gave them voice. As the Grammarian parody suggests, the *Fantastique* (especially its last movement) was a site of linguistic assertion rather than simply disintegration, one in which Berlioz set himself up as a new Girault-Duvivier, a musical *grammarien-patriote* reactivating a syntax of revolt akin to that of Domergue and Mercier and, in more modern terms, Hugo and Hoffmann. That he chose hell as the place in which to take such a stand is not entirely surprising. La Harpe, Edmund Burke, and other counterrevolutionary theorists had famously dubbed the language of revolution demonic and even apocalyptic, the stuff of infernal invention.[104] Berlioz (as with many of his romantic contemporaries, notably Byron) took his cue from – indeed, embraced – this denunciation, reclaiming hell as a symbol of political and linguistic resistance. His *fantastique* inferno is not, we might argue, a site of damnation or alienation, but instead of emancipation, a place animated by revolutionary spirit, lexical individualism, and what Jacques Attali terms "noisy" resistance.[105]

Syntax beyond the *Fantastique*

Complaints around phraseology did not by any means end with the *Fantastique* and its sequel, but instead persisted through the reception of later works, finally emerging, alongside "imitation," as central to the perceived threat of Berliozian sound. Blaze, in his 1838 overview of the composer, heard in the symphonic works at large – especially *Harold en Italie*, the Overtures, and the recently premiered *Benvenuto Cellini* – evidence of the same disordered grammar that had produced the first symphony. In this sense, he argued, all of these were *fantastique* works, all were engaged in the same form of linguistic conjuring. They were not, of course, all on supernatural themes; indeed, fantasy is not a matter merely of thematics for Blaze, but of shared grammar – incantatory, foreign, radical. By invoking it, Berlioz's compositions invoke a pernicious code, their real meaning seeming to hover just below the surface, poised to work a musico-neological magic drawing into being other worlds with the same revolutionary potential as the *Fantastique*.

---

[104] Blakemore notes the satanic language in Burke's essay "Reflections on the Revolution in France" in *Burke and the Fall of Language*, 57–58. On similar rhetoric in La Harpe's writing and that of other counterrevolutionaries, see Rosenfeld, *A Revolution in Language*, 181–226.

[105] Attali, *Noise*.

Mainzer made much the same argument in his own 1838 profile of Berlioz, tying the melodic language of the first symphony to that of Berlioz's later compositions. He, like Blaze, cited *Harold en Italie* as a key example, a work whose rhythmic dislocation – especially the relentless syncopation and metrical unhinging of the finale – qualified it as a *symphonie fantastique*. The *Messe des morts*, too, fell into this category, its "disjointed ideas" (*idées décousues*) and metrical disjunctions rendering it not just unintelligible, but dangerous. The fantastic ethos of this work, its otherworldly landscape, was not the product either of faith or naïve supernaturalism for Mainzer (the stuff of the old marvelous tradition), but instead of a new and violent realism, a "foul doctrine" (*mauvaise doctrine*) championed by Hoffmann and Hugo and appealing only to "degenerate men with a taste for gross and brutal emotions." Rather than a divine representation, the *Messe des morts* was a vehicle for neological invention; it was not just a commemoration of the July Revolution, Mainzer argued, but a grammatical analogue of it.[106]

Syntax was also at the center of arguments made in defense of Berlioz, these too beginning to mobilize around 1838, partly in response to attacks by the composer's detractors. Once again, it was Joseph D'Ortigue who emerged as the composer's staunchest proponent, publishing several large-scale articles and, in 1840, a book-length study in which issues of melodic and rhythmic form play a central role. Here, as earlier, defending Berlioz meant in large part championing his grammar. D'Ortigue's 1840 study, titled *Du Théâtre Italien et de son influence sur le goût musical françois*, elaborates on a binary already central to Berlioz's own criticism (and that of his denouncers, including Blaze), pitting the so-called Italian School, champions of melodic symmetry and rhythmic regularity, against the German School (what Blaze had termed the *école fantastique*), defenders of melodic freedom and rhythmic variety.[107] Extending the political rhetoric that had long since become central to discussions of phraseology, D'Ortigue denounces *carrure* (an "Italian" convention embraced by conservative French institutions) as a form of repression: "The Italians, in enclosing

---

[106] "les hommes dépravés qui cherchent des émotions grossières et brutales." Mainzer, *Chronique musicale*, 40. Blaze also tied the language of the *Messe des morts* to the syntactical errors of the first symphony: "M. Berlioz écrivait une messe tout comme il aurait composé une symphonie" ("De l'École fantastique," 113).

[107] D'Ortigue, *Du Théâtre Italien et de son influence sur le goût musical françois*. Here, D'Ortigue invokes what Carl Dahlhaus later termed the "twin styles," with Rossini in one camp and Beethoven/Berlioz in the other (*Nineteenth-Century Music*, 8–14). The historical construction and leveraging of this binary has been the subject of sustained recent attention; see especially Mathew and Walton, *The Invention of Beethoven and Rossini*.

themselves in a static frame, that is to say, in four-square phraseology and rhythmic uniformity, create an absolutist system."[108]

The problem with this system is not just that it eradicates free expression, but that it violates the principles of organicism. Nature, as D'Ortigue argues, abhors relentless symmetry, embracing instead an energized comingling of balanced, imbalanced, whole, fragmentary, simple, and complex shapes. Rather than being pretty, its forms are vital; rather than simply pleasing the eye and ear, they move the soul. (Later, and along similar lines, Gautier will position symmetrical musical phraseology as a symbol of "things past, conventions imposed and suffered" and irregular lines as symbols of "restlessness, aspiration, search for the infinite, presentiments of the future."[109]) Echoing Berlioz, D'Ortigue traces truly natural grammar to Gluck, situating him as a resolute resister of *carrure* whose rhythmic innovations led directly to Beethoven and Weber. The composer of the *Fantastique* extends this melodic trajectory, his much-maligned asymmetries and rhythmic experiments not the stuff of illegibility but of "truthful" musical discourse – the grammar of creation itself and therefore of a God-given moral and political order. And Berlioz's large-scale forms are, for D'Ortigue, extensions of the same melodic fluidity, growing from the free phrases that constitute them (*le jet primitif et spontané de la pensée de l'auteur*). Taking unusual, even unidentifiable shapes, they map the contours of a free consciousness, resisting the generic strictures of a repressive aesthetic system, embracing instead the neological imperative of true artistry.[110] These arguments are, of course, not new, but summative, returning to Berlioz's aesthetic claims, Hugo's still-resonant Preface, D'Ortigue's own earlier critical essays, as well as the wider discourses around musical form and syntax we have already encountered.[111]

---

[108] "Les Italiens, en se renfermant dans un cadre invariable, c'est-à-dire dans la carrure de la phrase et l'uniformité du rythme, créèrent un système absolue." D'Ortigue, *Du Théâtre Italien*, 40.

[109] "Sans doute, les nombres impairs ont quelque chose de mystérieux et d'incomplet qui représente l'inquiétude, l'aspiration, la recherche de l'infini, le sentiment de l'avenir; tandis que les nombres pairs symbolisent, par leurs décompositions symétriques, les choses accomplies, les rites acceptés et subis." In a review of Berlioz's *La Damnation de Faust* in *La Presse* (7 December 1846). Here, Gautier supports Berlioz's rhythmic innovations – his resistance to "formules prévues d'avance" – although also warns him of the dangers of "enjambemens perpétuels."

[110] D'Ortigue, *Du Théâtre Italien*, vi–viii. D'Ortigue is reacting in part to fixed conceptions of form and genre as conceived by Restoration aestheticians. Bonald, in particular, generated a hierarchy of genres with the "impersonal" heroic, tragic, lyric, and epic styles at the top and the "personal, fragmented" elegiac, erotic, bacchic, comic (and fantastic) modes at the bottom. Fixity of language was inextricable, for him, from coherent form. For more, see Klinck, *The French Counterrevolutionary Theorist Louis de Bonald*, esp. chaps. 1, 3, and 4.

[111] D'Ortigue's defense of Berliozian phraseology dates to his reviews of the *Épisode de la vie d'un artiste*, where he already aligns his friend with German melodic profundity rather than empty Italian routine: "Rossini et son école nous ont accoutumés à une mélodie, en quelque sorte toute extérieure, à un chant dont le corps et la forme saisissent dès l'abord. Il n'en est pas ainsi

Grammatical Imaginaries

For D'Ortigue, as for Berlioz and his "romantic" contemporaries, grammar remained central to the idea of imaginative liberty, and once again, to modern fantasy. What Berlioz took from his "liberated" models, as D'Ortigue put it, was "this rhythm of ravishing fantasies and the most unexpected caprices" and (going back to Gluck) a phraseology whose expressive variety ushered in "all the fantasies of instrumental music."[112]

Connections among melodic irregularity, political volatility, and fantastic vitality persisted, surfacing in virtually every substantial French profile (encyclopedia entry, critical overview, biography) of Berlioz published before the end of the century.[113] They shaped the assessment of the composer's later works – *Roméo et Juliette* and *La Damnation de Faust*, for instance, were both subject to charges of melodic deficiency and therefore *fantastique* disorder[114] – and, over time, began to affect the critical reception of other composers. Wagner is a case in point, a figure who, as David Trippett has pointed out, was charged with the same kind of melodic absence associated with Berlioz, the same tendency toward fractured, quasi-prosodic lines. Nietzsche even dubbed him "the Victor Hugo of music as language" – of course, some fifty years after Berlioz had held the title.[115] Small wonder, then, that Wagner was also tarred, in France, with the

---

de la mélodie allemande moins cadencée, moins rythmée, d'un dessin moins arrêté, mais aussi d'une expression plus profonde." *La Quotidienne* (4 January 1833).

[112] "ce rythme de ravissantes fantaisies et des caprices les plus inattendus"; "toutes les fantaisies de la musique instrumentale." D'Ortigue, *Du Théâtre Italien*, 39, 100.

[113] See, for instance, Clément on Berlioz and his "school" in the panoramic *Musiciens célèbres depuis seizième siècle jusqu'à nos jours* (1868), where we find recycled the architectural denunciations familiar from Reicha: "Ils [the members of l'école fantastique] démolissent l'édifice harmonique, et quand tous les matériaux sont à leur pieds, ils tentent de le reconstruire d'après un nouveau plan. Mais ils ont négligé de numérateur les pierres, de sorte qu'au lieu d'un édifice bien ordonné, ils reviennent fatalement à une architecture primitive, fantaisiste et naïve, mais point belle" (516–17). In late-century musical grammars, Berlioz's work emerges as a key example of improper or absent melody; see Noel, *Clef de la langue et des sciences* (1861), which contains the following in an entry under "Mélodie": "On ne peut nier que M. Berlioz ne soit un grand harmoniste, mais qu'il laisse à désirer sous le rapport de la mélodie!" (66) The problem, as Noel argues, was that Berlioz had not spent enough time listening to Racine at the Théâtre français (!)

[114] See the reviews of *Roméo et Juliette* in *Le Constitutionnel* (28 November 1839) and *La France musicale* (1 December 1839); also see Jules Janin's review of *La Damnation de Faust* in *Le Ménestrel* (12 December 1846), which ties the charges of melodic and formal incoherence levied by the "ultra-melodists" directly to their denunciation of the *genre fantastique*.

[115] Trippett, in *Wagner's Melodies*, notes that both German and English critics complained of an absence of symmetry (and therefore legibility) in Wagner's melodic language, as well as a tendency toward "eternal psalmodically reciting declamation" (what Berlioz had termed *chant récitatif*), arguing that his work was "totally barren of rhythmical melody." See chap. 1 (here, 27 and 33). And for more on Wagner's connection, in the 1850s, to Hugo and his "characteristic" or "ugly" forms, see 51–57.

fantastic brush. Larousse, among others, placed him squarely in this category in his entry under "fantastique" for the *Grand dictionnaire universel* (1866–72), describing Wagner's music as even more outlandish than that of Berlioz. He saw in the composer of the music dramas the same orchestrational excess, metaphysical error, and, above all, melodic incomprehensibility resonating back to the *Fantastique*; indeed, Wagner was a composer whose language was so fantastic that even the foremost French champion of the mode could no longer comprehend it. Berlioz's "future of rhythm" (what Gautier called his "presentiments of the future") was, Larousse implied, in some sense inextricable from Wagner's "future of music" – and it was a dire future indeed. *Tristan und Isolde*, rooted in the same "barbaric words" that had conjured romantic literary fantasy, was poised to invoke a version of the neological hell showcased in Berlioz's first symphony – a place of ugliness, disorder, and aesthetic collapse.[116]

It was in large part "new words," to sum up – both literary and musical – that conjured fantasy's other worlds, words with "the power to save or the power to kill," organized in grammatical shapes that called into being spaces of otherworldliness, idealism, dream, or imagination. They coalesced into a language not only describing, but *materializing* new political and philosophical realities, drawing on what some called a cabbalistic and others a vital or electric power. Fantasy was rooted not just in pantheistic listening, but equally clearly in theories of organic or originary speech, not just in foreign philosophy, but in radical politics. Its semiotics were linked, in French discourse, to notions of emancipated literary grammar, which were themselves inextricable, going back to Domergue and Mercier, from the natural rights of man. Eradicating stylistic and lexical boundaries, fantastic syntax replaced the fixed language of rationalism with a fluid idiom borrowing the generative properties of nature itself. At its heart was a transformative power, a capacity to generate spaces of Callot-esque juxtaposition, rhetorical unworking, and revolutionary remaking.

---

[116] Larousse, "Fantastique," 95.

Of Demons and Fairies

5   ❧   Listening in Hell

O sonder foul, sonder foul leimi,
Sonder rak simoun irridor!
Muk lo meror, mul lunda merinunda
Farerein lira moretisfò. O sonder foul!!!
Rake liri merinunda, fime lotou lirirein
Sonder rak simoun irridor,
Muk lo meror, muk landa merinunda
Ni farerein lira moretisfò.
Nir mulich dotos!!! Fime nerina,
Fereno riko lu lu chun nerino,
Faretra sitti sitti mombo
Irmensul for gas meneru,
Sol Irmensul for gas meneru.

This is the text given to a "Choeur d'ombres irrités" ("Choir of Angry Shades") in the second movement of Berlioz's 1832 *mélologue Le Retour à la vie*. It is a language of the composer's own invention invoked in an episode depicting the ghost scene from *Hamlet*, during which the king returns from beyond the grave to reveal the circumstances surrounding his murder. His message, given to a chorus of infernal spirits, is couched in a tongue marked by awkwardness, hyperbolic punctuation, exotic spelling, and vaguely primitivist repetition ("lu lu chun" and "sitti sitti mombo"). For Berlioz, this was the language of the dark afterworld, the realm inhabited by Shakespeare's king, "doom'd for a certain term to walk the night, / And for the day confined to fast in fires, / Till the foul crimes done in my days of nature / Are burnt and purged away."[1] It was an object of considerable interest in the 1830s, in part because of its novelty (then, as now, it seemed a good gag), but, more importantly, because of its tantalizing realism: discrete phrases, inflecting accents, even the outward show of poetic meter and form. Was it in some sense legible? Did it "mean"? Where had it come from?

According to a colorful (and probably fictitious) passage from Berlioz's memoirs, these were the questions that occupied the Italian censors, who

---

[1] William Shakespeare, *Hamlet*, act 1, scene 5, 9–13.

delayed publication of the score of *Le Retour* for several months as they scrutinized its peculiar language. In the end, so the composer claimed, they were stymied:

> My leisure at La Côte Saint-André was spent in copying the orchestral parts of the monodrama which I had written during my wanderings in Italy and which I now wished to have performed. I had had the chorus parts copied in Rome, where I had become embroiled in a dispute with the papal censorship over one of the movements, the Chorus of Shades. The text of this piece (which I mentioned earlier) was in an "unknown tongue" – the language of the dead, unintelligible to the living. When I applied to the censor for a license to print it, the question of the precise meaning to be attached to the words caused consternation among the philologists. What was this language and how was this strange speech to be interpreted? A German was sent for, but declared he could make no sense of it; after him, an Englishman, with no better luck. Then a Dane, a Swede, a Russian, a Spaniard, an Irishman, and a Bohemian – each confessed himself mystified. Confusion in the censor's office, the printer unable to proceed, the publication in abeyance until further notice. At last one of the censors hit upon an argument the soundness of which impressed all his colleagues. "Since none of the interpreters, English, Russian, Spanish, Danish, Swedish, Irish or Bohemian, can understand this mysterious language," said he, "it is very probable that the Roman people will not understand it either. It seems to me therefore that we can safely authorize the publication without serious risk to morals or religion." So the Chorus of Shades was printed. Rash censors! It might have been in Sanskrit.[2]

If this anecdote highlights Berlioz's pleasure in the befuddlement of his text's first readers, it underscores equally clearly his own fascination with and knowledge of languages – and the degree to which philology itself continued to be wrapped up with his conception of imaginary, including infernal, sound. This connection lasted through the remainder of his career; indeed, the spirit language of *Le Retour*, which has so often been dismissed as a bit of caprice or another example of Berliozian eccentricity, was part of a sustained practice of neological invention. It was the first of several other fictitious tongues, each carefully constructed, whose sources, attributions, and interconnections reveal something important about the nature of Berlioz's demonic fantasy.[3]

The composer of *Le Retour* was far from forthcoming about the provenance of his spirit language; in fact, his remarks on the subject were (intentionally?) murky. In the original libretto of the work, his artist-hero

---

[2] Berlioz, *Memoirs*, trans. Cairns, 213–14. There is no record of an Italian publication of *Le Retour*, which casts doubt on the veracity of this story.

[3] For commentaries on Berlioz's ghostly language, see Bloom, "A Return to Berlioz's 'Retour à la Vie'"; Micznik, "The Musico-Dramatic Narrative of Berlioz's *Lélio*"; and Wotton, "'Infernal Language.'" Bloom returns to the issue in the foreword to *NBE*, 7:ix–xi.

refers to the idiom as "incomprehensible," the sound of an "unknown world" (*un monde inconnu*). But a footnote to the text revises this claim, identifying it as an "ancient dialect of the North" (*Ancien dialecte du Nord*), a language with a more concrete philological pedigree. From the outset, then, Berlioz's text hovered between the fictional and the historical, between art and artifact. His friend Joseph D'Ortigue obfuscated matters further in an article for *La Revue de Paris* published just after the premiere of *Le Retour*. Here, he told the story of the censors for the first time, adding his own fanciful ending: when the Italians had exhausted their experts, they interviewed Berlioz himself, who revealed that the spirit language was "an ancient dialect once spoken in Iceland, at the foot of Mount Hekla."[4] Surely riffing on Berlioz's own suggestion that the invented idiom had northern roots, D'Ortigue went one step further, giving it a discrete geographical source. The inhabitants of Berlioz's inferno were both imaginary, he suggested, and in some sense terrestrial, just as the fires of his otherworldly hell were also those of Iceland's uneasy volcano.

D'Ortigue's reference to Iceland was whimsical, probably inspired by contemporary fascination with Hekla (the volcano was active for several stretches through the early-mid nineteenth century, and its periodic spewings closely reported in the French press). But had he examined the history of the "Choeur d'ombres" more carefully, he would have discovered that the connection he had drawn between real and imaginary geographies was not so far off the mark. The place that hovered around and behind the work was not, however, Iceland, but Egypt. Berlioz had drawn the music for the piece, with minor alternations, from the final section of his cantata *La Mort de Cléopâtre*, written for the 1829 Prix de Rome competition.[5] Here, in a section marked *Méditation*, Cleopatra prepares herself for death following the suicide of her husband, Mark Antony. A recitative announces her utter resignation ("Il n'en est plus pour moi que l'éternelle nuit!") and is followed, in the *Méditation*, by a plea to the great pharaohs to grant her a resting place beside them. Marked *pianissimo* and *Largo misterioso*, Cleopatra's text, delivered *sotto voce*, seems already to emanate from the deathly world to which she seeks entry. It is accompanied by sustained winds and a pizzicato rhythmic ostinato in the low strings, a figure that persists throughout, catching the ear in part because its sound is so remote from the lyrical world of the strings, conjuring instead a distant drum tattoo – the sound of ancient death rites? Against it, Cleopatra makes a quivering, semi-declamatory appeal to her ancestors resting in their funerary pyramids.

[4] "Il [Berlioz] dit que c'est un ancien dialecte jadis en usage en Islande, et qu'on parlait au pied du mont Hécla." *La Revue de Paris* (23 December 1832), as part of a biographical sketch of Berlioz.
[5] On a text by Pierre-Ange Viellard. This was Berlioz's third failed attempt to win the prize.

Example 5.1a Berlioz, "Méditation," *La Mort de Cléopâtre*, mm. 11–13

When Berlioz composed his "Choeur d'ombres" some three years later, it was to the textural and harmonic world of the *Méditation* that he turned. A new rising figure in the strings ushers in the "Choeur," marking the moment when Berlioz's artist-hero "hears" his imaginary orchestra begin (*Oui, je l'entends!*), but from thereon in the music is that of Cleopatra. The same sustained *pianissimo* winds are heard, and the familiar string ostinato, whose rhythm will later be taken up by an expanded percussion section (bass drum and gong in addition to the original muted timpani).[6] Cleopatra's solo line is, of course, divided among the chorus, but their *sotto voce* register links them directly to her, as does Berlioz's unison vocal scoring; clearly, he is thinking of his choir as an amplified solo voice (see Examples 5.1a and 5.1b for a comparison). It was his vanquished queen – and, more broadly,

---

[6] Berlioz specifies sponge-headed drumsticks – *baguettes d'éponge* – in both works.

Example 5.1b Berlioz, "Choeur d'ombres," mm. 12–14

ancient Egypt – that he was hearing when he imagined the otherworldly soundscape and language of his infernal realm. For him, the fiery region inhabited by Shakespeare's king was connected, not to an ancient European north, but to an African one, the world of the pharaohs.

As Berlioz reports in the *Memoirs*, he eventually removed his ghostly language from *Le Retour*, having decided "to reserve the device for the Pandemonium scene in *La Damnation de Faust*."[7] Here, the quasi-language is given not to "angry shades," but to a related group –

---

[7] Berlioz, *Memoirs*, trans. Cairns, 213. For an overview of the musical and literary evolution of *La Damnation*, see Rushton's foreword in *NBE*, 8b:455–61.

demons – who celebrate Méphistophélès's triumphant arrival in hell with Faust. The first printed score gives the text for the scene as follows:

Les démons portent Méphistophélès en triomphe
Tradioun Marexil fir
Trudinxé burrudixé!
Fory my Dinkorlitz,
Ô merikariu Omévixé merikariba.
Ô merikariu Ô midara Caraibo lakinda,
Merondor Dinkorlitz, merondor.
Tradioun marexil,
Tradioun burrudixé
Trudinxé Caraibo.
Fir omévixé merondor.
Mit aysko, merondor mit aysko! Ô!

Ils dansent autour de Méphistophélès
Diff! Diff! merondor,
Merondor aysko!
Has! Has! Satan.
Has! Has! Belphégor.
Has! Has! Méphisto.
Has! Has! Kroix.
Diff! Diff! Astaroth,
Diff! Diff! Belzébuth,
Belphégor, Astaroth, Méphisto!
Sat, sat rayk irkimour.
Has! Has! Has! Has! Has!
Irimiru Karabrao!

This is clearly a new iteration of Berlioz's demonic tongue, although it has much in common with the first, featuring similar lurching rhythms and consonant jumbles, and even variations on familiar "words": "rak" has become "rayk"; "merinunda" has become "merondor"; "irridor" has become "irkimour." Elements of syntax and punctuation are also shared, including a tendency toward exclamatory line openings ("O sonder foul" in *Le Retour* and "Ô merikariu" in *Faust*) and exclamation points in general, which give the impression of overall noise as though every phrase is being shouted. Other characteristics, including weird morphology and spelling, have been intensified, as if Berlioz is aiming in *Faust* for something even more outlandish than in *Le Retour*: alongside the foreign letter k, words featuring x figure prominently. The second section of text, sung while the inhabitants of hell dance around Méphistophélès, slides more clearly into the realm of legibility than the first, containing the names of a series of demons derived from biblical, fictional, and pseudo-scientific writing, including the Old Testament, Milton's *Paradise Lost*, and Collin de Plancy's *Dictionnaire infernal*.[8] Here, more strongly than in *Le Retour*, we have the sense of grotesque rhetoric, an idiom hovering between meaning and monstrosity, just outside rational control.

This sense of hesitation is deepened by yet another layer of attribution: now Berlioz tells us, in a footnote to the Pandemonium text, that his language is indebted to eighteenth-century scientist and mystic Emanuel Swedenborg. The reference is surely to Swedenborg's *Heaven and Hell*, originally published in 1758, in Latin, and available in French by the early 1820s. It records a series of visions in which Swedenborg visits first heaven, then hell, documenting the inhabitants, geographies, customs, and languages of both places. Swedenborg describes the idiom of the inferno only in the vaguest terms (he is reluctant, he claims, to communicate the "frightful horrors" of the place), positioning its speech simply as "opposite" to that of heaven: "The language of evil and hellish spirits ... comes from evil affections and ... foul concepts, which are utterly repugnant to angels. This means that the languages of hell are opposite to the languages of heaven. Evil people cannot stand angelic speech, and angels cannot stand hellish speech." The only further detail Swedenborg offers concerns the "language of hypocrites," which "sounds like a grinding of teeth."[9] But his account of angelic dialects – on which topic he is much more forthcoming – provides us (and presumably Berlioz) with a negative model:

The speech of heavenly angels is like a gentle stream, soft and virtually unbroken, while the speech of spiritual angels is a little more resonant and crisp. Then too, the vowels U and O tend to predominate in the speech of heavenly angels, while in the speech of spiritual angels it is the vowels E and I. ... the language of heavenly angels lacks any hard consonants and rarely puts two consonants together without inserting a word that begins with a vowel.[10]

If we want to know what Swedenborg's hellish language sounded like, theoretically we can simply reverse all of these qualities: rather than airy vowels, harsh consonants; rather than an unbroken stream of sound, a halting

---

[8] Most of the fiends to whom Berlioz refers are described (and their literary, mythological, or biblical provenances traced) in Collin de Plancy's *Dictionnaire infernal*, France's best-known work on demonology.

[9] Swedenborg, *Heaven and Its Wonders and Hell Drawn from Things Heard and Seen*, 420, 210. Swedenborg's works were first systematically translated into French by J. P. Moët, librarian at the Royal Library at Versailles, between 1819 and 1824. Expanded and alternative translations appeared through the 1830s and 1840s, and a second complete-works series by J.-F.-E. Le Boys des Guays was published in the 1850s.

[10] Ibid., 208.

and crude one; rather than gentle resonance, unpronounceable noise. These are, of course, the attributes of Berlioz's Faustian tongue, and its "ghostly" predecessor; in this sense, then, Swedenborg may have been a model.

Berlioz's critics noted his Swedenborgian reference, although some – particularly the composer's most literary reviewer, Théophile Gautier – found it unsatisfying. Swedenborg might have offered an aesthetic template, but where had Berlioz obtained a concrete grammar and vocabulary (*la syntaxe et le dictionnaire*)? This question was more pressing for Gautier than for later listeners, since he was responding to an earlier version of the Pandemonium scene given in the first edition of the libretto, which was published several weeks in advance of the premiere. Here, the illusion of realism was heightened by an extended dialogue between the demonic choir, the "Princes of Darkness," and Méphistophélès himself, which implied "actual" communication[11]:

Choeur infernale:	Has! Irimiru Karabrao!
	Omidaru Caraibo!
	Merikariba
	Myriak mereada.
Les Princes des ténèbres à Méphistophélès:	Irkimour sat rahyk? . . . Irkimour Méphisto? . . .
Méphistophélès:	Irkimour sat rahyk.
Les Princes:	Rial mir orakai Faust undo voll isto? . . .
Méph:	Faust undo voll isto.
Les Princes:	Uraraiké? . . .
Méph:	Uraraiké.
Les Princes:	Muraraiké? . . .
Méph:	Muraraiké.

Rather than a mystical idiom, this seemed to Gautier like a spoof, whose very proximity to realistic dialogue highlighted its status as gibberish. In an article for *La Presse*, he dismissed it as a Berliozian invention akin to that of Molière in the Act IV "Turkish" dialogue of *Le Bourgeois gentilhomme* (here, the Frenchman Cléonte poses as a royal Turk, speaking exotic babble in order to impress the foolish Monsieur Jourdain).[12] Gautier mused again on the Berlioz–Molière connection in a second piece on *Faust*, also for *La Presse* (this one responding to the first performance), expanding his thoughts on the subject of the infernal tongue and its surrounding music:

---

[11] Reproduced in *NBE*, 8b:490–91. Suspension points are original to the text.

[12] *La Presse* (23 November 1846). Act 4, scenes 3 and 4 of *Le Bourgeois gentilhomme* do indeed contain made-up gibberish, although the subsequent "Turkish Ceremony" draws on Lingua franca, a fact of which Gautier may have been unaware. My thanks to Jonathan Bellman for pointing this out.

The *Course fantastique* [*Course à l'abîme*] has that breathless speed, that stumbling, broken rhythm, that vertigo, that terror that M. Berlioz excels in rendering. The choir of demons, in an infernal language, is perhaps a touch long. In the announcement we made several days ago about the *Damnation de Faust*, we raised some doubts about the authenticity of this part of the libretto. This diabolical language, which we think resembles a bit too closely that of the Turc of Covielle, is the invention of M. Hector Berlioz. The real language of demons is known. Father Kircher gives the alphabet and grammar in his *Oedipus Aegyptiacus*; its purpose is to record pacts and covenants. The learned Mezzofanti, who is familiar with all languages, speaks it fluently, and no doubt he would have found it a genuine pleasure to furnish M. Berlioz with exact words for this important scene.[13]

If Gautier's mind had leapt first to Turkey, now he gestured toward another (familiar) locale: Egypt. Demonism and exoticism are clearly intertwined for him and, even more interestingly, demonism and *realism*. He suggests, only partly tongue in cheek, that an infernal language actually exists, deciphered by seventeenth-century orientalist Anathasius Kircher and recorded in his *Oedipus Aegyptiacus* (1652–54). This text, often considered a landmark work in the field of Egyptology, contained Kircher's "translations" of Egyptian hieroglyphs and his descriptions of later forms of the language, including Coptic (a written idiom that adapted Egyptian sounds to the Greek alphabet). The Coptic tongue, according to Kircher, was significant in that it preserved the last development of ancient Egyptian. He published a grammar for the language in 1636, the *Prodromus coptus sive aegyptiacus*, touting it as the only remaining repository of hieroglyphic sound, and therefore of lost magic and power.[14] This was surely the body of work Gautier had in mind; for him, the "real language of demons" was synonymous with that of ancient Egypt. Berlioz should have availed himself of Kircher's discovery, according to Gautier, turning to the only living speaker of Coptic, the great linguist Giuseppe Caspar Mezzofanti (1774–1849), for

---

[13] "La course fantastique a cette rapidité haletante, ce rythme saccadé, brisé, ce vertige, cet effarement que M. Berlioz excelle à rendre. Le choeur des démons, en langage infernal, est peut-être un peu long. Dans l'annonce que nous avons faite, il y a quelques jours, de la Damnation de Faust, nous élevions quelques doutes sur l'authenticité de cette partie du livret. Ce langage diabolique, que nous trouvions un peu trop ressemblant au turc de Covielle, est de l'invention de M. Hector Berlioz. La vraie langue des diables est connue. Le père Kircher en donne l'alphabet et la grammaire dans son Oedipus Aegyptiacus; elle sert à rédiger les pactes et les conjurations. Le savant Mezzofanti, qui sait toutes les langues, la parle couramment, et nul doute qu'il ne se fût fait un vrai plaisir de fournir à M. Berlioz des paroles exactes pour cette scène importante." *La Presse* (7 December 1846).

[14] Kircher's translations of hieroglyphs proved inaccurate, as did many of his claims surrounding Egyptian language and culture; nevertheless, he is regarded as an important pioneer of Egyptology whose work laid the foundation for later scholars and scientists. See Stolzenberg, *Egyptian Oedipus*; and Findlen, *Athanasius Kircher*.

a sample; he should have looked to "reality" and modern science, in other words, rather than mere fancy.

But Berlioz, as we have seen, was well aware of the exotic-demonic connection (and the wider philological and historical backdrop) alluded to by Gautier. Surely it was part of the reason he had set his first infernal tongue – that of *Le Retour* – to Cleopatra's music; indeed, the sounds and images of ancient Egypt had underpinned the composer's linguistic conception of the inferno from the outset, if only tacitly. He made the link explicit in a third language invented and set to music a decade later in the fourth act of *Les Troyens*: that of Nubian slaves, who sing and dance for the entertainment of Dido and her entourage. They come, of course, from northeastern Africa, from an area in the Nile Valley that includes the lower portion of Egypt. The inhabitants of this region sing the following text:

Ha! Ha!
Amaloué
Midonaé
Faï caraïmé
Deï beraïmbé
Ha! Ha!

None of the "words" included in this idiom is carried over from the invented languages of *Faust* or *Le Retour*, although there are clear similarities in tone and construction, even in this brief sample. The passage is framed by the same kinds of exclamatory gestures that open and close the original Pandemonium dialogue. Has! Has! has become Ha! Ha!, but both have the quality of prelinguistic noise-making or perhaps demonic laughter (or both). Certain words seem vaguely related, as though the same sounds and spellings are marked "infernal" and "foreign" in Berlioz's imagination: "caraïbo" in the Faustian tongue and "caraïmé" in the Nubian scene, for instance. And the general cadence of the languages is similar, tending toward line-endings marked by an accented "e": "uraraiké" and "burrudixé" in Pandemonium, "amaloué" and "beraïmbé" in Nubia.

Taken together, we might think of Berlioz's three invented idioms as overlapping moments of linguistic fantasy connecting make-believe languages to "real" ones, supernatural creatures to actual speakers. Demonic speech, in these instances, hovered for him on the edge of human, if culturally alien, utterance. It was not the mere babbling of medieval and Renaissance fiends – creatures defined, in part, by their estrangement from the God-given realm of language[15] – but a newly rational mode. Marked, as

---

[15] See Armando, *Satan's Rhetoric*.

we have seen, by the appearance of stable syntax and phraseology, Berlioz's infernal tongues smacked of the scientific; indeed, nineteenth-century linguists would have classed them within the same language "family." They held out the promise of translation – and the intimation of terrestrial origin. At the same time, they resisted rational reading, the semantic never quite emancipating itself from the merely noisy. At the heart of their novelty lay a new liminality, a hesitation between Molière and Mezzofanti, between Swedenborgian fantasy and modern philology.

The epistemological uncertainty marking Berlioz's demonic linguistics is significant, in part, because it is mirrored in the composer's *musical* demonism; it provides us with a starting point for interpreting the compositional language of *Les Francs-juges*, the *Huit Scènes de Faust*, and *La Damnation de Faust*, among other pieces. Works of this ilk draw on a mode that Berlioz termed the *fantastique terrible*, a phantasmagorical but also realist idiom characterized (as are the languages with which it is associated) by a complicated allegiance to the human. His newly semantic hell was also a quasi-ethnomusicological place that moved away from the undifferentiated din or purely imaginary sound of older infernos toward a conflation of "natural," exotic, and supernatural effects. This combination was, I suggest, what rendered Berlioz's darkest works especially compelling and frightening (his infernal pieces quickly became his most famous), but it was not confined to him alone. As we shall see, an aesthetics of hesitation underpinned the musical hells of many other nineteenth-century composers, lending them a newly materialist, newly *fantastique* cast. The fiends inhabiting these worlds were no longer simply imaginary creatures but earthly ones, products of entrenched theological fantasy as well as an emerging imperial reality.

A Tale of Two Gluckian Effects

At several points in his critical writing, Berlioz makes reference to two poles of fantastic expression, one associated with the demonic or "terrible," the other with the gracious and fairy-like. In *À Travers Chants*, a collection of essays and fictional pieces published in 1862, he positioned Weber's *Der Freischütz* at one end of the spectrum and the same composer's *Oberon* at the other: "*Oberon* is the counterpart of *Der Freischütz*. The one belongs to the dark, violent, demonic fantastic; the other belongs to the domain of smiling, gracious, enchanting fairies."[16] The same dichotomy surfaces in the

---

[16] Berlioz, *À Travers chants*, 242.

Memoirs, now applied to Berlioz's own work. But here an interesting substitution happens. In the *féerique* category Berlioz places an obvious piece, his Queen Mab scherzo (modeled on both Weber's and Mendelssohn's fairy music); but in the demonic category he places a work with no otherworldly connotations, the orgiastic finale of *Harold en Italie*.[17] The relationship between Weber's opera and Berlioz's symphonic movement – musical, geographical, programmatic – is unclear. Berlioz suggests an overlap between the demonic characters of the Wolf's Glen and the "real" bandits of the Abruzzi mountains, positioning his own infernal mode in both places at once.

This wavering resonates back to Berlioz's earliest references to the *fantastique terrible* in the critical writing of the mid-1830s. Here, he positions Gluck as a crucial model, drawing attention to passages from two separate works: in *Alceste*, the oracle and forest scenes; in *Iphigénie en Tauride*, the Scythian sequence. The *Alceste* scenes involve a series of supernatural events and characters: Alceste, queen of Pherae in Thessaly, prays to Apollo to restore her dying husband, Admetus, to life. The god's presence fills the temple, causing a circle of light to appear, the ground to shake, and the altar to sway. He speaks through the oracle – a stone statue – telling Alceste that Admetus will die unless another dies for him. The queen resolves to sacrifice herself and (several scenes later) keeps her promise, going alone into a dark wood "sacred to the Gods of the Underworld," where she is received by a chorus of otherworldly spirits. For Berlioz, these moments in Gluck's score represented a *locus classicus* of the dark fantastic: "What could be more terrible than the oracle scene, more fantastic than the measured recitative ('Ove fuggo, ove m'ascondo') which was so unfortunately cut from the French *Alceste*."[18]

The music animating these passages draws on a collection of related topical gestures. Act 1, scene 4 (the oracle scene), opens with a recitative in which Alceste appeals to Apollo in minor mode over chromatically slippery sustained strings. When the high priest announces that the god is present, we hear a leaping triadic figure in E flat in the strings, doubled at the unison and octave. The priest's description of the swaying altar and shaking ground are marked by a return to the minor mode, a rising dynamic level, diminished harmonies, and restless triplet and tremolo figures in the strings. All of this paves the way for the oracular pronouncement introduced by open octaves in the muted strings, horns, and trombones, and delivered in a sustained monotone. This same collection of effects reappears in Act 2, scene 2, when Alceste ventures into the dark

---

[17] Berlioz, *Memoirs*, trans. Cairns, 311.   [18] *Journal des débats* (20 February 1835), in *CM*, 2:69.

wood to give herself up to the infernal Numi. As she moves into their otherworldly terrain, diminished harmonies and agitated string figures paint both her own fear and the "mute horrors" (*muti orrori*) of the landscape. The underworld spirits greet her in much the same musical language spoken by the oracle: slow, repeated-note declamation doubled by low brass. Terrified by their voices and spectral forms, Alceste attempts to flee ("Ove fuggo, ove m'ascondo"), but finds herself transfixed. The agitated string figures return, their effect heightened by the heroine's broken, gasping text.[19]

These musical tropes, taken together, are old signifiers of horror. They have their roots, as W. J. Allanbrook has argued, in the popular "ombra scenes" of sixteenth-century *intermedi* – those "set in hell with oracular voices and choruses of infernal spirits." Allanbrook (along with Birgitte Moyer, Clive McClelland, and others, following Leonard Ratner) refers to an "ombra topic," a mode of otherworldly evocation passed down through Italian opera of the seventeenth century and disseminated through theatrical and symphonic works by later composers from Gluck to Beethoven.[20] David J. Buch, writing more recently on the subject of operatic terror, cites the same gestures, now parsing them into several overlapping categories of otherworldly sound: "noisy" effects depicting storms or hellish landscapes (often marked "bruit" or "bruit de tonnerre" in French works from Rameau onward); "noble" invocations of the classical underworld in Jommelli and Traetta, often featuring low brass; and monotone, chant-like utterances associated with oracles or statues in both French and Italian works (and linked to the sacred or "high" style). These effects were distinct but often intertwined, the product of cross-fertilization among eighteenth-century French, Italian, and German traditions of marvelous evocation. Buch jettisons the term *ombra*, pointing out that sources, both musical and aesthetic, of the period refer instead to a "terrible" or "terrifying" style:

Composers devised a designated "terrifying" style for depicting violent storms, Furies, flying dragons, infernal scenes, and similar horrific episodes. By the middle of the eighteenth century, rapid scale passages, sustained bursts in the brass instruments, disruptive *alla zoppa* syncopation, diminished chords, minor keys, tremolo, octave- and-unison sonority, and sharply contrasting dynamics were the typical devices of

---

[19] Berlioz gives a detailed description of the vocal and orchestral effects of this passage in *À Travers chants*, 187–88.

[20] Allanbrook, *Rhythmic Gesture in Mozart*, 361; Moyer, "Ombra and Fantasia in Late Eighteenth-Century Theory and Practice"; McClelland, *Ombra*; and idem "Ombra and Tempesta." All of these texts expand on Ratner's foundational work on musical topics in *Classic Music*. Moyer notes that the term *ombra* to describe the characteristic effects of supernatural scenes entered musicological discourse only as recently as Abert's *Niccolò Jommelli als Opernkomponist* (1908).

musical terror. These techniques also appeared in choruses with chantlike monophonic writing (both in unison and in octaves) and repeated-note declamation.[21]

As Buch notes, Gluck's "terrifying" evocations, especially the oracle and underworld scenes in *Alceste* and the depiction of the Furies in *Orfeo ed Euridice*, synthesized many of the key tropes of the style, providing important models for later eighteenth- and early nineteenth-century composers, including Mozart (Berlioz, among others, traced the statue music of *Don Giovanni*'s second act to Gluck) and Weber (whose Wolf's Glen music amplified the gestures of terror found in *Alceste* and *Orfeo* to an unprecedented degree).[22] It is hardly surprising, then, that Berlioz should have identified Gluck as critical to his own demonic mode; indeed, in doing so he suggested that his "dark fantastic" idiom was simply an extension of the old *ombra* tradition.

Complications arise, however, when he points to another, quite different moment in the same composer's work as equally paradigmatic: Act 1, scene 3 of *Iphigénie en Tauride*. Here, instead of the supernatural, we encounter the base natural – not the noble vistas associated with *ombra*'s sublime realm (the peaks, vast oceans, and murky deeps that Burke had hailed as stimulators of transcendental experience), but the ignoble spectacle of human savagery, a kind of bestial realism. In Gluck's scene, a great storm at sea has cast two young Greeks, Orestes and his friend Pylades, on Scythian shores. They are discovered by the natives of the region, servants of King Thoas, who call for the death of the two men in a chorus invoking the Scythian law condemning all strangers to ritual sacrifice ("Les Dieux apaisent leur couroux"). Set almost entirely syllabically, the chorus is a fierce Allegro in 2/4 whose most striking effect is the clashing of cymbals on strong beats (Scythian hatchets, according to Berlioz), reinforced by a persistent eighth-note pattern in the drum. Piccolos double the ornamented turn figures in the oboes, clarinets and upper strings, producing a high-pitched whistle. Iphigénie, Priestess of Diana, bemoans the fate of the captives in a brief aside following the chorus, while Thoas orders the men brought to the temple altar, adjuring his subjects to "sing hymns of war to our guardian gods." The Scythians comply, performing a second chorus ("Il nous fallait du sang") even more vicious, according to Gluck's marking, than the first (the piece is to be delivered with "joie barbare"). Here again, the text setting

---

[21] Buch, *Magic Flutes and Enchanted Forests*, 175. For Buch's discussion of the subcategories of terrifying sound, see 48–57.

[22] Buch explores Gluck's influence on later scenes of terror in Ibid., 81–102. Berlioz cites King Thoas's aria "De Noir pressentimens" (*Iphigénie en Tauride*, Act 1) as a direct precedent for Mozart's statue scene, linking both to the "terrible" style; see his letter of 7 December 1834, *CG*, I: 469.

is relentlessly syllabic, its intransigence underscored by doubling across the upper winds and strings. And the strong-beat cymbal and drum strokes have been amplified by a ringing triangle. Together, these instruments, along with the piccolo, generate the popular eighteenth-century "janissary" sound, against which the natives renew their call for blood. A final Scythian ballet extends the ferocity of the chorus, although it begins quietly, scored for strings and winds alone, adding the janissary instruments one by one: first the ringing triangle, then the piccolos, cymbals, and tambourine (standing in for the drum).

These effects are not associated with *ombra* scenes nor with Buch's terrifying sound at all, but with quite a different, albeit equally entrenched mode: the exotic. (The "janissary" sound was an imitation of Turkish military music, but, as Ralph P. Locke (echoing Jonathan Bellman) has pointed out, the percussive noise and primitivist phraseology and text setting with which it was associated evolved into a blanket topic for ethnic otherness – "the first codified expression of the strange and exotic."[23]) This topic was equally central to Berlioz's *fantastique* mode, according to an early and lengthy essay on *Iphigénie* in which he singled out the Scythian music:

Here, for the first and last time, Gluck used the piccolos, cymbals and basque drum. When one sees this troupe of cannibals come on stage, barking out jerky, syllabic harmony coupled with the metallic noise of the cymbals (which seems to come from the forest of hatchets brandished and waved in the air by the Scythians) it is difficult not to feel a profoundly violent shock. The second chorus, "Il nous fallait du sang," is in style still more bold and brutal, if such a thing is possible. . . . The phrases are heavy and brutish; one might imagine a chorus of drunken butchers. The tragic horror evoked to so great a degree by the voices is not at all diminished when the orchestra is heard alone. The ballet of the Scythians is universally admired, and rightly so. This light and staccato air, accompanied by a triangle and by other instruments, all playing *pianissimo*, while dancers of hideous cast pass rapidly across the scene like shades, makes one tremble. The *genre fantastique* appears here in all its power. [But] one must not say so too loudly; some of Gluck's admirers might style us blasphemers, and regard the application of such an accursed term to one of his works as a grave insult.[24]

For Berlioz, the bloodthirsty Scythians are in some sense "like" the shades of the operatic *ombra* tradition; demonism is interlinked with cannibalism, the otherworldly with the Other. The Scythians of Gluck's (originally

---

[23] Locke, *Musical Exoticism*, 110–26 (here, 110). For Bellman's remarks, see *The "style hongrois" in the Music of Western Europe*, 24–25. Other relevant discussions include Meyer, "*Turquerie* and Eighteenth-Century Music"; and Hunter, "The *Alla Turca* Style in the Late Eighteenth Century."

[24] *Gazette musicale* (7 December 1834), in *CM*, 1:469–70. This was the last in a series of four essays on *Iphigénie en Tauride* published that year; the others appeared on 9, 16, and 23 November.

Euripides') story were, obviously, a real people whose exploits – particularly their prowess in war – were recorded by the fifth-century historian Herodotus. They controlled an empire reaching, at its peak, from west Persia through Syria and Judaea to the borders of Egypt, a territory bordering on that of the Turkic tribes to the east and the peoples of the Mediterranean and North Africa to the south. They take us back to the same general neighborhood of Cleopatra and to the exotic-demonic overlap underpinning Berlioz's infernal languages. Clearly, these associations carried over into his conception of infernal *music*; indeed, the effects associated with Gluck's Scythians are cited repeatedly in Berlioz's critical writings as markers of a newly defined "terrifying" style.

The Orchestration Treatise makes this connection clear, linking the instrumental effects of the "cannibal" choruses – particularly their percussive clashing – directly to the sounds and imagery of demonic terror. In his remarks on the piccolo, for instance, Berlioz notes that the shrieking effect of the instrument's top range is appropriate for scenes "of ferocious, satanic character," especially when coupled with cymbals and percussion. Gluck's Scythian music serves as his prime example: "In the *Choeur des Scythes* ... two piccolos double the violins' turns an octave higher. These shrill notes, combined with the baying of the savage horde and the incessant rhythmic clatter of cymbals and small drum, have a terrifying effect."[25] Gluck's effect was taken up, in modified form, by Spontini, who pared it down (for the first time, according to Berlioz) to a cymbal and piccolo clash in a bacchanale written for the Parisian version of Antonio Salieri's *Les Danaïdes* (1817):

> It was Spontini, in the magnificent *Bacchanale* he wrote for Salieri's *Les Danaïdes* (which later became an orgiastic chorus in *Nurmahal*), who first thought of coupling a brief piercing cry on the piccolos with a cymbal clash. The unique relationship thus established between two such dissimilar instruments had not been suspected before. It causes an instantly lacerating, stabbing sensation, like a swordthrust.

Spontini's effect was, as Berlioz noted, striking, although he goes on to argue that the full "Scythian" clash found in Gluck is stronger: "This [Spontini's] is a very characteristic effect even if only the two instruments in question are used. But with a staccato entry of the timpani and a short chord on all the other instruments its force is greatly increased" (here, Berlioz gives an example modeled on *Iphigénie*, complete with piccolo grace notes).[26]

---

[25] Berlioz, *Orchestration Treatise*, trans. Macdonald, 147.
[26] Ibid., 147. Macdonald notes that Berlioz's example does not derive directly from Gluck, but instead seems to capture his memory of the composer's effect.

Like Gluck's Scythian music, Spontini's bacchanale is an exotic evocation laced with violent intent. Incorporating a "Hymne à Bacchus," and a danced chorus, it sets up the moment when the Danaïds (daughters of Danaus, according to Greek legend) kill their unwanted Egyptian husbands, first seducing them with wine and dance. The sequence is marked *Allegro con fuoco* (A minor/D minor; 2/4 time) and characterized by an incrementally increasing tempo, presumably evoking the escalating ferocity of the Danaïds (and, when the bacchanale appears later, in *Nurmahal*, the burgeoning rage of Dsheangir, emperor of the Mongols[27]). According to the manuscript score of Spontini's/Salieri's *Les Danaïdes*, "The dance accelerates by degrees and becomes a kind of bacchanale."[28] Its exotic/erotic frenzy is conjured both by the partial "Scythian clashes" that Berlioz notes and by the ringing of a triangle – the same janissary instrumentation Gluck employed. In the Orchestration Treatise, as in his later critical writing, Berlioz repeatedly marked this collection of sounds as productive of musical terror, even calling the bacchanale "the archetype of satanic and orgiastic frenzy."[29]

The importance, not just of the cymbal/piccolo/drum combination, but the triangle, is confirmed in his entry for the instrument, which brings us back to the Scythian music as well as folding in yet another moment of exotic evocation: "Its [the triangle's] metallic sound is only suitable for loud sections in extremely brilliant pieces, or for playing softly in strange, bizarre passages. Weber made the most felicitous use of it in his Gypsies' Chorus in *Preciosa* and Gluck's use was even better in the *maggiore* section of the terrifying Scythians' Chorus in Act I of *Iphigénie en Tauride*."[30] Here, we see clearly the degree to which the sounds of cultural and geographical otherness had become intertwined with Berlioz's conception of horror. His version of the "terrifying" style was more capacious than that of his eighteenth-century predecessors. No longer associated only with the invocation of gods, oracles, ghosts, or storms, it embraced the sounds of Turks, Scythians, Egyptians, and even Gypsies (themselves fantasized and therefore interchangeable markers of alterity).

---

[27] Spontini's *Nurmahal oder das Rosenfest von Caschmir* (on a libretto by Carl Alexander Herklots, after Spicker's German translation of Thomas Moore's *Lalla Rookh*) originated as a series of *tableaux vivants* written in honor of Tsar Nicholas's visit to the Prussian court in 1821. The composer expanded it into a full opera the following year.
[28] The full indication reads as follows: "Scène IV. La danse s'anime par degrés et devient une espèce de bacchanale. Les Danaïds versant à boire à leurs époux, et les enivrant d'amour et de vin. Le jour commence à baisser. Hymne à Bacchus. Choeur dansé." For more on Spontini's additions and changes to Salieri's opera, see Parodi, "*Les Danaïdes* di Salieri diretta da Gaspare Spontini (Parigi, 1817)."
[29] In *Les Soirées de l'orchestre*, 220.   [30] Berlioz, *Orchestration Treatise*, trans. Macdonald, 290.

The *fantastique terrible*, in Berlioz's new formulation, had broadened to encompass both the transcendental and the material, both unearthly and human horrors. Its raw materials, however, were by no means unprecedented, but were grounded (as we have seen) in well-established systems of musico-topical signification. What *was* novel about Berlioz's demonic mode, what rendered it *fantastique*, was its conflation of these systems. It forced together the sublime realm of *ombra* (that of divinity, nobility, and the "high style") with the burlesque realm of exoticism (that of the barbaric and often comic).[31] It was, in other words, the product of a topical and more broadly stylistic and epistemological convergence, a new kind of permeability. To come back to José Monleón's definition of the fantastic, it placed "two incompatible systems in one single sign."[32] As we shall see, this same conflation marked Berlioz's infernal music from the earliest period of his career, generating exotic demons of a specially nineteenth-century cast.

Berlioz's Demons

Berlioz's first foray into the realm of musical horror was an opera set in fifteenth-century Germany featuring the activities of the secret Vehmic tribunals (self-appointed vigilante judges), *Les Francs-juges*. The topic was a popular one in the 1820s, at the height of the craze for Gothic-tinted *romans noirs*, having already featured in a *mélodrame historique* by J.-H.-F. de Lamartelière and a historical sketch by François Adolphe Loève-Veimars. Berlioz's opera, riding the coattails of these works, was composed in 1825–26 on a libretto by Humbert Ferrand (it was revised in 1829–30 and again in 1833–34, but never performed; Berlioz finally abandoned it, destroying or recycling much of the composed material).[33] In keeping with the aesthetic of the moment, he downplayed the historical

---

[31] As Locke notes, Turks were usually represented on the eighteenth-century theatrical stage as ridiculous, appearing "in operatic genres that were more or less comic" (*Musical Exoticism*, 111, 116). Head, in *Orientalism, Masquerade and Mozart's Turkish Music*, makes the same point, arguing that once the Ottoman Empire ceased to pose a serious military threat to Western Europe (by the mid-eighteenth century at the latest), Turks became the stuff of operatic ridicule, depicted as socially and intellectually backward. A letter from Mozart to his father describing the character of Osmin in *Die Entführung aus dem Serail* confirms the tradition, claiming that Osmin's rage was "rendered comical by the use of Turkish music" (58).

[32] Monleón, *A Specter is Haunting Europe*, 40.

[33] J.-H.-F. de Lamartelière, *Les Francs-juges, ou les temps de barbarie* (Paris: Barba, 1807). François Adolphe Loève-Veimars, *Précis de l'histoire des tribunaux secrets dans le nord de l'Allemagne* (Toul: Carez, 1824). The play by Lamartelière, first performed in 1807 and revived at the Théâtre de l'Ambigu-Comique in 1823 (where Berlioz saw it), is the obvious template for Ferrand's libretto. See *NBE*, 4:viii.

in favor of the phantasmagorical, figuring the *francs-juges* as hooded, quasi-demonic specters. Their story begins with the nefarious Olmerick, who has seized the throne of Breisgau by murdering his brother, the king. In order to eliminate his last remaining rival, he tasks the Vehmic judges to hunt down and kill his nephew Arnold. We learn of Olmerick's villainy and Arnold's flight in the first two acts which, set in an ancient castle surrounded by a forest, emphasize the sinister hold of the judges over the local peasantry. In the climactic third act, Arnold faces the black-hooded tribunal in a cavern furnished with a circle of twelve black chairs and lit by the reflections of a distant moon. The ritual proceedings are presided over by a bronze statue – an emissary of hell – sent to exact final judgment on the accused. At the last moment, just as Arnold's fate seems sealed, soldiers storm in, saving the day. Olmerick refuses to be taken alive, instead leaping into the arms of the statue, which is engulfed in flames.

The influence of *Don Giovanni*, with its avenging statue, is transparent, as is that of *Der Freischütz*, whose Wolf's Glen provides a clear model for Berlioz's midnight cavern scene.[34] And *Les Francs-juges* borrows all the familiar *ombra* tropes of Mozart's and Weber's supernatural music – those of the old terrifying style – from trembling and rushing strings, to blasting low brass and rumbling timpani. But Berlioz also incorporates effects absent from Weber and Mozart: those of Gluck's Scythians, most obviously their trademark drum, cymbal, and piccolo clash. It appears at several points in the fragmentary remains of the opera, notably in the reprise of the "Hymne des francs-juges" at the climax of the cavern scene, when Olmerick admonishes the judges to carry out their task of vengeance. They stand immobile in the presence of the statue, their eyes lit by a "sublime flame" and their ears deaf to all pleas. Their hymn opens with sustained brass and muffled timpani, to which shivering and sharply rising figures in the strings are soon added – familiar *ombra* gestures. But midway through the hymn, Berlioz calls for the two flutes to be replaced by piccolos and, as the avengers announce their intention to strike ("Frappons, frappons!"), we hear the sound of Scythian hatchets: *fortissimo* "janissary" chords decorated – as were Gluck's – with grace notes in the piccolo (Example 5.2). The effect is arresting, suggesting that Ferrand's judges are, in Berlioz's mind (or ear), both supernatural emissaries and human savages.

This conflation of otherworldliness and Otherness is showcased even more clearly in the overture, which provides a foretaste of the opera's key instrumental effects and themes. Composed last, and representing Berlioz's

---

[34] Holoman emphasizes Weber's influence in *Berlioz*, 83. Rushton also notes echoes of Spontini, Le Sueur, and Gluck (in the solo oboe part) in *The Music of Berlioz*, 12. Cairns highlights the work's indebtedness to opera of the Revolution and the Empire in *Berlioz*, 1:227–33.

Example 5.2 Berlioz, "Hymn des Francs-juges" with janissary strikes, mm. 46–48

most polished writing of the period, it was the only portion of *Les Francs-juges* to enter the permanent repertory (it was first performed in May 1828 and reappeared on Berlioz's Parisian programs routinely through the mid-1830s).[35] Cast in F minor, it opens with a quiet dotted figure in the violins, which, soon doubled in the bassoons, rises chromatically over a string tremolo to a threatening *fortissimo*. Our sense that the world of the opera is to be a supernatural one is confirmed a few measures later by octave-unison blasting in the trombones and ophicleides: *ombra* writ large.

[35] Performances of the Overture (often alongside other extracts from *Les Francs-juges*) included those on the following dates: 26 May 1828; 1 November 1829; 5 December 1830; 3 December 1832; 12 March 1833, 2 May 1833, 24 November 1833, 14 December 1834, 25 June 1835, 18 December 1836.

The low brass theme – Olmerick's musical marker – charges upward to a series of repeated-note climaxes followed by chromatically darkened descents. Its final upsurge drives toward a cadence marked, unexpectedly, by a Scythian clash. Berlioz introduces the piccolos, cymbals, and timpani for this single chord, its steely D-flat major punctuating a turn from the harmonically dark realm of the supernatural to the major-mode world of Gluck's "joyous" barbarians. Immediately afterward, the low brass (and the minor mode) reasserts itself, but the same D-flat major cadence brings the janissary instruments back, now for a series of *fortissimo* clashes moving swiftly from D-flat to a distant C major (mm. 45–49) as if to suggest timbral and harmonic estrangement (Example 5.3). Once again, *ombra* tropes return, but the introduction culminates in yet another moment of "Scythian" intrusion (m. 57), this one on the heels of a dominant lock on C clearly meant to prepare a tonic (F minor) beginning for the Allegro section. The clash – a diminished seventh chord on B-natural – derails things, jerking us away from C major, which Berlioz then reasserts, *piano*. The chord reads as a harmonic and topical grinding of gears, an intrusion of savagery into the "high style" of supernatural *ombra*.

If the clashes dominating the slow introduction seem like moments of topical dissonance, the remainder of the overture begins to synthesize Berlioz's exotic and *ombra* material, welding them into a new whole. As the Allegro begins, we move away, temporarily, from the otherworldly/Other dialectic of the opening, toward a topically remote theme in the strings (perhaps representing Arnold's flight) and a lyrical melody in the violins and winds (the pastoral realm of the peasants). A timpani solo (mm. 308–35) recalls the old *bruit* or *bruit de tonnerre* effects of French scenes of terror – a storm, perhaps, since it is embedded in pastoral material. Here, and elsewhere through the lyrical material, the low-brass *ombra* effects return, and when they do, the Scythian clashes are also heard. The two effects are showcased most clearly in mm. 457–71, now no longer separate but overlapping, the descending three-note motive in the brass accompanied in each case by a janissary clash. Thus far, Berlioz has called for the piccolo only during these characteristic chords, but by m. 457 he assigns the instrument its own staff, integrating it into the orchestral texture as though diffusing its sound – now wedded to the exotic clash – across the sonic landscape.

As the piece draws to a close, the tempo begins to increase *con furore*, from *animato* in m. 580, to *Più vivo* in m. 588, and finally *Molto vivo* in m. 604. Now the *ombra* and janissary instruments are fully integrated, brass blasting accompanied by cymbals and timpani in a frenzied tutti roar. The two topical worlds have converged, low trombone and ophicleide

Example 5.3 Berlioz, *Les Francs-juges*, Overture, fortissimo clashes (in context), mm. 42–49

chords graced with Gluck's familiar piccolo flourishes as if a band of marauding Scythians had wandered into the Gothic world of the *francs-juges*. This is not simply a case of the *tutta forza* noise-making Berlioz associated with Rossini's overtures (pieces that sometimes draw on the same complement of instruments); indeed, the composer of *Les Francs-juges* explicitly condemned such "abuse," arguing that percussion should not be used indiscriminately, nor should any instrument (especially the low brass) be employed simply to amplify sound.[36] These instruments, and the topics with which they are associated, are strategically deployed in Berlioz's Overture. Their careful highlighting in the early portion of the work invites us to hear them as independent entities even when they are combined – or, to put it differently, to be aware of their conflation as hermeneutically charged. The culminating din of Berlioz's Overture does more than just assault the ear, it also complicates conventional musico-rhetorical listening, combining the gestures of supernaturalism with those he identified with savage naturalism to produce the new *fantastique terrible*.

Les Francs-juges is important in part because it is the first place in which Berlioz showcases this exotic-demonic interface. Clearly practice preceded theory; his first opera was composed several years before mention of a dark fantastic mode appeared in his critical writings and long before the Orchestration Treatise formalized this mode (and made it prescriptive) by linking the two topical traditions at its heart. The connection does not appear to have been inherited; it is absent, as I have already noted, from the scenes of terror that Berlioz knew and admired: those of Gluck, Mozart, and Weber. In his own work, however, the interface continued to feature; indeed, the effects Berlioz associated with barbarism (particularly the telltale Scythian clash) become a permanent feature of his infernal terrains and the demons therein.

Consider, for instance, *La Damnation de Faust*, written some twenty years after *Les Francs-juges*. The work is a quasi-opera (Berlioz titled it *Légende dramatique*) calling for an enormous orchestra, chorus, and four soloists: Faust, Marguerite, Brander, and Méphistophélès. The latter character – the century's best-known demon – appears for the first time in Part II following the "Chant de la Fête de Pâques." At this point, Faust, who begins the work jaded and dissatisfied, has been buoyed by the warmth of spring and the Easter hymn of the townsfolk. Against a backdrop of sustained strings he announces that "heaven has won me back," but the minute the

---

[36] Complaints surrounding gratuitous orchestral noise-making and ill-considered instrumentation weave through the Orchestration Treatise, which draws special attention to misuse of the bass drum and cymbals, as well as unmotivated deployment of the percussion in general, and of brass instruments. As Macdonald points out, these kinds of complaints date to the earliest years of Berlioz's career, becoming increasingly insistent through the 1830s and 1840s. Characteristic is his essay in the *Journal des débats* (14 December 1841), which excoriates the abuse of instruments in works by minor composers Alexandre Monfort and P.-L.-P. Dietsch. Here, Berlioz winds up with a familiar anti-Rossinian diatribe: "It is the present leader of the so-called School of Melody [Rossini] whom we have to blame for this horrible instrumental abuse, while Beethoven and Weber, the leaders of the rival school regarded as the School of Violence and Noise, were alone in upholding the principle of moderation and the intelligent use of instruments." Berlioz, of course, counts himself a member of the "rival school." Qtd. in Macdonald, *Berlioz's Orchestration Treatise*, 225–26.

words have left his mouth, Méphistophélès appears and begins to undermine his restored faith. The demon is accompanied by a sudden (familiarly Gluckian) clash: a single chord for upper winds, brass, and cymbals anticipated by a descending motive in the trombones and a grace-note flourish in the piccolo, all underpinned by a *fortissimo* tremolo in the strings. This is, of course, the amplified Scythian clash (minus the timpani). It happens in a flash, clearly meant as a timbral shock rather than a harmonic entity, although the string tremolo persists, against which the initial trombone motive is developed. Here, encapsulated in a single moment, we encounter the same topical wedding permeating the *Francs-juges*: a convergence of *ombra* instruments and effects (low brass, tremolo, diminished harmonies, chromatic motion) and exotic ones (the cymbal/piccolo strike) (Example 5.4).

Méphistophélès's bidirectional topical sign will stay with him throughout *La Damnation*, reappearing whenever he does. It (and he) returns, for instance, just after the sacrilegious fugue following Brander's drinking song. Again, the chord has the quality of an orchestrational shock, emerging without warning from the quasi-religious plagal cadence (emphasized by a *ritenuto*) at the end of the choral "Amen." This time – presumably to maximize the effect – Berlioz cuts out the strings entirely, producing a focused *fortissimo* "sword thrust" in the upper winds, brass, and cymbals, with the same piccolo/brass anticipation and sneering trombone after-effects.[37] Méphistophélès is not simply a phantasmagorical demon, but, like the *francs-juges*, a savage one, hovering midway between the barbaric "real" and the theological imaginary.

When we arrive with Faust at Méphistophélès's domain, Pandemonium, we find that it too is shot through with markers of exotic ferocity. The movement opens with a reinforced version of the demon's chord, cymbal and piccolo now accompanied by bass drum and gong and trombones doubled by ophicleides. This sonority permeates the opening several systems, establishing itself as the dominant timbre of hell, the sonic backdrop against which Berlioz's infernal language is heard. It thins, momentarily, when the Princes of Darkness ask Méphistophélès the crucial question: "Are you master and lord over this proud soul [that of Faust] forever?" (*De cette âme si fière / À jamais es-tu maître et vainqueur, Méphisto?*). Here, Berlioz gives us conventional *ombra* tropes: unison scoring in the chorus, doubled by trombones, ophicleides, and bassoons, against a bass tremolo (shades of the oracular pronouncement in *Alceste*). When Méphistophélès answers in the affirmative, the amplified Scythian clashes return in

---

[37] Macdonald draws attention to the cymbal/piccolo clashes in both *Les Francs-juges* and *La Damnation de Faust*, noting that "a characteristic of these 'satanic' shrieks is the grace note (or notes) on the piccolo" (*Berlioz's Orchestration Treatise*, 148).

Example 5.4 Berlioz, *La Damnation de Faust*, Méphistophélès's first appearance, Part II, scene v

a frenzied explosion – again, the "joie barbare" of Gluck's chorus – as the demons carry him aloft in triumph, speaking their infernal tongue. Berlioz alternates between exotic effects (paired with his incomprehensible idiom) and *ombra* gestures (for the intelligible question and answer), between the literally foreign and the conventionally marvelous.

There follows a demonic celebration, a shift to Allegro and to triple time as the infernal horde dances around Méphistophélès. This section, too, opens with an amplified clash, now complete with Gluckian grace notes in the piccolo. Berlioz sets his demonic language almost entirely syllabically as a series of quarter notes organized into short, repeating melodic/harmonic units – the same approach taken by Gluck in his Scythian choruses and by many other Western composers of "primitive" music.[38] As the hellish revelers invoke the names of fictional and biblical demons ("Diff! Diff! Merondor / Merondor aysko! / Has! Has! Satan / Has! Has! Belphégor / Has! Has! Méphisto"), Berlioz lightens the orchestral texture, generating the illusion of speed. Our sense that the dance is accelerating is heightened by the piling up of names in the final measures of the section ("Diff! Diff! Belzébuth, / Belphégor, Astaroth, Méphisto!") and by consistent downbeat accents. The scene hurtles toward a final prolonged Scythian clash (sustained in a blast of sound over a single bar marked *maestoso*) before ratcheting up several notches in tempo for the final *Allegro vivace*, now in common time, which culminates in an explosion of tutti clashes degenerating into sheer clamor: a bass drum solo, prolonged timpani rolls, and racing scalar figures in the bass.

Berlioz's demonic dance borrows the orchestral effects of Gluck's exotic choruses as well as the incremental tempo increases of Spontini's bacchanale (the same is true of the *Francs-juges* overture, whose *con furore accelerandi* now seem as much like tropes of Berlioz's new demonic mode as excitement-building devices routine to operatic overtures). Clearly, he conceived of the infernal world and its ceremonies, whether enacted by hellish judges or whirling fiends, in terms of exotic ritual: exultant demons behave much like bloodthirsty Scythians and vengeful Danaïds or Mongols. Not just the sounds, then, but the forms, tempi, and expressive markings he associates with Otherness have become native to his *ombra* characters and landscapes.[39]

---

[38] See Locke's summary of "exotic" effects in *Musical Exoticism*, 51–54.

[39] The Scythian clash appears in two other movements in *La Damnation*: the "Marche Hongroise" (also known as the Rakoczy March) and the scene in Auerbach's cellar. I deal with its appearance in the latter passage in the final section of this chapter. The janissary instrumentation of the March is more straightforward. It serves, on one hand, simply to mark Hungary as an exotic place, a world outside the realm of European "civilization" (this was an association on which Liszt had already capitalized). On the other hand, it reflects the absorption of janissary instruments into European, particularly Austrian, military ensembles of the eighteenth century, perhaps (as Matthew Head suggests) as a way of "absorbing their [the Turks'] military strength" while also celebrating their neutralization as a military power (*Orientalism, Masquerade and Mozart's Turkish Music*, 33). A similar conflation of janissary effects with military topoi happens in the works of other composers; see, for instance, Rossini's overture to *La Gazza Ladra*, whose opening section (marked *Maestoso marziale*) also features "Turkish" instrumentation.

The same infiltration also happens in the opposite direction in Berlioz's *oeuvre*: the tropes of supernatural terror begin to appear in evocations of *terrestrial* savagery. A clear example of this reverse penetration is to be found in the much earlier *Harold en Italie* (1834), whose finale depicts the life of Italian bandits – lawless savages of the Abruzzi mountains, according to Berlioz's descriptions. His "Orgie des Brigands" opens with precisely the sonority we might expect: the tutti Scythian clash, whose timbral jolt is intensified by a dissonant seventh. The bandits' theme follows, marked by short, jerky units doubled across the strings, and offbeat accents that destabilize our sense of meter, suggesting a kind of chaotic abandon. Taking a page from Beethoven's book, Berlioz moves through a series of reminiscences of the symphony's previous movements beginning with a snippet of the introductory material from "Harold aux montagnes," then melodies from the Pilgrims' March and Serenade, and Harold's own viola theme.[40] Each of these is cut off by the brigands' music, which grows more violent with every recurrence, moving from the *con frenetico* effect of the opening to *con fuoco* at m. 71 (the latter marking echoes Spontini's bacchanale as well as the *con furore* of the *Francs-juges* Overture). Already, its appearance following the first-movement quotation has a frenzied feel, culminating in multiple accelerating repetitions of a rising fourth (mm. 29–33) whose brutishness calls to mind Gluck's cannibals. The serenade music lasts only eight measures, silenced by the tutti clash heard at the movement's opening. Finally, Harold's theme meets the same end – *he* is now the trespasser on foreign soil, annihilated by a version of the same musical blade that threatened Orestes.

Once the reminiscences have been dispatched, the "orgy proper" (as Julian Rushton puts it) can begin.[41] Now the brigands' music unfolds without interruption, marked by the same rhythmic instability and stabbing octave drop we encountered in the opening. Berlioz varies and explores this material before arriving at a related theme in m. 177, a march. It, too, begins with a tutti Scythian clash, drawing on the octave drop and rushing triplet figures already associated with the brigands. And now the exotic instruments are brought more overtly to the fore, their characteristic steel-on-steel sound marking the beginnings and endings of phrases. This theme originated in a sketch for "Le Retour de l'armée d'Italie" (a piece depicting Napoleon's triumphant return from his Italian campaign). It draws our attention to the appropriation of janissary instruments and effects by European military ensembles – the sounds of the subdued appropriated

---

[40] For more on this feature of the finale, see Bonds, "*Sinfonia anti-eroica.*"
[41] Rushton, *The Music of Berlioz*, 268.

by the subduers – suggesting, perhaps, that, foreign savagery could also be domestic. More transparently, the march invests Berlioz's "exotic" bandits with military ferocity, giving them the hatchets and swords he associated with the Gluckian/Spontinian clash (the telltale piccolo grace notes underscore this connection).

But all of these violently exotic tropes – the sounds of murder, rape, and pillage – give way, as does the janissary orchestration, around m. 208 when Berlioz introduces a dissonant tremolo (E-flat/D in the first violins against octave Ds in the seconds). This trembling sonority, sustained over the following twenty-three measures, marks a drastic change in topical language, ushering in sustained chords, *forte*, in the brass, and a triplet motive doubled at the octave/unison in the trombones and low winds. The jubilant major mode of the brigands' march dissolves, replaced by minor and diminished harmonies, the earlier *con fuoco* marking exchanged for *con gravità*. The tropes Berlioz is invoking here are, of course, those of a conventional *ombra* scene, the same collection of gestures he had already applied to Olmerick and his vigilante judges (and would later attach to Méphistophélès). Suddenly, *Harold*'s brigands no longer seem simply like terrestrial outlaws, but figures of a darkly supernatural cast; the Abruzzi mountains are tinged with the shadows of the Wolf's Glen (Example 5.5).[42] This passage ends as quickly as it began, yet another Scythian clash (m. 231) wrenching us out of the volatile C-minor realm of the trombones and ophicleides as if by force. (The topical jolt here is similar to the ones we encountered in the introduction to the *Francs-juges* overture.) After a bit of harmonic casting about and a melancholic string theme (the anguish of the brigands' victims?), we are back in the realm of orgiastic celebration. A written-out repeat of the exposition, minus the opening reminiscences, allows us to hear the entire sequence again.

As in both *Les Francs-juges* and *Faust*, the topical and orchestrational worlds set most clearly in relief in the symphony's exposition – those of the exotic and the otherworldly – converge as the piece comes to a close.

---

[42] Rushton hears the orgy differently, as a piece of irony, calling the brass motive in the section beginning at m. 208 a "drunken trombone theme" (*The Music of Berlioz*, 268–69). An element of burlesque may indeed underpin the movement, the Turkish/military topic of its opening section hearkening back to the comedic flavor of certain exotic scenes in eighteenth-century opera. But I hear less humor in the *ombra* section, whose trembling opening ushers us unmistakably into the *seria* realm, yoking the brigands' brutality with intimations of supernatural evil. Many nineteenth-century critics agree: a report in *L'Artiste*, for instance, highlighted the "verve infernale" of the movement (November 1834) and a piece in *Le Figaro* called the Orgie "satanique et terrible" (25 November 1834), with both reviewers attributing its hellish effects to novel orchestration.

Example 5.5 Berlioz, "Orgie des brigands," *Harold en Italie* IV, *ombra* music with entry of trombones, mm. 211–16

Harold tries one final time to assert himself (or perhaps his religious sentiments) in a passage recalling a snatch of the pilgrims' music (the solo viola is heard as part of a string quartet texture). But the chant, and with it the hope that heroism or faith will prevail, is finally and absolutely vanquished with the Scythian clash of m. 501. We are left in the world of the brigands, which is also, Berlioz suggests, that of demons. He brings back the orgy/march music, punctuated by janissary effects, its triplet figure appearing in diminution in the strings, then in shorter note values, finally escalating into a headlong rush – a quasi-accelerando gesturing back to Spontini's bacchanale as well as forward to the frenetic close of Pandemonium. But against this backdrop, the low brass also returns in long notes over a chromatic descent recalling the *ombra* texture of the exposition. The same convergence happens again beginning in m. 563, although now the brass have adopted the triplet rhythm of the orgiastic strings, and the strings the long notes of the brass. The two topics and their respective instrumentations have, in other words, intermeshed, joining forces for a crashing close.

That Berlioz located both *Der Freischütz* and the finale of *Harold* at the same dark end of the fantastic spectrum now seems more logical. For him, the musical worlds of lawless savagery and demonic revelry were synonymous, occupying the same topical and affective terrain. He underscored the conflation in an excited report on *Harold*'s 1843 performance in Brunswick (one of the stops on his German tour) figuring the players and even their instruments as dancers in a bacchanale tinged with supernaturalism:

> [I]n this furious brigands' orgy, where the intoxications of wine, blood, joy and rage mingle – where the rhythm seems now to stumble, now to rush furiously forward and the mouths of the brass to spew forth curses, responding with blasphemy to the voices of supplication, laughing, drinking, striking, destroying, killing and raping – in this brigands' scene, the orchestra *became a veritable pandaemonium*. There was something supernatural and terrifying in the frenzy of its [the players'] exhilaration, violins, cellos, trombones, drums, cymbals, all singing, leaping, and roaring with diabolical accuracy and precision, while from the viola (the dreamer Harold) a few faint echoes of the trembling evening hymn were still heard hovering in the distance.[43]

Here, the brigands (and their music) teeter between human sadism and otherworldly evil, occupying the same semi-real Pandemonium as does Méphistophélès. This was not the torturous fire pit of Christian theology nor the gloomy classical underworld, but a new and quintessentially *fantastique* locale. Clearly, something had shifted in the perception and construction of hell – something that produced Berlioz's radically "real" demons.

The beginnings of an explanation are to be found in the musical narrative (the "program") of *Harold* itself, which borrowed not just from Byron's epic poem, but, as Berlioz claimed, from his own direct experiences of Italy and its inhabitants. His bandit-fiends were the product of a new kind of ethnographic impulse, a species of foreign reporting undertaken during Berlioz's sojourn to Rome and its environs as a Prix de Rome winner in the early 1830s. He kept a detailed journal of his adventures, highlighting his forays into the "wild Abruzzo" mountains (the alleged home of the bandits), which provided the basis for several published articles – contributions to the popular travel writing genre – including a piece commissioned by the *Revue européenne* (1832) and an essay in a collection titled *Italie pittoresque* (1836). Berlioz later recycled this material into his book-length *Voyage musicale en Allemagne et en Italie* (1844) and his *Mémoires*, where he linked his experiences in Italy directly to his production of *Harold*.[44]

---

[43] Berlioz, *Mémoires*, 2:110.
[44] Inge van Rij has also explored Berlioz's engagement with travel writing, including tales of New Zealand and Tahiti and the Italian narratives he associated with the song "La Captive"; see *The Other Worlds of Hector Berlioz*, 14–69.

The mountainous region that Berlioz associated with the symphony's brigands is among the most intensely described in his Italian writings, where it is figured as a world so distant from modern civilization that "neither art nor industrialism had penetrated." Of the mountains and their inhabitants, Berlioz wrote:

The villages of Vico-Var, Olevano, Arsoli, Genesano and a score of others whose names I have forgotten are almost identical to look at: the same huddle of greyish houses plastered like swallows' nests against the same barren and almost sheer mountainside, the same half-naked children running up at the sight of strangers. ... Streets or paths, where they exist, are mere ledges in the rock, barely discernible from the rest. You encounter men loafing about, who stare oddly at you; women driving pigs, which, with maize, form the entire wealth of the region ... and all so wretched, downtrodden and squalidly dirty that in spite of the natural beauty of the people and the picturesque cut of the native dress, it is hard to look at them and experience any feeling but pity.[45]

Even worse were the rural places he encountered on the way back from a trip to Castellammare: one village was full of "appalling hovels" and inhabited only by "a pair of young pigs wallowing in black mud on the rough boulders which served the wretched place for streets." Outside of it Berlioz and his companions encountered a shepherd whose "guttural speech was more like a gargle than any language known to man." The bandits operating in this rural landscape were also shaped by it, less noble (and less literary) than those Byron had immortalized. Coming back from a visit to Tasso's island, Berlioz reflected "on the attractions of the brigand's life ... thinking that despite the hardships it would be the only really decent career left for an honest man, if there were not so many wretched, subnormal and vile-smelling creatures even in the smallest gangs."[46]

These descriptions, saturated with xenophobia, tell us much about the political and aesthetic impulses underpinning Berlioz's new conception of the demonic. His brigands are more than just foreign or otherworldly creatures; they are specimens of colonialist ethnography, members of a backward society seen through the lens of a "cultured" observer. In conjuring them, Berlioz adopts the tone of the imperial travelogue, a vaguely Napoleonic disdain for everything outside the French capital that allows him to dismiss rural Italy as a land estranged from modern Europe, awaiting (but perhaps impervious to) enlightenment. Its inhabitants are both fascinating and repulsive, their gargling subhumanism tied, in Berlioz's symphony, to a new brand of evil. It was this conflation of imperial reality and the infernal imaginary – a new mode of colonialist looking and

---

[45] Berlioz, *Memoirs*, trans. Cairns, 179.   [46] Ibid., 99, 200, and 195–96.

hearing – that shaped Berlioz's infernos, locating and populating them. The devilry we encounter in *Harold*'s finale is mild (Italy's brigands still have a certain romantic appeal and a literary familiarity), but Berlioz's most terrifying infernos were, as his invented languages suggest (and as I shall argue in the next section), associated with more distant geographies and with "demonic" natives more foreign than the Italian pillagers: figures hovering on the edge of an expanding French empire.

The Imperial Inferno

The sun had just set, leaving behind it darkness and gloomy thoughts. I was conscious of nothing but fear; the desert, hunger, and dangers of every kind presented themselves before me to frighten me.[47]
  –T. Arbousset and F. Daumas, *Relation d'un voyage d'exploration au nord-est de la colonie de Cape de Bonne-Espérance*

The relationship between demonism and imperialism is a familiar one, much explored by colonial and postcolonial theorists, who have described from various angles the processes of darkening inherent in that of colonizing: the establishment of civilized-savage binaries that relegate certain groups to the level of Calibans; the practices of projection that transfer the least desirable qualities of dominant cultures onto those they subjugate; the rhetorical devices that inscribe such subjugated groups within a language of abjection; and the manipulation of discourse itself (the idioms of history, science, and philosophy) such that the objects of imperial desire are constructed through and enfolded by them.[48] These are universal tactics, by no means particular to the romantic period. But they were implemented with special force in France in the first decades of the nineteenth century during a time of renewed imperialist ambition – the first stirrings of the so-called second colonial empire. This was a period in which a new and especially damning weapon was added to the imperial arsenal: a theory of racial difference that opened up an unbridgeable gap between self and other, a chasm filled with fear and loathing. More radically than ever before, the act of colonizing became one of demonizing, a locating of darkness (moral, intellectual, spiritual) within the body itself. The fiends that resulted – those menacing Berlioz's generation – were no longer just the stuff of imagination, they were also products of reason, "discovered" and constructed by the

---

[47] Translations of this work are adapted from those of Brown in *Narrative of an Exploratory Tour*.
[48] See, for instance, the following classic and more recent texts: Mannoni, *Psychologie de la colonization* (in English as *Prospero and Caliban*); Curtin, *Image of Africa*; Said, *Orientalism*; Cohen, *The French Encounter with Africans*; and Spurr, *The Rhetoric of Empire*.

burgeoning physical and social sciences. Their threat derived from their newly liminal status, their (partial) release from the realm of mythology into that of scientific modernity.

France's renewed focus on colonial expansion in the early part of the nineteenth century was, in part, a response to the string of territorial losses it suffered in the second half of the eighteenth century. Overseas conflict with Britain (beginning with the War of the Austrian Succession and the Seven Years' War) had stripped it of most of its "first" colonial empire: its Indian outposts, a good deal of its North American territory, and a portion of its West Indian holdings. And the slave uprising in Saint-Domingue, France's most lucrative colony, had wrenched the island from metropolitan control, resulting in the creation of the first black republic, Haiti. Weakened overseas, France also found itself – in the wake of Napoleon's defeat – humiliated at home. In an attempt to regroup, it turned its attention back to the place that had provided its West Indian slave labor: Africa. Interest in the continent came from several interrelated groups, including French administrators already serving there (largely in France's existing enclaves in Senegal), missionaries and members of the political left (both of whom saw the "uplift" of Africa as a moral duty), and explorer-geographers eager to map out and claim new territory. A series of scouting missions to the Mediterranean coast and into the western interior around the turn of the nineteenth century paved the way for more formal expansion: the invasion of Algeria in 1830, followed by a slow move into the western and central regions of the continent through mid-century and, finally, the clinching of French imperial control in the 1880s and 1890s.[49] For most of the century, then, Africa stood at the center of France's imperial program, looming large in the political as well as popular imagination as a place of wealth, desire, and insistent disquiet.

The emissaries sent to the continent in the 1810s and 1820s (some by the government, others by the church or by various scientific societies) traveled to a place already steeped in negative mythology. As far back as Herodotus, Africa had been associated with the monstrous and unearthly: stories of hydra-headed beasts, men with tails, and savages who "eat locusts and snakes and screech like bats."[50] Ideas of this sort were passed down and amplified through the following centuries, gaining traction in part because Africa remained largely unexplored by the West. Sixteenth-century accounts associated the dark skin of its inhabitants with the earth, baseness, and distance from God, some arguing that Africans were descendants of the cursed

---

[49] For two fairly recent histories of French imperialism, see Singer and Langdon, *Cultured Force*; and Evans, *Empire and Culture*.
[50] Cohen, *The French Encounter with Africans*, 1–34 (here, 1).

biblical figure Ham. Even the eighteenth-century philosophes perpetuated the notion of a barbarous continent, although they had little or no firsthand knowledge of Africa. Diderot, in the 1780 supplement to the *Encyclopédie*, denounced its governments as despotic and its people as ferocious, lazy, cruel, and cowardly. When romantic explorers *did* experience the continent directly, they reinscribed rather than challenged these ideas. Their travelogues recycled many of the negative images already associated with Africa, lending them an aura of factuality, a truthful sheen associated with eyewitness reporting.[51]

The confirmation of African savagery was part of a broader rationalization of French imperialism; nineteenth-century observers were preconditioned to see (in Berlioz's words) an absence of "art and industrialism" and, of course, also eager to *produce* this image as a justification for France's ongoing practice of slavery and its percolating plans for incursion. But it was also, in many ways, a form of exorcism, a way of ridding the West of unwanted baggage. Demons in their old, theological incarnation had long since been condemned by Enlightenment reason, along with the entire superstructure of Christian supernaturalism. By the late eighteenth century, the influence of materialism, empiricism, and various forms of deism had almost entirely deconstructed the Devil as a religious adversary, recasting him in some quarters as a trivial figure (the stuff of satire and comedy) and in others as a political symbol (a force of revolutionary resistance). There was no longer a place in educated Europe for the fantasies of otherworldly evil, sadism, and depravity that had once been contained and focused by the Christian inferno. They floated around in the collective consciousness, attaching to ("confined" to, in Foucauldian terms) the fringes of European society (the poor, criminal, mad) and, increasingly, to distant, dark bodies beyond the boundaries of the enlightened world.[52] Africa and other, equally murky, places including Australia, Polynesia, and the West Indies, became favorite dumping grounds for them, places to offload sinister impulses and images. They were filled by Western explorers not only with barbarians awaiting civilization, but with supernatural fantasies in need of extermination. The two were, of course, related and eventually, as H. L. Malchow has argued, became inextricable, producing the newly "natural" demons of early romanticism – figures no

[51] See Cohen, *The French Encounter with Africans*, chap. 3 (60–99); also Miller, *Blank Darkness*, Part One (3–61), which moderates Cohen to some degree, arguing that a "dual, polarized" perception of Africa existed from classical antiquity onward, sometimes noble, sometimes monstrous (5). For one of the first French-language accounts of France's reception/construction of Africa, see Fanoudh-Siefer, *Le Mythe du nègre et de l'Afrique noire*.

[52] For an account of the deconstruction of the Christian hell in eighteenth- and nineteenth-century discourses, see Russell, *Mephistopheles*, 128–213; also Turner, *The History of Hell*, 199–232. The notion of rationalism's "confinement" of evil is fleshed out in Foucault, *Folie et déraison*.

longer separate from the civilized world but increasingly absorbed into it as unsettling colonial extensions of the "enlightened" center.[53]

The slippage between a projected and witnessed Africa, between fantasized fiends and foreign savages, can be felt in early eyewitness descriptions of the interior that began to filter back to France in the first decades of the nineteenth century. Consider, for instance, Gaspard Théodore Mollien's account of the Senegambia (among the first to reach French readers), written following a trip in 1818 whose purpose, as defined by the government, was to discover the sources of the Senegal, Gambia, and Niger Rivers.[54] Despite his prefatory claims to objectivity and "scientific" purpose, the Africa to which Mollien introduces us is, from the outset, a phantasmagorical place – the stuff of nightmare. In his opening chapter, he recalls his first encounter with the continent, a voyage of two years earlier, which was fraught with disaster. It began with the wreck of his frigate off Cape Blanco and his southward struggle through the Sahara to the French outpost at St. Louis. Having survived the hardship of the desert, he found himself at the mouth of the Senegal River, which would also be the starting point for his commissioned journey. What he encountered there on his first trip, and what he seems again to see in 1818, is not just a perilous terrain, but a demonic one:

[W]henever the wind blows from the east, a kind of sirocco is generally felt on the coast; the horizon assumes the whiteness of a heated furnace; a devouring flame seems to circulate through the air we breathe; and the water we drink to quench the continual thirst which torments us, seems only to provoke it anew. The frightful silence which reigns throughout desolate nature is interrupted only by the lengthened groans of panting herds; and the Moor, shut up in his tent, has no means of allaying the fire which consumes him but by remaining in a state of complete immobility.[55]

This Africa is, quite clearly, the inferno; indeed, Mollien's imagery and rhetoric are so reminiscent of Dante that we find ourselves, right away, caught between the theological past and the geographical present. Equally slippery are the figures who inhabit his hell, themselves both victims and propagators of its torments (both demons and damned):

It is not astonishing that these people, constantly at risk of falling prey to famine or being surprised by enemies, should be cruel and perfidious. Wherever the soil is

---

[53] Malchow, *Gothic Images of Race*. See also Leonard, ed., *Into Darkness Peering*.
[54] Mollien had been preceded by renowned British explorer Mungo Park, whose route he originally hoped to retrace. My translations of his account, *Voyages dans l'intérieur de l'Afrique*, are adapted from those of Bowdich in *Travels in the Interior of Africa*.
[55] Mollien, *Voyage dans l'intérieur de l'Afrique*, I:5–6.

ungrateful, man is gloomy, barbarous, and greedy of plunder; the spoils of the victims which necessity or ferocity impel him to immolate are the only harvests which he reaps in these desolate regions.[56]

As Mollien's story continues, the infernal Africa he remembers becomes synonymous with the one he observes. His report proper, which details his journey westward to Sedo, then south through Fouta Djallon, then back eastward to the European colonies on the coast, confirms the vicious temperament of African natives by offering readers firsthand evidence. Many of the tribesmen he encounters display "natural" indolence and apathy, others animalian ferocity. The Ouladahmins, who inhabit "the neighborhood of the Portendic" on the Senegal River, are inherently cruel: "The look of an Ouladahmed, like that of a tiger, indicates a thirst for blood which nothing can allay; his haggard eyes roll from side to side, as if in quest of prey; his beard is thin, but stiff and bristly; his body is small but full of vigor."[57] Later, Mollien assigns the same ferocity to the people of Fouta Djallon, whom he characterizes as "in general ugly" and "as ferocious as ... a tiger." Among the most repugnant are the Djalonkés, who, in Mollien's eyes, are little more than bestial scavengers: "With these people, everything is good; the leaves of trees, the juice of wild fruits, a handful of pistachio nuts, appease their hunger."[58] Modern African savages are inextricable, it seems, from Dantesque fiends.

But Mollien's account is not entirely dark; here and there he assigns redeeming features to the Senegambians, including generosity, kindness, and bravery. One of his early positive examples involves a "Moorish" boy – a prince – who, at the age of ten, already challenges his enemies and rallies his troops courageously. He has grown up in a state of savagery, but "in ten years ... a European education would make this child a hero."[59] Here Mollien suggests that, despite the darkness hanging over the continent, civilization is possible; barbarism can be eliminated, and perhaps with it, the specter of the inferno itself. But his belief in the power of enlightened uplift – in France's ability to elevate Africa's savages to European moral and intellectual standards – dwindles in travelogues of the 1830s and 1840s. Here, we encounter an even darker Africa, a place leached of virtually all redeeming features, figured not only as backward, but as depraved and murderous. This new sensationalism was rooted not just in claims of empirical objectivity, but, increasingly, in scientific authority,

---

[56] Ibid., I:7. Echoes of eighteenth-century climate theory linger in this passage – the notion that physical and moral temperament were shaped by environment – although by 1820 such ideas were antiquated, having already been supplanted by a belief in racial predetermination.
[57] Ibid., I:17. [58] Ibid., I:179 and 2:62. [59] Ibid., 1:9.

a burgeoning rhetoric of physical difference that located African barbarism as corporeal and therefore permanent.

An 1842 account by missionary Thomas Arbousset describing a voyage to South Africa through the region northeast of the Colony of the Cape of Good Hope is typical of the decade. Here, we encounter a description of the interior much more frightening than Mollien's. Virtually all of the natives Arbousset encounters are "atheists," and many are also cannibals; indeed, the entire region he and his party survey seems infested with man-eaters, whose activities he describes in salacious detail. The Marimos, one of Arbousset's most striking exhibits, consume human flesh, not out of exigency, but by choice, fattening the elderly for consumption and, when foreign targets are scarce, even preying on their own wives and infants, whose deaths form part of a hideous, quasi-religious ritual:

As soon as they have seized upon a victim, they cut off his third finger, and allow the blood to flow from the wound until life is extinct; they then tear off the hands and the feet; they empty the skull and make a cup of it; they fill the bladder with wind, and hang it as a trophy on their heads or on the walls of their dwellings.[60]

These descriptions had nothing to do, of course, with the nineteenth-century Africa Arbousset was observing, but instead with the infernal *European* past he was imagining. The imagery he invokes derives from legends of the Witches' Sabbath, including "confessions" of demonic activity made by women accused of witchcraft during sixteenth- and seventeenth-century witch trials.

For Arbousset, as for Mollien, African savages are synonymous with demons, although Arbousset's fiends are much less susceptible to rehabilitation. Their viciousness is inscribed on the body itself, inescapable, immutable. In a passage on the tribe called the Bastaards (so-named for their mixed Dutch and Hottentot heritage), Arbousset links despotism and depravity clearly to physicality – a particular nose shape, forehead type, etc. – suggesting that the group's most "African" (Hottentot) features are those that relegate it to savagery:

The Bastaard is of middling stature, and rather thin in his person; he is of a tawny complexion ... he has a flattened nose, sunken cheek, high cheekbone, small eyes deeply set, and a flat forehead: the distinctive characteristics of the Hottentot race.... Anger alone can rouse him from his habitual sluggishness. But when that passion animates him, he is a true Hottentot – treacherous, malicious, and passionate – and he gives himself up to unrestrained rage and revenge.[61]

[60] Arbousset and Daumas, *Relation d'un voyage*, 114–15.   [61] Ibid., 21.

Other accounts of the 1840s, among them a report on the Senegambia by Anne Raffenel, home in even more acutely on the bodies of Africans, generating what we might call a taxonomy of demonism, a continuum of features separating the less from the more bestial. Raffenel gives the following description of members of the Peul tribe (a subgroup of the Foulahs):

Their color, brown tinged with red, is midway between that of the Moors and the Toucouleurs; their noses, less impressed than those of the Negroes [the Torodos], are cartilaginous, of a character particular to the Caucasian race but absent from the Ethiopian race; their thin lips, oval face, their more generous forehead and less acute facial angle (*angle facial*), clearly suggest a different race [than either the Moors or Toucouleurs], but a somewhat hybrid one.[62]

This rhetoric derives, of course, from the burgeoning scientific theory of race, which rendered not just biblical or mythological but biological the connection between physical and moral darkness. Arbousset's and Raffenel's descriptions have their roots in a system of classification established in the last quarter of the eighteenth century – the era in which the groundwork for racist ideology was laid – resonating, in particular, with the work of Dutch anatomist and zoologist Petrus Camper, who (perhaps influenced by the work of French naturalist Louis-Jean-Marie Daubenton) distinguished human varieties on the basis of facial physiognomy. Camper's *Dissertation sur les variétés naturelles qui caractérisent la physionomie des hommes* (1764, published in French in 1791) argued that the placement and projection of the upper and lower jaws were most crucial, introducing the idea of the "facial angle" (to which Raffenel also referred) – a line extending from the most prominent point of the forehead to the front of the upper incisor teeth and, on the horizontal plane, from the opening of the ear to a point under the root of the nose. The most obtuse facial angles were associated with Europeans (in their most "ideal" form, with the profiles of ancient Greek sculptures), while the most acute ones were found among Africans, orangutans, and monkeys.[63]

Camper's facial index was taken up in France by naturalists Georges Cuvier and Etienne Geoffroy Saint-Hilaire, who placed it at the center of a theory of race that linked the lower angles of non-Europeans, especially Africans, to diminished brain capacity and therefore intelligence. Cuvier's *Leçons d'anatomie comparée* (1800–05) gave the facial slope of Negroes as synonymous with that of young orangutans (70 degrees), suggesting that

---

[62] Raffenel, *Voyage dans l'Afrique Occidentale*, 262–63.
[63] For more on Camper's ideas and their eighteenth-century roots, see the following: Claude, *Race and Aesthetics in the Anthropology of Petrus Camper*; Staum, "The Facial Angle, Physiognomy, and Racial Theory," in *Labeling People*, 23–48; and Curran, *The Anatomy of Blackness*.

blacks were closer to animals than to other humans. This idea, derived from the "science" of physiognomy, was shored up in later writing on human types, particularly that of Julien-Joseph Virey and Jean-Baptiste-Maximilien Bory de Saint-Vincent, who drew on other indices of physical difference (some derived from the dubious field of phrenology): skull size and shape, nose type, body proportions, and hair texture. Unsurprisingly, flat noses and wide lips, along with "wooly" hair and allegedly small crania, were found to correlate with acute facial angles, confirming the inferiority of Negroes. Members of this group were not inclined toward thinking (as were white Europeans), but, as their jutting mouths and noses suggested, toward tasting, smelling, and other sensual pleasures.[64] These perceived physical differences fueled the ascendance of polygenist theories of human origins, the notion that humanity derived not from a single root (monogenism), but as separate races, some with greater moral and intellectual capacity than others. No longer were all people advancing along a single continuum toward enlightenment (the Great Chain of Being); instead, some were condemned to perennial deficiency. Most abhorrent were dark-skinned human types, from Moors and Turks to the even blacker African Bushmen and Hottentots, who were relegated by the emerging disciplines of anthropology and ethnology to the lowest rungs of humanity. Shackled by their own bodies, they would, as Cuvier argued, "always remain barbarous."[65]

Far from vanquishing demons, then, the human sciences of the nineteenth century modernized and reanimated them. Malchow shows, in his pioneering study of the "racialized" Gothic, that dark-skinned fiends were quick to proliferate, wandering out of travelogues and scientific reports into fiction of the period – the novels of Matthew Lewis, Mary Shelley, and Bram Stoker, among others – and, from there, back into journalistic and anthropological writing, make-believe villains mingling inextricably with "actual" ones. The sexually deviant, bloodthirsty, and misshapen antiheroes of late eighteenth- and nineteenth-century horror stories were pervasively coded black, infused with the perceived physiognomic and phrenological deficiencies of the African (Australian, Polynesian) peoples. Frankenstein's monster

[64] Cuvier, *Leçons d'anatomie comparée*; Bory de Saint-Vincent, *L'Homme (homo) ou Essai zoologique sur le genre humain* [1825] (Paris: Rey et Gravier, 1827); Virey, *Histoire naturelle du genre humain*, 3 vols. (Paris: Couchard, 1824). For a detailed discussion of these sources and their impact on French thought, see Staum, *Labeling People*, esp. 23–84; and Cohen, *The French Encounter with Africans*, 210–62.

[65] Cuvier, *Le Règne animal distribué d'après son organisation* (Paris: Deterville, 1817), 95, qtd. in Staum, *Labeling People*, 29. Racist thought hardened through the middle and late nineteenth century, culminating in a series of now-infamous writings, including Figuier's 1872 *Les Races humaines*, which cemented the notion of Africa as a locus of the most fearful and vicious human types, exaggerating – even caricaturing – existing discourse surrounding Caffres, Hottentots, and Negroes; see Gilman, *Difference and Pathology*.

is an obvious example, his physical enormity, black hair and lips, yellowish eyes, and oversized sex organs gesturing clearly toward the physical markers of the "degenerate" races. Shelley's bogeyman is a creature of nightmare, but also a creation of modern science, born quite literally of nineteenth-century medicine, chemistry, and anatomy.[66]

The scientific impulses shaping literary demons were clearly also at work in the musical world. Berlioz's hells, with their newly exotic overtones – their generically Turkish effects and more pointedly Egyptian and Nubian resonances – were responding to the same imperial discourses that produced Gothic villainy. But the proto-anthropological rhetoric hovering behind Shelley's literary monster (the images of black physiognomy) do not explain fully Berlioz's sounding demons, who were marked less by monstrous appearance (the fiends of *Le Retour*, for instance, are invisible, and those of *Faust* uncostumed) than by incomprehensible language. It was not the physical sciences alone that shaped Berlioz's infernos and their inhabitants, but also the social sciences, particularly the discipline of comparative philology, whose role in the emergence of racist theory has been much explored.

Philip D. Curtin, in his classic study of British–African interaction, traces the close association between anthropology and linguistics during the early nineteenth century, noting the various ways in which philologists borrowed approaches from biology:

One effort was to arrange languages on an absolute scale of value, not unlike the Great Chain of Being. In another direction, linguists were trying to arrive at an evolutionary theory of language. A third effort was to discover the familial relations between similar languages, showing, for example, whether related languages were parent and offspring or collateral descendants from a common ancestor language. The influence of biological thought is obvious.[67]

The process Curtin describes began in Germany with the generation of Friedrich Schlegel, Jacob Grimm, and Franz Bopp, and continued with one of Bopp's students, August Friedrich Pott. Pott's work highlights clearly the mapping of racist taxonomy onto philological theory, separating languages

---

[66] For Malchow's reading of *Frankenstein*, see "Was Frankenstein's Monster 'a Man and a Brother'?" His notion of a "racialized" Gothic builds on Brantlinger's exploration of an "imperial Gothic" in *Rule of Darkness*, and has been followed by a wealth of more recent writing on the connections among race, empire, and Gothic literary culture.

[67] Curtin, *The Image of Africa*, 394. Said drew the same connection somewhat later (although more famously) in *Orientalism*, claiming "I do not think it wrong or an exaggeration to say that a typical page of [Ernest] Renan's Orientalist *Histoire générale* was constructed typographically and structurally with a page of comparative philosophical anatomy, in the style of Cuvier or Geoffroy Saint-Hilaire, kept in mind" (142).

by genus and species to indicate separate patterns of inheritance and descent. For Pott, the richest idioms were those of the Indo-European family, whose speakers had risen to positions of cultural dominance by virtue of "the exquisite word bestowed upon them, queen over all language families, a wonderful, agile, and adaptive organ, and the true likeness of their very spirit." Less "agile" were the so-called Semitic languages – those associated with the Middle East and Northern Africa, including Aramaic, Hebrew, and Arabic.[68]

Theorization of the Semitic family is most closely associated with later French philologists, especially Ernest Renan and Arthur Comte de Gobineau, purveyors of the infamous term "Aryan." Renan argued for language as the clearest distinguisher of racial type, claiming that "enormous cross-breeding" among humans had rendered the physical body an inaccurate barometer. For him, "race became a matter of language, religion, laws and customs more than of blood." He denied the Semitic tongues any connection with Indo-European forms, claiming that the latter were fundamentally "active" (inflected) or "energetic" languages while the former were "inactive" (uninflected), devoid of grammatical organicism or nuance. Even lower on the linguistic hierarchy were Chinese, Native American idioms, and finally western and sub-Saharan African tongues. For Renan, as for many contemporary German and English philologists, these languages were so primitive as to be virtually prelinguistic (Pott wrote that Africa was "irrefutably of all corners of the world the most unwieldy, a truly unarticulated and dismembered stump").[69] Negro languages, like Negro bodies, were considered ill-suited to creative, moral, or scientific thought, their underdeveloped grammar reflecting disorganized family structures, barbaric political and religious systems, and limited intellect.[70] Though this idea was not fully fleshed out until mid-late century, its roots were old. As early as 1801, Virey had already tied African "savagery" to both physical deformity and underdeveloped language.[71]

Philology, then, was a key weapon in the imperial arsenal, underpinning not just the Orientalist culture excoriated by Edward Said, but a more

---

[68] For a discussion of the German school of comparative philology, including Pott's work, see Benes, *In Babel's Shadow*. The quotation from Pott is taken from his *Etymological Studies of Indo-Germanic Languages* (1833), given in Benes at p. 201.
[69] Benes, *In Babel's Shadow*, 197–240 (here, 224–25 and 211).
[70] Irvine, "The Family Romance of Colonial Linguistics"; see also idem, "Mastering African Languages"; and "Subjected Words." Curtin notes that the inability among European philologists to master the grammar of African languages lay partly in their failure to recognize some of these idioms as tonal (*Image of Africa*, 394–413).
[71] Virey, *Histoire naturelle du genre humain*, 434–35, discussed in Cohen, *The French Encounter with Africans*, 214.

particular brand of African demonism. From the early nineteenth century onward, French explorers of the continent were enjoined by their scientific colleagues (members of the new *Société ethnologique* and, later, the *Société d'anthropologie*) to observe both the physical features of African tribes and the peculiarities of their *languages* (and, implicitly, to connect the two). Many complied, providing detailed accounts of the linguistic sounds and forms they encountered. Mollien drew a parallel between the savage disposition of the Djalonké people and their speech, which was "extremely harsh, and ... difficult to articulate." Elsewhere, he traced the genealogical links between West African groups (the Poulas, Joloffs, and Serreres) by noting shared words, arguing that the Serreres "are evidently the most ancient inhabitants of this part of Africa. Their language, which is extremely simple, is probably one of the oldest, and their wild manners have not undergone any change."[72] Arbousset also included a section devoted to language in his account, in which he traced similarities and differences among several South African tongues. Complaints of harshness and barbarism weave through his analyses, particularly the passage on Seroan (the language of the Bushmen), which is "too much loaded with consonants ... and little varied in form," and features a "horrible aspiration" that suggests that the Bushmen "bark rather than speak."[73]

In many cases, the authors of travelogues included vocabulary lists and rudimentary grammars, the raw material with which early comparative philologists worked. Mollien, for instance, included tables of Ioloff (Wolof), Poula, and Serrere terms, and Arbousset gave vocabularies of the Seroan, Zula, and Sesuto languages. As early as the mid-1820s, the first translation dictionaries and grammars were available in Paris, notably those of Jean Dard, a French government official and educator posted in Senegal, who published a *Dictionnaire français-wolof et français-bambara* (1825), followed by a *Grammaire Wolofe* (1826).[74] By the early 1840s, a great number of vocabularies were available, as were the earliest multi-language African concordances. Often hodgepodge collections of nouns, short phrases, and verbs, these were gobbled up by general readers along with the travelogues in which they were so often embedded, becoming part of

---

[72] Mollien, *Voyage dans l'intérieur de l'Afrique*, 296, 158.

[73] Arbousset, *Relation d'un voyage d'exploration*, 507–08. This characterization of African languages reached back, as we have seen, to classical antiquity and persisted through the end of the nineteenth century. Figuier, in *Les Races humaines*, figured Bushmen as the "lowest of mankind," and their language as "a mixture of chattering, hissing, and nasal grunts" (500).

[74] Dard, *Dictionnaire français-wolof et français-bambara, suivi du dictionnaire wolof-français* (Paris: Imprimerie royale, 1825); *Grammaire Wolofe ou méthode pour étudier la langue des noirs en Sénégambie suivie d'un appendice* (Paris: Imprimerie royale, 1826).

French Africanist discourse – a window onto the quasi-supernatural speech of cannibals, warlords, and "primitives."

It seems quite possible that these were the texts hovering behind Berlioz's infernal languages, providing him with a model (conscious or unconscious) for demonic utterance. Indeed, when paired with some of the earliest African vocabularies, his infernal morphology begins to appear less fanciful, more scientific – and more ominous. Consider, for instance, the opening several pages of Dard's French-Wolof/French-Bambara Dictionary. Here, we encounter many of the sound combinations found in Berlioz's Faustian tongue: the persistent consonant jumbles and unusual spellings, including prominent use of the letter k. Berlioz's term "dinkorlitz," for instance, resonates immediately with the Bambara "donkili," "dofraka," and "dikessey." His "rayk" (in the ghostly tongue of *Le Retour*, "rak") finds a parallel in the Wolof "rék." In many cases, the connections seem not just sonorous, but also semantic. The terms "merikariu/merikariba" and "lakinda" in the phrase "Ô merikariu Omévixé merikariba / Ô merikariu Ô midara Caraibo lakinda," sung by demons "avec un enthousiasme furieux" as they dance around Méphistophélès and the damned Faust, bear more than a passing resemblance to the Wolof words "merrekat" and "lakite." Dard defines "merrekat" as "Colérique, celui qui se fâche souvent" (volatile, one who is often angry), linking it to the noun "merre," meaning "La colère, la fureur, la rage, passion démesurée" (anger, rage, unmeasured passion). And "lakite" he translates as "cendre" (ash), relating it to "lakă," meaning "Brûler, mettre en combustion, incinérer" (burn, set on fire, incinerate).

The connections between these terms and Berlioz's scene are too close to be entirely accidental, although of course he does not borrow verbatim from either Wolof or Bambara. The sense one gets is that he is riffing on (while maintaining a certain distance from) African vocabularies, borrowing their spellings and sounds and in some cases flirting with their actual meanings such that we can *almost* imagine a translation. His texts hover between reality and the unreal, all the more terrifying for their semi-legibility. They gesture not just toward Dard's dictionary, but toward other, later vocabularies. Many of his "invented" words in the Faustian and Nubian languages (especially those he capitalizes, as if to indicate proper nouns) share a similar cadence, marked by a final, accented e: Amaloué, Omévixé, Midonaé. They recall the place and chief names listed in Arbousset's South African account: Amazouazés, Onjobé, Mauéué, Pongolé, Thlasaioé. Also in Mollien: Boqueuquillé, Longué. African geography seems uncannily close to Berlioz's infernal topography, his demons echoing the names of desert villages and chieftains. The speech rhythms of his murky afterworld are also, it would seem, those of the dark continent.

That Berlioz should have made these kinds of connections is, given the scientific and aesthetic histories I have been tracing here, unsurprising; indeed, the fact that he conceived of his hells *linguistically* makes sense. They are modern, even scientific infernos as much as phantasmagorical ones, emerging from theories of human demonism (philological, anthropological, geographical) already well entrenched by the time of *Le Retour* and *Les Francs-juges*. More so than many of his musical contemporaries, Berlioz is likely to have been aware of these theories; he was, after all, an avid producer and consumer of travel literature. Precisely which travelogues and word lists crossed his path (Dard? Mollien?), or whether Africanist imagery and language was hovering in his imagination in a more diffuse sense, we may never know. What is clear, and perhaps more significant, is that certain listeners and critics *heard* his music in this context; for them, the link between Africa and demonism, Africa and the *fantastique* Berliozian soundworld, was unambiguous.

Among the earliest places in which this set of associations is delineated is a tale by novelist and librettist Joseph Méry titled "La Fontaine d'ivoire," published in 1835 as one of the series of *contes fantastiques* commissioned by Maurice Schlesinger for the *Gazette musicale*. These tales, as I argued in Chapter 3, were key vehicles for Berlioz criticism, places in which fiction was pressed into service to explain and contextualize the modern, the romantic, and especially the fantastic. Méry's story is based on the true tale of a giraffe sent by Mehmet Ali, pasha of Egypt, to Charles X as a gift – an exotic bribe meant to persuade the king to abandon his support of Greece in the War of Independence. It arrived by boat at the port of Marseille in 1826 along with its Arab groom (Hassan), and was met by naturalist Geoffroy Saint-Hilaire (in Méry's version, also by Georges Cuvier), men at the heart of Paris's burgeoning scientific community. Their mission was to lead the giraffe overland some 900 kilometers to Paris, where it was to be installed in the menagerie of the Jardin des plantes.[75]

Méry's tale opens by referencing this historic journey, although it departs almost immediately from the realm of fact. His two scientists and their unnamed stenographer (presumably the narrator/protagonist) decide to acclimatize the giraffe by traveling through the most familiar – the most "African" – landscape possible. They lead it toward the medieval village of Mazargue, entering a world described in barren, even apocalyptic terms: "a country devastated by grasshoppers, wind, and sea sand," whose "horizon is barricaded, at noon, under high mountains bleached by six thousand years

---

[75] An account of the giraffe's trip is given in Allin, *Zarafa*. Among the nineteenth-century paintings immortalizing the journey is Jacques Raymond Brascassat's *Le passage de la girafe à Arnay-le-Duc* (1827).

of burning sun." Pine trees clustered in valleys provide the only color, giving off "burning freshness under sudorific shadows."[76] This place, in Méry's telling, is utterly foreign, utterly unknown: "It is Africa, not that of the Dey d'Alger [Turkish Algeria], nor of the Hottentots, but the mysterious, interior, unknown, unrecorded Africa."[77]

Once in this place, the giraffe breaks free of its captors and, pursuing it, Méry's protagonist loses his way, struggling through savage terrain, among rocks, along precipices, through pine forests. As the day fades, the landscape moves from frightening to demonic; the stenographer finds himself at the edge of a rocky gorge, "already black as midnight," in a place that seems "ever more satanic." For Méry, as for so many of his contemporaries, Africa (in this case quasi-Africa) has become synonymous with the inferno. He pauses, inviting us to listen to its soundworld – one to which Berlioz seems to have special access:

If I had the honor of being Berlioz, I would steal from nature the symphony that she then performed for me, even were she to charge me with forgery. The instruments were few, but they gave forth an ample harmony; a stream wept; the pine needles shivered; the saxifrage murmured with melancholy; the dry yellow leaves turned in the breeze; the cricket performed his nocturne; the mountain drew chords from all its caverns, the sea from all its reefs. A gigantic pine lowering and raising one of its long, bare branches resembled the Habeneck of this mysterious orchestra of the woods. In this ravishing overture to the night drama, there was not a single wrong note, not a chord that disobeyed the rules; not one error of composition. Nature orchestrates her oeuvres flawlessly; she combines with incomparable art all the players who perform her unpublished scores.[78]

---

[76] "[le giraffe entra dans] une campagne dévastée par les sauterelles, le vent et le sable marin. L'horizon est barricadé au midi, sous de hautes montagnes blanchies par six mille ans de coups de soleil; par intervalle, elles laissent couleur vers la plaine quelques vallons vêtus de pins, forêts d'une fraîcheur brûlante, aux ombrages sudorifiques." Joseph Méry, "La Fontaine d'ivoire," *Gazette musicale* (25 January 1835).

[77] "C'est l'Afrique, non pas celle du dey d'Alger, ni des Hottentots, mais l'Afrique mystérieuse, intérieure, non visitée, recueillie." Ibid. If this landscape seemed quasi-African to Méry, it was also decidedly French; the "fontaine d'ivoire" is a water source located in a cave at the bottom of a limestone outcropping outside the ancient town of Mazargue (now part of Marseille).

[78] "Si j'avais l'honneur d'être Berlioz, je volerais à la nature la symphonie qu'elle exécutait alors pour moi, dût-elle m'attaquer en contrefaçon. Les instrumens étaient peu nombreux, mais ils versaient une large harmonie; un ruisseau pleurait; les aiguilles des pins frissonnaient, les saxifrages murmuraient avec mélancolie; les feuilles jaunes et sèches tourbillonnaient à la brise; le Grillon exécutait son nocturne: la montagne tirait des accords de toutes ses cavernes, la mer de tous ses écueils; un pin gigantesque, en inclinant et relevant un de ses longs rameaux dépouillés, ressemblait à l'Habeneck de cet orchestre mystérieux des bois. Dans cette ravissante ouverture du drame de la nuit, il n'y avait pas une fausse note, pas un accord contre les règles; pas une erreur de composition; la nature orchestre supérieurement ses oeuvres musicales; elle combine avec un art incomparable tous les sujets qui exécutent ses partitions inédites." Ibid.

Here, Méry does more than situate Berlioz as the potential recorder of his infernal scene, he shows how he (and Berlioz) "hear" hell. Its music is synonymous with natural sound, the ambient noises of an exotic landscape. These are not the *ombra* effects of old, but those of the new "real" supernatural, an "orchestre mysterieux du bois" – Berlioz's orchestra. Méry even imagines the composer's first conductor, Habeneck, at the scene; indeed, the "symphony" and "ravishing overture of the night" to which he alludes draw to mind two pieces first led by Habeneck: the *Symphonie fantastique* and the *Francs-juges* Overture. These infernal soundworlds, and Berlioz's hells more broadly, are not, Méry suggests, imaginary spaces, but physical locales mapped by overseas exploration (and, in his tale, absorbed into France itself in a moment of vertiginous superimposition – or anticipatory colonialist expansion). He places Berlioz alongside Cuvier and Geoffroy Saint-Hilaire as a scientific traveler, a kind of orchestral anthropologist whose natural supernaturalism is tantamount to sounding ethnography, an imprint of empirical/imperial modernity.

As Méry's tale continues, it imitates and exaggerates the Gothic tropes weaving through so many African travelogues. His narrator stumbles into a giant cavern full of water, a "natural coliseum" (*un colisée naturel*), full of infernal sights and sounds. He attempts to flee via a mountain path, but claps of thunder start a landslide, sending enormous blocks tumbling to his feet. "Disheveled pines" seem to descend from the mountain's peak "like a troupe of bandits in pursuit of a traveler" (Méry's brigands, like Berlioz's, are interchangeable with demons).[79] Finally, he comes across a hermit's hut that promises him shelter, thus ending his travails and the first part of the story.

The second portion of Méry's narrative is more pointedly musical, picking up at a point "several years later" when his protagonist, haunted by the sights and sounds of his "African" journey, decides to return to the "fontaine d'ivoire." He arrives at eleven o'clock at night, bringing with him a group of 100 musicians, three wagons of brass instruments, and an enormous clock. When the clock strikes midnight, the musicians perform a series of infernal works beginning with the Overture to *Der Freischütz* and the nuns' scene from Act 3 of *Robert le diable*. This music calls forth a response from the cavern itself and its exotic environs, which echo back Weber's and Meyerbeer's infernal harmonies, allowing natural sounds to mingle with supernatural effects:

[T]he air was inundated with all the vibrations of desolate places; we heard thumps of gravediggers; ... brushing of lush grass; beating of diaphanous wings; sighs of

---

[79] "des pins échevelés semblent descendre des cavernes du pic comme une troupe de bandits qui courent au voyageur." Ibid.

ghouls; bursts of deranged sound; cries of vampirized virgins; ripping of shrouds; clicking claws of black cats; ... distant trios of ospreys, horned owls, and hyenas. Our hands were clamped to our ears, but the subtle flow of these harmonies invaded us through our very pores.[80]

The concert ends with the Act 1 finale of Rossini's *Semiramide*, the moment when King Nino's ghost rises from his tomb. Now the music seems to come directly from the rocky landscape itself: "the doleful cry of Ninus emanated from the mountain as from a Babylonian pyramid." Looking outside the cavern, Méry sees Babylon itself, "the hanging garden of Semiramis; the sea roiling with solemn waves like the Euphrates; the demon of the night sprinkling his oriental perfumes in the heavy air, encouraging adultery."[81]

Here, Rossini's ancient Mesopotamia blurs without comment into Méry's pseudo-African (and modern *French*) landscape. Weber's Wolf's Glen and Meyerbeer's graveyard are relocated to the same place, the sounds of their ghouls and demons made to intermingle with the rustling of desert grasses and the braying of hyenas. Méry shows us how modern listeners are (re)hearing existing hells as well as how new composers are orchestrating them. Past and present, imaginary and actual infernos converge in his make-believe Africa, transported from the realm of the marvelous to the semi-terrestrial space of the fantastic via a new mode of imperial listening. Berlioz, as Méry suggests (and as I have been arguing thus far), was especially tied to this mode, but he was by no means the only composer to recast hell along materialist lines. Méry's tale adds "African" sounds to Meyerbeer's graveyard scene, but, as I will suggest in the following section, he hardly needed to do so, for exotic impulses are already present in *Robert*'s demonic music, lending it what critics were quick to label a newly *fantastique* sound. Later infernos, including those of Liszt and Gounod, are equally indebted to the imagery and instrumental effects of human savagery. Berlioz was the earliest theorizer of the *fantastique terrible*, but by no means the mode's sole practitioner; rather, his hells are symptomatic of a broader reconceptualization of hellish sound, a wave of terrestrial infernos populated by overtly racialized musical demons.

---

[80] "l'air fut inondé de toutes les vibrations des lieux désolés; nous entendîmes des coups sourds de fossoyeurs ... des frôlemens d'herbes grasses; des battemens d'ailes de phallènes; des soupirs de goules; des éclats de timbre fêlé; des cris de vierges vampirisées; des déchiremens de suaires; des cliquetis d'étincelles de chats noirs; ... des trios lointains d'orfraies, de grands-ducs et d'hyènes; nos mains se collaient sur nos oreilles, mais le flot subtil de ces harmonies nous envahissait par tous les pores." Ibid.

[81] "Je regardai en dehors de la caverne; c'était une véritable nuit de Babylone ... on aurait cru voir le jardin suspendu de Semiramis; la mer roulait des flots solennels comme l'Euphrate; le démon de la nuit éparpillait dans l'air tiède, ces parfums orientaux qui conseillent l'adultère." Ibid.

Dark Nature, Black Magic, Bacchanale

Among the best-known and most-emulated demonic evocations of the early nineteenth century were the infernal chorus (*Valse infernale*) and nuns' music (*Bacchanale des nonnes*) in Act 3 of *Robert le diable*. These passages were the subject of persistent critical attention, lauded for their chilling supernatural imagery and unusual instrumentation – features aligning them, according to many, with the new aesthetics of the fantastic. Fétis, for instance, in a review following the opera's premiere in 1831, described the entire third act as a *monde fantastique*, arguing that "there, effects of a mysterious ilk produced by new [orchestral] techniques spark in the audience sensations completely different from those they experienced in the first two acts." Meyerbeer's fantastic soundworld not only set his third act apart, but differentiated his opera from well-known earlier models of hellish evocation, particularly Weber's. For Fétis, the nuns' music had "nothing in common with the second act of *Freyschütz*," but nevertheless, "expressed not less well than Weber the character of infernal beings."[82] Observations linking the opera's fantastic soundworld with its revised conception of hell echoed through other reports, among them a review for *Le Courrier de l'Europe*, which hailed Meyerbeer's "orchestre fantastique" as the vehicle for a newly visceral inferno, an ensemble conflating "not only the accents of all the passions, but also all the sounds of nature, [and] the voices of spirits and genies."[83] A critic for *Le Moniteur universel*, in a passage on the demonic chorus, insisted that "never had our musicians produced a comparable idea of the inferno, nor had the imagination of poets stretched so far. One is frozen with terror, the coarseness and savagery of the singing adding to the artificial contrivances [the

---

[82] "Au troisième [acte], l'action est engagée, et le spectateur est introduit dans un monde fantastique: la, des effets d'un genre mystérieux, produits par des moyens nouveaux, procurent aux spectateurs des sensations absolument différentes de celles qu'ils ont éprouvées dans les deux premiers actes. ... M. Meyerbeer, en écrivant cette partie de son ouvrage, a joui d'un rare bonheur d'inspiration. Sans avoir rien de commun avec le deuxième acte de Freyschütz, il n'a pas moins bien exprimé que Weber le caractère des êtres de l'enfer qu'il avait à mettre en scène." *Gazette musicale* (3 December 1831). That Fétis praises the *fantastique* effects in Meyerbeer is striking, since he denounces them so vehemently in Berlioz. The implication is that unusual instrumentation is more acceptable on stage (where it justified by dramatic action) than in the concert hall.

[83] "Monsieur Meyerbeer porte le génie des combinaisons au plus haut dégré; aussi, non seulement les accents de toutes les passions, mais encore tous les bruits de la nature, les voix des esprits et des génies sont exprimés par cet orchestre fantastique." *Le Courrier de l'Europe* (23 November 1831). References to *fantastique* sounds and effects weave through other early reviews of the work, including those in *La Revue de Paris*, *Le Corsaire*, and the *Journal des débats*; see Coudroy, *La Critique parisienne des "grands opéras" de Meyerbeer*.

instrumentation] employed by Meyerbeer."[84] On the subject of this instrumentation, Castil-Blaze, writing for the *Journal des débats*, drew attention to the combination of *ombra* tropes in the winds and brass heard against persistent clanging in the percussion:

In the infernal sabbath [the *Valse infernale*] ... the reeds whistle in the upper range and quiver in double chords in the lower, while one hears the din of timpani, cymbals, and triangles, the high-pitched cries of oboes and piccolo, [and] the rumblings of the chalumeau. At the same time all the trumpets in the cavern strike a formidable dominant, and the orchestra underpins these infernal cries with harrowing chords.[85]

This dazzling profusion of effects was not (as Castil-Blaze and his contemporaries rightly pointed out) found in Weber's *Der Freischütz*, nor was it typical of hellish evocations of the previous generation; instead, it smacked of a new inferno, a soundscape already foreshadowed, as we have seen, by Berlioz.

Berlioz himself, in an 1835 essay for the *Gazette musicale*, remarked on the special use of instruments in Meyerbeer's opera, noting in general that orchestration – rather than either harmony or melody – was at the core of the work's novelty: "the instrumentation must necessarily strike the audience with astonishment and pleasure at the same time, since this is the first time, I am convinced, that we have had the opportunity to hear a theatrical work orchestrated in this manner."[86] Among other notable effects, Berlioz singled out Meyerbeer's use of percussion and low brass, which, he claimed, were carefully implemented from the very outset of the opera. The trombones were not always doubled by an ophicleide, whose low growl was added only at strategic moments. And in the overture, Meyerbeer avoided using the bass drum and cymbals in the usual "ridiculously unregulated" manner, instead reserving them for the final measures, where they were united with the low-brass motive (the opera's infernal theme) to produce a sudden and colossal effect: a "terrible clash" (*terrible*

---

[84] "Jamais nos musiciens n'avaient donné une pareille idée de l'enfer, jamais l'imagination des poètes n'a été aussi loin. On est glacé d'effroi, la rudesse, la sauvagerie du chant ajoutent encore aux moyens artificiels que Meyerbeer a employé." *Le Moniteur universel* (24 November 1831).

[85] "Dans ce sabbat infernal ... les anches sifflaient à l'aigu, et frémissaient en double corde au grave, tandis qu'on entendait le fracas des timbales, des cymbales, des triangles, les cris aigus des hautbois et de la petite flûte, les mugissements du chalumeau. Ainsi toutes les trombes de la caverne attaquent un sol formidable, et l'orchestre pose des accords déchirants sur ces appels de l'enfer." *Journal des débats* (16 December 1831).

[86] *Gazette musicale* (12 July 1835), in *CG*, 2:209–215 (here, 211). Berlioz's claim is found in many earlier and later reviews of *Robert*; indeed, as Newark argues in his "Metaphors for Meyerbeer," the opera (particularly its third act) was perceived as much as a staging of modern instruments and orchestration as it was of dramatic events.

coup). Here and throughout *Robert*, the orchestration was not just mechanical or noisy, Berlioz insisted, nor was it merely the product of "laborious science and meditation" (common complaints levied against the *genre fantastique*), but guided by "the most immediate and instinctive inspiration."[87]

Meyerbeer's carefully orchestrated "clash" was, of course, crucial to Berlioz's own conception of demonic sound, and to his new *fantastique terrible*, and this is surely why he drew attention to it. It returns in the Act 3 infernal music, whose "savage" effects (vocal and percussive) earlier critics had so much remarked on. These effects are embedded in a conventional *ombra* soundworld, itself associated (unsurprisingly) with a Gothic setting. As Act 3 opens, "the stage depicts the rocks of Saint Irene, a gloomy, mountainous landscape. In the foreground, on the right, are the ruins of an ancient church and a cavern whose entrance is visible. On the other side is a wooden cross." The cavern marks the entrance to hell, where Bertram will meet with his infernal masters to discuss the future of Robert. Once he has gotten rid of Raimbaut (bribing him to abandon his rendezvous with Alice), he meditates on his task in a recitative shot through with diminished harmonies, string tremolo, and monotone brass:

Roi des anges déchus! mon souverain ... je tremble!
Il est là! ... il est là qui m'attend! ... Oui, j'entends les éclats
De leur joie infernale! ... Ils se livrent ensemble,
Pour oublier leurs maux, à d'horribles ébats!

(King of fallen angels! My sovereign ... I tremble! / He's there ... he who awaits me is there! ... Yes, I hear the cries / Of their infernal joy! ... To forget their suffering / They give themselves over to horrible revels!")[88]

So far, so Weberian. But the *ombra* effects give way to a different set of tropes once we *hear* the "infernal revels" that Bertram describes. The demons themselves are ushered in by an extension of the monotone brass fanfare that punctuates the recitative (Castil-Blaze's "formidable dominant"), which emanates from an offstage band "within" the cavern. This figure develops into a pedal tone, now in 3/8 time, over which the chorus enters in unison. Accompanied by a ringing triangle, they deliver their text in awkward syllabic fashion to a repeating rhythmic/melodic figure whose jerkiness is intensified by offbeat accents: "Noirs *dé*mons, fantômes, / Ou*bli*ons les cieux, / Des *som*bres roy*au*mes / Célé*brons* les jeux!" (Black demons, phantoms / Forget the heavens, / Let's enjoy the amusements / Of this dismal realm!). Each phrase ends with a version of the

---

[87] Ibid. [88] Suspension points original to text.

Example 5.6 Meyerbeer, "La Valse infernale (Choeur dans la caverne)," *Robert le diable*, Act III, scene ii (offstage orchestra only)

"clash," a cymbal strike preceded by the now-familiar piccolo flourish and amplified by tutti brass. The total effect is that of aural savagery – the steel-on-steel sound and primitivist declamation that will become so central to Berlioz's infernal idiom (Example 5.6).

Hovering outside the cavern, Bertram announces his intention to "brave Hell" and, in the main orchestra (which has none of the exotic instrumentation of the infernal band), the rushing strings of his *ombra* mode begin to echo the intractable phrasing of the demons. As the scene unfolds, the mainstage Gothic-medieval world and the savage realm of the cavern become increasingly proximate. Bertram sings of his eclipsed glory and his beloved son against the rhythmic tattoo of the demons celebrating their *Valse infernale*: "Gloire au maître qui nous guide! / A la danse qu'il préside!" (Glory to the master who leads us! / In the dance over which he presides!). Finally, their whirling waltz absorbs him. A ringing triangle in the offstage band ushers in a *stringendo* marking the convergence of offstage and main orchestras during which the open-fifth drone associated with the demons is taken up by the pit orchestra, now dominated by

Example 5.6 (cont.)

a syncopated semi-tone oscillation (a modal, vaguely non-Western motive). Meyerbeer gradually ratchets up tension, shifting to 12/8 time and adding whirling strings. The demons and their hidden band return, now entirely divested of melody, reducing to atomized syllabic shouting in praise of the Master of the Dance. All culminates in a mad, *fortissimo* close (with a bit of old-school *tonnere*). As Bertram enters the cavern itself, it shoots out flames, the metaphorical climax of the cavern orgy as well as a signal of traditional fire and brimstone.

What sets Meyerbeer's scene apart from the infernal soundworlds of his predecessors (and what yokes it to Berlioz) is, of course, its conflation of *ombra* and exotic modes. It highlights – indeed, dramatizes – the topical convergence by placing their instruments and effects in two competing ensembles, which, as they gradually intersect, showcase the power of the orchestra itself to remake the inferno along *fantastique* lines. Meyerbeer's demons are contained within, though also held apart from, the safely fictional realm of the main stage, singing on the fringes of the opera's visible world like distant, raucous natives. Small wonder that critics perceived the scene as novel; certainly, Meyerbeer was the first to stage so viscerally the topical and ontological hesitation at the heart of the modern inferno, its new conflation of temporal, intellectual, and geographical distance. But we should remember that *Robert*'s exotic demonism was not entirely new; it had already been hinted at in Berlioz's *Francs-juges* Overture, a work Meyerbeer surely knew (indeed, the low-brass motive in *Robert*'s Overture, with its culminating "clash," bears a remarkable resemblance to Olmerick's trombone/ophicleide theme). Clearly, both composers were responding, roughly simultaneously, to the same set of cultural impulses: those of Gothic imperialism, which allowed the sounds of the racialized "real" to creep into the realm of dark imagination.[89]

The same convergence marks the height of Meyerbeer's nuns' music (the Act 3 finale), set, once again, in a Gothic landscape: a graveyard in the courtyard of an ancient moonlit monastery featuring a statue of Saint Rosalie. Bertram has lured Robert to this sacred spot, convincing him to commit a sacrilege – to pluck the evergreen branch on Rosalie's tomb, which will grant him immortality and unlimited power. Again, it is *ombra* music that accompanies Bertram's recitative as he calls the unholy nuns sleeping beneath the monastery stones to awake and aid him in his plan. But as they come slowly back to life, the familiar sounds of primitivist revelry return. Meyerbeer's nuns, like his demons, are dancers, whose famous scene opens with a ringing triangle and a quiet, staccato motive in the upper strings. To this accompaniment, the nuns rediscover in their graves the objects of pleasure to which they were attached during life, including wine and dice. Some make offerings to an idol while others adorn their heads with crowns of cypress. Fully restored to the material world, "they are soon aware of nothing save the allurement of pleasure, and the dance becomes a wild bacchanal." The opening texture gives way to the dance proper, which shifts from D minor to a raucous D major, from *piano* to *fortissimo*, recasting the light motive of the opening as a heavy-footed theme marked by percussive downbeat clashing – the familiar bass drum and cymbal strikes of the demons' chorus, now amplified by tutti orchestra. The end of the first eight-measure phrase is marked by a series of four emphatic clashes, now with characteristic grace notes: first a single neighbor-note decoration, then, when the figure repeats, a four-note slide in the upper winds. Gone is our sense of airy spirits or ghosts, replaced by the sounds of Gluck's "joyous" barbarism (Example 5.7).

As in the *Valse infernale*, the nuns' dance accelerates as it unfolds. Whirling strings introduce a coda-like *Vivace* (increasing the tempo from

---

[89] The question of who influenced whom is unanswerable, partly due to the complicated compositional chronology of *Robert*; see Everist, "The Name of the Rose."

Example 5.7 Meyerbeer, "Bacchanale des nonnes," D-major section with line-end clashing, *Robert le diable*, Act III, scene vii

the opening *Allegro con moto*), which quickly begins to careen out of control, sixteenth-note passagework in the upper winds and strings heard against near-constant clanging of the cymbals, bass drum, and triangle: a frenzied, orgiastic sound that mirrors the close of the *Valse*. All comes to a sudden standstill when Robert appears and the nuns hide themselves, waiting to see how he will proceed. They lure him into temptation with a series of three dances, the first enticing him with drink, the second with gambling, and the third with pleasures of the body. When Robert eventually succumbs and plucks the branch, the bacchanale music returns, now even more frenetic. The nuns are transformed into specters and joined by demons, who rise from beneath the ground forming "a disordered circle"

Example 5.7 (cont.)

around Robert. The sound of steel on steel accompanies the return of the infernal horde, whose syllabic shouting and unison part-writing recall the primitivist vocal textures of their earlier chorus. Again, the demons' line is mindlessly repetitive, dotted with offbeat accents (marked by clashes), which render their text declamation unnatural and, in places, jerkily incomprehensible: "*Il* est à nous / il est *à* nous / il est *à* nous." The same sense of whirling acceleration that marked the end of the nuns' (truncated) bacchanale resumes in the final danced chorus, which races toward a now-predictable *fortissimo* end marked by metallic frenzy.

Both of Meyerbeer's most famous infernal scenes, then – those involving the demonic chorus and the unholy nuns – are percussive dances that move well outside the topical realm of the traditional *ombra* scene incorporating an array of exotic effects. Especially notable is the title Meyerbeer gives to his nuns' demonic round: bacchanale. The term brings us back once again to Berlioz, who, in the Orchestration Treatise and elsewhere, cites Spontini's bacchanale from *Les Danaïdes* (and, later, *Nurmahal*) as a model of demonic frenzy and an early source for the infernal "clash." As we have seen, he drew on many of the features of Spontini's dance (not just its percussive orchestration, but also its expressive markings, repetitive phraseology, and incremental accelerandi) in his own demonic evocations, implying a link between exotic revelry and demonic ritual. And clearly, a similar connection was hovering in Meyerbeer's mind; indeed, well before the bulk of Berlioz's infernal music, the composer of *Robert* had already embraced the bacchanale as a demonic form. He was apparently the first composer to include a piece bearing this title in an infernal scene and in so doing initiated an important trend, forging one of the musical building blocks of the new imperial inferno. His Gothicization of the bacchanale speaks, as we shall see, to the complex history of the form, whose evolution in visual and literary as well as in musical culture is relevant here.

Originally, bacchanales were associated with the followers of Bacchus/Dionysius, the Roman/Greek God of wine. In the ancient world, the term referred to the orgiastic revels of the bacchantes, who held danced celebrations marked by drunkenness, sexual abandon, and violence. But, as historian and anthropologist Christopher B. Steiner has shown, the idea (and especially the visual imagery) of the bacchanale became broader and looser over time, enlarging to include various other sorts of blasphemous and ribald revelry.[90] He points, for instance, to the borrowing of its iconography in sixteenth-century depictions of Old Testament idolatry. Lucas van Leyden's "The Dance Around the Golden Calf" (1529–30) and Gabriello Simeoni's "Adoration of the Golden Calf" (1565) show the ancient Israelites revolving in a circle around (or beside) an elevated calf, their arms flung wide and legs upraised in bacchanalian fashion. Around them, onlookers engage in lascivious and gluttonous behavior, echoing the orgiastic abandon of Greek revelry (Steiner gives the woodcut from Simeoni, by Eskrich, which I reproduce as Figure 5.1). Similar images of uncontrolled dancing were appropriated by other artists at roughly the same time to depict the cavorting of the peasantry who, "like the heathen worshipers of the Old Testament ... were portrayed as a 'godless' people who heeded neither spiritual nor temporal authority as they feasted in a savage and untamed manner" (among Steiner's examples are Sebald Beham's woodcut "The Nose Dance at Fools' Town" of 1534 and Pieter Bruegel the Elder's "The Wedding Dance" of 1570).[91]

---

[90] Steiner, "Travel Engravings and the Construction of the Primitive."   [91] See ibid., 215.

Figure 5.1 "Adoration of the Golden Calf." From Gabriello Simeoni, *Figure de la Biblia, illustrate de stanze Tuscane*, Illustration XXXII (Lione: Appresso G. Rouillio, 1577), Woodcuts by Pierre Eskrich. © British Library Board, Shelfmark C.51.b.2.

More obviously, bacchanalian imagery – now inextricable from blasphemy and peasant debauchery – began to be transferred to images of "primitive" societies, marking the final stage of a transformation that stretched across several centuries. Steiner locates an early example in Theodor de Bry's engraving "The Manner of Serving Food and Drink, and the Dance of the Savages Before Their King" (1619), which borrows the familiar circle of dancers, adding a drum. Images of similar type proliferated through the following centuries, becoming a staple of non-Western representation. Steiner tracks iterations of de Bry's engraving, only marginally altered, through a series of travelogues including Peter Kolben's *The Present State of the Cape of Good Hope* (1731), where it is associated with "Hottentot Dancing and Music"; Jean-Frédéric Bernard's *Histoire générale des cérémonies, mœurs, et coûtumes religieuses de tous les peuples du monde* (1741), alongside a description of "Aztec" ceremony; Antoine François Prévost's *Histoire générale des voyages* (1754), in connection with "Mexican" ritual; and Jean-Baptiste-Léonard Durand's *A Voyage to Senegal* (1806), as part of a description of native "ritual" in Sierra Leone. (I reproduce the third and fourth of these images as Figures 5.2 and 5.3). Such illustrations were not the fruit of observation or experience, but were recycled from one travelogue to the next as default constructions of Otherness. Nevertheless, they carried the sheen of scientific realism,

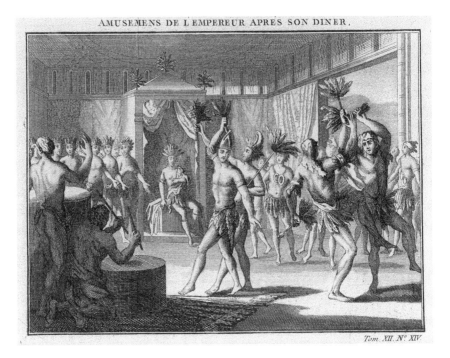

Figure 5.2 "Amusemens de l'empereur après son dîner." From Antoine François Prévost, *Histoire générale des voyages, ou nouvelle collection de toutes les relations de voyages par mer et par terre*. Volume 12, Plate 14 (Paris: Didot, 1754). Harvard University, Baker Library.

ensuring that bacchanalian dancing (now a distant relative of actual Bacchic ritual) would become inextricable from modern notions of barbarism.

The appropriation of the bacchanale as an ethnographic form, a tool of colonialist representation, happened not just in visual culture, but also in the literary realm. Late eighteenth- and early nineteenth-century travelogues recording journeys to Africa, Australia, and other "savage" lands are permeated with references to dance, often figured as *bacchanalian* and described in horrified (and titillated) detail. As early as Pierre-Joseph-André Roubaud's *Histoire générale de l'Asie, de l'Afrique et de l'Amérique* (1770–75), we hear of "celebrations similar to Bacchanales" (*fêtes semblables aux Bacchanales*) involving frenzied circles of intoxicated dancers.[92] Mollien and Arbousset give similar reports, as does Anne Raffenel, who underscores the popularity of such events "down the [Senegal] river" and "in St. Louis," where women perform body movements of disgusting shamefulness" and increasing frenzy, lured on by the "shouting, beating of hands, and encouragement of the

[92] Roubaud, *Histoire générale de l'Asie, de l'Afrique et de l'Amérique*, 2:223.

Figure 5.3 "The Cullemgee of the Negroes." Jean-Baptiste-Léonard Durand, *A Voyage to Senegal; or, Historical, philosophical, and political memoirs relative to the discoveries, establishments and commerce of Europeans in the Atlantic Ocean, from Cape Blanco to the river of Sierra Leone*. Plate facing p. 104. (London: Richard Phillip, 1806). Manuscripts, Archives and Rare Books Division, Schomburg Center for Research in Black Culture, The New York Public Library, Astor, Lenox and Tilden Foundations.

crowd."[93] By the last quarter of the century, ribald ring dancing had become associated with virtually all dark-skinned peoples. Louis Figuier, in his infamous *Les Races humaines* (1876), gives an elaborate (and entirely derivative) account of such revelries amongst the natives of Fiji:

Dancing is the popular diversion of the Fiji Islands. The chant by which it is usually regulated is of monotonous rhythm, its words recalling either some actual circumstance or historical event. The dancers' movements are slow at first, growing gradually animated, and being accompanied by gestures of the hands and inflections of the body. There is always a chief to direct the performers. ... Two bands, one of musicians, the other of dancers, take part in the regular dances of the solemnities at Fiji; the first usually numbers twenty, and the other from a hundred and fifty to two hundred individuals. These latter are covered with their richest ornaments, carry clubs or spears, and execute a series of varied evolutions, marching, halting, and

---

[93] Raffenel, *Voyage dans l'Afrique Occidentale*, 295.

running. As the entertainment draws towards its close their motions increase in rapidity, their action acquires more liveliness and vehemence, while their feet are stamped heavily on the ground, until at last the dancers, quite out of breath, give a final "Wa-oo!" and the antics cease.[94]

These kinds of descriptions were, for obvious reasons, enticing to musicians who, from the late eighteenth century onward, produced a profusion of exotic bacchanales borrowing many of the tropes later enumerated by Figuier: incremental *accelerandi*, rhythmic repetition, heavy-footed stamping, and percussive clashing. No longer confined to scenes of Greek ritual (those involving Bacchus himself), the bacchanale became associated with "primitive" geographies more broadly. Spontini's 1817 Egyptian (1822 Mongolian) bacchanale and Cherubini's 1833 Arabian bacchanale (from the opera *Alibaba*; adapted from *Achille à Scyros*, 1804) were well-known examples. They were followed by a host of similar dances (independent character pieces as well as operatic set pieces) up to and including the famous one by Saint-Saëns for *Samson et Dalila* (1875), which linked bacchanalian dance inextricably to foreign sensuality and violence. Clearly, composers were responding (and contributing) to the same culture of imperial darkening perpetuated in the visual and literary arenas: a process by which old, originally Western tropes of amorality were reassigned to racially "inferior" groups.

The final stage in this process of musical darkening was the absorption of the exotic bacchanale into infernal scenes – a collapsing of demonic and "ethnographic" revelry, of the *Ronde* (or *Valse*) *du sabbat* with the features of the dark-skinned circle dance. Not just barbaric, colonial dance was now satanic, the dancers themselves not just uncivilized humans, but specters and fiends. Idolaters, heathens, cannibals, and Gothic ghouls converged in the soundworld of the romantic bacchanale, which began to hover between the anthropological and phantasmagorical. Meyerbeer's opera was the first work to render such connections explicit, transporting the sounds of "actual" revelers to hell itself and, in so doing, articulating a new kind of racialized loathing and terror. His innovation was enormously influential, shaping the demonic evocations of a host of later composers (among them, as we have seen, Berlioz). Through the middle decades of the nineteenth century, bacchanales (and the exotic effects associated with them) became common tropes of infernal landscapes and creatures, not just in the realm of opera, but also ballet and instrumental music. The result was a permanent modernization of the old *ombra* landscape in favor of a quasi-realist collection of sounds and images: those associated with Berlioz's *fantastique terrible*.

[94] Figuier, *Les Races humaines*, 580.

The best-known ballet composer to embrace the new bacchanalian demonism was Adolphe Adam, whose evil Wilis in *Giselle* (1841) – the spirits of jilted brides – lure men into voluptuous and deadly dance. As Marian Smith has pointed out, the work's specters, as conceived in Gautier's original libretto (full title, *Giselle ou les Wilis, ballet fantastique en deux actes*), were not innocent or purely imaginary waifs (the *ballet blanc* figures they would become in later stagings of the work), but exotic temptresses, including Indian, Persian, and Spanish figures.[95] Like *Robert*'s nuns, on whom they were surely in part modeled, the Wilis rise from their graves at midnight on a mission of seduction and destruction.[96] In the 1841 scenario, we first encounter them in Act 2 (following Giselle's madness and death) in a *ballet fantastique* led by the queen of the Wilis, who calls forth each of her dancers one by one. Their dark magic is, from the outset, conflated with exotic sounds and gestures: first to appear is "Moyna, the Odalisque, executing an oriental step; then Zulmé, the Bayadère, who displays her Indian poses." Giselle, newly buried, is raised from her tomb and inducted into the group, which attempts to entice a band of passing villagers with "voluptuous poses," then quickly moves on to the gamekeeper Hilarion (onetime suitor of Giselle), whose appearance marks the beginning of the Wilis' most famous scene.[97] Hilarion is first enticed by the queen herself, who touches him with her scepter, forcing him to imitate her own dance. She is followed by each of the Wilis in turn, who impel Hilarion to continue, finally surrounding him in "a vast circle, which contracts little by little, closing in on him and then changing into a fast waltz movement, in which a supernatural power obliges him to partake." As the tempo of the scene accelerates, Hilarion dances "with an ardent frenzy," finally "tumbling into the abyss" – the pool in the midst of the forest – where he sinks to a watery death. Delighted by their success, the Wilis "commence a joyous bacchanale."

---

[95] Smith, *Ballet and Opera in the Age of Giselle*. The sources for Gautier's libretto, as Smith points out, were Victor Hugo's poem "Fantômes," which describes a Spanish girl whose love for dancing leads to her death, and a passage from Heinrich Heine's *De l'Allemagne*, which tells the Slavic myth of the Wilis. The latter source characterizes the spectral brides as bacchantes: "They laugh with a joy so hideous, they call you so seductively, they have an air of such sweet promise that these dead *bacchantes* are irresistible" (*Ballet and Opera*, 171–72). This idea was taken up by Gautier, who first imagined the balletic Wilis of *Giselle* as unabashedly exotic figures: "a cacucha dancer from Seville, a gitana, twisting her hips and wearing a skirt which is tight with flounces of cabalistic signs; a Hungarian dancer in a fur bonnet, making the spurs on her boots, like teeth chatter in the cold; a *bibiaderi* [bayadère] in a costume like that of Amani, a bodice with a sheath of sandalwood, gold lamé pants, a belt and a necklace of mirror-bright metal plates ... bizarre jewels, rings in her nose, bells around her ankles" (Ibid., 174).

[96] On the literary and musical links between Adam's Wilis and Meyerbeer's nuns, see ibid., 168; also see Edgecombe, "Meyerbeer and Ballet Music of the Nineteenth Century."

[97] These and subsequent quotations from the original libretto are given in Smith's translation, included as Appendix Two of *Ballet and Opera in the Age of Giselle* (227–38); she gives the original French in the same Appendix (213–26).

The music for the *Scène des Wilis* opens with the string tremolo and creeping chromatic lines of the *ombra* world, which accompany Hilarion's entrance into the spooky woods. But once the demonic spirits have begun their dance, the expected topical shift happens: the dynamic changes from *piano* to *fortissimo* and the trembling *ombra* effects to heavy, percussive clashing (the familiar bass drum, here with triangle rather than cymbal), amplified by brass and overlaid by shrill trilling in the piccolo, flute, and upper strings. Echoing Meyerbeer's title, Adam marks the passage "Bacchanale des Wilis," moving the piece from the end of the scene (as in the libretto) to its heart; his Wilis perform their dance *during* rather than after the seduction of Hilarion. Marked by downbeat thumping and insistent triangle ringing, their revelry conjures not ghosts or virginal spirits, but barbarians; we *see* vaporous figures onstage while *hearing* a group of heavy-footed revelers. The result is a classic moment of bacchanalian hesitation. Adam's "magic circle," like Meyerbeer's "disordered ring," conjures both the rites of Gautier's demons and the erotic revelry of Figuier's Fijians (Example 5.8). As his dance increases in intensity, Adam's music moves through a series of tension-building crescendos and then a final Presto with whirling strings – the "musique toujours plus rapides" described in the libretto – and, finally, a fiercely percussive close complete with banging drums and cymbals and rolling timpani. The "rire satanique" that marks its final measures is also a "rire éxotique," a moment when Hilarion is overcome not just by demonic but by savage forces, by the threat and lure of the uncivilized world. Once he has been dispatched, we return to the *ombra* landscape, echoes of imperial realism shading fluidly back – as in Meyerbeer – into supernatural medievalism.[98]

On the operatic stage, bacchanalian hells were equally prominent, particularly in settings of *Faust*, which, in the wake of Berlioz's *La Damnation*, never returned to the purely imaginary musical topoi – the old marvelous soundscape – of Louis Spohr's 1818 setting. Gounod's *Faust*, which premiered in 1859 at the Théâtre Lyrique, offers us an interesting example of the new inferno. Its depiction of hell happens at the beginning of Act 5, when Méphistophélès transports Faust to the Walpurgisnacht, the witches' sabbath, celebrated (as he puts it), in his own "empire." The scene opens, as does Berlioz's Faustian hell, with the telltale "Scythian" clashes: *fortissimo* drum, cymbal, wind, and brass blasts. These quickly give way to standard *ombra* tropes: shivering *pianissimo* figures in the strings, monotone invocation by a chorus of spirits, diminished harmonies, and the calls of night birds. None of these Weberian effects was, as

---

[98] Meglin offers us a different and intriguing reading of the *Scène des Wilis* focusing on its link to Gautier's *conte fantastique*, "La Cafetière," and to a fantastic waltz tradition in "Resurrection, Sensuality, and the Palpable Presence of the Past in Théophile Gautier's Fantastic."

Example 5.8 Adam, "Bacchanale des Wilis," *Giselle ou les Wilis, ballet fantastique en deux actes*, Act II, scene xiv

critics complained, particularly frightening; indeed, they seemed derivative and rather routine. Whether Gounod's witches' music got scarier or more original as it progressed we shall never know since he cut the majority of it before the opening performance, partly in order to provide more solo material for Faust.[99] But a clue as to its content may lie in the set piece with which Gounod replaced it: a "Chant bachique" (perhaps substituting for an original witches' bacchanale?) allowing the sounds of foreign ribaldry to infiltrate the world of dark supernaturalism.

In Gounod's sung bacchanale (as in Adam's erotic/infernal dance), the link to exotic culture is made explicit. Méphistophélès has converted the

[99] Huebner describes in detail the compositional process of *Faust* and its evolution in the several years following its premiere in *The Operas of Charles Gounod*, 99–132.

dismal landscape of hell into a beautiful, glittering palace populated by the "queens and courtesans of antiquity," including the famous seductresses Cleopatra and Laïs. Just as Robert was lured into sacrilege by the sounds of erotic carousing and Hilarion to death by the same mechanism, Faust succumbs to intoxication in an aria with all the familiar tropes of Otherness. His song opens with a version of the familiar clashes, heard *fortissimo*, with decorated wind flourishes and a ringing triangle, and becomes more raucous as it proceeds. When Méphistophélès and the chorus join in, the exotic clamor intensifies, bass drum and cymbal joining the triangle to produce the full-throated clashing we expect. For Gounod, as for so many of his contemporaries, the sounds of primitivist excess seem to have been bound inextricably to those of fantasized evil (Example 5.9).

The bacchic element of the Walpurgisnacht scene was much expanded in German premieres of *Faust*, notably those in Darmstadt and Dresden (both 1861). In these performances, Faust's aria was extended into a full, danced bacchanale, perhaps to compensate for the paucity of Gounod's own Walpurgisnacht material (while exploiting the resources of the German theatres), and – equally possibly – to satisfy public demand for a hell cast in the Meyerbeerian mold. The replacement bacchanale was written by conductor and clarinetist Louis Schindelmeisser, Hofkapellmeister in Darmstadt from 1853 onward, and the author of several operas, instrumental works, and incidental pieces. It opens with a nod to Gounod – an introductory section borrowing the thematic material and expressive marking of Faust's bacchic aria (*Allegretto maestoso*, 6/8, B flat), although Schindelmeisser abandons the soft effect of Gounod's harp (the signal of Faust's intoxication), instead introducing the drum, cymbals, triangle, and piccolo immediately (Example 5.10). When the dance proper begins, it shifts into D major and accelerates to the tempo *Allegro molto vivace*, displaying all the established features of the bacchanale genre, from gracenote clashes and ringing triangle to furious motivic repetition, whirling string figures, and gradual tempo increases. A central Adagio introduces a languid string theme (shades of softer seduction?), but quickly gives way to a return of the opening material, which grows increasingly frantic, culminating in a final Coda, *Più mosso*, which races toward a close over a persistent tonic drone, the dance whirling out of control amidst thunderous percussion.

When Gounod himself revised his infernal scene, for the 1863 premiere of *Faust* at the Opéra, he added a series of his own dances (a bit of *de rigueur* spectacle) that have much in common with Schindelmeisser's piece; in fact, several are bacchanales in all but name, performed by the exotic figures of antiquity as part of Faust's infernal seduction. Consider, for instance, the

Example 5.9 Gounod, "Chant bachique," *Faust*, Act V, scene i ("From this bewitching goblet / Let us drink everlasting oblivion!")

Danse antique and the Danse de phryné, both of which borrow all the familiar Spontinian tropes: heavy-footed pulse, relentlessly reiterative phraseology, percussive instrumentation, and incremental accelerandi culminating in orgiastic finishes.

Example 5.10 Schindelmeisser, Bacchanale for Gounod's *Faust*, mm. 1–5

Later settings of Faust collapse demonic and exotic dance entirely, many containing ring dances for infernal creatures showcasing – now seemingly as a matter of routine – the sounds and effects of Meyerbeer's, Adam's, and Schindelmeisser's bacchanales. Boito's *Mefistofele* (1868, revised 1875) provides a good example. At the heart of its Walpurgisnacht scene, Mefistofele sings a "Ballata del mondo" ("Ballad of the world"), in which he derides the wickedness of the Earth and its inhabitants and celebrates his own sure victory over them, finally flinging to the ground a glass globe he holds in his hands (the action is adapted from the "Witch's Kitchen" episode in Goethe's *Faust*, Part I). In response, a host of witches and warlocks commence a circle dance (*ridda infernale*), whirling about Mefistofele in triple-time, *Allegro focoso*. Their vocal line is all but tuneless, marked by furiously syllabic text-repetition ("riddiamo, riddiamo, riddiamo"), its rising phrases culminating in

Example 5.11 Boito, Witches' dance ("Ridda e fuga infernale"), *Mefistofele*, Act II, scene ii

predictable downbeat clashing. Suddenly interrupted by a vision of Marguerite, the dance returns once Mefistofele has convinced Faust that she is nothing but an illusion. Now even more frenzied, Boito's infernal creatures abandon intelligible language altogether, lapsing into gibberish: "Sabba, Sabba, Saboè... Saboè har Sabbah!... Sabbah, Sabbah, Sabbah! har Sabbah!" These made-up words are highlighted in a series of passages of antiphonal pounding with full-throated bacchanalian percussion (Example 5.11). Our sense of primitivism intensifies as the piece races toward a close, accelerating through a *Più presto* section dominated by more meaningless shouting ("Sabba, Sabba, Sabba, Sabba"), and then a final instrumental *Prestissimo*. As much as witches or warlocks, we are invited to imagine foreign circle-dancers casting a spell in some unknown tongue as they twirl in escalating frenzy around a fire, their savage sound united – as in Berlioz – with degraded speech.

Interestingly, Boito intersperses the percussive clashing of his dance with contrapuntal passages; the second portion of the piece is labeled "Ridda e fuga infernale," perhaps a nod to Berlioz's fugal witches' dance in the *Symphonie fantastique*. Equally derivative of Berlioz is Boito's musical marker for Mefistofele: the same percussive shock that had, decades earlier, been a novelty in *La Damnation* and a marker of the new *fantastique* inferno. We first encounter this effect in Act 1, where Faust and Wagner, enjoying the Easter celebration of the village folk, notice a grey friar wending his way toward them. Wagner insists that the man is just what he seems, but Faust recognizes him as a demon in disguise, noting that "flames spurt up from his feet!" (*orme di foco imprime al suol!*). His terrified "Ah!" as he becomes aware of the friar's true identity – his first intimation of Mefistofele – is marked by a sudden tutti clash, the brass, bass drum, cymbal, and piccolo attack that had announced Berlioz's demon. The effect returns when Mefistofele is first revealed, divested of his disguise by the power of Faust's incantation. Boito marks the moment with ironic self-awareness: as the trademark clash sounds, his demon exclaims "Che baccano!" (What a noise! – Example 5.12). We are hardly surprised to encounter the same effect, the old sound of Gluckian and Spontinian savagery, punctuating the end of the introductory phrase of Mefistofele's first solo piece, the so-called Whistling Aria, whose *Allegro focoso* marking anticipates that of the Act 2 witches' round (and, of course, echoes the many *focoso* movements we have already encountered).

Boito was not the first to borrow Berlioz's Mephistophelian marker; indeed, if we look beyond staged versions of Goethe's drama to the realm of instrumental music, we find that Liszt's *Faust* Symphony (1854) had, almost fifteen years earlier, adopted the same trope. The telltale clash, complete with familiar grace-note flourish, appears at the outset of the work's third movement, titled "Mephistopheles" (see Example 5.13, which also borrows the rising bass figures of Berlioz's *Ronde du sabbat*). It is clearly a moment of homage, an acknowledgment of the timbral innovation of *La Damnation*, which Berlioz had dedicated to Liszt (having himself introduced the pianist to Goethe's drama in 1830). The erotic exoticism of the Berliozian/Meyererian hell continued to inform Liszt's depiction of Mephistopheles for the remainder of his career, notably in the first of his four Mephisto Waltzes ("Der Tanz in der Dorfschenke," No. 2 of the *Zwei Episoden aus Lenaus Faust*, composed in the late 1850s). Here, we encounter yet another bacchanalian dance – the term appears in the program for the work, taken by Liszt from Nikolaus Lenau's version of the Faust legend. In this excerpt, Mephistopheles has transported Faust to a wedding feast at a village inn. Snatching a fiddle from the hands of a lackluster player, he produces irresistibly seductive music, impelling all who hear it to join in a wild ring dance:

Listening in Hell

Example 5.12 Boito, Mefistofele revealed ("What a noise!"), *Mefistofele*, Act I, scene i

Example 5.13 Liszt, *Faust* Symphony III ("Mephistopheles"), opening gesture with Berliozian clash, mm. 1–5

> And ever more ardent, more raucous and tempestuous,
> Like men's cries of joy, or maidens' moans,
> The violin's seductive melodies resound,
> And all are swept into a bacchanalian circle.[100]

Faust, who had at the outset of the scene been too timid to approach the maiden of his choice, now loses all modesty, seizing his "brunette," joining the whirling circle, then dancing out of the tavern itself into the countryside, where he is engulfed by a "roaring ocean of pleasure" (*Und brausend verschlingt sie das Wonnemeer*).

Liszt's demonic waltz opens with a drone (shades of Meyerbeer's *Valse infernale*) and a reduced orchestra (winds and strings only), conjuring the pastoral setting and peasant dancers of Lenau's tale. But as it accelerates into bacchanalian whirling (racing strings, blasting brass), it also begins to

---

[100] "Und feuriger, brausender, stürmischer immer, / Wie Männergejauchze, Jungferngewimmer, / Erschallen der Geige verführende Weisen, / Und alle verschlingt ein bacchantisches Kreisen." Nicolaus Lenau, *Faust. Ein Gedicht*, 47–51.

incorporate the savage orchestration associated with the genre (the drum/cymbal effect with grace-note flourishes) and the familiar expressive markings: *wild, furioso*. A central, lyrical section follows, showcasing the seductive power of Mephistopheles's melody, after which we return to the *Vivace* dance music of the opening, which begins to increase in tempo, its clashing now near-continuous, underpinned by a ringing triangle. A final cadenza lets us hear Mephistopheles's magical violin one last time, then a trilled flute solo – the nightingale – as Faust, in the grip of demonic enchantment, whirls out of the inn into the countryside itself. After that, all is madness. The dance quickens into a final Presto rush, then an even hastier Accelerando, racing toward a percussive close, the sound of Faust's utter sensual abandon. Clearly Liszt was "hearing" infernal dance in much the same Spontinian terms – those of primitivist revelry – as were Meyerbeer, Berlioz, and their mid-century musical contemporaries.

But the Mephisto Waltz differs in at least one important respect from the bacchanalian rings we have already encountered: it is not performed by Gothic fiends, evil spirits, or exotic inhabitants of hell, but instead by peasants, who seem equally adept at the erotic whirling associated with Adam's Wilis and Boito's witches. The sound of country carousers shades fluidly, in Liszt's dance, into that of dark-skinned circle-dancers, the two becoming inextricable. (Something similar might be said of Meyerbeer's *Valse infernale*, whose metallic percussion is preceded by an opening string drone with the flavor of a rustic dance; indeed, it was surely this mixture that caused critics to hear, both in this piece and in the related nuns' bacchanale, echoes of both peasant dancing and exotic revelry.[101]) This connection is significant, since it complicates the idea of barbarism – and of the new demonism – reminding us that its models might be homely as well as foreign, domestic as well as colonial.

Homegrown Savages

My statements will serve ... to prove that the Blacks, whom we consider as barbarians, so far from being wholly destitute of intelligence, are very little behind the generality of the peasantry of Europe.
    –T. G. Mollien, *Voyage dans l'intérieur de l'Afrique*

Steiner's genealogy of primitivist iconography draws our attention, as I have already noted, to a historical link between peasant carousing and exotic dancing forged in the mid-sixteenth century when the imagery surrounding ancient bacchanalian ritual was transferred to depictions of rural savagery

---

[101] See the review of *Robert* in *Le Journal des débats* (16 December 1831), which underscores the link between the nuns' ballet and the peasant "farandole," a ring dance popular in Nice.

(on its way to being reinvented as colonial revelry). The peasantry, as Steiner points out, were widely perceived as the link between contemporary and primitive man, between European modernity and its murky past.[102] This notion, forged in the early modern period, persisted into the nineteenth century, when it was deepened – and also crucially altered. Now scientists began to situate the European underclasses not just as a developmentally arrested, but as biologically distinct from the nobility and the emerging middle classes. They were cast by anthropologists and philologists as economically and socially as well as *racially* alien, shackled by the same moral and intellectual limitations associated with the Semitic and Negro peoples. This shift divested them of their Rousseauian glow – their access to a noble, prelapsarian purity – recasting them as homegrown savages inhabiting a newly barbaric world.

Malchow, drawing on work by Christopher Herbert, Lee Sterrenburg, and others, underscores this theoretical transference, noting that "by midcentury, sociocultural evolutionism was investing elements of the working classes in Britain with a mental primitivism whose characteristic impulsiveness, improvidence, and general childishness exactly paralleled the construction of the racial primitive in the expanding empire."[103] The same was true in France, where "middle-class commentators viewed the poor, underprivileged classes in the country and in the cities as forming a different race; the color of their skin, the shape of their skulls, and their innate intellectual capacities were seen as fundamentally different from those of their more fortunate fellow citizens."[104] Not just mentally and morally deficient, the poor classes (rural and urban) were increasingly regarded as dangerous, consumed by the same blood lust and carnal appetite of the lesser races. Popular acts of violence and rage, particularly those perpetrated in the interest of revolutionary reform, were compared to the violent, even cannibalistic behaviors of slaves and dark-skinned foreigners.

The racial degradation of paupers and revolutionary peasants was accompanied, as Liszt's Waltz demonstrates, by a contemporaneous musical darkening – a resignification of conventional pastoral tropes, especially those of rustic dance, such that they became intertwined with the sound of foreign ritual, *both* emerging as models for demonic evocation. This was true not just

---

[102] Steiner, "Travel Engravings and the Construction of the Primitive," 216.
[103] Malchow, *Gothic Images of Race*, 70. See, more broadly, Malchow's sections "Folk Cannibalism" (55–61) and "Cannibalism and the Working Class" (61–76); also his more recent *Taming Cannibals*. Malchow relies in part on Sterrenburg, "Mary Shelley's Monster"; and Herbert, *Culture and Anomie*.
[104] Cohen, *The French Encounter with Africans*, 216. See also Monleón, *A Specter is Haunting Europe*, chaps. 2 and 3, which return repeatedly to the link among barbarians, specters, and paupers.

in Liszt's work, but in the wider realm of operatic Fausts, many of which foreshadow the topical and formal language of their new primitivist infernos in earlier scenes of peasant or lowlife ribaldry, linking domestic with foreign savagery – and cementing their dual tie to the new racialized infernal imaginary. These aural connections can be traced back at least as far as Berlioz's *La Damnation*, whose Scythian clashing is heard first in the scene in Auerbach's cellar (Part 1, scene 6), where Méphistophélès has transported Faust in an attempt to reawaken his taste for worldly pleasure. Marked *Allegretto*, then *Allegro con fuoco* (the Spontinian marking we will encounter again in Boito), the episode opens *fortissimo*, its first sonority a percussive shock amplified by full orchestra. A chorus of common revelers raises a toast to Rhinish wine, and Méphistophélès introduces Faust to the "wild company" (*folle compagnie*) amidst yet more orchestral noise-making: a monotone fanfare in the strings underpinned by crashing timpani, drum, and cymbal. This is much the same sonority (including monotone fanfare) we will encounter at the beginning of Pandemonium: the sound of savage orgiastic din. The scene continues with a Chorus of Drinkers and a solo song sung by Brander, to which his fellows append a facetious fugal Amen. Listening to all of this, Méphistophélès encourages Faust to attend closely to the sound of "sheer bestiality" (*la bestialité dans toute sa candeur*). He goes on to contribute a song of his own (the famous "Song of the Flea" – another *Allegretto con fuoco*), which brings the evening to a peak of hilarity. As the scene draws to a close, the discourse grows not only coarser in tone, but also less intelligible, legible speech dissolving into laughter (Ha! ha!). It can hardly be accidental that "Ha!" will also be the first syllable we hear in Pandemonium, the initial "word" spoken in Berlioz's infernal tongue. (It is also uttered several times by the Choeur de Follets, the Chorus of Spirits, who accompany Méphistophélès's Serenade in Part 3). Clearly, for Berlioz, both the sound and *language* of urban depravity are intertwined with imagined evil, working-class barbarism collapsing into "foreign" primitivism, which together provide the musico-linguistic template for his new demonism.

Gounod's *Faust* makes a similar, although also more elaborate, set of connections, tracing not just the link between peasants and "exotic" demons, but filling in the other stages in Steiner's genealogy: the move from Bacchic dance to peasant revelry, Old Testament idolatry, primitivist dance, and finally, hellish ritual. Like Berlioz, Gounod first introduces the sonority of hell in an early scene featuring debauched townsfolk, although now they are *en plein air*, celebrating the Easter holiday. The scene opens with familiar clashing (that of Gluck's Scythians and Berlioz's demons), clearly meant to evoke the "orgy" for which Faust had called at the close of the previous act:

"I'll have pleasure / I'll have young mistresses! / Their caresses! / Their desires! / I'll have the energy / Of powerful instincts / And the mad orgy / Of the heart and senses!"[105] Cast as a *fortissimo* Allegretto, the revelry of Gounod's crowd is marked by downbeat thumping of the drum, cymbal, timpani, and triangle, to which the participants toast wine, beer, sex, and the delights of war. They do so, tellingly, outside an inn bearing "the mark of Bacchus"; indeed, the old heathen god is the metaphorical source of their celebration and its characteristic orchestral effects – those of sensuality, violence, and inebriation. Gounod thus rolls two stages of Steiner's genealogy into one, underscoring the historical connection between the excesses of the ancient bacchanates and those of the modern peasantry.

The next time we hear the orgiastic instrumentation is in Méphistophélès's first aria, the "Ronde du veau d'or" (Round of the Golden Calf). Here, the tempo is quicker, but the topical language immediately familiar: the same relentless downbeat clashing intensified by a repeating, whirling figure in the strings. The Ronde is a celebration of idolatry, the worship of the golden calf by the ancient Israelites. Their error, according to Méphistophélès, has been passed down through generations of sinners who continue to circle the false God: "The golden calf, / is still standing, / his might / is celebrated / from one end of the world to the other! / Nations and kings mix together / to hail the infamous idol / and to the sinister clink of coins / they whirl in a frenzied ring / round and round his pedestal! / And Satan leads the dance!"[106] When we hear the same orchestral effect in the opening measures of Gounod's Walpurgisnacht scene, our ear takes us back to both the Bacchic revelry and blasphemous dance of Act 2 – and of course, these images and sounds hover equally clearly around Faust's "Chant bachique" (and, later, Schindelmeisser's danced bacchanale). Gounod invites the attentive listener to make a series of musico-historical connections, laying bare (consciously or otherwise) the historical logic underpinning the new savage demonology.

Boito, whose *Faust* echoes many of the key innovations of the previous several decades, casts a similar aural web – although with a few notable twists. His Act 1 Easter scene (featuring, as in Gounod, the celebration of "vulgar" common folk, as Wagner calls them), prefigures not just the savage sonority of the witches, but also their circle dance. Here, the peasantry celebrate drink, wild affairs, and easy women, then perform an Obertas, a rapid-tempo folk dance of Polish origin. The dance, as we might expect,

---

[105] "A moi les plaisirs, / Les jeunes maîtresses! / A moi leurs caresses! / A moi leurs désirs! / A moi l'énergie / Des instincts puissants, / Et la folle orgie / Du coeur et des sens!"

[106] "Le veau d'or est toujours debout; / on encense / sa puissance / d'un bout du monde à l'autre bout! / Pour fêter l'infâme idole, / rois et peuples confondus, / au bruit sombre des écus, / dansent une ronde folle / autour de son piédestal! / Et Satan conduit le bal!"

evidences many of the tropes of the bacchanale, including its characteristic accelerations – the same effect that will mark the witches' dance in Act 2. It begins with a *più mosso* section (a tempo increase from the previous Allegro vivace), leading to a Vivacissimo passage, and then a final stretch of percussive noise-making marked "precipitando il più possibile." As Boito's peasant dancers whirl around, they – like Berlioz's "bestial" drunkards – lapse into the realm of inarticulate ("uncivilized") speech:

Juhé! Juhé! Juhé! Juhé!
Juhé! Juhé! Juhé! Juhé!
Ah! Ah! Ah! Ah!
Tutti vanno alla rinfusa
Sulla musica confusa.
Tra la la ra la ra la ra, etc.
Alla rinfusa tutti van, cantiamo.
La danza scalpita sul suol,
La danza rotonda.
Tutti vanno alla rinfusa.
Heisa hé!

(Juhé! Juhé! Juhé! Juhé! / Juhé! Juhé! Juhé! Juhé! / Ah! Ah! Ah! Ah! / Everyone moves in a jumble to the confused music / Tra la la ra la ra la ra, etc. / Into a jumble everyone goes, let's sing. / The dance stomps on the ground / The round dance / Everyone moves in a jumble / Heisa hé!)[107]

The trope of incoherence reappears in Boito's demonic characters, including Mefistofele, who, in his Whistling Aria, sums himself up in the monosyllable "No," as a denier of everything, from "the star" and "the rose" to light, life, and language itself. At the height of his aria, he abandons meaningful speech entirely in favor of "roaring," "hissing," and finally whistling. His vocalized noise foreshadows the semi-incoherent speech of the witches and warlocks, whose sound Mefistofele describes as he and Faust enter the Brocken (the site of the Walpurgisnacht): "From the valley's abyss I hear the howling of a thousand voices" (*Ad imo della valle un ululato / Di mille voci odo sonar*). As in Berlioz's *Faust*, the first syllable uttered by Boito's infernal horde points back at the language of the carousing peasants: "Ah!" And, as I have already noted, the witches themselves demonstrate the same propensity toward gibberish – now much exaggerated – in their bacchanalian round, itself an echo of the peasant ring dance. Clearly, for Boito the sonorous realm of demonism was wrapped up not just with savage musical effects and forms – the echoes of debauched peasants and foreigners – but with the philological degeneracy associated with both racial groups.

---

[107] Translation by Gary Moulsdale.

All of this brings us full circle to Berlioz's infernal languages and the novel soundscapes in which they were embedded, suggesting that his *fantastique* conception of the demonic was far from unique. The topical conflation at its heart was produced, as I have argued here, by France's imperial machine, its encounter with places hovering outside the boundaries of the "civilized" and the human. These worlds, once virtually unknown, became, over the course of the late eighteenth- and early nineteenth centuries, radically visceral and immediate, not just explored, but increasingly absorbed into the metropolitan center. They redefined and relocated evil, generating a new template for the demonic rooted in terror and guilt. The hells that resulted were shaped, on one hand, by a widespread fear of savage colonies and rebellious slaves and, on the other, by a paranoia surrounding racial distinction – a creeping sense that whiteness could be compromised from both within and without. "Enlightened" Europeans might be drawn into the revolutionary bacchanalia of the peasantry or – even worse – succumb to the licentious rites of distant savages, "go native," be absorbed (like Joseph Conrad's hero) into a dark sensuality that lay just beneath the crust of their lucid selves.

Ralph Locke, in his most recent study of exoticism, argues that imperial activities were seldom openly represented on the European operatic stage ("nineteenth- and early twentieth-century Oriental operas almost never ... directly portray recent or current imperial and colonial encounters carried out by the composer's own country"). At most, these pieces made vague, historically distanced references to imperialist endeavor and to a geographically nebulous "East." "Black Africa," Locke contends, despite its importance to France's imperial plan, "found relatively little immediate echo in Western musical life."[108] The first of these claims is surely accurate, but the last seems worth revisiting; indeed, this chapter has argued that France's nineteenth-century relationship with the dark continent played a crucial role in the evolution of its musical and theatrical cultures. Its African interactions were not, of course, "directly" represented in the repertory I have been examining here, but hovered just beneath the surface, sublimated, cast as imaginary, and at the same time made terribly proximate. They generated a new notion of sounding hell which, collapsing into the old *ombra* landscape, produced romantic infernos hovering between ethnography and imagination, reality and phantasmagoria. No longer confined to theological or mythological terrains – the dark world of eighteenth-century marvels – their demons emerged as actual and *rational* creatures, science itself locating them in the murky and frightening demi-light of Berlioz's *fantastique terrible*.

---

[108] Locke, *Musical Exoticism*, 176, 178.

As we shall see in the chapter to follow, the same empirical imagination that materialized demons also recalled more benign creatures: the fairies of Weber's *Oberon*, Mendelssohn's *Midsummer Night's Dream* music, and Berlioz's *La Reine Mab*. These figures, conjured via Berlioz's "gracious fantastic" were (like romantic demons) rationalized, rendered partially real, although their recuperation had less to do with anthropology and philology than it did with botany and entomology. Fairies were not products of imperialism's artificial nature, but, like Berlioz's dream beloved in the *Épisode de la vie d'un artiste*, of idealism's enchanted nature. And yet a hint of the threatening hovered even around even their miniature domain, its "scientific" sounds challenging music's status as a purely aesthetic medium, generating a now-familiar form of confusion and resistance: a sense that *fantastique* composers were moving beyond the legitimate boundaries of music into spaces of noise, incoherence, and disorder.

6 ∾ Fairyology, Entomology, and the *Scherzo fantastique*

> The originality of his portrayal of fairy life has become typical; all later composers have, in similar subjects, followed in his footsteps.
>
> –Eduard Devrient, on Mendelssohn[1]

Consistently, both during and after his lifetime, Felix Mendelssohn was figured as the pioneer of a novel fairy sound – an instrumental idiom linked to the third movement of his Op. 20 Octet (1825), the *Midsummer Night's Dream* Overture (1826), and the incidental music for the same play (1843), especially its opening scherzo. Fanny Mendelssohn traced this sound to "the ethereal, fanciful, and spirit-like scherzo" of the Octet, describing it as "something quite new." The movement's presto, *pianissimo* wind and string textures had been inspired, she claimed, by the Walpurgisnacht Dream of Goethe's *Faust*, a fanciful episode in which Ariel, Puck, and a host of other airborne fairies perform a masquerade in celebration of the golden anniversary of Oberon and Titania.[2] Many of the same elfin folk, including Shakespeare's fairy king and queen, reappeared less than a year later in Mendelssohn's *Midsummer Night's Dream* Overture, which featured a similar gossamer soundscape generated by rapid, staccato strings and pointillistic winds. The Overture (initially more widely known than the Octet) was received both in Germany and England as a striking innovation. Johann Christian Lobe, in conversations with Mendelssohn published in 1855, remembered "what excitement this Overture caused due to your [Mendelssohn's] surprising originality and honesty of expression." It seemed to Lobe to have "no sisters, no family resemblance," to "surpass all of your earlier works in originality."[3] His memory of the Overture's reception is borne out by London critics who, in 1839, described it as "full of originality, of invention, and indication of the highest genius." Years later, after Mendelssohn's death, they were still insisting that "there is more that is new in this one work than in any

---

[1] Devrient, *Meine Erinnerungen an Felix Mendelssohn-Bartholdy*, trans. Macfarren as *My Recollections of Felix Mendelssohn Bartholdy*, 247.
[2] Hensel, Mendelssohn-Bartholdy, and Mendelssohn Hensel, *The Mendelssohn Family*, 1:131.
[3] Qtd. and trans. in Nichols, *Mendelssohn Remembered*, 106, 103. Mendelssohn agreed that "the idea for the subject of this Overture" had sparked a new approach to sound, although the work's form (the concert Overture) was indebted to Beethoven.

other one that has ever been produced."[4] Claims surrounding the Overture's novelty were, from the early German performances onward, linked to its elfin subjects and their "fantastic" representation in sound. According to Ludwig Rellstab, the piece was "a fantastic intellectual work that allows Shakespeare's romantic play to shimmer through in a happy tone painting" (1832). Later, Gottfried Wilhelm Fink lauded its "fantastic transformations" (1834) and its ability "to express itself in sound more fantastically" than any of Mendelssohn's other Overtures (1835).[5]

Similar ideas surrounding both the novelty and the fantastic mien of Mendelssohn's new fairy idiom also surfaced in France, not around Felix's own elfin music, but in connection with Berlioz's Queen Mab scherzo, written a little more than a decade after the *Midsummer Night's Dream* Overture and several years before the related incidental music. Another Shakespearian fairy evocation, Berlioz's *La Reine Mab* (included as the central movement of his dramatic symphony *Roméo et Juliette*, 1839), seems clearly to have been influenced by Mendelssohn's Overture and perhaps also the scherzo of the Octet. It features a familiar set of wind and string textures as well as a collection of new orchestral effects, imitating as well as extending the scherzo sound that critics had already identified as characteristically Mendelssohnian and unmistakably elfin. French reviewers, who were less familiar with Mendelssohn's work than their German and English counterparts, heard this sound as unique. Berlioz's scherzo was, according to *Le Constitutionnel*, "the most original, the most inspired piece that has ever been composed." In *Le Ménestrel*, it was deemed so novel as to preclude analysis, and in *L'Avant-Scène*, its "astonishing innovations" in instrumentation and harmony opened up the miniature fairy world "as no music had done before."[6] Again, and more clearly than in Germany, these innovations were tied to the aesthetics of the fantastic; indeed, French critics assigned Berlioz's

---

[4] The first quotation is taken from an anonymous "Life of Felix Mendelssohn Bartholdy," *Musical World* (1837), ix. The second comes from an obituary published in the same journal (1849), by the critic Macfarren, who located Mendelssohn's originality not only in the Overture, but in a new kind of "intermezzo or scherzo" (37), which was "a form and style of movement entirely his own" (36). For a substantial excerpt from this article, see Brown, *Portrait of Mendelssohn*, 437–46.

[5] In Rellstab's description of the Overture: "Sie ist ein phantastisches, geistvolles Werk, welches Shakespeares romantische Dichtung in einem glückliche Tongemälde überall durchschimmern lässt." *Iris im Gebiete der Tonkunst* (23 November 1832). In Fink's writing, we encounter references to the work's "phantasievoll Veränderlichen" and its "phantastische" expression; see his reports in the *Allgemeine musikalische Zeitung* of 25 June 1834 and 6 May 1835.

[6] *Le Constitutionnel* (8 December 1839); *L'Avant-scène* (28 November 1839); *Le Ménestrel* (8 December 1839). For similar assessments, see the *Gazette musicale* (28 November 1839) and *La Quotidienne* (26–27 December 1839). The single exception to this overwhelming rhetoric of originality was a review by A. Specht, who was aware of Mendelssohn's *Midsummer Night's Dream* Overture and noted that Berlioz's scherzo was a work of related type; see *L'Artiste* (1 December 1839).

Mab music a new label summing up both its unusual compositional language and its otherworldly content: *scherzo fantastique*.

The designation appeared in accounts of the scherzo's premiere in both the *Gazette musicale* and *La France musicale*, as well as in other journals, which dubbed the piece "tout fantastique" and "ultra-fantastique," charging it with a collection of now-familiar tropes: extravagant sonority, imitation, melodic deficiency, and problematic phraseology.[7] It generated a sense of unease and excitement, seeming to hover between real and imaginary soundworlds, imitative "effects," and poetic expression. These were, of course, all the signposts of the *genre fantastique* and indeed, Berlioz himself connected the piece with modern fantasy. His scherzo drew on a mode he termed the "gracious fantastic" whose roots lay in part in Weber's *opéra fantastique*, Oberon, a fairyscape in which "the supernatural is so well blended with the real world, that one cannot tell exactly where one ends and the other begins." Both Weber's orchestral texture and his fluid phraseology, Berlioz wrote, underpinned a musical language "which one seems never to have heard before."[8] This new elfin sound proved transformative, resonating through the remainder of the nineteenth century and on into the twentieth, shaping not only Mendelssohn's and Berlioz's scherzi, but a series of other elfin evocations marked with the same fantastic sensibility, and in many cases the same "fantastique" rubric – works stretching from Franz Liszt and Antonio Bazzini to Benjamin Godard and Igor Stravinsky. Together these pieces constitute a strand of *fantastique* evocation wedded to the scherzo form itself, a modern mode of *féerique* hearing and listening. Conflating fiction and science, magical miniaturism and microscopic realism, modern fairy scherzi generated soundworlds at once natural and fanciful. As we shall see, they were products of a wider reinvention of elves – literary, visual, and scientific – which recalled such creatures from the realm of marvels, ushering them into the liminal domain of romantic fantasy.

The Fairy Revival

The intelligible forms of ancient poets,
The fair humanities of old religion,
The power, the beauty, and the majesty
That had their haunts in dale or piny mountain,
Or forest by slow stream, or pebbly spring,

---

[7] See the *Gazette musicale* (28 November 1839); *La France musicale* (1 December 1839); the *Journal de Paris* (27 November 1839); and the *Gazette de France* (*Édition de Paris*) (1 December 1839).

[8] *Journal des débats* (6 March 1857), reprinted in *À Travers chants*, trans. Csicsery-Rónay as *The Art of Music and Other Essays*, 161.

Or chasms and wat'ry depths; all these have vanished,
They live no longer in the faith of reason

–Friedrich Schiller, *The Piccolomini*[9]

Fairies were originally conceived as spirits of air, water, earth, and fire – elemental beings whose powers fueled the wondrous transformations of the visible world. They are so described in the writings of Paracelsus (the sixteenth-century physician-chemist Theophrastus von Hohenheim), who classed them as "intermediate" creatures, entities hovering between the human and divine, preserving a true knowledge of nature. Dwelling within and in a sense born of their native elements, fairies formed the basis of all physical objects, animating and regulating them. Their magic – the magic of nature itself – could be appropriated by those of sufficient learning, including priests of the old religion and magus-kings, whose knowledge of occult lore gave them access to the realm of spirit. Elemental enchantment and human authority were intertwined, the domain of man fluidly connected with that of Paracelsian magic.[10]

It was this old fairy ontology that shaped the dramatic representation of such creatures when they began to appear on the operatic stage in the seventeenth century. Here, elves assumed roles akin to the superhuman characters of conventional mythological and pastoral genres, operating as personifications of elemental magic. Their music, costumes, and gestural language differed little from that of the lords and princes with whom they interacted; indeed, the power of fairies and the authority of the nobility were contingent, natural enchantment the province of divine right, and fairies themselves reinforcers of prevailing power structures. But as magic began to dwindle in the Age of Reason, fairies were increasingly separated from notions of reality, figured as imaginary (sometimes satirical) creatures, the products of dream, make-believe, and childhood reverie – of immaturity and irrationality. As David J. Buch has shown, the musical and visual tropes governing their representation were, over time, carefully distinguished from those associated with human characters and lived events, becoming part of a "distinct category for magical topics" – the category of the marvelous – which was situated, in theoretical writing, in direct opposition to rational and "natural" depiction. Mid-eighteenth-century fairies were held apart from their surroundings via a new language of otherness: hushed wind sonorities linked with enchantment or sleep, modal harmonies, pseudo-archaic contrapuntal textures, and elaborate ornamentation tied by listeners either to the mannerisms of *preciosité* or the decadence of the exotic – to imagined and distant realms. They were defined as

---

[9] In Coleridge's translation, in *The Dramatic Works*, 225–26.
[10] Paracelsus, "On Nymphs, Sylphs, Pygmies, and Salamanders, and on the Other Spirits."

well as confined by the language of the marvelous, banished from the grown-up world, which no longer had room for the pagan deities of old.[11]

By the late eighteenth century, this exile had begun to wear thin, generating a widespread sense of loss, a yearning for the enchantment, wonder, and proximity to nature that magical creatures represented. Europe at large was gripped by a fairy revival, a vogue for the elfin folk of *A Midsummer Night's Dream* and *The Tempest* as well as the gnomes and sprites of German *Märchen* and the farfadets of French *contes de fées*. These miniature beings exercised a curious fascination over artists and audiences, beckoning them toward a place in which queens consorted with insects, plants produced intoxicating elixirs, dewdrops were drunk from golden goblets, and all of nature was animated by enchantment. Elves held out the promise of something hidden, a portal back to a world once known but now forgotten. It was this promise and the nostalgia underpinning it that fueled nineteenth-century fairy writers, whose musings are shot through with tropes of loss and memory.

In France, Collin de Plancy's popular *Dictionnaire infernale* reported wistfully on the enchanted prairies and forest groves that had once housed "lutins" and "fées." These places, old druid haunts, had long been abandoned, their magical inhabitants fading first into invisibility and then into legend. Émile Montegut, a few decades later, linked the elfin folk not only with lost history, but with lost innocence. Sylphs, gnomes, and other magical creatures belonged to a golden age in human history, a luminous world untainted by knowledge or reason. In the modern world, men retained only a distant recollection of their stories, which manifested as a sense of vague longing: "How many times have we yearned to recover that tale whose traces we have lost." Similar sentiments underpinned German and English writing on the elfin folk. Friedrich Schiller, in his trilogy *Wallenstein*, bemoaned the "faith of reason" that had banished fairies and their "fable existences." And John Ruskin argued that "railroads, gasworks, mowing machines, [and] telegraph poles" had "despoil[ed] the landscape of fairyland."[12]

---

[11] See Buch, *Magic Flutes and Enchanted Forests*, where he traces debates surrounding the proper sphere of the marvelous, its relationship with the "real," and its impact on musical style back to the early 1700s. But only, he argues, toward mid-century, when music at large ceased to be associated with the otherworldly – when "theorists and critics could define music in purely rational terms and divest it of its mystery" (74) – could a separate category for the musical marvelous emerge. For detail, see in particular chap. 1, "L'Académie Royale de Musique" (43–102) and chap. 2, "Opéra-comique" (103–52).

[12] Schiller, *Piccolomini*, 225–26. For Collin de Plancy's descriptions of the lost fairy tribes, see the entries under "Fée," "Farfadet," "Lutin," and "Elfe" in his *Dictionnaire infernal*. Montegut's remarks form part of an essay titled "Des Fées et de leur littérature en France," published in the *Revue des deux mondes* (April 1862). Ruskin's claim is quoted in Bown, *Fairies in Nineteenth-Century Art and Literature*, 40. The link to earlier German forms of philosophical yearning (*Sehnsucht*) as explored in Chapter 2 is obvious.

Over the course of the century, artists struggled to rematerialize not just elves themselves, but the magical world they represented, producing a barrage of fairy poetry, painting, and music. But the sprites they restored were not those of a distant past; instead, they were creatures of the romantic present, products of a *féerique* mode invented and sustained by the technologies of the modern world. Their resuscitation was rooted, paradoxically, in rationalization, in the reconciliation of archaic faith with contemporary fact. As Carol Silver puts it, nineteenth-century fairy lovers were "wavering between a somewhat outmoded but not abandoned belief in such creatures as fairies and an enlightened skepticism," and, seeking compromise, "use[d] the sciences ... to heal the breach."[13] Rather than exiled by Ruskin's industrial reality, fairies became intertwined with it; indeed, their return was predicated on a new kind of magical materialism. Artists used the very tools of modernity – the evolving disciplines of botany, entomology, and archeology – to reveal and even produce elfin creatures, collapsing the realm of reverie with that of reality in a dizzying mixture, a kind of ontological collision. They recuperated – or reinvented – the old Paracelsian ontology by dint of a new fantastic theology, a form of real supernaturalism rooted (as we have already seen) in idealist as well as revolutionary impulses. Dissolving the boundary between seen and unseen worlds, fantasy allowed elves to balance at the tipping point between make-believe and materiality, science and imagination. This was true for fairies of all stripes – seen, read, and heard – although it is especially obvious in the visual world.

Look, for instance, at Joseph Paton's *The Quarrel of Oberon and Titania*, among the nineteenth century's best known fairyscapes, and one that offers a clear model of the fantastic "wavering" Silver describes. Paton's piece, produced at the height of the golden age of fairy painting (first version, 1846), features the same elfin couple that caught Mendelssohn's fancy: Shakespeare's Oberon and Titania, shown here in the throes of their legendary dispute (Figure 6.1).[14] They are strongly illuminated and positioned in the middle of a darkened frame – an overtly theatrical effect suggesting an imaginary space. Our sense of otherworldliness is heightened by the density and microscopic scale of Paton's imagery. Oberon and Titania are surrounded by a host of miniscule fairies, some of whom lounge

---

[13] Silver, *Strange and Secret Peoples*, 32.

[14] My reading of Paton's painting takes its cue from Maas's essay "Victorian Fairy Painting" and from the entry for Paton by Gere and Lambourne, both found in Maas et al., *Victorian Fairy Painting*, 10–21 and 108–12. Paton's painting has been much discussed by other fairy scholars, who have used it to draw attention to diverse, often intersecting strands of nineteenth-century fairy culture. See Bown, *Fairies in Nineteenth-Century Art and Literature*, 91–94, for an exploration of scale, size, eroticism, and escapism in Paton's piece; see also Silver, *Strange and Secret Peoples*, 160, for remarks on its "fairy malevolence."

Figure 6.1 Sir Joseph Noel Paton, *The Quarrel of Oberon and Titania*, 1849. Oil on canvas, 99 cm × 152 cm. Reproduced by permission of the National Gallery of Scotland.

in the hollows of tree trunks, while others lie in the petals of flowers, play with insects, or bathe among water lilies, inextricable from and emblematic of the natural utopia in which they are ensconced. Paton encourages us to lean inward toward the painting in order to penetrate their intricately wrought world – to make sense of the mass of intertwined fairies behind Titania, the smaller collections of creatures on the riverbank, and the even more elusive bodies concealed in crevices and leafy nooks. As we do so, we find ourselves in a space of virtuosic detail where the normal rules of scale, size, and perspective seem not to apply. This is the realm of the miniature, the home of the fairies, in which, as Susan Stewart has argued, "reduction in scale ... skews the time and space relations of the everyday lifeworld":

> The depiction of the miniature moves away from hierarchy and narrative in that it is caught in an infinity of descriptive gestures. It is difficult for much to happen in such depiction, since each scene of action multiplies in spatial significance in such a way as to fill the page with contextual information.[15]

The elaborate surface – the "contextual information" – of Paton's landscape confounds our sense of depth and spatial orientation. Tiny fairies are grouped next to even tinier ones, suggesting infinite regression or worlds

---

[15] Stewart, *On Longing*, 47.

within worlds. Images, gestures, and events are jumbled together, collapsing background and foreground, cause and effect. We are absorbed, transfixed, drawn out of what Stewart calls "lived historical time" into "the infinite time of reverie" – the time of childhood, of imagination, of long-ago-and-far-away.[16]

But if Paton's painting transports us to the realm of make-believe, it also locates us firmly in the world of reality. As we move closer to his Shakespearian landscape – as we begin to succumb to the vertigo of the miniature – we recognize that it is also a scientific place. Each leaf, flower, and insect is depicted realistically. Each plant and even the bark of the tree aspire to botanical accuracy. Paton's fairy world is simultaneously the real world, which has been magnified and sharpened with the aid of nineteenth-century technology. It reflects innovations in photography and microscopy – new ways of seeing – that were rendering the invisible world increasingly visible. Its naturalistic detail relies on advances in botany and entomology, which had begun to plumb the secrets of the vegetable and animal worlds. Science, Paton's painting suggests, was not separate from but productive of fantasy, capable of penetrating and even rematerializing the miniature world of the fairies. This positions his work far from the realm of the marvelous, and from eighteenth-century notions of fairyland altogether, and squarely within the category of the fantastic (in this case, a species of otherworldly realism that prefigured Pre-Raphaelitism).[17] His elfin world is imaginary while also clearly tangible and accessible; he shows us a landscape hovering between fiction and reason, history and modernity – an idyllic past recalled by the industrial present.

Paton's painting provides us with a useful model for reading Mendelssohn's and Berlioz's fairy scherzi, which, as we shall see, draw on similar strategies. Both composers produced elfin soundscapes at once actual and fictional, rooted as much in empirical as in otherworldly sound. Their pieces escaped (or recast) the tropes of the musical marvelous, locating fairies within the realm of the "real" supernatural, that of miniature nature. Like Paton, they drew on the devices of modernity to penetrate this world – to capture its elusive effects – recording the results with the aid of new textural and timbral effects. Pressing into service modern instruments and playing techniques, their *fantastique*

---

[16] Ibid., 66.
[17] See Maas et al., *Victorian Fairy Painting*, 108–12. Paton was not a member of the Pre-Raphaelite brotherhood, although he was connected to it through his friend John Ferdinand Millais. Among the key tenets of the group was that direct and truthful representation of nature could reveal a supernatural reality concealed beneath the surface. Science, Pre-Raphaelite ideology posited, could operate as a tool to facilitate acute observation and therefore revelation, opening a modern portal back to an imagined past. For more on this strand of Pre-Raphaelite aesthetics, see Werner, *Pre-Raphaelite Painting and Nineteenth-Century Realism*.

scherzi revealed, in effect, a Paton-esque space of musical miniaturism, a realm of inaudibility amplified by orchestral machinery.

Mendelssohn, Berlioz, and the Technologies of Fairyland

He [Berlioz] was the incomparable initiator of the entire generation to which I belong. He opened the golden door through which soared and invaded the world that host of dazzling and enchanting fairies that is modern orchestration.
–Camille Saint-Saëns[18]

In France, in theatrical productions from the seventeenth century onward, fairies were associated with dance music, especially minuets, gigues, and, later, waltzes. More broadly, both in and outside of France, elfin scenes (as with those depicting enchantment or transformation) were quiet, often scored for strings and upper winds and bearing the label "soft" or "doux." In some cases, as in the stage works of Rebel and Francœur, they also contained rapid, contrapuntal passages featuring sixteenth-note figurations and elaborate ornamentation.[19] At least some of these tropes carry over into Mendelssohn's earliest known fairy music – the third movement of his Op. 20 Octet – where we encounter a persistently quiet dynamic level (*sempre pp*), delicate ornamentation, and fleet contrapuntal elaboration. But in the Octet, the "elegant" lyricism of earlier elfin evocations has been replaced by a texture too quick and skittish to qualify as melodious or to operate as functional dance music – a sound marked by continuous *staccato, pizzicato,* and breathless motivic exchange underpinned by chromatic hovering (Example 6.1). Mendelssohn's fairy music, here and elsewhere, is cast as a scherzo, a form that (in its instrumental guise) had been popularized by Haydn and taken up by a host of later composers. Mendelssohn borrowed it for his fairy music and, to some degree, relied on an existing strand of scherzo sound. Indeed, if we are looking for clues surrounding the musical building blocks of his elfin mode, we must take into account not just an old theatrical tradition, but a newer instrumental one.

Flashes of Mendelssohn's gossamer aesthetic appear in both Haydn's and Beethoven's scherzi; see, for instance, the airy wind and string texture and swift contrapuntal elaboration at the beginning of the Eroica's scherzo, the similar effect found at the outset of the third movement of Beethoven's Sixth Symphony and, earlier, in the *Presto e scherzando* finale of Haydn's Symphony

---

[18] "Discours lu à l'inauguration du Musée Berlioz, à la Côte-Saint-André," trans. adapted from Rose, *Berlioz Remembered*, 295.

[19] Buch, *Magic Flutes and Enchanted Forests*, 23 and 48; for a discussion of Francœur, Rebel, and their contemporaries, see 46–57.

Example 6.1 Mendelssohn, Octet, Op. 20, mm. 1–10

No. 46.[20] But, as with fairy dances in eighteenth-century French opera, these pieces only hint at Mendelssohn's elfin aesthetic rather than constituting clear models. Their delicate textures quickly give way to contrasting material: *fortissimo* explosions, tuneful homophonic themes, and tutti passages. Scherzi of this ilk, as Tilden A. Russell has argued, are defined by dynamic and textural

---

[20] Krummacher, in his discussion of precedents for Mendelssohn's scherzo sound, offers other examples drawn from the chamber music of Beethoven and his contemporaries; see his "Thematische Substanz und motivische Figuration in raschen Binnensätzen," in *Mendelssohn der Komponist*, 235–59.

incongruities; they draw on a tradition of German humor mingling seriousness and capriciousness, *Ernst* and *Scherz* (the latter quality having long been associated by literary critics with the flightiness of fairies).[21] It is this element of contrast that is eradicated in Mendelssohn's elfin scherzi, which have a more homogenous texture; we might call them single-affect pieces. They capture and sustain the fleeting moments of *scherzhaft* found in Beethoven and elsewhere, generating something peculiarly Mendelssohnian – what Friedrich Krummacher has dubbed the *Elfenton*.[22] Rather than simply an extension of operatic fairy music or a variation on Beethoven's and Haydn's scherzo style, this was (as critics were so quick to point out) a substantially new mode – one that Mendelssohn himself traced not to existing musical templates, but to literary description and natural sound.

As I have already noted, Fanny Mendelssohn reported that her brother drew inspiration for the Octet's scherzo from the Walpurgisnacht Dream of Goethe's *Faust*, a whimsical episode mingling imaginary creatures with real ones. The celebratory masquerade performed in honor of Oberon and Titania is attended by a miniature orchestra composed largely of insects, who provide music for the event: "Fly-Snout and Gnat-Nose, here we are, / With kith and kin on duty: / Frog-in-the-Leaves and Grasshopper – / The instrumental tutti!"[23] To their accompaniment, Puck dances, Ariel sings, and other supernatural creatures flit and hover. At the first light of morning, the *pianissimo* orchestra fades as do the characters themselves. Fanny quoted the final stanza of the episode as an explanation for the feather-light ending of Felix's scherzo: "A breeze in the leaves, a wind in the reeds, / And all has vanished."[24] The scherzo at large, as R. Larry Todd

---

[21] Russell traces the history of the scherzo as a vocal and instrumental form in his "Minuet, Scherzando, and Scherzo." Well before Mendelssohn had rendered the scherzo a "fairy" form, Johann Adam Hiller, in a discussion of dramatic genres (1767), had identified a "scherzhaft" mode of writing associated with romanesque comedy, including fairy tales or Märchen-type plots (ibid., 124).

[22] Krummacher associates this sound with "raschestes Tempo, pikante Rhythmik, fliegende Staccati, getupfte Akkorde ... Perpetuum mobile," identifying the scherzo of the Octet as an early and key example, then tracing the texture through other scherzi and pieces of scherzo-like quality, including the *Midsummer Night's Dream* music, certain of the keyboard caprices and Konzertstücke, and the middle movements of the "Scottish" and "Italian" Symphonies. See *Mendelssohn der Komponist*, 235–59, and, for a more technical discussion of Mendelssohn's scherzo construction, 423–59.

[23] Goethe, *Faust*, Part One, trans. David Luke, 135.

[24] This is the translation Sebastian Hensel gives in *Mendelssohn Family*, 131. Luke's translation (see note 23) is: "Leaves rustle, and the reeds are stirred – / And all is blown away now" (140). The dream itself, with its fairy characters, disappears with the scherzo's final gesture, but of course the scherzo music returns in the finale as one of a series of recollections from earlier movements. These moments of recall and, more broadly, the sense of integration (thematic, extra-musical) they suggest are partly what prompts Todd's suggestion that the whole Octet

suggests, was meant to capture Goethe's Shakespearian fairy scene by reproducing the effect of its insect orchestra: "leaping figures at the opening for the crickets and frogs, buzzing trills for the flies, and brisk *spiccati* for the stinging mosquitoes."[25] These were the sounds that made Fanny feel, as she put it, "so near the world of spirits, carried away in the air, half inclined to snatch up a broomstick and follow the aerial procession."[26] For Mendelssohn and his sister, the sound of fairies was synonymous with the sound of insects, which were rendered into music by the new transparent texture of the scherzo. If Paton's painting implied that the artist who looked closely enough at nature might *see* fairies, Mendelssohn's scherzo suggested that the composer who listened with a keen ear might *hear* them.

The connection between fairies and insects (between the supernatural and the microscopic natural) that underpinned the Octet was solidified in the Overture to *A Midsummer Night's Dream*. This was not, of course, cast in the form of a scherzo, but drew obviously – especially in its opening material – on the sounds and textures of the Octet's third movement. Sebastian Hensel, in his history of the Mendelssohns, described the summer of the Overture's composition as one spent largely in the garden of the family home, where the children enjoyed what he called a "fantastic, dreamlike life" dominated by outdoor activities.[27] Drawing was among Mendelssohn's favorite pastimes, his sketches from the period demonstrating early signs of an interest in botanical forms and textures.[28] This preoccupation with nature extended to his ear as well as his eye, according to Mendelssohn's friend Julius Schubring, who recalled the acute sense of hearing the composer developed that summer:

On the sole occasion I rode with him, we went to Pankow, walking thence to the Schönhauser Garden. It was about that time when he was busy with the Overture to *A Midsummer Night's Dream*. The weather was beautiful, and we were engaged in animated conversation as we lay in the shade on the grass when, all of a sudden, he seized me firmly by the arm, and whispered: "Hush!" He afterwards informed me

---

might be read as a Faustian narrative (see *Mendelssohn: A Life in Music*, 151–52). It also underpins Taylor's recent essay on time in the Octet, in which he reads the piece as an enactment of the "organic, evolving spiral" central to the temporal and narrative unfolding of *Faust* and, more broadly, to Goethe's notion that a "higher unity" of time might be achieved via a conflation of past and present; see Taylor, "Musical History and Self-Consciousness in Mendelssohn's Octet, Op. 20," 157.

[25] Todd, *Mendelssohn: A Life in Music*, 151.   [26] Hensel, *The Mendelssohn Family*, 131.
[27] Ibid., 130. Todd also remarks on this passage in *Mendelssohn: A Life in Music*, 161.
[28] Clive Brown reproduces some of Mendelssohn's early sketches and comments on the composer's eye for natural detail in *A Portrait of Mendelssohn*, 47–53. The visual nature of Mendelssohn's music more broadly has been much discussed; see Grey, "Tableaux vivants"; idem, "Fingal's Cave and Ossian's Dream"; Todd, "On the Visual in Mendelssohn's Music"; and Kimber, "Reading Shakespeare, Seeing Mendelssohn."

Example 6.2 Mendelssohn's "buzzing fly," *Midsummer Night's Dream* Overture, Op. 21, mm. 264–70

that a large fly had just then gone buzzing by, and he wanted to hear the sound it produced gradually die away. When the Overture was completed, he showed me the passage in the progression, where the cello modulates in the chord of the seventh of a descending scale from B minor to F-sharp minor, and said: "There, that's the fly that buzzed past us at Schönhauser!"[29]

The sound of Mendelssohn's fly (Example 6.2) is joined, in the Overture, by other whirring and humming effects with an onomatopoeic flavor, as if a variety of insects have been caught and amplified in the work's musical web. Nineteenth-century audiences were quick to make just this observation; following the Overture's 1827 premiere, a reviewer for the *Berliner allgemeine musikalische Zeitung* wrote, "An excellent effect was created by the whisper of divided violins, which an artistic and witty lady compared, certainly not inappropriately, to a swarm of gnats that raise a delightful tumult of life in the last rays of the evening sun."[30] The gnat-like effect that introduces Mendelssohn's Shakespearian scene ushers us into the fleet, *pianissimo* soundworld familiar from the Octet, one seemingly populated by the same cast of insect-fairies. Too quick to be melodic, the opening violins (*staccato* and *pizzicato*) produce a humming sound, a kind of microscopic noise.

---

[29] Schubring, "Reminiscences of Felix Mendelssohn-Bartholdy," *Musical World* 31 (12 and 19 May, 1866), reprinted in Todd, *Mendelssohn and His World*, 225.

[30] *Berliner allgemeine musikalische Zeitung* 4 (1827), trans. Brown, in *Portrait of Mendelssohn*, 335.

Twice, in the first sixty measures, Mendelssohn's insect-fairies pause, alighting on pre-dominant chords (mm. 39 and 56) that hold us in dissonant suspense before the elfin creatures take off once again. Later, when they return at the close of the development, their music is interspersed with other noises: *fortissimo* interjections in the horns, hushed timpani rolls, high-pitched wind interjections, and chromatic murmuring in the low strings. We get the strong sense that the wider soundscape of the gnat-fairies has been reproduced here: the clicking of beetles, buzzing of bees, rustling of leaves, and perhaps even the sudden growl of a small animal. Indeed, the Overture's fairy music invokes a catalogue of natural effects beginning with the famous opening chords themselves, which, tapering from *piano* to *pianissimo*, suggest the whispering of the wind, inviting us into a near-inaudible landscape.

But the world into which Mendelssohn's inaugural chords introduce us is also, of course, a fantasy space. Recalling Paton's painting, we recognize it easily as the realm of the miniature, an elaborately detailed terrain crammed with trills, leaps, and passagework heard at breakneck speed. We listen ever more closely – we lean inward to catch every nuance of Mendelssohn's *pianissimo* soundworld – becoming absorbed in its descriptive density. Our attention to large-scale form wavers as we enter its miniscule terrain and is further muddled by the periodic return of the wind chords, which delay the unfolding of Mendelssohn's sonata form, introducing periods of temporary stasis. The chords themselves are harmonically ambiguous: as the Overture begins, they allow both key and mode to hover in a space of uncertainty, holding us suspended, evoking "a timeless quality" – the sound of long-ago-and-far-away.[31] Mendelssohn's music, like Paton's painting, locates fairies in a dream world while also placing them in the actual world. It conflates the miniature space of fantasy with the microscopic realm of reality, calling on a new palette of instrumental effects (a new set of musical technologies) to capture and materialize Shakespeare's elfin folk.

Weber had already introduced some of these colors and textures in *Oberon*, a work that exerted considerable influence on Mendelssohn.[32]

---

[31] Todd, *Mendelssohn: A Life in Music*, 162. Grey describes these chords as "a kind of curtain that slowly opens onto, and draws us into, the fantasy world of the play and of the Overture alike" in "The Orchestral Music," 465. Both his and Todd's remarks resonate with Liszt's description of the initial chords as the eyes closing and reopening onto a dream state in "Über Mendelssohns Musik zum Sommernachtstraum." We might also link them to magical moments in opera, including sleep, enchantment, and transformation, which, as Buch points out, were often set apart from the surrounding music by hushed wind chords. Among other examples, he cites the oracle scene of Mozart's *Idomeneo* (act 3, scene 10); see *Magic Flutes and Enchanted Forests*, 318.

[32] See Todd, *Mendelssohn, The Hebrides and Other Overtures*, 39–42, where he documents several "striking resemblances" between Weber's opera and Mendelssohn's Overture and suggests that Felix may have had access to a piano-vocal score of *Oberon*.

Melodic echoes of (and, in some instances, direct quotations from) Weber are woven into the fabric of the Overture, but above all, it was the work's orchestration that Mendelssohn borrowed: muted strings, *pianissimo* and *staccato* winds, violin tremolos, and the sound of Oberon's magic horn. In Weber, orchestration is no longer a secondary concern, an afterthought applied to an existing melodic/harmonic framework, but a primary compositional tool – texture and timbre are everything. Mendelssohn was struck by the novelty of Weber's instrumentation both here and in earlier works; according to Schubring, he "used to speak with astonishment of what the man did with a strange orchestra."[33] Berlioz responded similarly (although much later) in an 1857 review of *Oberon*, writing, "Of Weber's instrumentation I will say only that it is of an admirable richness, variety, and novelty."[34] While the form and sound of the evolving scherzo tradition – including the fairy-like harmonies found in Beethoven's and Haydn's inner movements – influenced both Mendelssohn and Berlioz, it was Weber, it seems, who introduced many of the innovations in orchestral texture associated with fairy music. Mendelssohn amplified these effects and added new ones, among them ingenious combinations of bowed and plucked strings, divided violins paired in extended (often chromatic) passages of thirds and fourths, and the low vibration of the ophicleide, which punctuates the recapitulation of the elfin music as if giving voice to the earth itself. His Overture brings Weber's fairies more clearly into focus, its soundworld depending not only on a refined set of orchestral devices, but also on a new species of virtuosity, a technical facility that allowed for the conjuring of miniature aural landscapes. Mendelssohn's insect-elves were materialized by players with unprecedented precision – those shaped by the rigorous, increasingly mechanical conservatory training of the early nineteenth century. The result was a sharply honed sound that rendered the *Midsummer Night's Dream* Overture the century's paradigmatic elfin evocation. Along with Mendelssohn's earlier scherzi (including an orchestral reworking of the Octet's third movement inserted into Symphony No. 1 as an alternative to the minuet), it was performed repeatedly in England and Germany through the late 1820s and 1830s, emerging as his hallmark work.

Mendelssohn's fairy pieces reached France slightly later; the *Midsummer Night's Dream* Overture was performed for the first time in Paris in 1832 at the Conservatoire and "much applauded," according to Hiller, although

---

[33] Schubring, "Reminiscences of Felix Mendelssohn-Bartholdy," reprinted in Todd, *Mendelssohn and His World*, 229.

[34] *Journal des débats* (6 March 1857), reprinted in *À Travers chants*, trans. Csicsery-Rónay, 163.

Fétis remembered it less warmly.[35] It did not appear with any frequency on concert programs through the remainder of the decade, nor was Mendelssohn's other instrumental music well known, with the exception of the first symphony, which did make its way into the repertory of the *Societé des concerts*.[36] Rather than Mendelssohn's fairy evocations, it was Berlioz's Queen Mab music (the fourth movement of *Roméo et Juliette*) that popularized the new sound of the elfin scherzo in Paris. The relationship between it and Mendelssohn's fairy music has long been the subject of speculation. Berlioz missed the 1832 Parisian performance of the Overture – he was in Italy, installed at the French Academy as a Prix-de-Rome winner – but he may well have encountered it through Mendelssohn himself, who traveled to Rome while on his European tour, meeting Berlioz in 1831. The two exchanged musical ideas, playing Beethoven, Gluck, and excerpts from their own works. The idea that Mendelssohn introduced Berlioz to his Overture and perhaps even the Octet (including its Faustian "program") during this period is compelling, since it was then (according to an oft-quoted passage in the *Memoirs*) that the idea for the Mab scherzo was born:

> It was on one of my riding trips in the Roman Campagna with Felix Mendelssohn that I expressed surprise that no one had yet thought of writing a scherzo on Shakespeare's sparkling little poem Queen Mab. He showed equal surprise, and I repented at once having given him the idea. For many years after I was afraid of hearing that he had used this subject. He would certainly have made it impossible, or at least decidedly rash, the double attempt that I made in my symphony *Roméo et Juliette*. Luckily for me he did not think of it.[37]

If Berlioz linked fairies and scherzi for the first time in 1831, the connection resurfaced – indeed, became entrenched – by the late 1830s, when it wove through his reviews of the Beethoven symphonies, written in the two years before *Roméo et Juliette*'s premiere. The colorful instrumentation and motivic play in the scherzo of Symphony No. 2 conjured for Berlioz "the

---

[35] "There were already, in 1830, tendencies towards originality in his productions, particularly in the Overture to *A Midsummer Night's Dream*, which I heard in Paris, but it was easy to see that it was more the product of research and labor than of inspiration." Fétis, *Biographie universelle des musiciens*, 6:368. For Hiller's recollection, see his *Felix Mendelssohn-Bartholdy*, 20.

[36] For an account of Mendelssohn's reception in the leading Parisian music journal, see Ellis, *Music Criticism in Nineteenth-Century France*, 134–41. In France, as Ellis notes (and Fétis's remarks confirm), Mendelssohn was perceived as a composer of technical facility rather than inspiration. His scherzi contained what critics regarded as his only real flashes of genius; later than in either Germany or France, they emerged as a central focus of his reception. See, for instance, the reviews of 1841 and 1849 by Henri Blanchard cited by Ellis on 138.

[37] In a footnote to chapter 36 of the *Mémoirs*, adapted here from the translation by Cairns in Berlioz, *Memoirs*, 168, n. 4.

fairy gambols of the graceful spirits of Oberon," while the darker orchestral tints in the Fifth Symphony's scherzo recalled "the famous Blocksberg scene in Goethe's *Faust*."[38] Scherzi at large seem, for Berlioz, to have become saturated with otherworldly imagery – the same Shakespearian and Goethian scenes that had inspired Mendelssohn. And when he made his own "double attempt" at a fairyscape – the scherzetto in the symphony's opening section (for tenor solo and chorus) and the longer orchestral scherzo in Part Four – he relied unmistakably on Mendelssohn's gossamer texture; his debt to Felix was more apparent than that to Beethoven.

Critics, it must be noted, made no mention of either composer in their reports, hearing in Berlioz only Berlioz; for them, the scherzo represented a new and delicious strand of his *fantastique* idiom. And yet they tied the piece to the same entomological soundscape that had underpinned Felix's fairyscapes. In their reports, Berlioz's *féerique* language reproduced the whirring, fluttering, and murmuring of Mab's airborne retinue, from her gnat-wagoner to her little team of atomies. Merrau, writing for *Le Courrier français*, was one of several who heard Mab's cricket-horsemen in the sustained violin harmonics of the trio; here, he argued, "M. Berlioz imitates the cry of crickets with the cry of the first violins playing in the highest register of the E string."[39] An article in *Le Commerce* interpreted the metallic shimmering of Berlioz's antique cymbals as "the little cry of the cicada," linking both the instruments themselves and their insect-sound to Greek legend and the Pindaric ode.[40] Novelist and essayist Astolphe de Custine, in a private letter to Berlioz, wrote rapturously of "ce choeur de la fée" [the Scherzetto], in which "one sees charming butterflies flying through a network of spiders' webs."[41] Heller, critiquing the same piece for the *Gazette musicale*, described Berlioz's orchestration itself in entomological terms: "The flutes hover and flutter . . . in an almost supernatural fashion."[42] Not only do fairies and insects share the same miniature world, they become synonymous – insect sound *is* fairy sound. Berlioz himself underscored the link in an open letter to Heine

---

[38] *La Revue et Gazette musicale* (28 January 1838), in *CM*, 3:375, 379.

[39] "M. Berlioz imitera le cri des grillons en faisant crier l'archet des premiers violons sur la chanterelle aiguë," *Le Courrier français* (26 November 1839).

[40] "Ah! M. Berlioz! je ne vous pardonnerai jamais d'avoir réservé pour vos amis intimes la confidence de deux petites cymbales antiques dont, il est parlé dans tous les poètes de l'école de Pindare, imitation [sic] touchante du petit cri de la cigale amoureuse dans les bois." *Le Commerce* (1 December 1839).

[41] "J'espère penser toute ma vie à ce choeur de la fée où l'on voit de charmants papillons voler à travers un réseau de fils d'araignée." Custine to Berlioz, in *CG*, II:681 (between 24 November and 20 December 1839).

[42] "Les flûtes papillonnent et badinent . . . d'une façon presque surnaturelle." *Gazette musicale* (19 December 1839).

(the sixth in his series of missives from Germany) in which he reported on a performance of the Mab scherzo given by the Brunswick orchestra:

> Queen Mab in her microscopic chariot, drawn at full gallop by her team of little atomies and driven by the murmuring gnat that buzzes and hovers on summer eves, danced her mad revels to the admiration of the Brunswick audience. You, poet of sprites and fairies, blood-brother to all those delicate and mordant creatures, will realize my misgivings. You know only too well from what gossamer thread their gauzy wings are spun and how serene the sky must be before that inconstant swarm can sport without fear under the pale light of the stars. Well! The orchestra, defying our doubts, identifying itself completely with Shakespeare's exquisite fancy, made itself so small and fine and nimble that never, I think, did the insubstantial queen dart more gleefully among her soundless harmonies.[43]

Here, nature and the supernatural collapse; for Berlioz, as for Mendelssohn, insects existed in the same ontological space as fairies. The humming and buzzing figures that dominate Mab's music evoked for Berlioz, as for his listeners, both the entomological realm under the magnifying glass and the imaginary world of Queen Mab. Both were housed in a space of magical smallness – a place of invisibility and inaudibility, of transparent forms and "soundless harmonies" renderable only by an ensemble more nimble and quick than any before it.

As Berlioz reported to Heine, the Brunswick orchestra (led by Carl Müller) worked tirelessly in order to master the scherzo, meeting an hour before each scheduled rehearsal to practice the most difficult passages. In a program that included *Harold en Italie*, the overture to *Benvenuto Cellini*, and two movements from the *Grand messe des morts*, it was the scherzo that worried Müller.[44] Mab's fairy world was a place of unprecedented virtuosity and, according to both Müller and his French counterparts, of orchestrational novelty. Its *monde fantastique*, according to *L'Avant-Scène*, was also a *monde nouveau* – a new universe of sound in which "Berlioz combined, in the most bizarre and original fashion, the wind and string instruments." *La France musicale* made a similar claim, crediting Berlioz with the

---

[43] Berlioz, *Memoirs*, trans. Cairns, 311.

[44] Berlioz himself was wary, noting that this was "the first time since coming to Germany I had ventured to include it in the programme." Ibid., 311. The performance took place at the Ducal Theater on 9 March 1843 and was, by all accounts, a success. But the scherzo continued to be perceived as a difficult work. More than a decade later, when Carl Eckert, conductor of the Hofoper orchestra in Vienna, decided to perform it, he sent a letter in advance to the publisher, Brandus (from whom he hired the orchestral parts), asking for advice. Berlioz responded in person with several pages of detailed instructions on how to prepare and perform what he termed "ce diabolique morceau." See *CG*, V:2182.

invention of "a new manner of employing voices and instruments."[45] Descriptions of the symphony's fairy music dissolved, in virtually every early account, into a catalogue of orchestral effects. The *Gazette musicale* listed "the constant employment of mutes, ... the strange dance of the altos, the harmonic tones of the harp, [and] the piercing cry of the little antique cymbals."[46] *La Quotidienne* gave an even longer list, collapsing the scherzo into a string of textural and timbral novelties – the sum total of Berlioz's "féerie instrumentale":

> this constant *pianissimo* produced by mutes, these divided violins with harmonic tones in the extreme upper register under which this veiled English horn melody hovers; then these skipping violas, then again these harmonic tones in the harp when the harmonics in the violins cease; then these fanfares in the horns; then this rhythm in the timpani; then these capricious pedal points; then this confused murmur of a crescendo; then these echoes of the antique cymbals.[47]

In all of these reports, the experience of the supernatural was bound up with an awareness of the machinery producing it. Like the new gas lighting and elaborate levers and pulleys that produced fairy spectacles on English and French stages, Queen Mab had been materialized, according to French reviewers, by modern technology – by the Berliozian orchestra, creator of "the most original and unexpected sonorities."[48] The Shakespearian past was also the musical present; archaic fantasy had collapsed into modernity. But of course Berlioz's soundworld was not entirely new. Like Mendelssohn before him, he called on instrumental virtuosity to generate and sustain a nostalgic world – he transported listeners, particularly in Mab's opening pages, to a landscape both original and familiar: that of the musical miniature.

---

[45] In *L'Avant-Scène*: "Ici [dans le scherzo] Berlioz a combiné, de la façon la plus bizarre et la plus originale, les instrumens à vent et les instrumens à cordes" (8 December 1839). In *La France musicale*, both the scherzo and the scherzetto were linked with orchestral novelty: "Le scherzino vocal est un chef-d'oeuvre. On dirait que le compositeur a trouvé une nouvelle manière d'employer les voix et les instruments." And later: "Le scherzo, c'est la traduction par des effets de sonorité nouveaux" (1 December 1839).

[46] "L'exécution perpétuellement en sourdines, le prestissimo du trait principal ... la danse étrange des altos, les sons harmoniques de la harpe, le cri perçant des petites cymbales antiques" (28 November 1839).

[47] "Ne serait-ce pas folie de chercher à peindre l'effet de toute cette féerie instrumentale à propos de la reine Mab, de ce pianissimo constant des sourdines, de ces violons divisés tenant des notes harmoniques à l'extrémité de l'aigu, au-dessous desquelles plane cette mélodie voilée du cor anglais, puis ces altos bondissans, puis encore ces notes harmoniques de la harpe quand les note harmoniques des violons se taisent, puis ces fanfares de cors, puis ce rythme des tymbales, puis ces point d'orgues capricieux, puis ce murmure confus du crescendo, puis ces échos de la cymbale antique." *La Quotidienne* (26–27 December 1839).

[48] *Gazette musicale* (28 November 1839).

Fairyology, Entomology, and the Scherzo fantastique

Berlioz's scherzo opens onto the same densely detailed terrain conjured by the *Midsummer Night's Dream* Overture, but unfolds at greater velocity as if ushering us into a world of more radical smallness. It, like Mendelssohn's Shakespearian music, begins with a series of sustained wind chords that establish the *pianissimo* register – the magic whisper – of the fairy world. These give way to divided violins, now *prestissimo* and *saltato*, whose hovering motion is punctuated by occasional *pizzicati* and upper-wind flourishes. Berlioz's insect-fairies, like Felix's, alight twice in the opening section (mm. 29 and 57) on variations of the wind chords with which the piece opened. They are, it seems, waiting for us to catch up, to follow them into the secret recesses of fairyland (Example 6.3). Once we have arrived at its portals – and the real beginning of the scherzo (m. 70) – the pace quickens. Berlioz's orchestra generates a whirlwind (a "swarm," as he puts it). String triplets whir along, sometimes in dialogue with the winds, sometimes breaking off for a rapid-fire tossing of pitches from one instrument to the other. Chromatic slides heard *prestissimo* (the first at m. 177) have the effect of glissandi, gesturing toward microtonal sound – an intervallic universe too tiny to be notated. Buzzing and rustling effects emerge from the texture around m. 263, written-out trills passing between the upper winds and strings in what is clearly a conversation although it transpires so rapidly we hardly register it. Periodically, the opening wind chords return (again, as in Mendelssohn), holding the headlong flight of Berlioz's scherzo in temporary suspension. Time seems to loop back on itself, to collapse then and now, so that we are unsure where we are in the form.[49] We are in a space of furious activity and yet curious stasis – the fantasy world of the fairies.

Once we have arrived in the elfin realm, Berlioz ushers into a place still more secret: Mab's dream world itself. We follow her as she visits a slumbering page "who dreams of mischief / Or sweet serenading," then a soldier who has visions of battle, and finally a young girl who sees herself at a ball.[50] It is fairy enchantment of the most elusive kind that captures these reveries – musical magic that critics heard, woven through the scherzo at large, as the distant song of insects. Mab's nocturnal antics begin as the trio opens (m. 354) and the Mendelssohnian texture of the opening section gives way to a less familiar soundscape. Shakespeare's mischievous fairy herself

---

[49] The scherzo at large has resisted stable formal analysis. Julian Rushton calls it "kaleidoscopic," summing up scholarly opinion on the matter and offering a compellingly multivalent assessment of the work's structure in *Berlioz, Roméo et Juliette*, 42–46. For an earlier analysis focusing in particular on the relationship between form and orchestration, see Shamgar, "Program and Sonority."

[50] The "program" for the scherzo (a modified and much truncated version of Mercutio's Mab speech) is given in the earlier scherzetto for tenor and chorus. It is reproduced in Rushton, *Berlioz: Roméo et Juliette*, 93–94.

288 *Of Demons and Fairies*

Example 6.3 Berlioz, "La Reine Mab," *Roméo et Juliette*, mm. 1–40

hovers on the edge of the new section (the very end of the opening *Prestissimo*) on a trilled A sustained over five measures and extended by a fermata. Our attention narrows, focusing on this single creature; the effect is that of a close-up, a new degree of magnification both visual and aural, which leads into a section marked *sempre pppp* – a dynamic range virtually outside the realm of hearing (and playing). Here, the fluttering trill fades into a mere vibration over which sustained violin harmonics produce a scratchy shimmer – an otherworldly noise that critics associated with the song of the grasshopper (Example 6.4). What they heard as insect sound Berlioz described as fairy noise. He catalogued the violin effect in his *Treatise on Orchestration*, noting that he had produced it for the first time "in the scherzo of a symphony," and (to make matters clearer) excerpting mm. 354–88 of the Mab music. The harmonics in this passage produce a "crystalline timbre," which "makes them suitable for what I call 'fairy' chords ... effects which draw the listener into ecstatic dreams and carry the mind away to the imaginary delights of a poetic, make-believe world." Mutes played an important role in producing the slightly dulled effect (the "extreme delicacy") of the violin harmonics: "dampened in this way," Berlioz wrote, "they sound in the remotest regions of the audible scale." This was a soundworld so quiet it had hitherto evaded capture, a bit of fairy magic never before recorded; indeed, Berlioz complained that no serious study of harmonics had as yet been instituted at the Conservatoire.[51]

The section beginning in m. 610 (the episode of the young girl dreaming of a ball) explores other "soundless harmonies," including those produced by a pair of antique cymbals – instruments whose timbre, according to Berlioz, "is so high and soft that one would scarcely hear them unless every other instrument were silent."[52] For Janin, these cymbals conjured the smallest, most elusive soundworld of the scherzo and, in doing so, excavated spaces – both imaginary and actual – more remote even than Shakespeare's fairyland. He linked the instruments with both insect song and natural magic; they invoked "the lovelorn cicada in the woods" – the voice of Tithonus, according to Roman legend, who had been transformed into an insect by his lover Eos, goddess of the dawn. Tithonus, in cicada form, was a sacred creature worshipped by "the priests of Ceres," practitioners of druid ritual for whom the insect was a symbol of

---

[51] Berlioz, *Orchestration Treatise*, trans. Macdonald, 23–25. Macdonald does not reproduce Berlioz's example from *La Reine Mab* in his translation, although he makes note of it. Harmonics had, in fact, been treated and taught in Pierre Baillot's violin treatise (1835), but had yet to become a regular focus of French institutional instruction (my thanks to Louise Goldberg for pointing this out).

[52] Ibid., 278.

Example 6.4 Berlioz, "La Reine Mab," trills at the close of the scherzo leading into the opening of the trio, *Roméo et Juliette*, mm. 349–70

enchantment and longevity.[53] Janin suggested, in a fanciful *feuilleton*, that Berlioz had unearthed the cymbals themselves from the ruins of Pompeii, incorporating them into his new orchestral machine – an ensemble capable

[53] "les instruments ressuscités que vous entendez là, ce sont tout simplement ces petites cymbales antiques dont il est parlé dans tous les poètes de l'école de Pindare. Ces petites cymbales étaient restées enjoués, avec le dithyrambe, dans les centres de l'antiquité, lorsque, dans les ruines de Pompéi, Berlioz découvrit l'instrument humilié, qui depuis tant de siècles n'avait pas fait entendre son petit cri de cigale amoureuse dans les bois." *Journal des débats* (29 November 1839).

of prying open not only the most minute natural spaces, but the supernatural worlds hidden within them. Heller, in a slightly later review, echoed and embroidered Janin's tale. In his account (now set in Herculaneum), Berlioz had dug up not only the cymbals, but also the score of the scherzo itself. Heller appealed humorously to "all amateur antiquarians and ethnographers" to search for other antique scherzi "in the ruins where Berlioz had unearthed his own."[54] The Mab music emerged, in his account, as a relic of ancient history, but it was a history reanimated by nineteenth-century science. Berlioz's musical innovations had achieved what historians and archaeologists had attempted to do – they had rematerialized (exhumed, to borrow Heller's metaphor) a fairy past, a lost magic. His orchestra was a tool of amplification and metaphorical excavation, and its product (the scherzo) the result of modern *musical* science – the same orchestral machinations critics had associated with the *Épisode de la vie d'un artiste* and with Meyerbeer's *Robert le diable*. Re-invoking complaints long associated with these works, and with musical fantasy at large, many argued that Berlioz's *féerique* mode relied not on genius or imagination, but on the intellect – it was cerebral, technological. A reviewer for *Les Guêpes* complained that "it appealed to the head" rather than the heart; others argued that it was a "savant" medium facilitating only arranging rather than creating.[55] Berlioz's Mab music simply imitated natural sound, according to Merrau; it was rooted in materialism, converting worldly noise directly into orchestrational effects without the intervention of any higher poetic sense.[56] For Custine, too, Berlioz's insect sounds – the charming butterflies as well as the more amorphous "sounds of nature" featured in the scherzetto – were produced by musical science, although in his assessment it was a science "concealed beneath inspiration."[57] Even non-musicians made the connection between Berlioz's novel orchestration and the reproduction of natural sound at the heart of the Mab music. The idea became routine, seeping into popular fiction. Balzac used the scherzo itself to describe the pastoral vista of fairyland – a place

---

[54] "j'adjure tous les amateurs d'antiquités et d'ethnographie de se mettre en quête, sous le bon plaisir du roi de Naples, de scherzos antiques dans les fouilles d'où Berlioz a déterre le sien." *Gazette musicale* (19 December 1839). Both Janin's and Heller's accounts were fanciful embroiderings of the truth: Berlioz had seen "two pairs of little cymbals" in a museum in Pompeii, which had been found beneath the ashes at Herculaneum. As he explains in the *Orchestration Treatise*, "any bell foundry can make these little cymbals which are first cast in copper or brass and then turned to adjust them to the desired pitch" (trans. Macdonald, 279). See also the letter to his family of 7 October 1831 (*CG*, I:244).

[55] "La musique de M. Berlioz s'adresse à la tête." *Les Guêpes* (December 1839); the same reviewer wrote: "La science est un moyen et non pas un résultat. On dit que la musique de M. Berlioz est savante." In *Le Figaro* (1 December 1839), we encounter something similar: "La génie est un mot quit veut créer. –La science ne crée pas,–elle arrange."

[56] *Le Courrier français* (16 November 1839). [57] *CG*, II:681.

conjured by Princess Finna in his satirical tale "Les Amours de deux bêtes" (1841–42). Here, at a signal from the princess:

> there arose in the silence of that perfumed night a music absolutely akin to the scherzo of Queen Mab in *Roméo et Juliette*, where the great Berlioz has extended the limits of the art of instrument-making [i.e., used instruments to the utmost of their capacity], in order to capture the effects of the Cicada, the Cricket, and of Flies, and to evoke the sublime voice of nature at midday in the tall grass of a meadow, where a brook murmurs across the silver sand.[58]

In Balzac's tale, as in Berlioz's scherzo, supernaturalism was rooted in musical realism. The Mab music was made up of entomological and, more broadly, empirical sound revealed and amplified via the latest orchestrational machinery. It was the product of scientific fantasy – aural archeology or antiquarianism, in Janin's account, but much more clearly, a kind of musical microscopy.

Microscopy, Entomology, Magic

The perfect accord of every movement of the delicate and subtle tactile and telegraphic apparatus, the strong head, in fine, which seemingly thinks, completed the illusion ... Shakespeare's Queen Mab, in her nut-shell chariot, occurred to my mind. And more, the chronicles of the Hubers, those impressive and almost terrifying narratives which would lead us to believe that the ants are far advanced in knowledge of good and evil.

–Jules Michelet[59]

That queen of fairies, you know her very well: she is nature herself.

–George Sand[60]

Berlioz's insect-fairy conflation – the fantastic hesitation at the heart of his scherzo – may have been influenced by Mendelssohn, but more likely both composers (and their critics) were responding to images of fairies already circulating in wider literary and scientific arenas. Both had fashioned musical microscopes in response to *actual* microscopes, which, well before the 1820s, had begun to reveal unknown and robustly populated unseen realms whose descriptions invariably bled into the world of the fairies. Microscopy itself was a discipline teetering between the scientific and the fabulous in the first half of

---

[58] "Du plus loin qu'elle aperçut le prince, elle [La Princess Finna] fit un signe. A signal, il s'éleva dans le silence de cette nuit parfumée une musique absolument semblable au scherzo de la reine Mab, dans la symphonie de *Roméo et Juliette*, où le grand Berlioz a reculé les bornes de l'art du facteur d'instruments, pour trouver les effets de la Cigale, du Grillon, des Mouches, et rendre la voix sublime de la nature, à midi, dans les hautes herbes d'une prairie où murmure un ruisseau sur du sable argenté. Balzac, "Les Amours de deux bêtes," 434–35.

[59] *L'Insecte*, 149.   [60] "Le Manteau rouge," in *Contes d'une grand'mère*, 180.

the nineteenth century. Inexpensive and portable instruments along with improved magnifying technologies made microscopes available and attractive to an ever-widening public, and fostered an upsurge of interest in the natural sciences – botany, geology, mineralogy, and especially entomology.[61] But these emerging disciplines, and the idea of scientific microscopy itself, overlapped with older cultures of natural magic and sensational entertainment. Sophisticated high-magnification and achromatic microscopes (those correcting for the chromatic aberration that had distorted images produced by earlier instruments) existed alongside more primitive devices featured in traveling exhibits and purchased for home diversion. Among the most popular of these was the solar microscope, first presented to the Royal Society in 1739 by Nathaniel Lieberkühn of Berlin and, beginning in the late-eighteenth century, much used in public optical shows in England and France. It consisted of a mirror that reflected a beam of sunlight (later, artificial light) through a tube. A converging lens directed the beam onto an object – often an insect or insect-part in a transparent preparation – and a second lens magnified it, throwing an enlarged image on a screen in a darkened room.[62] The solar microscope was really a modified version of an old device: the magic lantern. It was connected in design and use to a long-standing tradition of phantasmagoria, bridging the supernatural optical illusions of the eighteenth century and the newer microscopic demonstrations of the nineteenth. What lanterns and other instruments of the *camera obscura* family had traditionally shown were devils, ghosts, goblins, and illustrations from fairy tales. The solar microscope promised to provide more "scientific" images – to rescue the magic lantern from its link with charlatanism – but instead it became part of a culture in which education and diversion were inextricably conjoined. Popular entertainers (who were sometimes also serious scientists) mingled supernatural lantern images with natural specimens – especially insects – projected by solar magnifiers, forging a relationship between entomology and magic that would endure through much of the nineteenth century.

Among the most famous of the microscope-showmen was Gustavus Katterfelto (nicknamed Dr. Caterpillar), a Prussian who came to London in 1782. As Deirdre Coleman has shown, insects played a key role in Katterfelto's act, which promised "Wonderful Wonders, Wonders and

---

[61] Classic and more recent histories of the microscope that have informed my work here include the following: Bradbury, *The Evolution of the Microscope*; Butler, Nuttal, and Brown, *The Social History of the Microscope*; Ford, *The Revealing Lens*; idem, *Single Lens*; Fournier, *The Fabric of Life*; Schickore, *The Microscope and the Eye*; and Wilson, *The Invisible World*.

[62] Lieberkühn is often cited as the inventor of the solar microscope, although devices using solar illumination had been described earlier. See Hankins and Silverman, *Instruments and the Imagination*, 54–58 passim. For an eighteenth-century account of the solar microscope's history, see Baker, *The Microscope Made Easy*.

Wonders." Using a solar microscope and other projection devices, Katterfelto promised to lay bare the "occult" forces of nature, magnifying beetles, fleas, and fly eyes to enormous sizes to reveal a hitherto unknown miniature world – a place both beautiful and monstrous. Katterfelto also magnified smaller creatures; in an advertisement published in *The European Magazine* he claimed that he would "shew in a drop of clear water (the size of a pin's head) upwards of 10000 live Insects." In the accompanying image, we see him stroking a black cat – his demonic sidekick – while pointing to the magnified insects (or animalculae, as other scientists called them), many of which have been given horns or winged, fairy-like forms.[63] The miniature world, Katterfelto suggested, was also an enchanted one, the home of creatures both entomological and imaginary. This idea was reinforced by French entertainers, including Nicolas Philippe Ledru and Etienne Gaspard Robertson, both of whom used the solar microscope (sometimes known as a megascope or, in Robertson's modified version, phantascope) to project insects and demonstrate other scientific marvels. These images, interleaved with and sometimes overlaid on projections of ghosts or other imaginary creatures, were billed as fabulous spectacles revealed by a new optical technology.[64]

The same convergence of miniature nature and the supernatural infiltrated fictional writing of the period, especially the tales of Hoffmann, which were well known to Mendelssohn and, as we have already seen, to Berlioz. In Hoffmann's "Master Flea" (1822), we encounter another solar microscope, this one wielded by seventeenth-century scientist Anton van Leeuwenhoek and his contemporary, entomologist Jan Swammerdam. The device not only plumbs the secrets of the natural world, but allows Hoffmann's scientist-magicians to reveal and materialize the fairy characters who inhabit it. Leeuwenhoek describes, first, the capturing of Princess Gamaheh during the dissection of a "lovely lavender and yellow tulip." Magnifying lenses reveal that a seed pellet hidden within the flower's cup is actually the princess, who is extracted, enlarged, and materialized:

With the aid of a fine Kuff solar microscope we projected her image and neatly detached the reflection from the white wall, smoothly and without any damage. As soon as the reflection floated free, it shot like a lightning flash into the lens, which was shattered in a thousand pieces. Before us stood the princess, fresh and full of life.[65]

A microscope of another sort also ensnares Master Flea, who to the naked eye is merely a "little monster" – an insect – but under the lens is shown to be a fairy.

---

[63] *The European Magazine* (June 1783), 406. For more on Katterfelto, see Coleman, "Entertaining Entomology," especially 111–14; also see Seibold-Bultmann, "Monster Soup."
[64] Hankins and Silverman, *Instruments and Imagination*, 63–64.
[65] Hoffmann, "Master Flea," 284.

The Flea himself describes his capture, which happens when he is flying over "two mages" (Swammerdam and Leeuwenhoek) using a microscope to observe the stars. One of their "magic instruments" focuses so sharply on the Flea that it blinds and immobilizes him, pulling him out of the sky:

> I was still too dazed to jump down off the mage's nose and get to complete safety, when the monster, that treacherous Leeuwenhoek ... neatly caught me with his fingers and put me directly under a Russwurm universal microscope. Despite the fact that it was nighttime and hence he had to light the lamp, he was far too practiced an observer and far too experienced in science not to recognize me at once as Master Flea.[66]

Having caught the Flea-King with his lens, Leeuwenhoek forces him and the insect-fairies under his command to perform in a flea circus for the entertainment of humans, an act, according to Hoffmann, that recalls the "equipage of Queen Mab." Secreted within miniature nature, his story suggested, was a supernatural space – the realm of fairytale and Shakespearian fantasy. For Hoffmann's readers, and the audiences of microscopic entertainments more broadly, new technology not only magnified this hidden universe, but revealed its true nature: it showed insects and even flowers to be fairies.

For many in the emerging scientific community, solar microscopes and the supernatural *frisson* that surrounded them were nonsense. British microscopist Dr. E. Goring insisted in 1827 that "the image of a common solar microscope may be considered as a mere shadow, fit only to amuse women and children."[67] And certainly, solar magnifiers themselves faded as newer technologies emerged, yet the insect-fairies revealed by them persisted; indeed, far from being eradicated by the work of later scientists, they proliferated. During the 1850s and 1860s, fairies were often linked with the entomological world.[68] French texts, particularly the widely read and translated works of Jules Michelet and Louis Figuier, played a key role in perpetuating such a connection, both authors describing the natural world of insects as a physical as well as an imaginary place.[69] Michelet's *L'Insecte* (1858) combines scientific scrutiny of

---

[66] Ibid., 300. [67] Qtd. in Altick, *The Shows of London*, 369.
[68] See Bown, *Fairies in Nineteenth-Century Art and Literature*, in particular the chapter titled "A few fragments of fairyology, shewing its connection with natural history," 98–162. This chapter shaped my own thinking about mid-nineteenth-century intersections between fairies and insects and drew my attention to important primary sources, although the readings of them given here are my own.
[69] Michelet and Figuier, who occupy the majority of my attention here, were by no means the first French naturalists to publish important studies on entomology; rather, they were purveyors of a brand of popular science particular to the 1840s and onward. Their work was preceded by that of Jean-Baptiste de Monet de Lamarck, whose treatise on invertebrates (including insects) was highly influential. It was rigorously factual in its description and classification (Lamarck is still recognized as the most important French pre-Darwinian taxonomist and evolutionary theorist), but, even here, fanciful rhetoric and a tendency toward anthropomorphizing had already begun

insects (descriptions of their anatomy, natural habitats, and metamorphoses) with pervasive anthropomorphizing (accounts of entomological loves, conflicts, and even weddings). The scientific world under the microscope transforms fluidly, in his account, into a tiny, fantastical kingdom – a place of fascination and desire. This shift is perpetuated, in part, by the sheer profusion of detail at the heart of the insect realm, its "abyss of imperceptible organisms" containing "myriads upon myriads of unknown beings and fabulous organizations."[70] Confounding the senses, this landscape produced in Michelet "a certain feeling of being dazzled" and later "a poetical charm which approaches the sublime."[71] Such disorientation was common in microscopical study, he argued, which not only required but produced "an isolation from the world, a point beyond time," ushering observers into a nostalgic place unmoored from experiential reality. This was, of course, the realm of the miniature, the fairyland of Paton's painting. The observer slipped, according to Michelet, between miniaturism and microscopy, between mental dazzlement and rational inquiry. He mapped this sense of duality onto a vacillation between feminine and masculine modes of experience. Entomology is a discipline best undertaken by women, who are "more poetical than men," more willing to attend to and even to be absorbed into a world of natural detail (the world "beyond time"), but female sensibility must be stabilized by masculine technology (the microscope). Together fantasy and reason open a true vista onto nature.[72]

This sense of double vision carries through Michelet's text at large, which introduces insects as natural specimens – indeed, insists on scientific rigor in the analysis of their behaviors – while also wandering repeatedly into supernatural description. In a chapter titled "A Phantasmagoria of Light and Color," he figured them as "beautiful beings, fantastic beings, admirable monsters." They are "clad in a hundred kinds of enamel ... some in burnished steel shot with yellow, others in silken hoods embroidered with black velvet." Looking through the microscope is akin to watching the phantasmagorical projections

---

to creep in. Lamarck claimed, for instance, that insect metamorphosis was "magical" and that, in its final stage (the flight stage), insects lived in a constant state of "gaiety and pleasure" ("Il semble alors ne respirer que la gaîté et le plaisir"), their ardor deriving from the knowledge that they had but a short time to live. See Lamarck, *Système des animaux sans vertèbres*, 188.

[70] From a passage on pioneering entomologist Jan Swammerdam, through whose microscope, "L'abîme de la vie apparut dans sa profondeur avec des milliards de milliards d'êtres inconnus et d'organisations bizarres qu'on n'eût même osé rêver." Michelet, *L'Insecte*, 92. This and the following translations are adapted from those of Adams in *The Insect*.

[71] In a passage describing "the lively infinity" ("l'infini vivant") of the insect world, *L'Insecte*, xxiii–xxiv, 115.

[72] "Enfin, pour résumer tout, ces études demandent ce qu'on a le moins aujourd'hui, qu'on soit hors du monde, hors du temps, soutenu par une curiosité innocente." Ibid., xi. This description of timelessness is embedded in a longer passage on microscopy and gender (xi–xii).

of an optical show: "With a burning brain," Michelet wrote, "I issued from the magic cave; and for a long time afterwards the sparkling, scintillating masks danced and whirled around me, pursuing me, and maintaining on my retina their wild, strange revel."[73] Repeatedly, he mapped the entomological world onto fairyland, partly, as I suggested earlier, in response to an insect-fairy connection already culturally engrained, and partly, as Bown posits, to render insects less frightening to amateur naturalists.[74] The bee, for instance, gathering pollen from flower-cups, "takes its stand at the bottom of these recesses worthy of the fairies, covered with the softest tapestry, under fantastic pavilions."[75] And arachnids, in Michelet's account, are themselves fairies. He describes a boyhood encounter with a domestic spider in his father's printing shop, during which the insect suggested that they might be friends. "The little black fairy," Michelet recalled, "said this in its own language, whispering low, very low (for it is thus that spiders speak)."[76] Insects seen under the microscope are akin not only to elfin folk, but to characters from medieval and Shakespearian tales. Two beetles locked in struggle are "equally provided with admirable defensive arms, after the fashion of the corselets, armlets, and cuisses of our ancient knights." Later, ants seen under the microscope call to mind Shakespeare's Queen Mab in her nutshell chariot.[77] Enlarging miniature natural creatures also seems, in Michelet's account, to materialize distant (even mythological) ones.

A similar kind of double-materialization – a tendency to link insect magnification with the recapturing of characters from myths or fairytales – pervades Louis Figuier's *Les Insectes* (1867). In Figuier, detailed drawings of entomological anatomy and scientific accounts of insect environments and behavior are intermingled with fictional anecdotes. Among these are Greek legends describing the magical powers of the cicada, including the rejuvenating effect of its "harmonious song." Another is the tale of the Comma butterfly, which excretes a red-colored liquid like "drops of blood" in the early stages of metamorphosis, producing "superstitious terror" among the

---

[73] "Elle [la nature] m'inondait et m'accablait d'êtres charmants, d'êtres bizarres, de monstres admirables, en ailes de feu, en cuirasses d'émeraudes, vêtus d'émaux de cent sortes ... les uns en acier bruni, glacé d'or, les autres à houppes soyeuses, feutrées de noirs velours ... Je sortis de l'antre magique la tête en feu, et longtemps ces masques étincelants dansaient, tournaient, me poursuivaient, continuant sur ma rétine leur bal effréné." Ibid., 156–57.

[74] Bown, *Fairies in Nineteenth-Century Art and Literature*, 125.

[75] "L'abeille s'établit au fond de ces réduits dignes des fées, tendus des plus doux tapis; sous des pavillons fantastiques." Michelet, *L'Insecte*, 321.

[76] "Comme la noire petite fée le disait en son langage, bas, très-bas, on ne peut plus bas (ainsi parlent les araignées)." Ibid., 205.

[77] "Toutefois ces deux ennemis étant également couverts d'armes défensives admirables, à l'instar des corselets, brassards et cuissards de nos anciens chevaliers." Ibid., 23; see also 120 for the link between Queen Mab and the ants.

untutored. Old wives' tales of the death's-head moth (the harbinger of doom) and of demonic locusts (connected to biblical punishment and, later, witchcraft) follow. Figuier did not suggest that these stories were true (in fact, he ascribed most of them to ignorance), and yet his elaborate recounting of them leant them fresh vigor, suggesting that they were hovering irresistibly in the popular and even scientific imagination.[78]

More playful was an earlier English text by L. M. Budgen titled *Episodes of Insect Life* (1849–51). Here, Budgen identified the discipline of entomology itself as "a powerful Genie, a light-winged Fairy," imbuing all of nature with elfin magic.[79] She couched her description of the insect world as a series of fanciful tales featuring spider-sirens, butterfly-sylphs, and beetle-knights. The insects in these stories not only have fairy-like appearances – they wear velvet cloaks and coats of mail, and sport wand-like piercers – but they are also associated with magical sound. In a section titled "Insect Minstrelsy," she claimed that the vibratory tremor of flies was similar to that of an aeolian harp string activated by "air playing on the membranaceous edges of the wings." And grasshoppers, rubbing their feet against their bodies, generated the effect of reeds, echoing the sound of Pan's mythological pipes. Borrowing Paracelsian rhetoric, Budgen called insects "the pipers and … the dancers [who] seemed in truth, to have taken complete possession of the three elements – air, earth, and water – together with a large portion of the fourth … and, in thus possessing, given apparent life to the elements themselves." Their music was "a veritable language" – the language of nature itself, which operated as a set of tiny incantations regulating the mysteries of birth, growth, transformation, and death.[80] In tandem, insect-musicians formed an elemental orchestra, an ensemble pictured in one of Budgen's many droll vignettes (Figure 6.2). Here, "the classic Cicada, the grassy Grullus, and the deep-toned Dor" play the lyre, double bass, and drum, each taking an instrument that approximates its

---

[78] Louis Figuier, *Les Insectes*. On Greek mythology and the cicada, see 103–04; on the Comma butterfly, see 192–93; on the Death's-head moth, see 208–09; on locusts, see 309. See also the extended discussion of flea circuses, 30–31, much of which is taken from an earlier entomological text: Walckenaer, *Histoire naturelle des insects*, 4:365–66.

[79] Budgen published this under the pseudonym Acheta Domestica (domestic spider). Page numbers given here refer to the 1867 edition; for the above quotation, see p. 9. The text was originally published in three volume's, 1849–51. For Bown's discussion of Budgen, see *Fairies in Nineteenth-Century Art and Literature*, 127–32. Bown's view of this text is rather darker than my own; she argues that Budgen uses fairy imagery and rhetoric as a way of "enchanting the natural world, of covering over 'the bare, the barren, and the death-like' and turning it into a fairyland" (127). Fantasy, in her reading, is pressed into service to mask the cruel realities revealed by science. My own research suggests a more complex relationship between the two modes. Fantasy was imposed on science by nineteenth-century entomologists, but science itself, as we have seen, also *produced* fantasy; microscopes had long since revealed fairies, not all of which were beautiful or reassuring.

[80] Budgen, *Episodes of Insect Life*, 236, 249.

Fairyology, Entomology, and the Scherzo fantastique

Figure 6.2 "The classic Cicada, the grassy Grullus, and the deep-toned Dor." From L. M. Budgen (Acheta Domestica), *Episodes of Insect Life* (London: Bell and Daldy, 1867), 237. *Episodes* was originally published by Reeve, Benham, and Reeve in three volumes, 1849–51. Reproduced by kind permission of the Syndics of Cambridge University Library. Classmark MA.14.33.

own sound. This group comes close to the ensemble Goethe described in *Faust* and Mendelssohn must have imagined while composing the scherzo of his Octet. Budgen, like Mendelssohn and Berlioz, suggested (however whimsically) that entomological music – the sounds of nature itself – could be captured with conventional instruments; indeed, she insisted that insects were *instrumentalists* rather than vocalists. They produced music not by singing, but by wing-beating or leg-rubbing. Their sound, as Greek legend reminds us, could even approach that of a human player. Budgen (and, later, Figuier) recounted the story of Eunomos, the famed cithara player who snapped a string during a competition. He was saved by a cicada who alit on his lyre and sustained the missing pitch, ensuring Eunomos' victory.[81]

[81] Ibid., 231; see also Figuier, *Les Insectes*, 131.

Not just cicadas but crickets emerge, in Budgen's text, as insects with magical musical powers. The last of her episodes of insect life, titled "The Spirits of Hearth and Home," tells the tale of a cricket who lives next to the fireplace in the cottage of a man called Caleb. Both Caleb's son and his old nurse, Dolly, hear the cricket singing and recognize the enchantment in its tune. Dolly comments on the unusually clear sound of the insect: "I can't say ... that I ever heard a cricket sing as plain as that; but there's no knowing, they're such wonderful creturs ... they must be of the natur of sperits or fairies."[82] The son hears and repeats several verses of the "Cricket Song," and is praised by Dolly, although Caleb rejects the notion of fairies as silly; to him, the cricket is nothing more than a chirping insect and he injures it, bringing ruin on his own house. This is a story with old roots and one that is important here not only because it underscores the connection between insect music and fairy song, but because it draws attention to a well-known fact about fairies: not everyone can perceive or understand them. Unaided or inborn access to fairies and fairy speech was, as we shall see, perceived as a rare commodity by nineteenth-century poets and composers alike – a mark of distinction and otherworldly inspiration.

On Fairy Perception and "Natural" Inspiration

When I told my teacher what I had heard, he declared that I was ill and that he needed to give me a purgative. But my grandmother forbade it, saying to him: "I pity you if you have never heard the roses speak. As for me, I long for the time when I heard them. It is a childhood facility. Be wary of confusing gifts with maladies!"
                                                                    –George Sand[83]

The notion that only the special few (the pure at heart, the innocent, the gifted) have access to fairyland permeates many nineteenth-century elfin tales, both English and continental. We encounter it in Nodier's writing, especially his 1822 novel *Trilby, ou le lutin d'Argail* (featuring another insect-fairy, a cricket-like *lutin* visible only to the story's heroine), and equally strongly in George Sand's tales, where children see fairies, but adults are barred except those endowed with unusual perception. One such grown-up features in a late Sand story titled "The Fairy with Large Eyes" ("Le Fée aux gros yeux," 1875), a work worth examining in some detail, since it draws together many of the strands of nineteenth-century fairy culture I have been tracing here, and – more importantly – underscores the way in which "fairy

---

[82] Budgen, *Episodes of Insect Life*, 418.
[83] "Ce que disent les fleurs," in *Contes d'une grand'mère*, 164.

sight" had begun to stand in, in nineteenth-century writing, for creative vision. The story features an Irish governess called Barbara who is afflicted, according to her employers, by visual impairment. She is unable to see anything not directly in front of her and routinely runs into people and furniture. Barbara seems, to the medical world, to be acutely myopic, although she claims that she has perfect vision and, indeed, that she sees more clearly than others. Sand explains that her eyes (which are unusually large) are actually microscopes that reveal a tiny universe inaccessible to adults and even to Elsie, the child she minds: "Her eyes were two lenses of a microscope that revealed in every instant the marvels unperceived by others."[84] Microscopic vision not only gives Barbara acute perception, it allows her to create wonderful objects: elaborate and magical pieces of embroidery composed of threads too fine to be seen by human eyes. She lives in a pavilion in the garden, where she can be seen at night walking about and conversing with invisible visitors. When Elsie (who has grown too old to believe in fairies) asks to be introduced to Barbara's friends, the governess tells her that she will be unable to see them or will see them badly. But finally she capitulates, inviting Elsie into the pavilion and giving her a strong magnifying glass. After dark, hundreds of beautiful moths fly in through the window, which under Elsie's glass are revealed as fairies. Barbara, of course, sees them without the aid of technology; she is gifted with natural microscopic vision – eyes that dim the human world (the material surfaces of things) while illuminating their fairy essences.

The issues raised by Sand's tale – issues surrounding the limitations of human sight, the relationship between "mortal" and "fairy" vision, and the role of technology in enhancing the human eye – resonate back to the seventeenth century and the first flowering of the microscope as a scientific tool. Early modern philosophers attributed perfect sight (true and complete perception) only to the select, including saints, those visited by divine presences, and Adam and Eve before the Fall. Prelapsarian vision, according to a 1661 tract by Joseph Glanvill, had provided access to both the microscopic and telescopic worlds without the aid of technology: "Adam

[84] "Elle voyait les plus petits objets comme les autres avec les loupes les plus fortes; ses yeux étaient deux lentilles de microscope qui lui révélaient à chaque instant des merveilles inappréciables aux autres." George Sand, "La Fée aux gros yeux," in *Contes d'une grand'mère*, 218; originally published in *Le Temps* (September 1875). Many of Sand's other tales figure fairies as interchangeable with insects, other animals, or natural objects, including rocks, flowers, and even dust. Among her *Contes d'une grand'mère*, see "Ce que disent les fleurs," "Le Marteau rouge," La Fée poussière," and "La Reine coax." In the wider literary world (including both Europe and the United States), fairies continued to be employed through the late nineteenth century as metaphors for scientific processes and microscopic entities. Increasingly, however, such connections were whimsical, calibrated to appeal to children; see, for instance, Meyer, *Real Fairy Folks*; and Buckley, *The Fairyland of Science*.

needed no Spectacles. The acuteness of his natural Opticks ... shew'd him much of the Coelestial magnificence and bravery without a Galileo's tube ... What the experiences of many ages will scarce afford us at this distance from perfection, his quicker senses could teach in a moment."[85] The notion that a "celestial" world existed alongside or behind the physical – a world inaccessible to sinful human eyes – persisted into the nineteenth century, when it became intertwined with debates surrounding fairy existence and the status of the supernatural more generally. Walter Scott, among the foremost fairy historians and fairytale editors of his generation, defended his own faith in the otherworldly (including fairies) by arguing that:

> Belief itself [in the supernatural], though easily capable of being pushed into superstition and absurdity, has its origin not only in the facts upon which our holy religion is founded, but upon the principles of our nature, which teach us that while we are probationers in this sublunary state, we are neighbors to, and encompassed by the shadowy world, of which our mental faculties are too obscure to comprehend the laws, our corporeal organs too coarse and gross to perceive the inhabitants.[86]

Most people were unable to perceive the "shadowy" fairy world, and those who could – as Sand's tale suggested and Scott's essay underscored – were regarded as oddities as much as visionaries. Barbara's fairy sight is wedded to pathology and seeming irrationality; her special skills set her apart, rendering her a lone figure whose world (and artistic work) is invisible or indecipherable to virtually all around her. Acute sight is wedded, in Sand's tale, to extraordinary creative production, but genius – or prelapsarian vision, as Glanville would have it – comes at a heavy cost.

Holding these ideas in mind, I want to turn back to Berlioz, and to a tale he wrote in 1849 titled "The Wandering Harpist" ("Le Harpiste ambulant"), in which he described not fairy vision, but a kind of fairy *hearing*. Here, Berlioz became a participant in his own reception history, telling concertgoers and critics alike how to hear his music well, while at the same time distancing them from the elite group of "fairy listeners" who had true access to it. The protagonist of his tale, Corsino, is Berlioz himself, thinly disguised. In the train station on the way to Austria, Corsino meets an itinerant harpist with an unusual history. As a young musician, the harpist became dissatisfied with the effects he could produce on his instrument, and fell into melancholy. He stopped playing, simply sitting outside with his harp beside him. One day, the wind blew across its strings, producing sounds unlike anything he had encountered: "After a few moments, a bizarre harmony, but

---

[85] Glanvill, *The Vanity of Dogmatizing*, 5–6. For a more detailed discussion of Glanvill, see Wilson, *Invisible World*, 63–64.
[86] Scott, "On the Supernatural in Fictitious Compositions," 52.

sweet, veiled, mysterious, like an echo of the hymns of heaven, seemed to reach my ear.... I listened entirely enraptured... It was the wind itself, in effect, that produced these extraordinary chords which I had never heard spoken about before!"[87] Sometimes the magical sounds of the harp transport him to a celestial sphere, in which he finds himself "in the midst of millions of white-winged angels crowned with stars" who sing to him in "an unknown language." Other times, the wind-harmonies plunge him into a state of profound sadness during which he seems to see "pale young girls with blue eyes clothed in their long blonde hair, more beautiful than the Seraphim."[88] The *pianissimo* whisper of nature – the music of fairies and angels – transfixes him, and he spends hours alone in the mountains listening to it and learning how to tune his harp so that the wind speaks most clearly. He loses touch with material reality, consumed by visions that grip him so profoundly he sometimes tears his hair and rolls on the ground in ecstatic agony (the description brings us back, of course, to Berlioz's nervous/idealist disorder as he constructed it in the 1830s; see Chapter 2).[89] Hunters who happen across the harpist assume that he is mad or intoxicated, as does his father, who isolates and punishes him. He realizes that others neither hear nor understand the incantatory sounds of the natural world and finally leaves his birthplace to wander across France and Germany. At a concert in Vienna, he hears Berlioz's (Corsino's) Queen Mab scherzo and recognizes immediately the magical chords of his harp translated – miraculously, so it seems to him – into orchestration: "Oh! a singular, most singular effect! It made me laugh, but laugh entirely wonderfully, and without being able to prevent it. I never believed that conventional instruments could produce such sounds, nor that an orchestra of a hundred musicians could give themselves up to such amusing little capers."[90] To most listeners, including a group the harpist encounters in a café in Vienna, the Mab music is simply perplexing. Only an equally sensitive listener could comprehend its language, the harpist insists, and empathize with his own experience. Corsino (Berlioz) himself is such a man, as is Weber, who "would have understood me ... he would not have taken me for a drunk, nor for a madman, nor for a saint." Indeed, one of the only

---

[87] Berlioz, "Le Harpiste ambulant," 58. [88] Ibid., 59.

[89] The convulsions and aural hallucinations suffered by Berlioz's itinerant musician recall the symptoms of his own "creative" malady described in *Memoirs* as the "mal de l'isolement" (chapter 40) and in the letters around 1830 as monomania. Clearly we are meant to associate the composer not just with Corsino, but also with the harpist.

[90] Berlioz, "Le Harpiste ambulant," 56.

other places in which the harpist claims to have heard similar magical sounds is in the Overture to Weber's *Der Freischütz*.[91]

In this story, Berlioz ascribes to himself (through both Corsino and the harpist) a kind of prelapsarian hearing – an aural acuteness available only to the privileged few. The language of the fairies (the Mab music), he implied, was an elemental idiom inaudible to the majority of listeners; only those with special senses perceived it, and still fewer could transcribe it. The story is both a defense of the unusual orchestration associated with the Mab scherzo and an attempt to explain the mode of transcendental listening Berlioz associated with its *fantastique* soundscape. It is also, of course, a response to those critics who, like the ignorant commentators in the café, rejected the scherzo as a collection of empty orchestral effects, an example of facile imitation or mere noise. They, Berlioz implied, were listeners of unrefined sensibilities, deaf to the language of nature. They subjected him to the same persecution suffered by the harpist (and later, by Sand's character Barbara), who was dismissed as a fool or a lunatic. To see or hear on a different plane, Berlioz suggested, was to live an isolated and misunderstood life. But it also meant enjoying access to an extraordinary realm of sound; indeed, his harpist, and Corsino himself, seem to hear and understand the whole of nature. Fairy language, in Berlioz's tale, encompasses all the subtle rustlings, whisperings, and sighings of the landscape, which are carried on the wind, communicated by ethereal spirits very much like Paracelsus' elemental beings. Berlioz's story restores the old enchantment associated with these creatures, making it part of the "real" and audible fabric of creation via the same pantheistic impulse – the visceralization of ideal sound – that gave voice to his dream beloved in *Le Retour à la vie* and to the realm of paradise in "Le Spectre de la rose" (*Les Nuits d'été*).[92]

The idea of a natural fairyscape was not, as we have seen, new, nor was the notion of fairy listening. As we might expect, it was prefigured by Hoffmann, whose "Master Flea" (available in French translation by 1830) introduced an aural fairyland distinctly similar to the one in Berlioz's tale. We encounter it toward the end of the narrative, when the protagonist, Peregrinus Tyss, is transported to an elfin grotto by Master Flea himself:

---

[91] Ibid., 61.
[92] "Sylphs" and "nymphs" were both identified in French dictionaries of the 1810s and 1820s as fairies in the Paracelsian sense: not simply otherworldly creatures, but repositories of scientific magic and secular divinity. Paracelsian rhetoric more broadly permeated romantic writing on the natural world, underpinning Berlioz's understanding of fairyland as well as Hoffmann's descriptions of supernatural nature, which are shot through with references to earth-spirits, sylphs, and salamanders. For a detailed account of the impact of Paracelsus in France between the sixteenth and eighteenth centuries, see Debus, *The French Paracelsians*. E. T. A. Hoffmann's relationship with elemental spirits is explored in Negus, *E. T. A. Hoffmann's Other World*.

> Mr. Peregrinus Tyss fancied presently that he was lying on the bank of a murmuring forest brook, listening to the rustling of the wind, the whispering of the bushes, and the buzzing of the thousands of insects that whirred about him. Then it was as if strange voices were becoming audible, distinct and ever more distinct, so that finally Peregrinus thought he could understand words. But only a confused chattering penetrated his ear, numbing his senses.[93]

Here, as in Berlioz, fairy language is synonymous with natural sound – insect song as well as rustling flowers and trees – but to mortal ears, it appears merely as confused babbling. Only when Peregrinus is changed back into fairy form (he is a human in disguise) is he able to decipher the idiom of his fellows, to perceive the "sweet words" of the flowers and of the "many-colored, light-winged insects."

This was a language barred to all but the most unusual humans, according to Hoffman, who ascribed it only to those suffering from madness or gifted with genius (the two, of course, went hand in hand). As we have seen in earlier chapters, his alter ego Kreisler was one such figure, a composer whose "fantastic" compositions were rooted in acute perception of the natural world. The essay titled "Johannes Kreisler's Certificate of Apprenticeship" makes this claim clearly, especially its central episode which, tellingly, Hoffmann couched in the form of a fairy tale. It is told by the musician-protagonist Chrysostomus and revolves around an ancient moss-covered rock that seems to contain and focus natural sound. The rock, according to legend, is bound up with a wondrous sonorous power capable of transforming all who hear it – revealing hidden truths, awakening occult knowledge, stimulating spiritual awareness and deep emotion. Chrysostomus is strongly attracted to it, numbering among the few who hears distinctly the melodies that seem to resonate from its mottled and mysterious surface: "Lying in the grass, or leaning against the rock, when the wind rustled through the tree's leaves, I often heard a sound like that of gentle spirit-voices."[94] Attracted to these voices as a child, he tries to reproduce them on the piano. But eventually he is taught to reject them as the stuff of fairy superstition, turning instead to "technical study" of music – harmony, counterpoint, physical exercises – at the local conservatory. Eventually, frustrated by the emptiness of such instruction, he returns to the rock, slowly learning to decipher and interpret its sonorous (Paracelsian) magic and in so doing discovering the "real" source of music. Conservatory training, as Hoffmann makes clear, only impedes perception of the natural soundscape, whose language cannot be taught but only intuited via the higher senses. His fairy story is both a definition of romantic genius and a metaphor for the maturation of the composer, whose apprenticeship is complete when he gains

---

[93] Hoffmann, "Master Flea," 395.   [94] Hoffmann, *Kreisleriana*, 163.

access to the "unknown language" of elemental spirits and can record the visions they inspire.

Not only did Berlioz, in his tale of the Wandering Harpist, figure himself, like Kreisler, as a composer who had achieved this inspired state but, perhaps more importantly, as one who had devised a way of transcribing the sounds of the natural world into orchestral effects – extending and honing the skills he had begun to develop as early as *Le Retour à la vie*. In this, his fictional harpist would have us believe, he was virtually alone – among the few musicians (Weber being the other) to have rendered fairy language accessible "on conventional instruments." Clearly, he regarded his scherzo as proof of his own coming of age, a piece that succeeded in both catching and amplifying the sounds of a near-inaudible landscape. It had much the same function as the magnifying glass that Barbara, in Sand's tale, gave to the child Elsie: it allowed the uninitiated (those without transcendental hearing) to perceive fairy sound, if only dimly and without always understanding it. Such a device was unnecessary for Berlioz himself, so he suggested, since he heard nature's music without the aid of artificial magnifiers, but it was crucial for most members of his audience. The scherzo was the lens that gave them access to the elfin world, the medium through which its elusive language had been amplified and translated into "modern" sound. Listeners embraced it eagerly, as did other composers, who borrowed the scherzo's textures and timbres – the technology of musical magnification – to materialize their own fairies. They no longer needed the elemental hearing that Berlioz, and in a sense, Mendelssohn, had ascribed to themselves, but could simply adopt the devices forged by these composers. They were like amateur naturalists who, with the aid of the latest microscope, gained access to a hitherto unavailable world, a place ripe for exploration and recording. The result was a proliferation of fairy scherzi, many derivative, which appeared in ever-greater numbers from the 1840s onward. Alongside Mab, Puck, and Ariel, a variety of other miniature creatures were restored to audibility; indeed, elfin scherzi became faddish both inside and outside of France, although they were particularly popular in Paris, where elves ran rampant and – as I shall argue in the following section – the musical and natural sciences grew increasingly proximate.

The *Scherzo fantastique* Takes Flight

The supernatural scherzi published through the middle and late decades of the nineteenth century were in large part independent character pieces meant for the salon or concert hall, and included the earliest works published under the title *scherzo fantastique* – a label, as I have already noted, first applied to Berlioz's *La Reine Mab*. Scherzi bearing this rubric (or those with supernatural titles or imagery) adapted the elfin effects associated with the *Midsummer Night's Dream* Overture and the Mab music, transferring them to solo instruments (keyboard or violin were most common) or, in some cases, inserting them into fresh orchestral settings. The result was a new instrumental subgenre, a tradition of *fantastique* scherzi distinct from the older, though still persistent, vocal scherzo (whose roots extended back to the early seventeenth century) and from other kinds of orchestral or pianistic scherzi, including pastoral and comic.[95] This tradition took flight in France soon after Berlioz's *La Reine Mab* with a piece by Stephen Heller, one of his supporters and confidantes, who published a *scherzo fantastique* in 1845. A virtuosic showpiece for keyboard, Heller's scherzo borrowed the 3/8 time signature and *prestissimo* tempo of the Mab music and its rambling form (sectional, with two contrasting 2/4 sections), as well as the E major/minor tonal center of Mendelssohn's Overture.[96] It was followed in 1846 by a second *fantastique* scherzo (also for solo keyboard), this one by Mendelssohn's friend Joachim Raff; the composer destroyed it in 1847. A third such work – and by far the best known of these early examples – was Antonio Bazzini's *scherzo fantastique* for violin and piano, published in 1852 just after he moved to Paris. Subtitled *Ronde des lutins* (*Round Dance of the Elves/Gnomes*), it was followed by a barrage of elf, farfadet, and gnome scherzi – pieces that cemented both the *féerique* status of the form and its crucial intermingling of science, fantasy, and instrumental technology.

In Bazzini's scherzo, we encounter a recognizable soundworld – the sustained *staccato*, *leggierissimo* landscape and hushed energy of both Mendelssohn's and Berlioz's fairy pieces. The violin enters with the light, impossibly fleet (*Quasi presto*) passagework of the elfin world and its gossamer *perpetuum mobile*. With the exception of a few robust passages to mark cadences (and an opening fanfare), the scherzo unfolds entirely in the *pp-ppp* dynamic range and it is this, combined with its sheer profusion of notes – its dazzling surface detail, to recall Susan Stewart – that gives us such

---

[95] Russell, "Minuet, Scherzando, and Scherzo," 30–36. The *scherzo fantastique* did not supplant these earlier scherzo types (indeed, it has certain features in common with both), but emerged as a later subspecies of the form.

[96] Fétis wrote a critique of the piece for the *Revue et Gazette musicale* (28 March 1847), praising it for its originality, but bemoaning its lack of melodic intelligibility. In a passage that easily recalls his complaints about Berlioz, he warned Heller that the *fantastique* mode was leading him down a wrong path, encouraging him to work in a genre divorced from "the spirit of song." Heller's work is, in many senses, a bridge between the *féerique* scherzo popularized by Mendelssohn and the concert scherzo associated with Frédéric Chopin, Sigismond Thalberg, and other Parisian pianists, combining the unprogrammatic virtuosity of the latter with the *fantastique* markers of the former.

a clear sense of smallness. Our absorption in its microscopic surface produces a familiar sense of stasis, reinforced by the rondo form itself, which dictates that we keep coming back to the opening material (ABACA); we literally go around in circles, mesmerized by the whirling fairy ring. But Bazzini's otherworldly sound is also overtly natural. His scherzo eschews melody, instead containing a wealth of chattering and buzzing figures. The B section (mm. 64*ff*) is dominated by oscillating double-stopped figures, *ppp*, connected by rapid scales – echoes of the insect-fairies that hover through earlier orchestral fairy music (Example 6.5). Here, and throughout Bazzini's piece, these creatures are conjured not just by the velocity of the passagework itself, but by a set of violinistic acrobatics, including ricochet bowing, right- and left-hand *pizzicati*, chromatic double and triple stops, and rapid consecutive harmonics. Via a technical *tour de force*, Bazzini reproduces the flitting, clicking, and shimmering sounds of the fairy orchestra on a single instrument. Reviewers were quick to connect his virtuosity with his elfin fantasy just as they had called attention to Berlioz's orchestral "machinery" in the Mab music. His scherzo, they noted, was indebted to Paganini (and Heinrich Wilhelm Ernst, its dedicatee), whose famous pyrotechnics rendered Bazzini's fairies visible while also lending them a slightly demonic tinge, a hint of "diablerie," as one critic put it.[97] They were not quite as benign as either Mendelssohn's or Berlioz's fairies.

Bazzini's scherzo was performed routinely in Paris (and across Europe) from mid-century onward alongside a host of similar elfin rounds, the majority of which were cast in scherzo form or marked *scherzando*. Among these was Liszt's *Gnomenreigen* (1862), published in France as *Danse des lutins*, a title clearly reminiscent of Bazzini's. Labeled *Presto scherzando*, Liszt's dance transfers the effects of the fairy scherzo to the keyboard, producing a sound so light and swift it seems airborne from the very outset. It opens *staccato e leggiero*, with another anti-melodic chattering motive played *pianissimo* – a flight of ornamented pitches ascending to the upper register of the keyboard and hovering there on a series of repeated C-sharps, as if waiting for us to follow (Example 6.6a). This tactic smacks of Berlioz (the measures preceding the trio of the Mab scherzo), as does the texture itself, which is so reminiscent of both his and Mendelssohn's elfin scoring that we almost hear their pointillistic flutes and *pizzicato* strings.

[97] G. M. Olivier Beauregard's review of the scherzo (as played by Jéhim Prumé) notes its Paganinian overtones, emphasizing the technical feats that conjure Bazzini's fairies: "Quelle pétulance et quelle diablerie dans cette *Ronde des Lutins* de Bazzini! C'est qu'aussi M. Jéhin Prumé s'en escrime à ravir. Il y a victorieusement enlevé toutes les difficultés du violon: le staccato, les *sons harmoniques*, le *staccato volant*, où Bazzini fait merveille, et particulièrement le staccato en tirant l'archet, tout a été exécuté de main de maître par M. Jéhin Prumé." *L'Univers musical, journal littéraire et artistique* (29 October 1863).

Fairyology, Entomology, and the Scherzo fantastique

Example 6.5 Adolphe Bazzini, *La Ronde des lutins, Scherzo fantastique pour violon avec accomp. de piano*, Op. 25 (Paris: Richault, 1852), mm. 64–79

Example 6.6a Liszt, *Gnomenreigen* [*Danse des lutins*], mm. 1–4

Liszt's breathless opening leads into a section of whirling 9/8 passagework – surely the fairy round proper – that challenges even Bazzini's virtuosity (Example 6.6b). It spins us around more and more quickly, taking us into a dizzy and magical space. Finally, the dance seems to careen out of control, exploding into a cascade of descending passagework, as if Liszt simply cannot keep up with the pace of the fairies themselves. He tries again, returning to the 6/8 grace-note hovering – the single fairy – of the opening, who leads us once more into the elfin ring. This time, the dance accelerates

Example 6.6b Liszt, *Gnomenreigen* [*Danse des lutins*], beginning of round dance proper, mm. 21–26

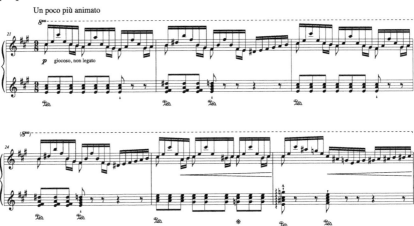

velocissimo before reeling into the same chromatic cascade, only to begin the pattern a third time, returning to the fluttering opening material and then plunging for a final attempt into the fairy round, now marked *Presto possibile*. This is a world of unprecedented detail, its speed seeming to translate into a new degree of magnification beyond the power of anyone but the composer himself. Liszt's virtuosic technique alone gains us access to the microscopic fairy circle. Here, all the tropes of the elfin scherzo are in evidence, but they are filtered through the pianist's own sensibility; this is no mere copy of the *Elfenton*, but a special transmutation of it. Still, Liszt is aware of his models; he closes with Mendelssohn's trademark feather-light gesture, in what was surely a nod to the earlier composer.

The *scherzando* designation attached to Liszt's elf dance was also associated with earlier fairy evocations. It was sometimes applied to scherzi themselves, but also to fairy dances in other forms – waltzes, polkas, and, more often (as with Liszt's and Bazzini's pieces), rounds. Clearly the *scherzo fantastique* was operating as both a generic subtype and a musical topic; the sound could be detached from the form. In fact, there is evidence that *scherzando* as a fairy-marking predated the emergence of the elfin scherzo itself as a formal type. It appears, for instance, in Ignaz Xaver Seyfried's score for Horschelt's "Grand Ballet-Pantomime," *Oberon Roi des Elfes*, produced at Schikaneder's Freihaus-Theater an der Wien in the mid-1820s. Seyfried attached the indicator *Vivace e scherzando* to one of the early numbers, titled "Szene der Elfen in Titania's Hain," which prefigures the light, quick motion and

Example 6.7 J. Ascher, *Les Diablotins, Polka fantastique pour piano* (Paris: Lemoine, 1858), mm. 1–20

continuous *staccato* of Mendelssohn's fairy scherzi.[98] The playful sound associated, here and elsewhere, with the *scherzando* marking was, Seyfried's music suggests, linked to fairy evocation by composers working slightly before (or independently of) Mendelssohn.[99] The marking persisted through the middle decades of the century, appearing in a multitude of *fantastique* fairy dances. An example for solo piano that foreshadows key elements of Liszt's fairy round is Joseph Ascher's *Les Diablotins, Polka fantastique* (1858). Here, we encounter the fluttering grace-note opening of Liszt's elf-round as well as the final anticipatory hovering before the dance begins. The polka itself is marked *scherzando*, combining the ornamental opening figures, now heard *piano*, with scalar passages (Example 6.7). Ascher's dance makes

[98] It is not clear when, precisely, Seyfried wrote his fairy music (although certainly before 1827, when he resigned the Kapellmeister post at the Freihaus-Theater) or whether he was aware of either Mendelssohn's *Midsummer Night's Dream* Overture or the Octet. The "scherzando" marking appears not at the top of his piece, but following a series of sustained chords; it is functioning clearly as a performance instruction rather than a movement title.

[99] The term *scherzando* has a complicated past, appearing from the 1760s onward (most famously in Haydn's Opus 33 quartets) as a movement title as well as a performance direction, and often seeming to function in both capacities simultaneously. See Russell, "Minuet, scherzando, and scherzo," 119–53. Many of the attributes of "scherzando" sound that Russell identifies in early nineteenth-century repertory are shared by later elfin music (including Seyfried's). Clearly, fairy composers appropriated and honed an existing set of musical tropes, gradually imbuing both them and the *scherzando* marking itself with *féerique* connotations and, in the wake of Mendelssohn's music, with a new collection of entomological sounds.

Example 6.8a Mendelssohn, Octet, Op. 20, closing ascent, mm. 237–41

nothing close to the virtuosic demands of Liszt's piece; it is clearly meant for the amateur market, requiring only a simplified version of the technique associated with earlier pianistic and orchestral elves. Things get slightly more difficult in the trio, which contains the now-predictable *staccato* and *leggiero* markings as well as the rapid repeated notes and humming figures – moments of micro-melodic chromatic vacillation – that recall Berlioz's entomological soundworld.

Many similar pieces were published by little-known composers as fodder destined for the salon and eagerly consumed by a fairy-entranced public. Ascher's choice of the polka (then a fashionable form) was not, however, the norm; most fairy dances were couched as rounds (the scherzo- or scherzando-rondo was most common), undoubtedly because fairy rings were so pervasively pictured in romantic fairy painting and poetry. Among these were a *Ronde fantastique* labeled *scherzando* (1849) by Camille Schubert (pseudonym of the much-maligned quadrille composer Camille Prillip), a *Ronde* labeled *scherzo* by cellist Friedrich August Kummer (1846; the third movement of his *Pièce fantastique* for cello and orchestra), and a *Rondo fantastique* with a central *scherzoso* section by virtuoso pianist Gennaro Perrelli (1869). These works, and others like them, contain all the flitting, *staccato* figures and the *leggiero, piano* markings we have already encountered. Most end with the final, *pianissimo* ascent associated with both earlier and later fairy dances: Examples 6.8a–e give the gesture in its familiar Mendelssohnian form, followed by parallel passages in Berlioz,

Example 6.8b Berlioz, "La Reine Mab," closing ascent (strings only), *Roméo et Juliette*, mm. 761–69

Example 6.8c Liszt, *Gnomenreigen* [*Danse des lutins*], closing ascent, mm. 165–68

Example 6.8d F. A. Kummer, *Ronde fantastique*, closing ascent (cello only), *Pièce fantastique pour le violoncelle avec acc. d'orchestre ou piano*, Op. 36 (Paris: Richault, 1846), mm. 243–56

Liszt, Kummer, and Perrelli. The latter two composers (like Berlioz) allow the quiet dynamic of the ascent to give way to a more rousing finish, tacking on robust cadential markers or, in Perrelli, repeating the entire ascending figure in a louder dynamic as the piece comes to a close. Kummer's *Ronde* shows us yet another variation; here the closing *pianissimo* flight is expanded into a series of emphatic trills in the cello part as if a few of his fluttering fairies have remained behind at the conclusion of the round.

Example 6.8e Gennaro Perrelli, *Rondo fantastique pour piano*, Op. 35 (Paris: Flaxland, 1869), closing ascent, mm. 376–86

Although fairy dances of all sorts, from rounds to waltzes, continued to bear the *scherzando* or *scherzoso* marking well into the 1870s and 1880s, it became more common for the scherzo sound and form to be united. A great number of fairy scherzi were published both inside and outside of France through the late nineteenth century and into the twentieth – too many to list in full. French examples include Benjamin Godard's scherzo *Les Farfadets* (the second movement of his *Sonate fantastique* Op. 63, No. 2; 1881), Louis Gregh's similarly titled scherzo-galop (1877; this piece also contains the *scherzando* indication), Francis Thomé's *Les Lutins, scherzo pour piano avec accompagnement d'orchestre* (1890s), Emile Nerini's *Ronde des lutins, scherzo* (1923), and Philippe Gaubert's *La Ronde sur la falaise, scherzo* (1931). To these we can add German examples – the fairy scherzo was by no means confined to Parisian composers – including Emil Hartmann's *Die Elfenmädchen und die Jäger, scherzo* (1879) and Hans Huber's *Elfenreigen, scherzo* (1885), as well as English pieces, among them John Francis Barnett's *Scherzo: The Elfin Page* (1874, from a larger work on Walter Scott's *The Lay*

of the Last Minstrel) and Ethel Barnby's *Will 'o the Wisp, scherzo* (1910).[100] These works, some for keyboard, others for orchestra, reproduce faithfully all the tropes of fairy sound that had, by this point, ossified into cliché. There is hardly a need to examine their fleet, *pianissimo* soundscapes individually, although each work does, of course, tweak the *Elfenton* slightly differently. Across Europe, the scherzo had, by the latter decades of the nineteenth century, emerged as a routine – we might even say default – form for the depiction of elves, farfadets, gnomes, and their ilk.

Queen Mab herself reappeared in the expected form in the works of both English and German composers, including William Cusins's *Queen Mab, scherzo* (1863), Oscar Beringer's *Queen Mab* (the first of three *Fairy Tales* for piano, ca. 1890s), and Richard Kleinmichel's *Fée Mab, scherzo* (1876) – all three for keyboard (the Cusins is for piano four hands). Often, as in the first and third of these works, composers drew attention to the scherzo itself by including the dance-type in their titles; in other cases (Beringer, for instance), they adopted the scherzo-trio form without comment. Of the late-nineteenth-century musical Mabs, Kleinmichel's is the most interesting. It has the distinct quality of a transcription, underscoring the degree to which fairy sound was still being conceived orchestrally even in solo pieces. The work's opening section is overtly un-pianistic, its sparse texture moving from buzzing figures in the cello range to rapid exchanges among the middle and upper registers that are clearly meant to invoke winds and pizzicato strings (Example 6.9). We do not hear the keyboard here (nor, I suspect, was Kleinmichel imagining a pianistic sound), but instead the Mendelssohnian and perhaps, given the Mab connection, Berliozian orchestras with their entomological effects.

The sense that insect sounds are echoing through this piece (and, as I have argued, through the fairy scherzi of Kleinmichel's contemporaries) is confirmed by the imagery associated with these works. Look, for instance, at the title page of Adolphe Le Carpentier's *La Ronde des farfadets, Danse fantastique* (1872, marked *scherzando*), given in Figure 6.3. Here, cherub-like farfadets (synonymous with "lutins," according to most French dictionaries of the period) hover in their customary ring just above the water. Their status as supernatural creatures is not much compromised by the little butterfly wings that hold them aloft, but their antennae align them unmistakably with the realm of the natural. These are not the pointed ears or horns of Shakespeare's Puck, but the delicate feelers of insects, which wave in different directions depending on which way each farfadet is inclined. As if underscoring their link

---

[100] Many other fairy works borrow the scherzo form (with or without trio) and sound, without identifying it or bearing the telltale "scherzando" marking; examples include Victor Moret, *Danse des lutins* (1882); and Benjamin Godard, *Tournoiement de fées* (1892).

Example 6.9 Richard Kleinmichel, *Fée Mab, Scherzo für piano*, Op. 27 (Mainz: B. Schott's Söhnen, 1876), mm. 1–17

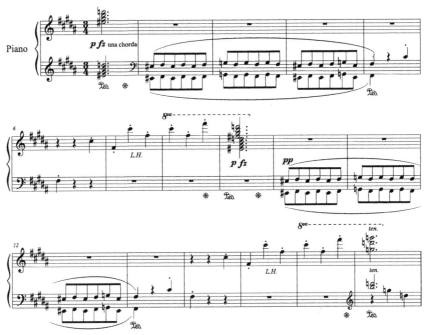

to the animal world, the left-most farfadet gazes at a pair of frogs on the bank. Across from him, one of his fellows prepares to launch into the sky, where pinpricks of light suggest a multitude of other fairy rings – far-off dancers who might easily be mistaken for fireflies.[101]

If the soundscapes and visual imagery of nineteenth-century fairy pieces confirm an ongoing overlap between musical fantasy and aural naturalism, a burgeoning repertory of *insect* scherzi published during the same period confirms it. While the form was becoming inextricable from elfin sound, it also emerged as central to entomological representation, with scherzi of both types drawing on a similar pool of textures and timbres. The connection is showcased especially clearly – and relatively early in the century – in a piece by Adolphe Blanc (the French violinist, conductor, and composer of chamber music) titled *La Farfalla* (*The Butterfly*), *scherzetto fantastique* (1853). Here, the magical-entomological overlap, the crucial

---

[101] For a similar scene, see the title page of Gregh's scherzo-galop *Les Farfadets* (Paris, 1877), although here the imagery is too small to allow for close scrutiny. A contrasting illustration appears on the cover of Ascher's *Les Diablotins*, which features a spiral of bat-like fairies – less like insects than miniature monsters. As his title suggests, these are creatures of a more demonic cast.

Figure 6.3 Title page of Adolphe Le Carpentier, *La Ronde des farfadets, Danse fantastique* (Paris: Meissonier, ca. 1872).

hesitation established in nineteenth-century scientific and fictional texts, is transferred overtly to the musical world. Insects are sacralized at the same time as fairies are naturalized, producing a typically *fantastique* soundscape. Blanc's butterfly scherzo is virtually indistinguishable from contemporary elfin scherzi; indeed, whole sections of it might almost have been taken from Bazzini's *Ronde fantastique* published the year before, although the level of difficulty is considerably lower (Blanc was writing for domestic performers rather than the concert stage). The work's *staccato* passagework, *perpetuum mobile*, and quiet dynamic (the opening *mezzo forte* giving way to *piano* and then *pianissimo*) generate a now familiar sound, confirmed by the trills and

Example 6.10 Adolphe M. Blanc, *La Farfalla, Scherzetto fantastique pour alto-viola avec acc. de piano*, Op. 7 (Paris: Richault, 1853), mm. 1–13

micro-melodic chromatic figures of its second half (Example 6.10). It ends with a version of the feather-light finish – in this case, the fluttering ascent is given to the keyboard, while the viola evokes, via a sustained chromatic tremor, the sound of humming wings receding into the distance. Fantasy generates science as readily as science produces fantasy: we find ourselves experiencing the double vision described by Michelet, hearing (and seeing) both insects and fairies, both the scientific world under the magnifying lens and the miniature realm of elfin magic. Blanc's butterfly evocation was followed by other insect scherzi bearing the *fantastique* label, including Adolfo Fumagalli's *Le Papillon, morceau fantastique* (ca. 1855) and a similarly titled piece by Alfred Jaell (1878). The same composers who produced fairy scherzi also, in many cases, wrote insect pieces in the same form or in free forms marked *scherzando*. Ascher, for instance, composed a caprice-scherzo for keyboard titled *Chasse aux papillons* a few years after his *scherzando*-labeled dance of the "diablotins," and Gregh published a piece titled *Les Joyeux papillons* (Op. 8, a keyboard caprice with the *scherzando* marking) in 1877, the same year as his scherzo *Les Farfadets*.

Alongside these butterfly dances, bee scherzi began to appear, including a piece by Parisian pianist Joseph Schiffmacher entitled *Les Abeilles, scherzo pour piano*, Op. 68 (1868). Following a brief, rhapsodic introduction, it launches into the dance proper, whose *presto, leggierissimo* passagework recalls both the delicacy and headlong rush of Liszt's *Gnomenreigen*. Occasionally, Schiffmacher allows the bass to drop out, highlighting

Fairyology, Entomology, and the Scherzo fantastique

Example 6.11a J. Schiffmacher, *Les Abeilles, Scherzo*, Op. 68. (Paris: Michelet, 1868), mm. 22–27

Example 6.11b Schiffmacher's "buzzing bee," *Les Abeilles, Scherzo*, Op. 68, mm 38–40

a chromatic turning figure in the middle register – a tiny, slightly dissonant buzzing clearly meant to represent a hovering bee. This passage, and others like it, are not aestheticizations of insect sound nor metaphorical representations of flight, but moments of "scientific" transcription that call to mind Mendelssohn's fly and Berlioz's swarm (Examples 6.11a and b give the opening measures of the dance and the later apiarian figure). No imagery accompanies Schiffmacher's scherzo, but many other insect pieces were published with fanciful vignettes or titles describing bee or butterfly dances, celebrations, "awakenings," and even weddings. These were largely written by French or Paris-based pianists and published in the French capital, and included Alphonse Leduc's *Le Réveil des abeilles* (1859), Louis Lefébure-Wély's *Fêtes des abeilles* (1859), Georges Lamothe's *La Reine des papillons* (1882), and Benjamin Godard's *Ballet des papillons* (1894). In the musical world, as in popular mid-century entomological texts, insects were given human sensibilities (love, desire, ambition) while also linked clearly to the magical world – the rites and dances of the fairy kingdom.

The tradition of microscopic scherzi and the insect-fairy convergence that perpetuated it persisted even into the twentieth century. As late as 1907, Stravinsky's *Scherzo fantastique*, Op. 3, reaffirmed it, drawing on both the magical and entomological strands of the scherzo's history. In communications to Rimsky-Korsakov during the period of the work's composition, Stravinsky reported that it had been inspired by Maurice Maeterlinck's *The Life of the Bees* (*La Vie des abeilles*, 1901):

> I am working a great deal. This work consists of orchestrating the Symphony and composing a fantastic scherzo, "The Bees," about which I'll tell you more. . . . As you know, I already had the idea of writing a scherzo in St. Petersburg, but as yet I had no subject for it. Then all at once here Katya [Stravinsky's wife] and I were reading "The Life of the Bees" by M. Maeterlinck, a half-philosophical, half-poetic work that captivated me, as the saying goes, from head to toe. At first I thought, for the sake of the fullness of the program, that I would choose some specific citations from the book, but I see now that this is impossible, since the scientific and literary language is too closely intermixed in it, and therefore I decided that I would simply allow myself to be guided in composing the piece by a definite program, but not use any citation as a heading. Simply "The Bees" (after Maeterlinck): Fantastic Scherzo. When we see each other I'll show you the spots I have taken from the program; in a letter I can't give you a complete idea.[102]

If Stravinsky decided against choosing specific quotations from Maeterlinck, a program note by the composer (undated) confirms that he had particular images in mind, including "the uninterrupted life of the swarm (hive) through the generations and the nuptial flight of the queen bee."[103] The second edition of the scherzo (Schott, 1931) contained a *Remarque préliminaire* that singled out the same images, now attaching them to particular portions of the scherzo: "the first section gives an impression of life and activity in the hive" while the middle section depicts "sunrise and the nuptial flight of the queen bee, the love fight with her chosen mate, and his death" and the third section "the peaceful activity of the hive continuing."[104] These descriptions point clearly to Maeterlinck's early chapters: Nos. 2–4 on the organization of life in the hive and No. 6, on "The Nuptial Flight." In these sections (and throughout the work), we encounter the same anthropomorphizing rhetoric and supernatural imagery associated with earlier French and English insect studies. The swarm, as it departs from the hive, is "like one of those magic carpets which, in

---

[102] Qtd. and trans. in Taruskin, *Stravinsky and the Russian Traditions*, I:7. In two later letters to Rimsky (1 July and 23 July), Stravinsky tracked his progress on the scherzo, continuing to refer to it as "Bees."
[103] Ibid., I:316. The program note, written in French, is held in the Stravinsky Archive.
[104] Ibid., I:7, n. 27.

fairytales, flits across space in response to its master's command," and the nuptials of the queen bee are themselves the stuff of legend – "the most fairylike that can be imagined."[105] For Maeterlinck and for Stravinsky himself – as his title suggests – the natural world of the bees was also a *fantastique* one.

Later, Stravinsky downplayed the role of Maeterlinck's text and finally attempted to eliminate it altogether, arguing that he had conceived the scherzo as "a piece of 'pure' symphonic music" – a deceit (as Richard Taruskin calls it) meant to distance the mature composer from programmatic musical aesthetics no longer in keeping with his artistic philosophy.[106] But of course the letters to Rimsky are clear counter-evidence to Stravinsky's denial, as is the title of the work itself, *Scherzo fantastique*, which by 1907 was freighted with more than half a century of extra-musical baggage. Even if Schott had not published the *Remarque*, listeners would have associated Stravinsky's piece with the many *fantastique* scherzi that had preceded it and with the butterflies, bees, elves, and farfadets hovering around such pieces.[107] Stravinsky himself was undoubtedly aware of the tradition and participating in it; indeed, the soundscape established in the opening pages of his scherzo is an easily recognizable one: muted and divided strings produce a delicate a-melodic whirring while pointillistic winds, *pianissimo*, flit and trill above them. Low brass and percussion have been omitted (although these instruments do play a part in Stravinsky's first symphonic scherzo, a piece with no supernatural associations) in the interest of generating a gossamer Mendelssohnian sound – one referenced by virtually every composer of a fantastic scherzo since the 1820s. Other elements of Stravinsky's orchestration are equally familiar; at m. 86, for instance, his hovering bees are temporarily stilled by

---

[105] The first of these quotations is from chap. 2 ("L'Essaim") of Maeterlinck, *La Vie des abeilles*; it describes the departure of the swarm with its new queen: "Enfin, l'un des pans se rabat, un autre se relève, les quatre coins pleins de soleil du radieux manteau qui chante se rejoignent, et, pareil à l'une de ces nappes intelligentes qui pour accomplir un souhait traversent l'horizon dans les contes de fées, il se dirige tout entier et déjà replié, afin de recouvrir la présence sacrée de l'avenir, vers le tilleul, le poirier ou le saule où la reine vient de se fixer comme un clou d'or" (96). The second is from chap. 5 ("La vol nuptial"); it describes the mating of the queen bee: "Voilà de prodigieuses noces, les plus féerique que nous puissions rêver" (237).

[106] Taruskin, *Stravinsky and the Russian Traditions*, I:8. Other scholars have taken Stravinsky's denial seriously, arguing that the scherzo was conceived without any programmatic influence; see White, *Stravinsky*, 141; and Lindlar, *Lübbes Strawinsky Lexikon*, 186.

[107] French reviewers reporting on the scherzo's Parisian premiere (November 1911, as part of the Concerts-Sechiari given at the Théâtre Marigny) were certainly aware of the work's entomological program; see, for instance, Robert Brussel's review in *Le Figaro* (13 November 1911): "M. Pierre Sechiari nous faisait connaître hier une pièce inédite du jeune musicien russe: un Scherzo fantastique. La lecture de la *Vie des abeilles* de M. Maeterlinck lui a suggéré l'idée de cette pièce." References to the Stravinsky–Maeterlinck connection persisted in Parisian journals over the following several years.

a stretch of sustained string harmonics (recalled at m. 102) over which the bassoon, the muted trumpet, and then the English horn exchange solo material. The shimmering timbre of the strings is ushered in by a single harp harmonic and rising arpeggio in the celesta, over which the solo winds do their *pianissimo, staccato* dance. This is a set of orchestral effects so reminiscent of Berlioz's Mab trio that one wonders whether Stravinsky was winking at his French predecessor. He gave no clear indication of this, although he did acknowledge the importance of Mendelssohn's work in the *Dialogues* with Robert Craft: "Mendelssohn's elegance," he admitted, "attracted me early in my career, as my *Scherzo fantastique* indicates." The question of influence comes up again in the *Conversations*, where Stravinsky identified both Russian and German models as important: "I see now that I did take something from Rimsky's *Bumblebee* (numbers 49–50 in the score), but the *Scherzo* owes much more to Mendelssohn by the way of Tchaikovsky than to Rimsky-Korsakov."[108] (In the passage Stravinsky ascribes to the *Flight of the Bumblebee* [beginning in m. 234], the orchestra is pared down to first violins alone, whose buzzing neighbor figures soon give way to fleet passagework in the flutes and piccolo, hovering motives in the clarinets, and staccato eighth notes in the middle winds – a collection of effects that does indeed bring to mind Rimsky-Korsakov's piece.) Several years after its premiere, the scherzo's apiarian sounds and images became the basis for a ballet titled *Les Abeilles* (*The Bees*) choreographed by Leo Staats, a work known to and ratified by Stravinsky (although he missed the first performance), which took Maeterlinck's "Nuptial Flight" as its centerpiece. It was first performed at the *Opéra* in 1917.[109]

The soundworld – especially the orchestration – of the Mendelssohnian and Berliozian *scherzo fantastique* hover around and behind Stravinsky's piece, but its harmony was more clearly inflected by Russian traditions. It was based almost entirely on octatonic and whole-tone scales – those

---

[108] Stravinsky and Craft, *Dialogues*, 115; and Stravinsky and Craft, *Conversations with Igor Stravinsky*, 41.

[109] Rimsky-Korsakov's "The Flight of the Bumblebee" had a different (in a sense, opposite) career. It was originally part of a theatrical work – the fairy opera *The Tale of Tsar Saltan* – becoming known as an independent instrumental piece (in the guise of arrangements for piano, violin, and virtually every other instrument) only later. That Stravinsky should have borrowed elements of Rimsky's "Flight" for his setting of Maeterlinck's *Life of the Bees* is hardly surprising, for both works were based on tales in which the miniature and magical realms overlapped: in Rimsky's opera, a prince became a bee, and in Maeterlinck's *Life*, a bee was figured as a queen. Rimsky's setting itself did what so many fantastic musical and literary works of the nineteenth century had already done and that Stravinsky's scherzo would also do: it allowed "scientific" sound (the famously realistic buzzing of a bee) to permeate the make-believe aural landscape of a fairy tale. It, alongside Mendelssohn's work (and the many *fantastique* scherzi in between), was an obvious model for Stravinsky, whose own scherzo opened up a similarly liminal space.

associated with Rimsky-Korsakov's magic operas and Russian supernatural evocation going back to Glinka. Stravinsky manipulates these scales virtuosically, producing elaborate symmetries and rotations meant in part to conjure the mathematical organization of the hive and in part to demonstrate his mastery of the technical procedures so beloved by his teacher.[110] Clearly, Stravinsky (like all composers of supernatural scherzi after Mendelssohn) was adapting and updating an entrenched fairy sound while also reconciling it with local influences. His scherzo was, as he himself acknowledged, a mongrel work, part Mendelssohnian, part Rimskian, even vaguely Wagnerian.[111] Taruskin's claim that the piece "owes nothing to Chaikovsky or Mendelssohn, and everything to Rimsky and the Belyayevets esthetic" seems, in light of the broader tradition I have been excavating here, open to question.[112] Stravinsky's work was part of a longer and more complex genealogy. Indeed, it was one of the last gasps of the truly entomological fairyscape – a scherzo that invoked, if only nostalgically, the magical miniature realm so beloved by the romantics.

As the twentieth century progressed, fairy belief dwindled – there was less and less talk of bee-like sylphs or of fairies at the bottom of the garden[113] – and yet the *scherzo fantastique* continued unabated. At least thirty scherzi bearing the rubric were published after 1900, many of which reproduced a version of the elfin soundscape I have been tracing here. These included Josef Suk's *Fantastické scherzo*, op. 25 (1903–04), Luís de Freitas Branco's *Scherzo fantastique* (1907), Louis Versel's *Scherzo fantastique* (1918),

---

[110] See Taruskin, *Stravinsky and the Russian Traditions*, I:323–33.

[111] Stravinsky identified Wagner as an influence on the diatonic music of the trio, particularly *Parsifal*, although Taruskin argues that *Die Meistersinger* may also have been in his mind (ibid., I:332).

[112] Ibid., I:315. Taruskin traces Stravinsky's *Scherzo fantastique* to a kuchkist tradition "that went back half a century, to the very beginning of the New Russian School, when Musorgsky and Cui had made their debuts with orchestral scherzi ... during the very first concert season (1859–60) of the Russian Musical Society" (323). But we should remember that Berlioz's *fantastique* scherzo had been performed in St. Petersburg well before this. *La Reine Mab* was heard both as an independent excerpt and as part of *Roméo et Juliette* at concerts in St. Petersburg at least four times in March 1847, and was well received. Berlioz himself, of course, along with the other members of the so-called New German School was warmly regarded by Musorgsky, Cui, and the kuchka at large.

[113] Among the last places in which such rhetoric is found is in the press surrounding the so-called Cottingley fairy photographs (1920), a series of images of girls and fairies taken by Elsie Wright and her cousin Frances Griffiths on the edge of Cottingley Beck, the stream in the Wright family's garden. These photographs seemed at first, to the few fairy believers who remained (among them Arthur Conan Doyle), to have done what romantic science promised: revealed and recovered elfin magic. But of course the photographs had been staged and were eventually debunked. The "fairies" they featured were cardboard cutouts, wistful rather than magical objects, products of a postwar reality in which technology could generate only the memory (or illusion) of fantasy.

Ernest Bloch's *Scherzo fantasque* (1950), and Eugène Goossens's *Scherzo fantasque pour flûte et piano* (1962). Of course, these pieces were increasingly removed from the cultural impulses that had produced the insect-like elves of the nineteenth century. Scientific thought had moved on, ceasing to entertain or even consciously remember the entomological-mythological yoking that shaped the writing of earlier microscopists and fairyologists. But echoes of that tradition and its fantastic language persisted in the form of musical topoi – sounds unmoored from their origins, preserved as compositional conventions inextricably encrusted onto the scherzo itself.

At the same time, and partly as the result of the dissolution of romantic naturalism, the form's programmatic associations broadened and loosened; no longer linked only to fairies, scherzi came to represent magic in a vaguer sense. This shift had certainly begun by 1897, when Paul Dukás couched his symphonic poem *L'Apprenti sorcier* as a scherzo, and must have inflected Gustav Holst's decision to cast the sixth movement of his orchestral suite *The Planets* (depicting Uranus, the Magician) as a scherzo, as well as Lothar Windsperger's choice to include a scherzo in his keyboard cycle *Lumen Amoris* (*Divine Love*, 1916). By mid-century, multi-movement works with fairytale themes had begun to incorporate the scherzo as a standard movement; examples include Hans Gál (*Zauberspiegel-Suite*, 1931), Lars-Erik Larsson (*Drei Opernbilder aus Die Prinzessin von Cypern*, 1939), and Henri Tomasi (*Les Noces de Cendres: Suite symphonique*, 1955). All manner of fantastic places and spaces could be conjured by the scherzo, whose magical ethos lingered on not only in the musical, but also in the literary sphere, where poets and novelists borrowed it to conjure imaginary soundtracks for passages of otherworldly description. This was especially true among French authors; Léon Roger-Milès, for instance, opened his hallucinatory poem "Pendant qu'elle rêve" ("While she dreams," from *Cent pièces à dire*, 1897) by inviting readers to "listen" to a scherzo:

Oh! le scherzo qui s'envolait
D'une maison voisine aux fenêtres décloses,
Tandis qu'auprès du lit où son corps sommeillait
Le songe trahissait son esprit, par ses gloses!

(Oh! the scherzo that floated
From a neighboring house with open windows
While on the bed where her body slumbered
The dream betrayed its meaning via glosses!)

Somewhat different, although equally predictable, was Maurice Renard's use of the term two decades later in the title of a science fiction tale – *Un*

Homme chez les microbes: scherzo (1928) – in which he transported readers to a space of fantasized miniaturism.

These moments in Roger-Milès and Renard – one evoking the scherzo as a dreamscape, the other as a microscope – take us back, of course, to the very beginning of this chapter and the origins of the *fantastique* scherzo itself. They point, however whimsically or ironically, to Mendelssohn, Berlioz, Liszt, Bazzini, and the fairy evocations of their lesser-known contemporaries, reminding us of the romantic tension at the heart of the fairy scherzo, the tug-of-war between artistic reverie and scientific reality, between archaic magic and musical modernity. It was this tension, as I have argued here, that produced and defined the strand of nineteenth-century fairy language pioneered by Mendelssohn – a fantastic mode that reactivated fairy enchantment by reconciling it with reason, opening up a space in which acute observation might lead to revelation or even magical transportation. The result was an elfin texture that linked the fluttering of Shakespearian fairies to the humming of Budgen's grasshoppers and the buzzing of Maeterlinck's bees, generating new kinds of hearing and orchestrating as well as reconfiguring notions of poetic expression and definitions of the "inspired" musician. The roots and genealogy of this fairy mode – the *scherzo fantastique* – cast new light on both Mendelssohn's and Berlioz's innovations, opening a window onto the intersections among nineteenth-century science, sound, poetry, and philosophy that rescued sylphs and sprites from intellectual and aesthetic exile, allowing them to creep back into – or at least hesitate on the edge of – reality.

Bibliography

Berlioz: Scores, Critical Writing, and Correspondence

New Berlioz Edition (*NBE*), general ed. Hugh Macdonald. Kassel: Bärenreiter, 1967–2006. Volumes cited:
4. *Incomplete Operas*, eds. Ric Graebner and Paul Banks (2002)
7. *Lélio ou Le Retour à la vie*, ed. Peter Bloom (1992)
8a–b. *La Damnation de Faust*, ed. Julian Rushton (1979–86)
15. *Songs with Piano*, ed. Ian Rumbold (2005)
16. *Symphonie fantastique*, ed. Nicholas Temperley (1972)
17. *Harold en Italie*, eds. Paul Banks and Hugh Macdonald (2001)
18. *Roméo et Juliette*, ed. D. Kern Holoman (1990)
24. *Grand traité d'instrumentation et d'orchestration modernes*, ed. Peter Bloom (2003)

CG: Correspondance générale, general ed. Pierre Citron, Paris: Flammarion, 1972–2003.
I: 1803–32, ed. Pierre Citron (1972)
II: 1832–42, ed. Frédéric Robert (1975)
III: 1842–50, ed. Pierre Citron (1978)
IV: 1851–55, eds. Pierre Citron, Yves Gérard, and Hugh Macdonald (1983)
V: 1855–59, eds. Hugh Macdonald and François Lesure (1988)
VI: 1859–63, eds. Hugh Macdonald and François Lesure (1995)
VII: 1864–69, ed. Hugh Macdonald (2001)
VIII: Suppléments, ed. Hugh Macdonald (2003)

CM: Critique musicale, 1823–63, general ed. Yves Gérard, Paris: Buchet/Chastel, 1996–present.
I: 1823–34, eds. H. Robert Cohen and Yves Gérard (1996)
II: 1835–36, eds. Anne Bongrain and Marie-Hélène Coudroy-Saghaï (1998)
III: 1837–38, eds. Anne Bongrain and Marie-Hélène Coudroy-Saghaï (2001)
IV: 1839–41, eds. Anne Bongrain and Marie-Hélène Coudroy-Saghaï (2003)
V: 1842–44, eds. Anne Bongrain and Marie-Hélène Coudroy-Saghaï (2004)
VI: 1845–48, eds. Anne Bongrain and Marie-Hélène Coudroy-Saghaï (2008)
VII: 1849–51, eds. Anne Bongrain and Marie-Héléne Coudroy-Saghaï (2014)
VIII: 1852–55, eds. Anne Bongrain and Marie-Héléne Coudroy-Saghaï (2016)

Nineteenth-Century Periodicals and Newspapers

Allgemeine musikalische Zeitung
L'Artiste: Journal de la littérature et des beaux-arts
L'Avant-scène
Berliner allgemeine musikalische Zeitung
Chronique de Paris
Le Commerce
Le Constitutionnel
Le Correspondant
Le Courrier de l'Europe
Le Courrier français
Dresdener Abendzeitung
The European Magazine
Le Figaro
La France littéraire
La France musicale
Gazette de France
Le Globe
Les Guêpes
Iris im Gebiete der Tonkunst
Journal des débats
Journal de Paris
Le Ménestrel
Le Mercure de France aux XIX siècle
Le Moniteur universel
Neue Zeitschrift für Musik
La Presse
La Quotidienne
Revue de Paris
Revue des deux mondes
La Revue et Gazette musicale
Le Temps
L'Univers musical, journal littéraire et artistique
Le Voleur

Books and Articles

Abert, Hermann. *Niccolò Jommelli als Opernkomponist*. Halle: Max Miemeyer, 1908.

Abrams, M. H. *Natural Supernaturalism: Tradition and Revolution in Romantic Literature*. New York: Norton, 1971.

Allanbrook, Wye J. *Rhythmic Gesture in Mozart: "Le nozze di Figaro" and "Don Giovanni."* Chicago: University of Chicago Press, 1983.

Allin, Michael. *Zarafa: A Giraffe's True Story, from Deep in Africa to the Heart of Paris*. New York: Walker, 1998.

Altick, Richard. *The Shows of London*. Cambridge, MA: Belknap Press of Harvard University Press, 1978.

Ameriks, Karl. *The Cambridge Companion to German Idealism*. Cambridge and New York: Cambridge University Press, 2000.

Andrès, Philippe. *La Fantaisie dans la littérature français du XIXe siècle*. Paris: L'Harmattan, 2000.

Arbousset, T. and F. Daumas. *Relation d'un voyage d'exploration au nord-est de la colonie de Cape de Bonne-Espérance*. Paris: Bertrand, 1842. Translated by John Croumbie Brown as *Narrative of an Exploratory Tour to the North-East of the Colony of the Cape of Good Hope*. Cape Town: A. S. Robertson, Heerengracht, 1846.

Armitt, Lucy. *Theorising the Fantastic*. New York: Arnold, 1996.

Attali, Jacques. *Noise: The Political Economy of Music*. Translated by Brian Massumi. Minneapolis: University of Minnesota Press, 1985.

Aubéry, Du Boulley, Prudent-Louis. *Grammaire Musicale ou méthode analytique et raisonnée pour apprendre et enseigner la lecture de la musique suivie d'observations sur les erreurs, préjugés et fausses opinions concernant la musique*. Paris: Richault, 1830.

Austin, J. L. *How to Do Things with Words*. Cambridge, MA: Harvard University Press, 1962.

Baker, Henry. *The Microscope Made Easy*. 2nd ed. London: R. Dodsley, 1743.

Balzac, Honoré de. "Les Amours de deux bêtes offerts en exemple aux gens d'esprit: Histoire animau-sentimentale." In *Scènes de la vie privée et publiques des animaux*. Edited by P. J. Stahl, illustrated by Grandville. Paris: Hetzel, 1867, 430–60.

La Peau de chagrin. Paris: Éditions Gallimard, 1974.

Barron, Neil, ed. *Fantasy and Horror: A Critical and Historical Guide to Literature, Illustration, Film, TV, Radio, and the Internet*. Lanham, MD: Scarecrow Press, 1999.

Barzun, Jacques. *Berlioz and the Romantic Century*, 2 vols. New York and London: Columbia University Press, 1969.

Beiser, Frederick C. *German Idealism: The Struggle against Subjectivism 1781–1801*. Cambridge, MA: Harvard University Press, 2002.

Bellman, Jonathan. *The "style hongrois" in the Music of Western Europe*. Boston: Northeastern University Press, 1993.

Benes, Tuska. *In Babel's Shadow: Language, Philology, and the Nation in Nineteenth-Century Germany*. Detroit, MI: Wayne State University Press, 2008.

Berger, Christian. *Phantastik als Konstruktion: Hector Berlioz's "Symphonie fantastique."* Kassel: Bärenreiter, 1983.

Bergström, Stefan. *Between Real and Unreal: A Thematic Study of E. T. A. Hoffmann's "Die Serapionsbrüder."* Studies on Themes and Motifs in Literature, vol. 49. New York: P. Lang, 2000.

Berlioz, Hector. *The Art of Music and Other Essays (À travers chants)*. Translated by Elizabeth Csicsery-Rónay. Bloomington and Indianapolis: Indiana University Press, 1994.

À Travers chants: études musicales, adorations, boutades et critiques. Paris: Lévy Frères, 1871.

Berlioz's Orchestration Treatise: A Translation and Commentary. Translation and commentary by Hugh Macdonald. Cambridge Musical Texts and Monographs. Cambridge: Cambridge University Press, 2003.

"Le Harpiste Ambulante." In *Les Soirées de l'orchestre*, 54–90.

Mémoires. Edited by Pierre Citron, 2 vols. Paris: Flammarion, 1991.

Memoirs. Translated and edited by David Cairns. London: Gollancz, 1969.

Selected Letters of Berlioz. Edited by Hugh Macdonald. New York: Norton, 1995.

Les Soirées de l'orchestre. Edited by Léon Guichard. Paris: Gründ, 1968.

Bernstein, Jay M., ed. *Classic and Romantic German Aesthetics*. Cambridge Texts in the History of Philosophy. Cambridge: Cambridge University Press, 2002.

Biran, Maine de. *Journal intime*. 2 vols. Edited by H. Gouhier. Neuchatel: Édition de la Baconnière, 1954.

Blakemore, Steven. *Burke and the Fall of Language: The French Revolution as Linguistic Event*. Hanover, NH: Brown University Press and University Press of New England, 1988.

Blaze (de Bury), Ange-Henri. "De l'École fantastique et de M. Berlioz." *Revue des deux mondes* (1 October 1838): 93–112.

Bloom, Peter. "A Return to Berlioz's 'Retour à la vie.'" *The Musical Quarterly* 64/3 (July 1978): 354–85.

"François-Joseph Fétis and the *Revue musicale* (1827–1835)." PhD dissertation, University of Pennsylvania, 1972.

"Orpheus' Lyre Resurrected: A 'Tableau Musical' by Berlioz." *The Musical Quarterly* 61/2 (April 1975): 189–211.

Bollnow, Otto Friedrich. "Der 'goldene Topf' und die Naturphilosophie der Romantik: Bemerkungen zum Weltbild E. T. A. Hoffmanns." In *Unruhe und Geborgenheit im Weltbild neuerer Dichter*. Stuttgart: Kohlhammer, 1953, 207–26.

Bonald, Louis Gabriel Ambroise de. "Législation Primitive considérée dans les derniers temps par les seules lumières de la raison." In *Oeuvres complètes de M. de Bonald*, vol. 1. Paris: Migne, 1864, 1050–1402.

Bonds, Mark Evan. *Music as Thought: Listening to the Symphony in the Age of Beethoven*. Princeton, NJ and Oxford: Princeton University Press, 2006.

"*Sinfonia anti-eroica*: Berlioz's *Harold en Italie* and the Anxiety of Beethoven's Influence." *Journal of Musicology* 10/4 (Autumn 1992): 417–63.

Bory de, Saint-Vincent, Jean-Baptiste-Maximilien. *L'Homme (homo) ou Essai zoologique sur le genre humain*. Paris: Rey et Gravier, 1827.

Bottigheimer, Ruth. "The Ultimate Fairy Tale: Oral Transmission in a Literate World." In *A Companion to the Fairy Tale*. Edited by Hilda Ellis Davidson and Anna Chaudhri. Cambridge and Rochester, NY: D.S. Brewer, 2003, 57–70.

Bourdieu, Pierre. *Ce que parler veut dire: l'économie des échanges linguistiques*. Paris: Fayard, 1982.

Bown, Nicola. *Fairies in Nineteenth-Century Art and Literature*. Cambridge: Cambridge University Press, 2001.

Bradbury, Savile. *The Evolution of the Microscope*. Oxford: Pergamon, 1967.

Brantlinger, Patrick. *Rule of Darkness: British Literature and Imperialism, 1830–1914*. Ithaca, NY: Cornell University Press, 1988.

Brittan, Francesca. "Berlioz and the Pathological Fantastic: Melancholy, Monomania, and Romantic Autobiography." *19th-Century Music* 29/3 (Spring 2006): 211–39.

ed. Etienne-Joseph Soubre, *Sinfonie fantastique à grand orchestra*. Middleton WI: A-R Editions, 2017.

"Liszt, Sand, Garcia, and the Contrebandier: Intersubjectivity and Romantic Authorship." *Journal of the American Liszt Society* 65 (December 2014): 65–94.

"On Microscopic Hearing: Fairy Magic, Natural Science, and the *Scherzo fantastique*." *Journal of the American Musicological Society* 64/3 (Fall 2011): 527–600.

Brooke-Rose, Christine. *A Rhetoric of the Unreal: Studies in Narrative and Structure, Especially of the Fantastic.* Cambridge: Cambridge University Press, 1981.

Brown, Clive. *A Portrait of Mendelssohn.* New Haven, CT and London: Yale University Press, 2003.

Brown, Hilda Meldrum. *E. T. A. Hoffmann and the Serapiontic Principle: Critique and Creativity.* Rochester, NY: Camden House, 2006.

Brown, Marshall. *The Shape of German Romanticism.* Ithaca, NY: Cornell University Press, 1979.

Brunet, François. *Théophile Gautier et la musique.* Paris: H. Champion, 2006.

Brunot, Ferdinand. *Histoire de la langue française des origines à 1900.* 13 vols. Paris: A. Colin, 1905–72.

Buch, David J. *Magic Flutes and Enchanted Forests: The Supernatural in Eighteenth-Century Musical Theater.* Chicago: University of Chicago Press, 2008.

Buchez, Phillipe-Joseph-Benjamin and Prosper-Charles Roux. *Histoire parlementaire de la révolution française.* 40 vols. Paris: Paulin, 1834–38.

Buckley, Arabella B. *The Fairyland of Science.* New York: Hurst, 1878.

Budgen, L. M. (Acheta Domestica). *Episodes of Insect Life*, 3 vols. London: Reeve, Benham, and Reeve, 1849–51.

Burwick, Frederick. *Poetic Madness and the Romantic Imagination.* University Park: Pennsylvania University Press, 1996.

Butler, Andrew M. "Psychoanalysis." In *The Cambridge Companion to Fantasy Literature*, 91–101.

Butler, Joseph. *L'Analogie de la religion naturelle et révélée avec l'ordre et le cours de la nature.* Paris: Brunot-Labbe, 1821.

Butler, Stella, R. H. Nuttal, and Olivia Brown. *The Social History of the Microscope.* Cambridge: Whipple Museum, 1986.

Cahusac, Louis de. "Féerie." In *Encyclopédie ou Dictionnaire raisonné des sciences, des arts et des métiers*, vol. 6. Paris: Briasson, 1760, 464.

Cailleux, Léon. "Études: Sur le fantastique." *L'Artiste* (13 February 1848): 227–31.

Cairns, David. *Berlioz.* Volume 1: *1803–1832, The Making of an Artist.* Berkeley and Los Angeles: University of California Press, 2000.

Berlioz. Volume 2: *Servitude and Greatness, 1832–1869.* Berkeley and Los Angeles: University of California Press, 2000.

Camper, Petrus. *Dissertation sur les variétés naturelles qui caractérisent la physionomie des hommes des divers climats et des différens âges, suivies de Réflexions sur la Beauté.* Paris: H.J. Jansen, 1791.

Castex, Pierre Georges. *Anthologie du conte fantastique français.* Paris: J. Corti, 1963.

Le Conte fantastique en France de Nodier à Maupassant. Paris: J. Corti, 1951.

Castle, Terry. *The Female Thermometer: Eighteenth-Century Culture and the Invention of the Uncanny.* New York: Oxford University Press, 1995.

Chantler, Abigail. *E. T. A. Hoffmann's Musical Aesthetics.* Aldershot, UK and Burlington, VT: Ashgate, 2006.

Charlton, David, ed. *E. T. A. Hoffmann's Musical Writings: Kreisleriana, The Poet and the Composer, Music Criticism.* Translated by Martyn Clarke. Cambridge Readings in the Literature of Music. Cambridge: Cambridge University Press, 1989.

Chateaubriand, François-René de. *Génie du Christianisme, ou Beautés de la religion chrétienne.* 5th ed., 2 vols. Lyon: Ballanche, 1809.

Claude, Miriam. *Race and Aesthetics in the Anthropology of Petrus Camper (1722–1789).* Amsterdam: Rodopi, 1999.

Clément, F. *Musiciens célèbres depuis seizième siècle jusqu'à nos jours.* Paris: Hachette, 1868.

Cohen, William B. *The French Encounter with Africans: White Response to Blacks, 1530–1880.* Bloomington: Indiana University Press, 1980.

Coleman, Deirdre. "Entertaining Entomology: Insects and Performers in the Eighteenth Century." *Eighteenth-Century Life* 30/3 (2006): 107–34.

Collin de Plancy, Jacques Albin Simon. *Dictionnaire infernal; Répertoire universel des êtres, des personnages, des livres, des faits et des choses qui tiennent aux esprits.* 6th ed. Paris: Plon, 1818.

Comini, Alessandra. *The Changing Image of Beethoven: A Study in Mythmaking.* New York: Rissoli, 1987.

Cone, Edward T. *The Composer's Voice.* Berkeley and Los Angeles: University of California Press, 1974.

ed. *Berlioz: Fantastic Symphony; An Authoritative Score, Historical Background, Analysis, Views, and Comments.* New York: Norton, 1971.

Conley, Tim and Stephen Cain. *The Encyclopedia of Fictional and Fantastic Languages.* Westport, CT, and London: Greenwood Press, 2006.

Constant, Benjamin. "De L'Esprit de conquête." In *Cours de Politique Constitutionnelle*, vol. 2. Paris: Guillaumin, 1872.

Copenhaver, Brian P. *Magic in Western Culture: From Antiquity to the Enlightenment.* New York: Cambridge University Press, 2015.

Cornwell, Neil. *The Literary Fantastic from Gothic to Postmodernism.* New York: Harvester Wheatsheaf, 1990.

Cosso, Laura. *Strategie del fantastico: Berlioz e la cultura del romanticismo francese.* Alessandria: Edizioni dell'Orso, 2002.

Coudroy, Marie-Hélène. *La Critique parisienne des "grands opéras" de Meyerbeer: Robert le Diable, Les Huguenots, Le Prophète, L'Africaine.* Etudes sur l'opéra français du XIXe siècle, vol. 2. Saarbrucken: Galland, 1988.

Curran, Andrew S. *The Anatomy of Blackness: Science and Slavery in an Age of Enlightenment.* Baltimore, MD: Johns Hopkins University Press, 2011.

Curtin, Philip D. *The Image of Africa: British Ideas and Action, 1780–1850.* Madison: University of Wisconsin Press, 1964.

Cuvier G. *Le Règne animal distribué d'après son organisation.* Paris: Deterville, 1817.

Leçons d'anatomie comparée. 4 vols. Paris: Baudoin, 1800–05.

Dahlhaus, Carl. *Nineteenth-Century Music.* Translated by J. Bradford Robinson. Berkeley: University of California Press, 1989.

Dard, Jean. *Dictionnaire français-wolof et français-bambara, suivi du dictionnaire wolof-français.* Paris: Imprimerie royale, 1825.

Grammaire Wolofe ou méthode pour étudier la langue des noirs en Sénégambie suivie d'un appendice. Paris: Imprimerie royale, 1826.

Davies, James. "Liszt, Metapianism, and the Cultural History of the Hand." In *Romantic Anatomies of Performance.* Berkeley, Los Angeles, London: University of California Press, 2014, 152–79.

Devrient, Eduard. *Meine Erinnerungen an Felix Mendelssohn-Bartholdy und seine Briefe an mich.* Leipzig: J.J. Weber, 1869.

Dramatische und dramaturgische Schriften, vol. 10. Translated by Natalia Macfarren as *My Recollections of Felix Mendelssohn Bartholdy and His Letters to Me.* New York: Vienna House, 1972.

Dill, Charles. "The Influence of Linguistics on Rameau's Theory of Modulation." In *Rameau, entre art et science.* Edited by Sylvie Bouissou, Graham Sadler, and Soveig Serre. Paris: École des Chartes, 2016, 397–408.

Dolan, Emily I. "E. T. A. Hoffmann and the Ethereal Technologies of 'Nature Music.'" *Eighteenth-Century Music* 5/1 (2008): 7–26.

The Orchestral Revolution: Haydn and the Technologies of Timbre. Cambridge: Cambridge University Press, 2013.

Dömling, Wolfgang. *Hector Berlioz: Symphonie Fantastique.* Munich: W. Fink, 1985.

D'Ortigue, Joseph. *Du Théâtre Italien et de son influence sur le goût musical françois.* Paris: Au Dépôt Central des Meilleurs Productions de la Presse, 1840.

Dowbiggin, Ian. *Inheriting Madness: Professionalization and Psychiatric Knowledge in Nineteenth-Century France.* Berkeley: University of California Press, 1991.

Duras, Claire de. "Édouard." In *Mademoiselle de Clermont, par Mme de Genlis et Édouard, par Mme de Duras.* Edited and with afterward by Gérard Gengembre. Paris: Editions Autrement, 1994.

Edgecombe, Anthony. "Meyerbeer and Ballet Music of the Nineteenth Century: Some Issues of Influence with Reference to *Robert le diable.*" *Dance Chronicle* 21/3 (1998): 389–410.

Ellis, Katharine. "Liszt: The Romantic Artist." In *The Cambridge Companion to Liszt.* Edited by Kenneth Hamilton. Cambridge: Cambridge University Press, 2005, 1–13.

——. *Music Criticism in Nineteenth-Century France: La Revue et Gazette musicale de Paris, 1834–1880.* Cambridge: Cambridge University Press, 1995.

——. "The Uses of Fiction: Contes and Nouvelles in the *Revue et Gazette musicale de Paris, 1834–1844.*" *Revue de Musicologie* 90/2 (2004): 253–81.

Esquirol, Etienne. *Des Maladies mentales: considérées sous les rapports médical, hygiénique et médico-légal.* 2 vols. Paris: Baillière, 1838. Translated by Raymond de Saussure as *Mental Maladies: A Treatise on Insanity.* A Facsimile of the English Edition of 1845. New York and London: Hafner, 1965.

——. "Monomania." In *Dictionaire des sciences medicales,* vol. 34. Paris: 1819, 117–22.

Esterhammer, Angela. *The Romantic Performative: Language and Action in British and German Romanticism.* Stanford, CA: Stanford University Press, 2000.

Evans, Martin, ed. *Empire and Culture: The French Experience 1830–1940.* New York: Palgrave Macmillan, 2004.

Everist, Mark. "The Name of the Rose: Meyerbeer's opéra comique, *Robert le diable.*" *Revue de musicologie* 80/2 (1994): 211–50.

Fanoudh-Siefer, Léon. *Le Mythe du nègre et de l'Afrique noire dans la littérature française de 1800 à la 2e guerre mondiale.* Paris: C. Klincksieck, 1968.

Fara, Patricia. "Marginalized Practices." In *The Cambridge History of Science,* vol. 4, *Eighteenth-Century Science.* Edited by Roy Porter. Cambridge: Cambridge University Press, 2003, 485–510.

Fénelon, François de Salignac de La Mothe. *Démonstration de l'existence de Dieu, tirée de l'art, de la nature, des preuves purement intellectuelles, et de l'idée de l'infini même, suivie des Lettres sur la religion.* Paris: Briand, 1810.

Fétis, François. "Berlioz." In *Biographie universelle des musiciens et bibliographie générale de la musique,* vol. 1. Brussels: Meline, Cans, et Compagnie, 1837, 150–52.

——— "De la mélodie." In *La Musique mise à la portée de tout le monde, exposé succinct de tout ce qui est nécessaire pour juger de cet art, et pour en parler sans l'avoir étudié.* Paris: Mesnier, 1830, 58–66.

——— "Mendelssohn." In *Biographie universelle des musiciens et bibliographie générale de la musique,* vol. 6. Brussels: Meline, Cans, et Cie., 1840, 367–69.

Findlen, Paula, ed. *Athanasius Kircher: The Last Man Who Knew Everything.* New York: Routledge, 2004.

Figuier, Louis. *Les Insectes. Tableau de la nature. La vie et les moeurs des animaux.* Paris: Hachette, 1867.

——— *Les Races humaines.* Paris: Hachette, 1872.

Ford, Brian J. *The Revealing Lens: Mankind and the Microscope.* London: Harrap, 1973.

——— *Single Lens: The Story of the Simple Microscope.* New York: Harper & Row, 1985.

Foucault, Michel. *Folie et déraison: Histoire de la folie à l'âge classique.* Paris: Plon, 1961. Translated by Jonathan Murphy and Jean Khalfa. Edited by Jean Khalfa as *Madness and Civilization: A History of Insanity in the Age of Reason.* London and New York: Routledge, 2006.

Fournier, Marian. *The Fabric of Life: Microscopy in the Seventeenth Century.* Baltimore, MD: Johns Hopkins University Press, 1996.

Gabay, Al. *Covert Enlightenment: Eighteenth-Century Counterculture and Its Aftermath.* Swedenborg Studies, vol. 17. West Chester, PA: Swedenborg Foundation, 2005.

Gall, Franz Joseph and Johann Gaspar Spurzheim. *Anatomie et physiologie du système nerveux en général et du cerveau en particulier.* Paris: F. Schoell, 1812.

Gamer, Michael. *Romanticism and the Gothic: Genre, Reception, and Canon Formation.* Cambridge: Cambridge University Press, 2004.

Gautier, Théophile. "La Cafetière." In *La Morte amoureuse, Avatar et autres récits fantastiques.* Edited by Jean Gaudon. Paris: Gallimard, 1981, 5–15.

——— *Histoire du romantisme suivie de notices romantiques et d'une étude sur la poésie française, 1830–1868.* Paris: Charpentier et cie, 1874.

Georget, E.-J. *Examen médical des procès criminels des nommés Léger, Feldtmann, Lecouffe, Jean-Pierre et Papavoine, dans lesquels l'aliénation mentale a été alléguée comme moyen de défense, suivi de quelques considérations médico-légales sur la liberté morale.* Paris: Migneret, 1825.

Gere, Charlotte and Lionel Lambourne. "Paton, Joseph." In Jeremy Maas, Pamela White Trimpe, Charlotte Gere, et al., *Victorian Fairy Painting*. Edited by Jane Martineau. London: Merrell Holberton, 1997, 108–12.

Gigante, Denise. *Life: Organic Form and Romanticism*. New Haven, CT and London: Yale University Press, 2009.

Gilman, Sander L. "Black Bodies, White Bodies: Toward an Iconography of Black Female Sexuality in Late Nineteenth-Century Art, Medicine, and Literature." *Critical Inquiry* 12 (Autumn 1985): 204–42.

Difference and Pathology: Stereotypes of Sexuality, Race, and Madness. Ithaca, NY: Cornell University Press, 1988.

Gioberti, Vincenzo. *Le Panthéisme de M. Cousin exposé par lui-même, traduites de l'italien par J. B. Ansiau*. Louvain: J. B. Ansiau, 1842.

Girault-Duvivier, Ch. P. *Grammaire des grammaires ou analyse raisonnée des meilleurs traités sur la langue française*. 6th ed. 2 vols. Paris: Janet et Cotelle, 1827.

Glanvill, Joseph. *The Vanity of Dogmatizing: Or, Confidence in Opinions Manifested in a Discourse of the Shortness and Uncertainty of Our Knowledge*. London: B. C., 1661.

Goethe, Johann Wolfgang von. *Faust, Part One*. Translated by David Luke. Oxford: Oxford University Press, 1987.

Goldstein, Jan. *Console and Classify: The French Psychiatric Profession in the Nineteenth Century*. New York: Cambridge University Press, 1987.

The Post-Revolutionary Self: Politics and Psyche in France, 1750–1850. Cambridge MA: Harvard University Press, 2005.

Gouk, Penelope. "Music and the Nervous System in Eighteenth-Century British Medical Thought." In *Music and the Nerves 1700–1900*. Edited by James Kennaway. Houndmills, Basingstoke, Hampshire: Palgrave Macmillan, 2014, 44–71.

Music, Science, and Natural Magic. New Haven, CT: Yale University Press, 1999.

"Music's Pathological and Therapeutic Effects on the Body Politic: Doctor John Gregory's Views." In *Representing Emotions: New Connections in the Histories of Art, Music and Medicine*. Edited by Penelope Gouk and Helen Hills. Aldershot: Ashgate, 2005, 191–207.

Grätz, Manfred. *Das Märchen in der deutschen Aufklärung: Vom Feenmärchen zum Volksmärchen*. Stuttgart: Metzler, 1988.

Grey, Thomas S. "Fingal's Cave and Ossian's Dream: Music, Image and Phantasmagoric Audition." In *The Arts Entwined: Music and Painting in the Nineteenth Century*. Edited by Marsha L. Morton and Peter L. Schmunk. Garland Reference Library of the Humanities 2099. Critical and Cultural Musicology 2. New York: Garland, 2000, 63–100.

"The Orchestral Music." In *The Mendelssohn Companion*. Edited by Douglass Seaton. Westport, CT: Greenwood, 2001, 395–550.

"Tableaux vivants: Landscape, History Painting, and the Visual Imagination in Mendelssohn's Orchestral Music." *19th-Century Music* 21/1 (Summer 1997): 38–76.

Hadlock, Heather. "Sonorous Bodies: Women and the Glass Harmonica." *Journal of the American Musicological Society* 53/3 (Autumn 2000): 507–42.

Hankins, Thomas L. and Robert J. Silverman. *Instruments and the Imagination*. Princeton, NJ: Princeton University Press, 1995.

Harpham, Geoffrey. *On the Grotesque: Strategies of Contradiction in Art and Literature*. Princeton, NJ: Princeton University Press, 1982.

Harries, Elizabeth Wanning. *Twice Upon a Time: Women Writers and the History of the Fairy Tale*. Princeton, NJ: Princeton University Press, 2003.

Head, Matthew. *Orientalism, Masquerade and Mozart's Turkish Music*. London: Royal Musical Association, 2000.

Hensel, Sebastian, Felix Mendelssohn-Bartholdy, and Fanny Mendelssohn Hensel. *The Mendelssohn Family (1729–1847) from Letters and Journals*. 2nd ed. Translated by Karl Klingemann, 2 vols. New York: Harper & Brothers, 1882.

Herbert, Christopher. *Culture and Anomie: Ethnographic Imagination in the Nineteenth Century*. Chicago: University of Chicago Press, 1991.

Hiller, Ferdinand. *Felix Mendelssohn-Bartholdy: Briefe und Erinnerung*. Cologne: M. Du Mont-Schauberg'schen Buchhandlung, 1874.

Hodson, Jane. *Language and Revolution in Burke, Wollstonecraft, Paine, and Godwin*. Aldershot, UK and Burlington, VT: Ashgate, 2007.

Hoffmann, E. T. A. "Automata." In *The Best Tales of Hoffmann*. Edited by E. F. Bleiler. Translated by Major Alexander Ewing. New York: Dover, 1967, 71–103.

"Casual Reflections on the Appearance of This Journal." In *E. T. A. Hoffmann's Musical Writings: Kreisleriana, The Poet and the Composer, Music Criticism*, 423–30.

"The Golden Pot." In *E. T. A. Hoffmann, The Golden Pot and Other Tales*. Translated by Ritchie Robertson. Oxford: Oxford University Press, 1992, 1–84.

Kreisleriana. In *E. T. A. Hoffmann's Musical Writings: Kreisleriana, The Poet and the Composer, Music Criticism*, 76–165.

The Life and Opinions of the Tomcat Murr. Translated by Anthea Bell. London: Penguin, 1999.

"Master Flea." In *Three Märchen of E. T. A. Hoffmann*. Translated by Charles E. Passage. Columbia: University of South Carolina Press, 1971, 251–402.

"The Mines of Falun." In *Tales of E. T. A. Hoffmann*. Translated by Leonard J. Kent and Elizabeth C. Knight. Illustrated by Jacob Landau. Chicago: University of Chicago Press, 1972, 149–72.

"A New Year's Eve Adventure." In *The Best Tales of Hoffmann*, 104–29.

"Princess Brambilla." In *E. T. A. Hoffmann, The Golden Pot and Other Tales*, 119–238.

The Serapion Brethren, 2 vols. Translated by Major Alexander Ewing. London: George Bell and Sons, 1908.

Hogle, Jerrold E., ed. *The Cambridge Companion to Gothic Fiction*. Cambridge: Cambridge University Press, 2002.

Hollander, John. *The Untuning of the Sky: Ideas of Music in English Poetry 1500–1700*. New York: Norton, 1970.

Holoman, D. Kern. *Berlioz*. Cambridge, MA: Harvard University Press, 1989.

The Nineteenth-Century Symphony. New York: Schirmer, 1996.

Horkheimer, Max and Theodore Adorno. *Dialectic of Enlightenment*. New York: Herder and Herder, 1972.

Hübener, Andrea. *Kreisler in Frankreich: E. T. A. Hoffmann und die französischen Romantiker*. Heidelberg: Winter, 2004.

Huebner, Steven. *The Operas of Charles Gounod*. Oxford: Oxford University Press, 1990.

Hugo, Victor. Preface to *Cromwell*. Translated by Charles W. Eliot in *Prefaces and Prologues to Famous Books*, vol. 39. New York: F. P. Collier & Son, 1909, 354–408.

Hunter, Mary. "The *Alla Turca* Style in the Late Eighteenth Century: Race and Gender in the Symphony and Seraglio." In *The Exotic in Western Music*. Edited by Jonathan Bellman. Boston: Northeastern University Press, 1998, 43–73.

Ironfield, Susan. "Creative Developments of the 'Mal de l'Isolement' in Berlioz." *Music and Letters* 59/1 (January 1978): 33–48.

Irvine, Judith T. "The Family Romance of Colonial Linguistics: Gender and Family in Nineteenth-Century Representations of African Languages." *Pragmatics* 5/2 (1995): 139–53.

"Mastering African Languages: The Politics of Linguistics in Nineteenth-Century Senegal." In *Nations, Colonies, and Metropoles*.

Edited by Daniel A. Segal and Richard Handler. Special Issue, *Social Analysis* 33 (1993): 27–46.

"Subjected Words: African Linguistics and the Colonial Encounter." *Language and Communication* 28/4 (October 2008): 323–43.

Jackson, Rosemary. *Fantasy: The Literature of Subversion*. London and New York: Methuen, 1981.

Jacob, Margaret C. *The Radical Enlightenment: Pantheists, Freemasons and Republicans*. London and Boston: George Allen & Unwin, 1981.

James, Edward and Farah Mendlesohn. *The Cambridge Companion to Fantasy Literature*. Cambridge: Cambridge University Press, 2002.

Janin, Jules. *La Confession*. Paris: Imprimerie-Librairie Romantique, 1830.

"Fantastique," *Dictionnaire de la conversation et de la lecture*, vol. 26. Paris: Béthune et Plon, 1832, 299–302.

"Kreyssler." In *Contes fantastiques et contes littéraires*. Beneva: Slatkine Reprints, 1979, 33–40.

Johnson, James H. "Beethoven and the Birth of Romantic Musical Experience." *19th-Century Music* 15 (1991): 23–35.

Listening in Paris: A Cultural History. Berkeley, Los Angeles, London: University of California Press, 1995.

Kastner, Georges. *Grammaire musicale comprenant tous les Principes élémentaires de Musique, la Mélodie, le Rythme, l'Harmonie moderne, et un aperçu succinct des voix et des Instruments. Dédiée à M. Giacomo Meyerbeer*. Paris: Lemoine, 1837.

Kayser, Wolfgang. *The Grotesque in Art and Literature*. Translated by Ulrich Weisstein. Bloomington: Indiana University Press, 1963.

Kennaway, James. *Bad Vibrations: The History of the Idea of Music as a Cause of Disease*. Farnham, Surrey, and Burlington, VT: Ashgate, 2012.

Kieckhefer, Richard. *Magic in the Middle Ages*. Cambridge: Cambridge University Press, 1989.

Kimber, Marian Wilson. "Reading Shakespeare, Seeing Mendelssohn: Concert Readings of *A Midsummer Night's Dream*, ca. 1850–1920." *The Musical Quarterly* 89 (2006): 199–236.

Klinck, David. *The French Counterrevolutionary Theorist Louis de Bonald (1754–1840)*. New York: Peter Lang, 1996.

Knittel, K. M. "Pilgrimages to Beethoven." *Music and Letters* 84 (2003): 19–54.

Kristeva, Julia. *La Révolution du langage poétique: l'avant-garde à la fin du XIX siècle, Lautréamont et Mallarmé*. Paris: Éditions du Seuil, 1974.

Krummacher, Friedrich. *Mendelssohn der Komponist: Studien zur Kammermusik für Streicher*. Munich: Wilhelm Fink, 1978.

Lacomb, Hervé and Timothée Picard, eds. *Opéra fantastique: Actes des colloque international, Rennes, 25–27 mars 2009.* Rennes: Presses universitaires de Rennes, 2011.

La Harpe, Jean-François de. *Du Fanatisme dans la langue révolutionnaire, ou de la persécution exercée par les barbares du XVIIIe siècle contre les ministres de la religion chrétienne.* Paris: Mignet, 1797.

Lamarck, Jean-Baptiste de Monet de. *Système des animaux sans vertèbres.* Paris: Deterville, 1801.

Lamartelière, J.-H.-F. de. *Les Francs juges, ou les temps de barbarie.* Paris: 1824.

Lamm, Julia A. "Romanticism and Pantheism." In *The Blackwell Companion to Nineteenth-Century Theology.* Edited by David Fergusson. Chichester, UK, and Malden, MA: Wiley-Blackwell, 2010, 165–86.

Larousse, Pierre. "Fantastique." In *Grand Dictionnaire Universel du XIX Siècle*, vol. 8. Paris: Administration du Grand dictionnaire universel, 1872, 93–95.

Le Dhuy (Ledhuy), Adolphe. *Nouveau manuel simplifié de musique; ou, Grammaire contenant les principes de cet art.* Paris: Roret, 1829.

Lehrich, Christopher I. *The Language of Demons and Angels: Cornelius Agrippa's Occult Philosophy.* Boston: Brill, 2003.

Lenau, Nicolaus. *Faust. Ein Gedicht.* Stuttgart and Tübingen: J.G. Cotta, 1836.

Leonard, Elisabeth Anne, ed. *Into Darkness Peering: Race and Color in the Fantastic.* Westport, CT: Greenwood Press, 1997.

Lesne, Melle. *Grammaire musicale, basée sur les principes de la grammaire française, par Melle Lesne, Professeur d'harmonie, de chant et de piano.* 2nd ed. Paris: Chez l'auteur, 1820.

Levin, Janet. *The Romantic Art of Confession: De Quincey, Musset, Sand, Lamb, Hogg, Frémy, Soulié, Janin.* Columbia, SC: Camden House, 1998.

Lindlar, Heinrich. *Lübbes Strawinsky Lexikon.* Gladbach: Lübbe, 1982.

Locke, Ralph. *Musical Exoticism: Images and Reflections.* Cambridge: Cambridge University Press, 2009.

Loève-Veimars, François Adolphe. *Précis de l'histoire des tribunaux secrets dans le nord de l'Allemagne.* Paris: 1824.

Lovenjoul, Charles de. *Histoire des oeuvres de Théophile Gautier*, 2 vols. Paris: Charpentier, 1887.

Maas, Jeremy. "Victorian Fairy Painting." In Jeremy Maas, Pamela White Trimpe, Charlotte Gere, et al., *Victorian Fairy Painting.* Edited by Jane Martineau. London: Merrell Holberton, 1997, 10–21.

Macdonald, Hugh. *Berlioz.* London: Dent, 1982.

Maeterlinck, Maurice. *La Vie des abeilles*. Paris: Charpentier, 1928.

Maggi, Armando. *Satan's Rhetoric: A Study of Renaissance Demonology*. Chicago: University of Chicago Press, 2001.

Mah, Harold. "The Epistemology of the Sentence: Language, Civility, and Identity in France and Germany, from Diderot to Nietzsche." *Representations* 47, Special Issue, *National Cultures Before Nationalism* (Summer 1994): 64–84.

Mainzer, Joseph. *Chronique musicale de Paris: De M. Berlioz, de ses compositions, et de ses critiques musicales*. Paris: Au bureau de Panorame de l'Allemagne, 1838.

Malchow, H. L. *Gothic Images of Race in Nineteenth-Century Britain*. Stanford, CA: Stanford University Press, 1996.

Taming Cannibals: Race and the Victorians. Ithaca, NY: Cornell University Press, 2011.

Mannoni, Octave. *Psychologie de la colonization*. Paris: Editions du Seuil, 1950. Translated by Pamela Powelsland with a foreword by Philip Mason as *Prospero and Caliban: The Psychology of Colonization*. London: Methuen, 1956.

Marcellin, Jean-Baptiste-Geneviève. *L'Homme (homo), ou Essai zoologique sur le genre humain*. Paris: Rey et Gravier, 1827.

Maret, H. L. C. *Essai sur le panthéisme dans les sociétés modernes*. Paris: Sapia, 1840.

Marmontel, Jean-François. "Merveilleux." In *Supplément à l'Encyclopédie, ou Dictionnaire raisonné des sciences, des arts et des métiers*. Amsterdam: M. M. Rey, 1776–77, 906–08.

Mathew, Nicholas and Benjamin Walton, eds. *The Invention of Beethoven and Rossini: Historiography, Analysis, Criticism*. Cambridge: Cambridge University Press, 2013.

McClelland, Clive. *Ombra: Supernatural Music in the Eighteenth Century*. Plymouth, UK: Lexington Books, 2012.

"Ombra and Tempesta." In *The Oxford Handbook of Topic Theory*. Edited by Danuta Mirka. Oxford: Oxford University Press, 2014, 279–300.

Meglin, Joellen A. "Behind the Veil of Translucence: An Intertextual Reading of the 'Ballet Fantastique' in France, 1831–41." Part One: "Ancestors of the Sylphide in the *Conte fantastique*." *Dance Chronicle* 27/1 (2004): 67–129. Part Two: "The Body Dismembered, Diseased, and Damned: The *Conte brun*." *Dance Chronicle* 27/3 (2004): 313–71. Part Three: "Resurrection, Sensuality, and the Palpable Presence of the Past in Théophile Gautier's Fantastic." *Dance Chronicle* 28/1 (2005): 67–112.

Mercier, Louis-Sébastien. *Néologie, ou Vocabulaire de mots nouveaux, ou pris dans des acceptions nouvelles.* Paris: Moussard, 1801.

Meyer, E. R. "*Turquerie* and Eighteenth-Century Music." *Eighteenth-Century Studies* 7/4 (1974): 474–88.

Meyer, Lucy Rider. *Real Fairy Folks: Explorations in the World of Atoms.* Boston: D. Lothrop, 1887.

Meyer, Stephen. "Marschner's Villains, Monomania, and the Fantasy of Deviance." *Cambridge Opera Journal* 12/2 (2000): 109–34.

Michelet, Jules. *L'Insecte.* Paris: Hachette, 1867. Translated by W. H. Davenport Adams as *The Insect. With 140 Illustrations by Giacomelli.* London and New York: T. Nelson and Sons, 1875.

Micznik, Vera. "The Musico-Dramatic Narrative of Berlioz's *Lélio*." In *The Musical Voyager: Berlioz in Europe.* Edited by David Charlton and Katharine Ellis. Frankfurt am Main: Lang, 2007, 184–207.

Miller, Christopher L. *Blank Darkness: Africanist Discourse in French.* Chicago and London: University of Chicago Press, 1985.

Miller, Margaret. "Géricault's Paintings of the Insane." *Journal of the Warburg and Courtauld Institutes* 4 (1941): 151–63.

Mitchell, Robert. *Experimental Life: Vitalism in Romantic Science and Literature.* Baltimore, MD: Johns Hopkins University Press, 2013.

Mollien, Gaspard-Théodore. *Voyage dans l'intérieur de l'Afrique, aux sources de Sénégal et de la Gambie fait en 1818 par ordre du gouvernement français; avec carte et vues dessinés et gravées par Ambroise Tardieu,* 2 vols. Paris: Coucier, 1820. Translated by T. E. Bowdich as *Travels in the Interior of Africa to the Sources of the Senegal and Gambia, Performed by Command of the French Government in the Year 1818.* London: Henry Colburn & Co., 1820.

Monleón, José. *A Specter is Haunting Europe: A Sociohistorical Approach to the Fantastic.* Princeton, NJ: Princeton University Press, 1990.

Montegut, Émile. "Des Fées et de leur littérature en France." *Revue des deux mondes* (April 1862): 648–75.

Moyer, Birgitte. "Ombra and Fantasia in Late Eighteenth-Century Theory and Practice." In *Convention in Eighteenth- and Nineteenth-Century Music: Essays in Honor of Leonard G. Ratner.* Edited by W. J. Allanbrook, M. M. Levy, and W. P. Mahrt. Stuyvesant, NY: Pendragon Press, 1992, 195–223.

Negus, Kenneth. "E. T. A. Hoffmann's *Der goldene Topf*: Its Romantic Myth." *Germanic Review* 34 (1959): 262–75.

——. *E. T. A. Hoffmann's Other World: The Romantic Author and His "New Mythology."* Philadelphia: University of Pennsylvania Press, 1965.

Newark, Cormac. "Metaphors for Meyerbeer." *Journal of the Royal Musical Association* 127/1 (2002): 23–43.

Nichols, Roger. *Mendelssohn Remembered*. London: Faber and Faber, 1997.

Nodier, Charles. *Dictionnaire raisonné des onomatopées françoises*. Paris: Delangle Frères, 1808.

"Du Fantastique en littérature." *Revue de Paris* (October 1830): 205–26.

"Jean-François les bas-bleus." In *Oeuvres complètes de Charles Nodier*, vol. 11. Paris: Eugène Renduel, 1837, 139–66.

"Piranèse, Contes psychologiques, à propos de la monomanie reflective." In *Oeuvres complètes de Charles Nodier*, vol. 11. Paris: Eugène Renduel, 1837, 167–204.

Smarra, ou les démons de la nuit. 2nd ed. Brussels: Meline, 1832.

Trilby, ou le lutin d'Argail. Paris: Garnier, 1822.

Noel, Léger. "Mélodie." In *Clef de la langue et des sciences, ou nouvelle grammaire française encyclopédique*, vol. 3. Paris: Dutertre, 1861, 66–67.

Nye, Edward. *Literary and Linguistic Theories in Eighteenth-Century France: From Nuances to Impertinence*. Oxford Modern Languages and Literature Monographs. Oxford and New York: Oxford University Press, 2000.

Olsen, Lance. *Ellipse of Uncertainty: An Introduction to Postmodern Fantasy*. Westport, CT: Greenwood, 1987.

Packham, Catherine. *Eighteenth-Century Vitalism: Bodies, Culture, Politics*. New York: Palgrave Macmillan, 2012.

Palisca, Claude. *Humanism in Italian Renaissance Musical Thought*. New Haven, CT: Yale University Press, 1985.

Paracelsus (Philippus Aureolus Theophrastus Bombastus von Hohenheim). "A Book on Nymphs, Sylphs, Pygmies and Salamanders, and on the Other Spirits." In *Paracelsus: Four Treatises*. Edited by Henry E. Sigerist. Translated by C. Lilian Temkin, George Rosen, Gregory Zilb, and Henry E. Sigerist. Publications of the Institute of the History of Medicine, the Johns Hopkins University Second Series. Texts and Documents 1. Baltimore, MD: Johns Hopkins Press, 1941, 213–57.

Parodi, Elena Biggi. "'Les Danaïdes' di Salieri diretta da Gaspare Spontini (Parigi, 1817)." *Musicorum* (2004): 263–95.

Patterson, H. Temple. "New Light on Dark Genius: The Influence of Louis-Sébastien Mercier on the 'Contemplations' of Victor Hugo." *The Modern Language Review* 43/4 (October 1948): 471–82.

Pemble, John. *Shakespeare Goes to Paris: How the Bard Conquered France*. London and New York: Hambledon and London, 2005.

Perot, Nicolas. *Discours sur la musique à l'époque de Chateaubriand*. Paris: Presses universitaires de France, 2000.

Petrey, Sandy. *History in the Text: "Quatrevingt-Treize" and the French Revolution*. Purdue University Monographs in Romance Languages, vol. 3. Amsterdam: John Benjamins, 1980.

Prod-homme, Jacques Gabriel. "Beethoven en France." *Mercure de France* 194 (1927): 589–626.

"Les Débuts de Beethoven à Paris." *Revue musicale* 2 (1921): 13–19.

Raffenel, Anne. *Voyage dans l'Afrique Occidentale comprenant l'exploration du Sénégal, depuis Saint-Louis jusqu'à la Falémé*. Paris: Bertrand, 1846.

Ratner, Leonard G. *Classic Music: Expression, Form, and Style*. New York: Schirmer Books and London: Collier Macmillan, 1980.

Raz, Carmel. "'The Expressive Organ within Us': Ether, Ethereality, and Early Romantic Ideas about Music and the Nerves." *19th-Century Music* 38/2 (Fall 2014): 115–44.

Reedy, W. Jay. "Language, Counter-Revolution and the 'Two Cultures': Bonald's Traditionalist Scientism." *Journal of the History of Ideas* 44/4 (October–December 1983): 579–97.

Reeve, Katherine Kolb. "The Poetics of the Orchestra in the Writings of Hector Berlioz." PhD dissertation, Yale University, 1978.

Reicha, Anton (Antoine). *Traité de mélodie, abstraction faite de ses rapports avec l'harmonie; suivi d'un supplément sur l'art d'accompagner la mélodie par l'harmonie, lorsque la première doit être prédominante. Le tout appuyé sur les meilleurs modèles mélodiques*. Paris: Scherff, 1814. Translated by Peter M. Landey as *Treatise on Melody by Anton Reicha*. Harmonologia Series No. 10. Edited by Thomas Christensen. Hillsdale, NY: Pendragon Press, 2000.

Reill, Peter Hanns. *Vitalizing Nature in the Enlightenment*. Berkeley: University of California Press, 2005.

Renwick, John, ed. *Language and Rhetoric of the Revolution*. Edinburgh: Edinburgh University Press, 1990.

Richards, Annette. *The Free Fantasia and the Musical Picturesque*. Cambridge: Cambridge University Press, 2006.

Ricken, Ulrich. *Linguistics, Anthropology and Philosophy in the French Enlightenment*. Translated by Robert W. Norton. London and New York: Routledge, 1994.

Ritchey, Marianna. "Echoes of the Guillotine: Berlioz and the French Fantastic." *19th-Century Music* 34/2 (Fall 2010): 168–85.

"Echoes of the Guillotine: Berlioz, Gautier, and the French Fantastic." PhD dissertation, University of California at Los Angeles, 2010.

Robson, Joseph P. *The Monomaniac and Minor Poems*. Newcastle-on-Tyne: Robert Ward, 1848.

Rodgers, Stephen. *Form, Program, and Metaphor in the Music of Berlioz*. Cambridge: Cambridge University Press, 2009.

Roger, Philippe. "The French Revolution as Logomachy." In *Language and Rhetoric of the Revolution*, 4–17.

Rose, Michael. *Berlioz Remembered*. London: Faber and Faber, 2001.

Rosenberg, Daniel. "Louis-Sébastien Mercier's New Words." *Eighteenth-Century Studies* 36/3 (2003): 367–86.

Rosenfeld, Sophia. *A Revolution in Language: The Problem of Signs in Late Eighteenth-Century France*. Stanford, CA: Stanford University Press, 2001.

Roubaud, Pierre-Joseph-André. *Histoire générale de l'Asie, de l'Afrique et de l'Amérique*, 2 vols. Paris: Des Ventes de la Doué, 1770–75.

Rousseau, George S. *Nervous Acts: Essays on Literature, Culture, and Sensibility*. New York: Palgrave Macmillan, 2004.

Rushton, Julian. *Berlioz: Roméo et Juliette*. Cambridge Music Handbooks. Cambridge: Cambridge University Press, 1994.

The Music of Berlioz. Oxford: Oxford University Press, 2001.

The Musical Language of Berlioz. Cambridge: Cambridge University Press, 1983.

Russell, Jeffrey Burton. *Mephistopheles: The Devil in the Modern World*. Ithaca, NY: Cornell University Press, 1986.

Russell, Tilden A. "Minuet, Scherzando, and Scherzo: The Dance Movement in Transition, 1781–1825." PhD dissertation, University of North Carolina, Chapel Hill, 1983.

Said, Edward W. *Orientalism*. New York: Pantheon Books, 1978.

Saint-Gérand, Jacques-Philippe. *Les Grammaires françaises 1800–1914: Répertoire chronologique*. Paris: Institut national de recherche pédagogie, service d'histoire de l'éducation, 2000.

Saint-Saëns, Camille. "Discours lu à l'inauguration du Musée Berlioz, à la Côte-Saint-André." In *Le Livre d'or du centenaire d'Hector Berlioz*. Edited by L. Lantelme. Paris and Grenoble: G. Petit, 1907, 173–82.

Sand, George. *Contes d'une grand'mère*. Paris: Calmann-Lèvy, 1876.

Sandner, David. *Fantastic Literature: A Critical Reader*. Westport, CT: Praeger, 2004.

Sanyal, Debarati. *The Violence of Modernity: Baudelaire, Irony, and the Politics of Form*. Baltimore, MD: Johns Hopkins University Press, 2006.

Schellhous, Rosalie. "Fétis's 'tonality' as a Metaphysical Principle: Hypothesis for a New Science." *Music Theory Spectrum* 13/2 (Autumn 1991): 219–40.

Schickore, Jutta. *The Microscope and the Eye: A History of Reflections 1740-1870*. Chicago: University of Chicago Press, 2007.

Schiller, Friedrich. "The Gods of Greece." Translation by E. A. Bowring in *The Poems of Schiller*. 2nd ed., revised. London: George Bell and Sons, 1874, 74.

The Piccolomini. Part 1 of *Wallenstein*. Translated by Samuel Taylor Coleridge in *The Dramatic Works of Samuel Taylor Coleridge*. Edited by Derwent Coleridge. London: Edward Moxon, 1857, 163-316.

Schleiermacher, Friedrich, *On Religion. Speeches to Its Cultured Despisers*. Translated by Richard Crouter. Cambridge Texts in the History of Philosophy. Cambridge: Cambridge University Press, 1996.

Schlobin, Roger. *The Aesthetics of Fantasy Literature and Art*. Notre Dame, IN: University of Notre Dame Press, 1982.

Schrade, Leo. *Beethoven in France: The Growth of an Idea*. New Haven, CT: Yale University Press, 1942.

Scott, Walter. "On the Supernatural in Fictitious Compositions; and Particularly in the Works of Ernest Theodore William Hoffmann." *Foreign Quarterly Review* 1 (July 1827): 60-98.

Scribe, Eugène. "Une Monomanie." In *Oeuvres complètes*, vol. 10. Paris: P.H. Krabbe, 1854, 161-72.

Seaton, Douglass, ed. *The Mendelssohn Companion*. Westport, CT: Greenwood, 2001.

Seibold-Bultmann, Ursula. "Monster Soup: The Microscope and Victorian Fantasy." *Interdisciplinary Science Reviews*, 25/3 (2000): 211-29.

Seifert, Lewis C. *Fairy Tales, Sexuality, and Gender in France, 1690-1715*. Cambridge: Cambridge University Press, 1996.

"Marvelous Realities: Reading the *Merveilleux* in the Seventeenth-Century French Fairy Tale." In *Out of the Woods: The Origins of the Literary Fairy Tale in Italy and France*. Edited by Nancy L. Canepa. Detroit, MI: Wayne State University Press, 1997, 131-51.

Shamgar, Beth. "Program and Sonority: An Essay in Analysis of the 'Queen Mab' Scherzo from Berlioz's *Romeo and Juliet*." *College Music Symposium* 28 (1988): 40-52.

Siebers, Tobin. *The Romantic Fantastic*. Ithaca, NY: Cornell University Press, 1984.

Silver, Carol. *Strange and Secret Peoples: Fairies and Victorian Consciousness*. Oxford: Oxford University Press, 1999.

Singer, Barnett and John Langdon. *Cultured Force: Makers and Defenders of the French Colonial Empire*. Madison: University of Wisconsin Press, 2004.

Sjödén, Karl-Erik. *Swedenborg en France.* In *Acta Universitatis Stockholmiensis*, vol. 27. Stockholm, Sweden: Almqvist and Wiksell International, 1985.

Smith, Marian. *Ballet and Opera in the Age of Giselle.* Princeton, NJ, and Oxford: Princeton University Press, 2000.

Soullier, Charles Simon Pascal. "Fantastique." In *Nouveau dictionnaire de musique illustré.* Paris: E. Bazault, 1855, 124.

Spitzer, John. "Metaphors of the Orchestra – The Orchestra as Metaphor." *The Musical Quarterly* 80 (1996): 234–64.

Spurr, David. *The Rhetoric of Empire: Colonial Discourse in Journalism, Travel Writing, and Imperial Administration.* Durham, NC and London: Duke University Press, 1993.

Staël, Anne-Louis-Germaine de. *De L'Allemagne.* Translated by O. W. Wight as *Germany.* 2 vols. New York: H. W. Derby, 1861.

Stafford, Barbara. *Body Criticism: Imaging the Unseen in Enlightenment Art and Medicine.* Cambridge, MA: MIT Press, 1991.

Devices of Wonder: From the World in a Box to Images on a Screen. Los Angeles, CA: Getty Research Institute, 2001.

Staum, Martin S. *Labeling People: French Scholars on Society, Race and Empire, 1815–1848.* Montreal and Ithaca, NY: McGill-Queen's University Press, 2003.

Steiner, Christopher B. "Travel Engravings and the Construction of the Primitive." In *Prehistories of the Future: The Primitivist Project and the Culture of Modernism.* Edited by Elazar Barkan and Ronald Bush. Stanford, CA: Stanford University Press, 1995, 202–25.

Sterrenburg, Lee. "Mary Shelley's Monster: Politics and Psyche in Frankenstein." In *The Endurance of Frankenstein.* Edited by G. Levine and U. C. Knoepflmacher, 1979, 143–71.

Stewart, Susan. *On Longing: Narratives of the Miniature, the Gigantic, the Souvenir, the Collection.* Baltimore, MD: Johns Hopkins University Press, 1984.

Stoeber, Louis-Adolphe. *Idées sur les rapports de Dieu à la nature et spécialement sur la révélation de Dieu dans la nature.* Strasbourg: Dannbach, 1834.

Stolzenberg, Daniel. *Egyptian Oedipus: Athanasius Kircher and the Secrets of Antiquity.* Chicago and London: University of Chicago Press, 2013.

Stravinsky, Igor and Robert Craft. *Conversations with Igor Stravinsky.* New York: Doubleday, 1959.

Dialogues. Berkeley and Los Angeles: University of California Press, 1982.

Sueur-Hermel, Valérie. *Fantastique!: L'estampe visionnaire de Goya à Redon.* Paris: Bibliothèque Nationale de France, 2015.

Swedenborg, Emanuel. *Heaven and Its Wonders and Hell Drawn from Things Heard and Seen.* Translated by George F. Dole. West Chester, PA: Swedenborg Foundation, 2000.

Sykes, Ingrid J. "Le corps sonore: Music and the Auditory Body in France 1780–1830." In Kennaway, *Music and the Nerves, 1700–1900.* Edited by James Kennaway. 72–97.

Taruskin, Richard. *Stravinsky and the Russian Traditions: A Biography of the Works through "Mavra."* 2 vols. Berkeley and Los Angeles: University of California Press, 1996.

Taylor, Benedict. "Musical History and Self-Consciousness in Mendelssohn's Octet, Op. 20." *19th-Century Music* 32/2 (2008): 131–59.

Teichmann, Elizabeth. *La Fortune d'Hoffmann en France.* Genève: E. Droz, 1961.

Thomas, Downing A. *Music and the Origins of Language: Theories from the Enlightenment.* Cambridge: Cambridge University Press, 1995.

Thormählen, Wiebke. "Physical Distortion, Emotion and Subjectivity: Musical Virtuosity and Body Anxiety." In *Music and the Nerves, 1700–1900,* 191–215.

Tilby, Michael. "New Words or Old? Balzac, Neologism, and Self-Conscious Narrative Discourse." *The Modern Language Review* 104/4 (October 2009): 976–91.

———. "Neologism: A Linguistic and Literary Obsession in Early Nineteenth-Century France." *The Modern Language Review* 104/3 (July 2009): 676–95.

Todd, Larry R. *Mendelssohn: A Life in Music.* Oxford and New York: Oxford University Press, 2003.

———, ed. *Mendelssohn and His World.* Princeton, NJ: Princeton University Press, 1991.

———. *Mendelssohn, The Hebrides and Other Overtures: A Midsummer Night's Dream, Calm Sea and Prosperous Voyage, The Hebrides (Fingal's Cave).* Cambridge: Cambridge University Press, 1993.

———. "On the Visual in Mendelssohn's Music." In *Cari amici: Festschrift 25 Jahre Carus-Verlag.* Edited by Barbara Mohn and Hans Ryschawy. Stuttgart: Carus-Verlag, 1997, 115–24.

Todorov, Tzvetan. *The Fantastic: A Structuralist Approach to a Literary Genre.* Translated by Richard Howard. Cleveland, OH: Case Western Reserve University Press, 1973.

Tomlinson, Gary. *Music and Renaissance Magic: Toward a Historiography of Others*. Chicago: University of Chicago Press, 1993.

Trippett, David. *Wagner's Melodies: Aesthetics and Materialism in German Musical Identity*. Cambridge: Cambridge University Press, 2013.

Trower, Shelley. *Senses of Vibration: A History of the Pleasure and Pain of Sound*. London and New York: Continuum, 2012.

Turner, Alice K. *The History of Hell*. New York: Harcourt Brace, 1993.

Van Rij, Inge. *The Other Worlds of Hector Berlioz: Travels with the Orchestra*. Cambridge: Cambridge University Press, 2015.

Van Zuylen, Marina. *Monomania: The Flight from Everyday Life in Literature and Art*. Ithaca, NY and London: Cornell University Press, 2005.

Virey, Julien-Joseph. *Histoire naturelle du genre humain*. 3 vols. Paris: Couchard, 1824.

Walckenaer, M. Le Baron. *Aptères*. In *Histoire naturelle des insects*, vol. 4. Paris: Librairie Encyclopédique de Roret, 1837.

Wallace, Robin. "French Beethoven Criticism." In *Beethoven's Critics: Aesthetic Dilemmas and Resolutions during the Composer's Lifetime*. Cambridge: Cambridge University Press, 1986, 105–25.

Warner, Marina. *Fantastic Metamorphoses, Other Worlds: Ways of Telling the Self*. New York: Oxford University Press, 2002.

No Go the Bogeyman: Scaring, Lulling, and Making Mock. New York: Farrar, Straus, and Giroux, 1999.

Watkins, Holly. *Metaphors of Depth in German Musical Thought from E. T. A. Hoffmann to Arnold Schoenberg*. Cambridge: Cambridge University Press, 2011.

Watts, Pauline. *Music: The Medium of the Metaphysical in E. T. A. Hoffmann*. Amsterdam: Rodopi, 1972.

Webber, Andrew J. *The Doppelgänger: Double Visions in German Literature*. Oxford: Oxford University Press, 2003.

Werner, Marcia. *Pre-Raphaelite Painting and Nineteenth-Century Realism*. Cambridge: Cambridge University Press, 2005.

White, Eric Walter. *Stravinsky: The Composer and His Works*. Berkeley and Los Angeles: University of California Press, 1966.

Whyte, Peter. "Théophile Gautier, poète-courtisan" In *Art and Literature of the Second Empire / Les Arts et la littérature sous le Second Empire*. Edited by David Baguley. Durham, NC: University of Durham, 2003, 129–47.

Wilkinson, Lynn R. *The Dream of an Absolute Language: Emanuel Swedenborg and French Literary Culture*. Albany: State University of New York Press, 1996.

Williams, Elizabeth. *The Physical and the Moral: Anthropology, Physiology, and Philosophical Medicine in France 1750–1850*. Cambridge: Cambridge University Press, 1994.

Wilson, Catherine. *The Invisible World: Early Modern Philosophy and the Invention of the Microscope*. Studies in Intellectual History and the History of Philosophy. Princeton, NJ: Princeton University Press, 1995.

Winter, Allison. *Mesmerized: Powers of Mind in Victorian Britain*. Chicago and London: University of Chicago Press.

Winter, Marian Hannah. *Théâtre du merveilleux*. Paris: Olivier Perrin, 1962. Translated as *The Theatre of Marvels*. New York: Benjamin Bloom, 1964.

Wotton, Tom S. "'Infernal Language': A Berlioz Hoax." *The Musical Times and Singing-Class Circular* (March 1937): 209–10.

Wurth, Keine. *Musically Sublime: Indeterminacy, Infinity, Irresolvability*. New York: Fordham University Press, 2009.

Yates, Frances. *Giordano Bruno and the Hermetic Tradition*. Chicago: University of Chicago Press, 1964.

Index

Abrams, M. H., 28, 37
Adam, Adolphe, 111
   Giselle ou les Wilis, ballet fantastique en deux actes, 251–52, 261
aeolian harp, 89, 90, 100–03, 108, 127, 172, 298
Africa
   and Berlioz's made-up languages, 233–34
   and comparative philology, 230–33
   in the *conte fantastique*, 234–37
   and demonic soundscapes, 234–37
   and demonism, 224–25
   and French imperialism, 222–24
   in French travelogues, 225–28, 232–33
   and racial theory, 228–29
   and "racialized" Gothic, 229–30
Allanbrook, W. J., 203
Arbousset, Thomas
   Relation d'un voyage d'exploration au nord-est de la colonie de Cape de Bonne-Espérance, 227–28, 232, 233, 248
Ascher, Joseph
   Les Diablotins, polka fantastique, 311–12
Aubéry Du Boulley, Prudent-Louis
   Grammaire musicale, 153–54

bacchanale
   as emblem of Otherness, 247–50
   as Gothic musical form, 250
   origins and evolution in travel writing, 246–50
   see also entries under individual composers
Bacchus, 206, 246, 250, 264
Balzac, Honoré de, 15, 33, 148
   "Les Amours de deux bêtes," 291–92
   La Peau de chagrin, 74–75
Barzun, Jacques, 134
Baudelaire, Charles, 15, 32
Bazzini
   Scherzo fantastique, 307–08, 309
Beethoven, Ludwig van, 39, 41, 62
   in the *conte fantastique*, 118–20, 122
   and "energized" musical grammar, 157–58, 163, 167, 186
   Fifth Symphony, 91–92
   in French reception, 104
   as "German Berlioz," 120
   and *idée fixe*, 120
   and imitation, 112
   as model for Berlioz, 123
   and nature music, 118–19, 126, 127
   as "Nouveau Colomb," 104

Pastoral Symphony
   Berlioz's defense of, 114–16
   French denigration of, 114
   and sublime, 97
   symphonic scherzi, 276, 283–84
Beham, Sebald
   "The Nose Dance at Fool's Town," 246
Bellman, Jonathan, 205
Berger, Christian, 5
Berlioz, Hector
   on conducting and electricity, 128–29
   on the *fantastique gracieux*, 201–02, 270, 282, 303–04
   on the *fantastique terrible*
     as conflation of topical modes, 208
     in Gluck's *Alceste*, 202–04
     in Gluck's *Iphigénie en Tauride*, 204–06
     in Meyerbeer's *Robert le diable*, 239–40
     in the Orchestration Treatise, 206–07
     as opposite of *fantastique gracieux*, 201–02
     in Spontini, 206–07, 246
     in Weber, 201–02
   as French Beethoven, 120
   "Le Harpiste ambulant," 302–04, 306
   on E. T. A. Hoffmann, 41
   on melodic grammar, *see* grammar, in Berlioz's critical writing
   on music and the nerves, 103–08, 116
   on musical imitation, 114–16, 134
   as "Nouveau Faust," 104
   and the *orchestre idéal*, 97, 104
   as Prospero, 105
   and uncategorizability, 134, 136–37
   and Victor Hugo, 137, 139–40
Berlioz Hector (works)
   Benvenuto Cellini, 44, 131, 184, 285
   La Damnation de Faust, 5
     and Berlioz's made-up language, 195–200
     and the dark pastoral mode, 263
     and melodic grammar, *see* grammar, in Berlioz's music
     Méphistophélès's musical sign, 213–14, 258
     Pandemonium, 214–16
   Les Francs-juges
     cavern scene, 208–09
     Overture, 209–13, 236, 243
   Harold en Italie, 5, 285
     brigands' music, 217–18
     and the *fantastique terrible*, 202, 220
     and melodic grammar, *see* grammar, in Berlioz's music

Berlioz Hector (works) (cont.)
   ombra music, 218–19
   and travel writing, 220–22
  Herminie, 65
  Huit scènes de Faust, 165
  Messe des morts, 5, 285
   and melodic grammar, *see* grammar, in Berlioz's music
  La Mort de Cléopâtre, 193
  La Mort d'Orphée, 102
  Le Retour à la vie, 88, 267, 291, 304
   Beethovenian references in, 97
   "Chant de bonheur," 97–100, 170–71, 172
   "Choeur d'ombres"
    and Berlioz's made-up language, 191–93
    connection to *La Mort de Cléopâtre*, 193–95
   "Fantaisie sur la tempête de Shakespeare," 104–8
   French reception of, 109–14
   in *contes fantastiques*, 117–31
   gestation of, 92–94
   "La Harpe éolienne," 100–03, 172
   and hesitation, 113–14
   idée fixe in, 108
   and imitation-expression binary, 111–17
   and melodic grammar, *see* grammar, in Berlioz's music
   and nature orchestra, 119, 124, 126, 127–29
   orchestration, 97, 109–11
   "Le Pêcheur," 94–97
   and vitalism, 126–31
  Neuf mélodies, 165
   "Élégie en prose," 171–73
  Les Nuits d'été, 304–05
  La Reine Mab scherzo, 267, 308, 322
   and fairy perception, 303–4
   and insect sound, 289–90
   and miniaturism, 287–91
   reception of, 269–70, 284–86, 291–92
   relationship with Beethoven's scherzi, 283–84
   relationship with Mendelssohn's fairy music, 283
   as *scherzo fantastique*, 270, 307
  Roméo et Juliette, 5, 170–71, 187
  Symphonie fantastique
   and autobiography, 79–81, 83–88
   in Berlioz's letters, 57–62
   French reception of, 41–43, 174–76
   and grotesque, 183–84
   and hell, 184, 236
   and E. T. A. Hoffmann's tales, 54–57
   idée fixe, 54–57, 59, 60, 62, 65, 88, 94, 108
   and melodic grammar, *see* grammar, in Berlioz's music
   and the *monde fantastique*, 57, 61, 94, 98
   and monomania, 57, 65–72, 85–88
   and *Sehnsucht*, 53, 57, 62–65
   and *vague des passions*, 55–57, 62–63, 88
  Les Troyens
   and Berlioz's made-up language, 200–1
  "Waverly" Overture, 165

Bernard, Jean Fréderic
  Histoire générale des cérémonies, moeurs, et coûtumes religieuses de tous les peuples du monde, 247
Blakemore, Steven, 149
Blanc, Adolphe
  La Farfalla, scherzetto fantastique, 316–18
Blaze (de Bury), Ange-Henri
  "De L'École fantastique et de M. Berlioz," 44–46, 131–35, 177–78, 184
Bloom, Peter, 93
Boito, Arrigo
  Mefistofele, 256–58
   and Berliozian effects, 258
   and the dark pastoral mode, 264–65
   and gibberish, 257, 265
  Ridda e fuga infernale, 256, 261
Bonald, Louis Gabriel Ambroise de, 146–47, 178
Bory de Saint-Vincent, Jean-Baptiste-Maximilien, 229
Boulanger, Louis, 16
Bown, Nicola, 297
Brantlinger, Patrick, 10
Bruegel, Pieter (the Elder)
  "The Wedding Dance," 246
Brunot, Ferdinand, 141
Bry, Theodor de
  "The Manner of Serving Food and Drink, and the Dance of the Savages Before Their King," 247
Buch, David J., 7
  on fairy representation, 271
  on the musical marvelous, 36
  on the terrifying style, 203–4
Buchez, Philippe-Joseph-Benjamin, 141
Budgen, L. M. (Acheta domestica)
  Episodes of Insect Life, 298–300
Burwick, Frederick, 73
Byron, Lord, 63, 184, 220, 221

Cabanis, Pierre-Jean-George, 66
Cailleux, Léon, 22–23
Cairns, David, 165
Callot, Jacques, 21, 33
  The Temptation of St. Anthony, 161–63, 183
Camper, Petrus
  on the "facial angle," 228
Castex, Pierre Georges, 3
Castil-Blaze (François-Henri-Joseph Blaze), 44, 239, 240
Charlton, David, 38, 39
Chateaubriand, François Auguste René de, 37, 63, 68
Cherubini, Luigi, 165, 182
  bacchanale from *Ali-baba*, 250
Clément, François, 136
Coleman, Deirdre, 293
Collin de Plancy, Jacques Albin Simon
  Dictionnaire infernal, 197, 272
Condillac, Étienne Bonnot de, 143, 160
Conrad, Joseph, 266
Constant, Benjamin, 63, 72

Index

Conte fantastique
  and Berliozian autobiography, 302
  early French examples of, 1–3
  and fantastic listening, 38–40, 45–46, 82, 90–92, 121, 123, 305–06
  featuring Beethoven, 118–20
  featuring Berlioz, 117–31, 234–36
  and imperialism, 127–28, 234–37
  and popular science, 294–95, 300–02, 304–05
  and psychiatric discourse, 53–55, 74, 86
  as title for French translations of E. T. A. Hoffmann's tales, 17
  as vehicle for French music criticism, 117–31
  and vitalism, 123–27
  see also tales listed under individual authors
Cornwell, Neil, 3, 34
Cosso, Laura, 5
Cousin, Victor, 37, 133
Curtin, Philip D., 230
Cuvier, Georges, 228–29, 234, 236

Dante Alighieri, 225
Dard, Jean
  Dictionnaire français-wolof et français-bambara, 232–33
Daubenton, Louis-Jean-Marie, 228
Delacroix, Eugène, 16, 33
De Quincey, Thomas, 82
Diderot, Denis, 142, 224
Dolan, Emily, 89, 90
Domergue, François-Urbain, 142–43, 161
Dömling, Wolfgang, 5
D'Ortigue, Joseph
  on the "Choeur d'ombres," 193
  on the *Symphonie fantastique*, 16, 43, 112–13, 179
  Du Théâtre Italien et de son influence sur le goût musical françois, 185–87
Dowbiggin, Ian, 66
Du Boys, Albert, 58, 59, 95
Dumas, Alexandre, 15
  "La Femme au collier de velours," 30
  Henri III et sa cour, 148
Durand, Jean-Baptiste-Léonard
  "The Cullemgee of the Negroes," 247–48
Duras, Claire de
  Édouard, 73

Ellis, Katharine, 116, 117
entomology, 295–300
Esquirol, Jean-Etienne-Dominique, 66–71

fairies
  and artistic inspiration, 300–06
  and entomology, 295–300
  and the marvelous, 271–72
  nineteenth-century reinvention of, 272–76
  in Paracelsus, 271
  on the seventeenth-century stage, 271, 276
fantastic (the)
  and aurality (as understudied), 4–5
  in contemporary Berlioz studies, 5–6
  Doppelgänger in, 81–88

fantastique gracieux, 10, see also fairies and *scherzo fantastique*
fantastique terrible, 10, 201, 202, 208, 213, 237, 240, 250, 266, see also Berlioz, Hector, on the *fantastique terrible*
French descriptions and definitions of, 14–25, 40–49
French emergence of, 1–3, 6–7
and Gothic, 30–31, 229–30, 236
and grotesque, 24, 33, 39, 138, 140, 161–63, 183–84
and hieroglyphs, 39, 46, 92, 102, 134
and idealist philosophy, 25–30
and imperialism, 6, 10, 32, 221, 222–37
as "intermediate world," 12, 15, 108
and natural sound, 38–40, 89–108, 117–31, 278–92, 306–25
and Neoplatonism, 28–29
and the orchestra/orchestration, 117–31, 201–08, 209–19, 238–61, 282–91
and pathology, 84–87
  in fantastic narratives, 53–62
  in French medical discourse, see monomania
  and *Sehnsucht*, 62–65
politics of, 30–33
resistance to, 44–49, 131–35
and revolution, 15, 21, 22, 24, 31, 33, 46, 139, 141–49
and science
  entomology, see separate entry
  grammatical sciences, see grammar
  microscopy, see microscope
  philology, 191–201, 230–34
  psychiatry, see monomania
  racial theory, 228–29, see also bacchanale
studies of, 3–4
and the *surnaturel vrai*, 37, 134
versus marvelous, 6, 11, 23, 34, 271, 275
and vitalism, 126–31, 132
Ferrand, Humbert, 41, 58, 59, 60, 63, 71, 208, 209
Ferrière, Théophile
  "Brand-Sachs," 130, 164–65
Fétis, François
  "De la mélodie," 154
  definition of fantastic music, 112
  on nature music, 133–34
  on *Oberon*, 282
  on the Pastoral Symphony, 114
  on *Le Retour à la vie*, 110–12
  on *Robert le diable*, 238
  on the *Symphonie fantastique*, 42–43, 136, 174–75
Fichte, Johann Gottlieb, 33, 37, 133, 160
Figuier, Louis
  Les Insectes, 297–98, 299
  Les Races humaines, 249
Fink, Gottfried Wilhelm, 269
Foucault, Michel, 31, 224

Gautier, Théophile, 11, 15, 32
  "La Cafetière," 1–2, 40
  on *La Damnation de Faust*, 186, 198–200

Gautier, Théophile (cont.)
   on the fantastic, 20
   "La Morte amoureuse," 30
Geoffroy Saint-Hilaire, Etienne, 228, 234, 236
Georget, Etienne-Jean, 71
Géricault, Théodore, 16, 69–70
Girardin, Saint-Marc, 18
Girault-Duvivier, Pierre
   Grammaire des grammaires, 147–48, 150, 152, 155, 179, 184
Glanvill, Joseph, 301
glass harmonica, 89, 91, 104–05, 127
   and *pédale céleste*, 104
Gluck, Christoph Willibald
   Alceste, 156, 202–04
   Iphigénie en Tauride, 156, 204–6, 207
   Orphée, 159, 204
Gobineau, Arthur (Comte de), 231
Goethe, Johann Wolfgang von, 20, 63, 161, 183
   Faust, 102, 256, 268, 278–92, 299
   "Der Fischer," 95–97
Goldstein, Jan, 66
Gouk, Penelope, 7, 34
Gounod, Charles, 237
   Faust
      bacchanalian expansions for German productions, 254
      "Chant bacchique," 252–55
      dances added for premiere at the Opéra, 254–55
      and the dark pastoral mode, 263–64
grammar
   in Berlioz's critical writing
      on Beethoven, 156–58
      on fantasy, 163–64
      on German inversions, 160–61
      on Gluck, 156
      in response to Fétis, 155–56
      on revolution, 164–65
      on rhythmic innovations, 159
      on J. Strauss, 158–59
   in Berlioz's music
      Benvenuto Cellini, 184
      La Damnation de Faust, 187
      Harold en Italie, 184, 185
      Huit scènes de Faust, 165
      Messe des morts, 185
      Neuf mélodies, 165
         "Élégie en prose," 171–73
      Le Retour à la vie, 170–71
      Roméo et Juliette, 187
      Symphonie fantastique, 166–70
      "Waverly" Overture, 165
   in Berlioz's reception, 174, 184–88
      Épisode de la vie d'un grammairien, 179–81
   in French music tutors, 149–55
   in literary culture
      grammairien-patriote, 142
      grammairien-philosophe, 142
      and rationalist paradigm, 147, 154
      Restoration policing of, 146–49
      and revolution, 141–46
      and sensationalist epistemology, 143

Habeneck, François, 235, 236
Haydn, Joseph, 276
Hegel, Georg Wilhelm Friedrich, 160
Heine, Heinrich, 128, 284, 285
hell
   and French travel writing, 225–27
   and imperialism, 222–25
   musical, *see* bacchanale
   and philology, 230–34
Heller, Stephen, 284, 291
   Scherzo fantastique, 307
Hensel, Sebastian, 279
Herbert, Christopher, 262
Herder, Gottfried, 27, 44, 132, 160
Hoffmann, E. T. A.
   "A New Year's Eve Adventure," 30
   "Automata," 54, 63–64, 73, 89–90
   on Beethoven, 39, 91–92, 163
   "Casual Reflections on the Appearance of This Journal," 120–23
   French reception of, 17–21, 55–56
   "The Golden Pot," 18–19, 29, 38, 82, 124–25, 134–35
   and Gothic, 30
   on the grotesque, 32, 161–63
   Kater Murr, 82, 90
   Kreisleriana, 38–40, 45–46, 82, 90–92, 121, 123, 305–6
   "Master Flea," 294–95, 304–5
   "The Mines of Falun," 30, 53
   and monomania, 73–74
   "Princess Brambilla," 53
   "The Sandman," 30, 81
   and *Sehnsucht*, 53–54, 64–65, 81–83
   The Serapion Brethren, 74
   and the *surnaturel vrai*, 20
Hogg, James, 83
Hübener, Andrea, 5
Hugo, Victor
   on the grotesque, 162–63
   Hernani, 137, 149
   Notre-Dame de Paris, 74
   Preface to *Cromwell*, 21, 137–39, 149, 161, 178, 183
   "Le Rhin," 128

Jackson, Rosemary, 32, 34
Janin, Jules, 15
   La Confession, 76, 83
   "Le Dîner de Beethoven," 118–20, 122
   on the fantastic, 22
   "Hoffman [sic]," 120–23
   "Kreyssler," 2, 40
   on *La Reine Mab*, 289–91
   on the *Symphonie fantastique*, 43, 112
Jean Paul, *see* Richter, Jean Paul
Johnson, James H., 114

Kant, Immanuel, 26, 44, 81, 132
Kastner, George
   Grammaire musicale, 154, 155
Katterfelto, Gustavus (Dr. Caterpillar), 293–94
Kayser, Wolfgang, 3

Kennaway, James, 132
Kircher, Anathasius, 199
Kleinmichel, Richard
   Fée Mab, scherzo, 315
Kolb, Katherine, 12
Kolben, Peter
   The Present State of the Cape of Good Hope, 247
Krummacher, Friedrich, 278

La Harpe, Jean-François, 15, 146
Lamb, Charles, 82–83
Larousse, Pierre, 28
   on the fantastic, 23–24, 47–49, 188
Le Carpentier, Adolphe
   La Ronde des farfadets, danse fantastique, 315
Le Dhuy, Adolphe
   Grammaire musicale, 154
Legouvé, Ernest, 80
Lenau, Nikolaus
   Faust, 258
Lesne, Mlle
   Grammaire musicale, 152–53, 155, 179
Lewis, Matthew, 30, 229
Leyden, Lucas van
   "The Dance Around the Golden Calf," 246
Liszt, Franz, 237
   Faust Symphony, 258
   and melodic grammar, 164–65
   "Der Tanz in der Dorfschenke," 258–61, 262
   and vitalism, 129–30
Lobe, Johann Christian, 268
Locke, Ralph P., 205, 266
Loève-Veimars, François Adolphe, 17, 208

Mab, Frédéric
   "Les Cignes chantent en mourant," 123–27
Maeterlinck, Maurice
   La Vie des abeilles, 320–21, 322
Mah, Harold, 160
Maine de Biran, François-Pierre-Gonthier, 72, 146
Mainzer, Joseph
   "Berlioz," in the *Chronique musicale*, 47, 136, 176, 185
Maistre, Joseph de, 133, 146
Malchow, H. L., 10, 32, 224, 229–30, 262
marvelous
   and *contes de fées*, 35
   as magical ontology, 34
   and musical topics, 36–37, 271
   "third age" of, 7, 37
   versus fantastic, 6, 11, 23, 34, 271, 275
McClelland, Clive, 203
Mendelssohn, Felix
   on Berlioz's temperament, 79–80
   A Midsummer Night's Dream Overture, 269, 307, 322
     and *fantastique* rhetoric, 268–69
     French reception of, 282–83
     and insect sound, 279–81
     and miniaturism, 281
     and Weber's *Oberon*, 281–82
   A Midsummer Night's Dream, Incidental Music, 267
   Octet, Op. 20
     and insect sound, 278–79, 280, 299
     and scherzo tradition, 276–78
Mendelssohn Hensel, Fanny, 268, 278, 279
Mercier, Louis-Sébastien, 144–46, 161
   Mon Dictionnaire, 146
   Néologie, 144–45
   Traité sur les inversions, 145, 169
Mérimée, Prosper, 15
   "La Vénus d'Ille," 30
Méry, Joseph
   "La Fontaine d'ivoire," 127–28, 234–37
Meyerbeer, Giacomo
   Robert le diable, 238, 291
     "Bacchanale des nonnes," 236, 238, 243–46
     and *fantastique* reception, 238–40
     and origins of Gothic bacchanale, 250
     Overture, 243
     "Valse infernale," 238, 240–43
Mezzofanti, Giuseppe Caspar, 199, 201
Michelet, Jules
   L'Insecte, 295–97
microscope
   and gender, 296
   and limitations of human perception, 301–02
   nineteenth-century popularization of, 292–93
   solar, 293–95
     description of, 293
     in E. T. A. Hoffmann's fiction, 294–95
     in popular entertainments, 293–94
Moke, Camille, 92–93
Molière (Jean-Baptiste Poquelin), 198, 201
Mollien, Gaspard Théodore
   Voyages dans l'intérieur de l'Afrique, 225–27, 232, 233, 234, 248, 261
Monleón, José, 31–32, 208
monomania
   and *consolations religieuses*, 69–71
   decline of diagnosis, 78–79
   in fiction, 72–81
   first identification of, 65–67
   and genius, 72–81
   and *idée fixe*, 66–67
   monomanie érotique, 67–71
   monomanie homicide, 71–72
   monomanie reflective, 84–87, 100, 104
Montegut, Émile, 272
Moore, Thomas, 94, 172
Moyer, Birgitte, 203
Mozart, Wolfgang Amadeus
   Don Giovanni, 204, 209
Müller, Carl, 285
Musset, Alfred de
   La Confession d'un enfant du siècle, 76–77, 83

Napoleon Bonaparte, 32, 146, 223
Nerval, Gérard de, 15
nerves
   and "material" musical effects, 91, 115–16, 129, 132–33, 157

nerves (cont.)
    and pathology, 56–61, 87, 108, 120, 126, 303
    and supernatural access, 88, 103, 104, 120, 130
    see also vitalism
Nodier, Charles, 12, 13, 32, 33, 148
    "Du Fantastique en littérature," 14–15, 21–22
    "Jean-François les bas-bleus," 86–87, 90, 100, 120
    "Piranèse, contes psychologiques," 84–87
    Trilby, ou le lutin d'Argail, 300

ombra music
    in the *conte fantastique*, 236
    as eighteenth-century topic, 203, 209, 210, 214, 252
    link to exoticism, 205, 211–13, 214, 215, 218–19, 239, 240–43, 252
    nineteenth-century extension of, 204, 208, 250, 266
    and "terrifying style," 203, 209

Palisca, Claude, 7
Paracelsus (Philippus Aureolus Theophrastus Bombastus von Hohenheim), 132, 304
Paton, Sir Joseph Noel
    The Quarrel of Oberon and Titania, 273–75, 279, 281
Pinel, Philippe, 66, 69, 71
Piranesi, Giovanni Battista, 85
Pott, August Friedrich, 230–31
Prévost, Antoine François
    Histoire générale des voyages, 247

race
    and the literary Gothic, 229–30
    and the musical Gothic, 238–67
    theories of, 228–29, 261–62
Raff, Joachim
    Scherzo fantastique, 307
Raffenel, Anne
    Voyage dans l'Afrique Occidentale, 228, 248
Ratner, Leonard, 203
Raz, Carmel, 103
Reicha, Anton (Antoine)
    Traité de mélodie, 150–52, 153, 154, 155, 165–84
Rellstab, Ludwig, 269
Renan, Ernest, 231
Renard, Maurice
    Un Homme chez les microbes: scherzo, 324–25
Richter, Jean Paul, 20, 48, 63, 64, 82, 161, 183
Ricken, Ulrich, 149
Rimsky-Korsakov, Nikolai, 320, 321, 323
    Flight of the Bumblebee, 322
Ritchey, Marianna, 5
Rivarol, Antoine de, 146
Rocher, Edouard, 58, 61, 71
Roger-Milès, Léon
    "Pendant qu'elle rêve," 324
Rosen, Charles, 167
Rossini, Gioachino, 212
    Semiramide, 237

Roubaud, Pierre-Joseph-André
    Histoire générale de l'Asie, de l'Afrique et de l'Amérique, 248
Rousseau, Jean-Jacques, 83
Roux, Prosper-Charles, 141
Rushton, Julian, 65, 165, 172, 181, 183, 217
Ruskin, John, 272, 273
Russell, Tilden A., 277

Said, Edward, 231
Saint-Chéron, Alexandre, 78, 81, 83
Saint-Saëns, Camille
    on Berlioz's orchestration, 276
    Samson et Dalila, 250
Sand, George, 15, 33
    "Ce que disent les fleurs," 300
    "La Fée aux gros yeux," 300–02
    "Le Manteau rouge," 292
Sandner, David, 3
Schellhous, Rosalie, 133
Schelling, Friedrich, 26, 126, 133
scherzo fantastique
    and Berlioz, 283–92
    as fairy form, 306–10
    and fairy round (*ronde fantastique*), 312
    and featherlight ending, 312–13
    and insect scherzi
        bee pieces, 318–23
        butterfly pieces, 316–18
        in Stravinsky, 320–23
        title-page imagery, 315–16
    and Mendelssohn, 276–82
    nineteenth-century proliferation of, 306–23
    and *scherzando* marking, 310–11
    twentieth-century extensions of, 323–25
    see also entries under individual composers
Schiffmacher, Joseph
    Les Abeilles, scherzo fantastique, 318–19
Schiller, Friedrich, 272
Schindelmeisser, Louis
    bacchanale for Gounod's *Faust*, 254
Schlegel, Friedrich, 30, 33, 34, 37, 38, 96, 133
    on the fantastic, 25–28
    and the grotesque, 161, 183
    and hieroglyphs, 28, 100
    and philology, 230
    on *Sehnsucht*, 63, 64, 91
Schleiermacher, Friedrich, 26, 27, 64, 81, 83, 85, 100
Schlesinger, Maurice, 117, 118, 164, 234
Schlobin, Roger, 3
Schubring, Julius, 279
Schumann, Robert
    review of the *Symphonie fantastique*, 169
Scott, Walter, 55–56, 57, 302, 314
Scribe, Eugène
    Une Monomanie, 75
Seifert, Lewis C., 35
Seyfried, Ignaz Xaver
    Oberon, Roi des elfes, 310
Shakespeare, William, 58, 97, 104, 105, 191, 195, 268, 269, 273, 281, 283, 285, 287–89, 292, 297, 315

Index

Shelley, Mary, 229–30
Silver, Carol, 273
Simeoni, Gabriello
  "Adoration of the Golden Calf," 246
Smith, Marian, 251
Smithson, Harriet, 42, 56, 58–62, 92–93, 103, 104, 172
Soullié, Charles, 12
Spinoza, Baruch, 26–27, 33, 44, 132
Spitzer, John, 128
Spontini, Gaspare
  Les Danaïdes, 206–7, 250
  Nurmahal, oder das Rosenfest von Caschmir, 206
Staats, Leo, 322
Staël, Anne-Louise-Germaine de, 21
  De L'Allemagne, 37, 95–97, 133
Stafford, Barbara, 3
Steiner, Christopher B., 246–48, 261
Stendhal (Marie-Henri Beyle), 148
Stéphen de La Madelaine, Nicolas, 56
Sterrenburg, Lee, 262
Stewart, Susan, 274–75, 307
Stoker, Bram, 229
Stravinsky, Igor
  Scherzo fantastique, 320–23
Swedenborg, Emanuel, 197–98
Sykes, Ingrid J., 150

Taruskin, Richard, 321, 323
Todd, R. Larry, 278
Todorov, Tzvetan, 3, 19, 24, 34, 140
Tomlinson, Gary, 7, 28
Trippett, David, 187–88

Van Rij, Inge, 12, 140
Viardot, Pauline, 64
Virey, Julien-Joseph, 229, 231
vitalism, 123–31, *see also* nerves

Wagner, Richard, 49, 187–88
Warner, Marina, 3, 81
Weber, Carl Maria von
  Der Freischütz, 304
    and the *fantastique terrible*, 201–02, 209, 236, 238, 239
    and melodic grammar, 159, 163
  Oberon, 267
    and the *fantastique gracieux*, 201, 270
    influence on later fairy music, 281–82
    and melodic grammar, 163, 169
  Preciosa (Incidental Music), 207
Wilhelm, B.
  Grammaire musicale, 155
Williams, Elizabeth A., 66
Winter, Marian Hannah, 7